Low-Income Housing: Suburban Strategies

The Center for Urban Affairs at Northwestern University is an interdisciplinary research center which promotes and facilitates policy research, teaching and social action on urban area issues through meaningful and mutually beneficial interaction among faculty, graduate students, undergraduates and community actors.

Low-Income Housing: Suburban Strategies +b

Published for the Center for
Urban Affairs, Northwestern University

Leonard S. Rubinowitz
Center for Urban Affairs
Northwestern University

Ballinger Publishing Company ● **Cambridge, Mass.**
A Subsidiary of J.B. Lippincott Company

International Standard Book Number: 0-88410-407-9

Library of Congress Catalog Card Number: 74-1182

Printed in the United States of America

Library of Congress Cataloging in Publication Data

Rubinowitz, Leonard S
        Low-income housing: suburban strategies.
        Bibliography: p.
          1. Housing—United States. 2. Suburbs—United States.
3. Poor—United States. I. Title.
HD7293.R8   301.5'4   74-1182
ISBN 0-88410-407-9

To Linda

Contents

Acknowledgments

This book represents a group effort. The members of the group do not all know each other, but I know all of them. And I thank them.

Louis Masotti, Director of the Center for Urban Affairs at Northwestern University and John McKnight, Associate Director, gave invaluable advice and assistance throughout the evolution of this book.

The Taconic Foundation and the Wieboldt Foundation provided financial support for the Metropolitan Low- and Moderate-Income Housing Project at the Center for Urban Affairs. This book is one of the products of that project.

Much of the research for this book was done by undergraduates, graduate students and law students at Northwestern University: Robert Abrams, Douglas Brooks, Gayle Claver, Wayne Cobb, Sue Cohen, Beth Fisher, Bob Fogel, Dave Freedman, Shirley Fujimoto, Sam Goldberg, Darel Grothaus, Melvin Jackson, Becky Johnson, Kathy Kaluzny, Don Kirihara, Anne Knipper, Wayne Kost, Jack Lawlor, Adrienne Levatino, Don Moran, Debbie Roxburgh, Steve Redicliffe, Pat Schauer, Robert Seigel and Linda Stoltz.

A special thanks to Roger Dennis, who undertook the difficult task of writing the Technical Appendix. And to Roger, Sarah Wolff and Mike Romansky for service above and beyond the call of duty. Their contributions ranged from initial research to final editing, and footnoting. Without them, the task would have been even more difficult and far less pleasurable.

Graduate students in the Urban and Regional Planning Department of the University of Illinois at Urbana also did research which was very helpful in preparing portions of the book: Claudia Benjamin, Fred Cooper, Rick Glance, Christine Moore and Tom Young.

A number of people made extremely helpful comments on part or all of an earlier draft of the manuscript. Many of their suggestions have been incorporated in the final version. Thanks to these people, who waded through a bulky document, the book is better than it would have been: Dick Babcock, Calvin Bradford, Mary Brooks, Herb Franklin, Kent Fuller, Darel Grothaus, Len Heumann, Kathy Kaluzny, Ed Levin, Jerry Muller, Alex Polikoff, Larry Rosser and Bill Rutzick.

Last, chronologically, were the people who typed the various drafts, creating order out of chaos, with great patience all the while: Carol Widrig, Joan Allman, Ann Flint and Sanna Hans.

With all that help, the book may still contain errors of fact. These are mine.

Introduction

This book describes and analyzes what has been called the "open suburbs movement." It proposes future directions for the effort to enable people with low or moderate incomes to choose where they wish to live. For housing choice to exist, there must be options. Providing suburban housing options is what this book is about.

In America, poor people have the same right as the rich to live in a slum. When it comes to living in the greener pastures of suburbia, however, it's a different story. The rich can afford to pay the price of admission there; the poor cannot. So the affluent move to suburbia, to the new housing, the quality schools and the jobs. The poor stay where they "belong," in the inner city. Their jobs have left town. They face an outrageous commute or an unemployment line. Their children are miseducated at inner city schools.

This pattern of metropolitan economic segregation must change. Poor people must have the same opportunity as the rich to live in the suburbs. It is both right and necessary that housing be made available in the suburbs for people with low and moderate incomes. The goal is to provide housing choice, not to disperse economic or racial minorities. Housing options must not cease for any income group at the artificial demarcation called the central city boundary.

It is no accident that most middle- and upper-income people live in the suburbs and most of the metropolitan poor live in central cities. Public policies and subsidies made it possible. The steady stream of the relatively affluent from the central cities in the past several decades has not been merely the coincidental result of massive numbers of private market decisions. Public funds built the roads which facilitated the trek to the suburbs, since commuting to central city jobs was often necessary. FHA mortgage insurance helped to finance the housing in the suburbs. Tax breaks, subsidies for public services and numerous other public benefits were bestowed on the suburbs, enticing the middle class out of the central city.

At the same time, public policies have insured that most people with low or moderate incomes remain in the central cities. Suburban municipalities' laws and practices serve to keep out those who cannot pay the stiff price of admission. Local communities have virtual autonomy in regulating the use of land within their boundaries. Since the Supreme Court decision upholding the constitutionality of zoning 50 years ago, the states have delegated this power to local jurisdictions. Most state enabling legislation authorizes localities to zone to further the public health, safety and welfare and puts no further restrictions on the latitude of local governments. Local communities abuse their autonomy by erecting complex sets of barriers to entry. Their land use regulations force up the price of housing beyond the means of those excluded. Whether the purpose is to exclude those people or the result is only incidental to other regulatory purposes, the effect is the same. Those on the outside of suburbia remain on the outside, with an extremely limited set of choices as to where they can live.

Who are the people who are so often excluded from suburbia? They have incomes as low as none at all and as high as $10,000 or $12,000 or more. For present purposes, low-income families will be thought of as those having incomes from zero to approximately $8,000 (for a large family in an area with high housing costs). Moderate-income families range in income from about $6,000 for a small family to around $12,000 for a very large family in a high-cost area. Low- and moderate-income people are employed, underemployed or unemployed. They are black, brown and white, although the excluded groups are disproportionately minorities.

Of course, some lower-income people do live in the suburbs. There are even suburban communities which consist almost entirely of poor people. For the most part, the suburban poor live in older housing. Because of increasing costs, new suburban housing is generally beyond the reach of low- and moderate-income families. Subsidies are necessary to enable these groups to have access to new housing. (The exception is that many moderate-income families can afford to buy mobile homes without any public subsidy.) The federal government has made housing available to low- and moderate-income families through a variety of subsidy mechanisms; some subsidized housing has even been built in the suburbs. Exclusionary practices are not universal. However, the barriers are very widespread and the flow of the relatively poor to suburbia has been a trickle compared with the flood of more affluent people out of the cities.

The exclusion of the poor from the suburbs is an old problem. What is new is the scale of the phenomenon and the widespread public recognition of this reality and its disastrous consequences. What is also new is a significant movement to alter the residential patterns of our metropolitan areas and to open the suburbs. Private nonprofit organizations such as the Suburban Action Institute have been formed specifically to increase suburban access. Pre-existing organizations like the National Committee Against Discrimination in Housing have broadened their focus to include overcoming obstacles to development of low- and moderate-income suburban housing. Litigation has been a major strategy of these groups. Increasingly, they are challenging in court the ordinances and practices of local communities.

At the same time, the public sector has begun to act. Two county governments have enacted legislation mandating the inclusion of some low- and moderate-income housing in large scale developments. A number of metropolitan and regional planning agencies and councils of governments have adopted plans for distributing new low- and moderate-income housing throughout their jurisdictions. Several state governments have made attempts to open the suburbs through administrative action as well as legislation. Similar tools have been identified, although not used extensively, at the federal level.

Most of the strategies employed have attempted to change practices without explicitly trying to alter the attitudes which underlie the exclusionary practices. However, some approaches have tried to develop political support for low- and moderate-income housing and to bring about voluntary acceptance of the concept of local responsibility in this area. Regional housing plans, for example, raise public consciousness concerning the housing issue and try to arouse support for sharing responsibility to provide needed housing. These efforts attempt to overcome the widespread stereotype of subsidized housing as the massive, crime-ridden, inner-city public housing project. In fact, much of the recently developed subsidized housing has been quality construction, aesthetically pleasing and indistinguishable from the privately developed housing in the community. Those seeking to change the attitudes of suburbanites have tried to convey this new reality about the character of subsidized housing.

In short, a movement is underway. It is early in the process and the steps to date have borne limited fruit in terms of the development of housing in hitherto exclusionary communities. However, many of the strategies have the potential to alter significantly the housing patterns of our metropolitan areas. The potential for change exists in part because of the wide range of possible allies in this struggle. Civil rights organizations have already become involved. Builders and their organizations have an interest in eliminating suburban obstacles so they can build more housing and make more money. Unions have an interest in getting housing near job sites for their workers. Companies need workers who stay on the job and can get there consistently. These and other groups will increasingly feel the need to see to it that housing for low- and moderate-income families is provided, in quantity, in suburbia.

This book focuses on the strategies for hurdling suburban barriers to the development of housing for lower-income people. The book outlines the suburban housing strategies attempted to date, evaluates their impact and recommends refinements as well as new approaches and combinations of approaches. It omits entirely or passes lightly over critical related questions such as conservation, rehabilitation and construction of housing for the poor in the central city; elimination of the dual housing market, one for blacks and the other for whites; access to existing housing by lower-income groups through the filtering process; and the need for comprehensive, integrated planning on a metropolitan or regional basis. This is not to suggest that these questions are less important than the issue of locational choice. For example, even if the suburbs become open to the whole spectrum of income groups, the cities will have to be made viable. Indeed, opening access to the suburbs and re-developing the central cities are inextricably related. As suburban housing opportunities increase, this relieves pressures in the cities which prevent rehabilitation of structures and neighborhoods.

Other questions involving suburban access are critical. If housing is to be built in the suburbs for low- and moderate-income people, it will have to be available to blacks. Otherwise, constructing the housing will merely accelerate the trend toward metropolitan apartheid; lower- income whites could reach the suburbs, but blacks would be forced to remain behind in the central city. Blacks must also have equal access to middle- and upper-income housing in suburbia if the trend toward increasing segregation and polarization is to be reversed.

To reverse the pattern of metropolitan economic and racial separa-tion, all of these related questions must be addressed. This book bites off the crucial piece of the problem involving suburban access. Part I identifies the critical need for increasing suburban housing opportunities. It focuses on the locational mismatch between suburban jobs and central city workers and the enormous costs involved for employee and employer alike; the disparities in educational quality between urban and suburban schools; the abundance of vacant land for new housing development in the suburbs and the relative scarcity of such land in central cities; and finally, the fundamental question of pro-viding people with a choice of where they can live, whatever their income.

Having shown why it is crucial to develop low- and moderate-income housing in suburbia, Part I then describes the obstacles that stand in the way of achieving that goal. Local exclusionary practices represent a major barrier, as do constraints built into the federal subsidy programs.

Parts II and III constitute the bulk of this book. They deal with strategies for overcoming the suburban barriers in order to achieve greater housing choice. Part II relates to the present and potential role of public bodies, from county governments to regional planning agencies and state and federal governments. Strategies available to the public sector include legislation, litiga-tion and administrative leverage, among others. Part III examines the other side of the coin, the role of voluntary organizations in increasing suburban access. These groups cover a broad spectrum from civil rights organizations to builders and developers. Their efforts rely heavily on litigation, but they can also lobby with public agencies, generate political support for distributing needed housing, and apply other kinds of leverage.

There are many actors in the movement to open the suburbs and just as many approaches at their disposal. The Conclusion attempts to distill from the strategies discussed those which have the most potential for success. It also identifies combinations of approaches which should be more powerful than any of the component parts used separately. This book explores largely uncharted waters and tries to help chart a course for the trip to the suburbs.

Part I

Keeping the Poor out of Suburbia

Chapter One

The High Cost of Suburban Exclusion

Public policies and subsidies have contributed enormously to the mobility of the relatively affluent within metropolitan areas. Given the choice of where to live, those people benefited by these policies increasingly have opted to move to the suburbs.

At the same time, low- and moderate-income families, particularly blacks and other minorities, have not generally had the option of moving into suburban housing. Federal subsidy policies and suburban land use practices have helped to insure that only middle- and upper-income people could choose suburbia as a place to live. The result is that economic segregation is prevalent in our metropolitan areas.

Continuing the present pattern of residential separation would be extremely costly, in social as well as dollar terms. First, employment opportunities, particularly for lower-income people, are moving to the suburbs, resulting in a disastrous geographical mismatch between the jobs and the people needed to fill them. Second, the large tracts of vacant land on which development of housing is most practical are located in suburbia. Third, suburban public schools are generally considered to be superior to those in the central cities. Achieving the national objective of equality of educational opportunity requires that the whole range of income and racial groups have access to quality public education, through residential mobility as well as other methods. Finally, continuing central city concentrations of the poor and the black means continuation of the attendant fiscal and social costs.

Enormous benefits would accrue from providing housing opportunities for low- and moderate-income people in the suburbs. The poor and the minorities would gain greater choice of where they could live in metropolitan areas. The promise of equality of opportunity in housing would move toward reality. There would be increased job opportunities for those moving to the suburbs, with the tremendous added payoff of a stable, dependable work force for suburban employers. Increased educational opportunities would also be available, for the new pupils as well as those previously attending the suburban schools. The new housing could be built on relatively abundant suburban land, thus saving the cost and time involved in redeveloping central city areas to meet housing needs.

In sum, if housing opportunities for low- and moderate-income families are to be significantly increased in this country, it is essential that housing be provided for these groups in the suburbs as well as in the central cities.

The Patterns

Metropolitan Economic Segregation.[1]   Low- and moderate-income people tend to live in central cities rather than the suburbs of metropolitan areas. This tendency becomes stronger towards the lower end of the income scale:

In 1969 one-fifth of all central city families had incomes below $5,000, or 1.7 times the proportion of such families in suburbia.[2]

In 1970 central cities contained 8.2 million people below the poverty line (12.9 percent of the population), while suburbs had 5.4 million people in this group (7.1 percent of the population). Thus, the absolute number of poor persons was 1.5 times as large in central cities as in suburbs in 1970. The percentage of total population defined as poor was 1.8 times as large in central cities as in suburbs.

Metropolitan Racial Segregation.   The pervasiveness of racial segregation in our metropolitan areas is widely recognized. In 1968 the President's Commission on Civil Disorders warned against the increasing polarization leading to largely black central cities and predominantly white suburbs:

> ... The nation is rapidly moving toward two increasingly separate Americas. Within two decades, this division could be so deep that it would be almost impossible to unite: a white society principally located in suburbs, in smaller central cities, and in the peripheral parts of large central cities, and a Negro society largely concentrated within large central cities. The Negro society will be permanently relegated to its current status, possibly even if we expend great amounts of money and effort in trying to "gild" the ghetto. In the long run, continuation and expansion of such a permanent division threatens us with two perils. The first is the danger of sustained violence in our cities. ... The second is the danger of a conclusive repudiation of the traditional American ideals of individual dignity, freedom, and equality of opportunity. We will not be able to espouse

these ideals meaningfully to the rest of the world, to ourselves, to
our children. They may still recite the Pledge of Allegiance and say
"one nation . . . indivisible." But they will be learning cynicism, not
patriotism. We cannot escape responsibility for choosing the future
of our metropolitan areas and the human relations which develop
within them. It is a responsibility so critical that even an unconscious choice to continue present policies has the gravest implications. . . . We must choose. Indeed, we are choosing.[3]

The President's Commission on Urban Problems also focused on the
racial aspects of this migration. "[T]he increase of nonwhites in central cities
is accompanied by just as big a movement of whites from the central cities to the
suburbs. The result is an almost unyielding pattern of segregation."[4]

Although the metropolitan economic segregation pattern in this
country is not as complete as the separation of the races, it is clear that lower-
income groups of all races are denied equal access to suburbia. This pattern
poses critical problems for these groups and for society at large, which cannot
be solved within the boundaries of central cities. Housing strategies must include
developing suburban alternatives for low- and moderate-income people.

Employment: The Jobs-Housing Mismatch

Although low- and moderate-income people are generally confined
to the central city, the jobs are not. Jobs for these groups are located increasingly in the suburbs, resulting in substantial and lengthening distances between
job sites and places where low- and moderate-income people are able to live.
Because of these distances and the informal methods by which people find jobs,
central city workers are often unaware of suburban job openings. They face
high rates of unemployment in the central city or, at best, lower wages than
they could receive on suburban jobs. Those workers that make the "reverse commute" from the central city to suburbia encounter inordinate costs in time and
money. The suburban employers suffer too, as jobs go unfilled and turnover and
absenteeism among low-skilled and unskilled workers hold at high levels. Thus,
it is essential to provide housing for these workers within reasonable proximity
to suburban job sites.

Decentralization of Jobs. The redistribution of jobs within metropolitan areas is a phenomenon of enormous proportions. The total number of
jobs in suburbia has climbed dramatically, while central city jobs have remained
relatively constant or declined in absolute terms. Large numbers of employers
have moved their establishments from the central city to the suburbs. In addition, almost all new metropolitan area jobs are being created in the suburbs. As
a result, the absolute number of suburban jobs has surpassed central city jobs
in some metropolitan areas and will shortly do so in others.

A 1968 study carried out for the President's Committee on Urban Housing found that:

> . . . it is impossible not to conclude that the most central parts of metropolitan areas are losing employment to outlying areas and that this process is, if anything, accelerating. Slow growth and not infrequent decline of central areas have accumulated to the point where absolute declines in central city employment are now commonplace.[5]

During the period from 1952 to 1966, for example, suburbs made relative gains in numbers of jobs:

In the New York region, covering parts of New York, New Jersey and Connecticut, New York City gained only 111,000 new jobs, while the remainder of the region gained 777,000 jobs.
San Francisco gained 25,000 new jobs in the 15 year period but its suburbs experienced an increase of 202,000 jobs.
Employment in the city of St. Louis suffered an absolute decline of 50,000 jobs while the number of jobs in the suburbs increased by 193,500.
Philadelphia's total jobs decreased by almost 15,000 during the period; almost 250,000 new suburban jobs were created.[6]

The trend continues. From 1968 to 1971 total suburban employment rose in 14 large metropolitan areas studied.[7] It increased by far larger absolute amounts than central city employment in all areas except one. Suburban percentage increases in jobs ranged from 2.3 percent to 33.7 percent. In contrast, central cities lost jobs in 12 of the 14 areas:

New York City lost 120,000 jobs in just three years (3.7 percent of its 1968 total), while suburban employment increased by 102,000.
St. Louis lost 35,000 jobs and its suburbs gained 50,000 jobs.
In the Philadelphia area, the city's jobs declined by 41,000 while the suburbs secured 46,000 additional jobs.[8]

The percentage of total metropolitan area employment located in the suburbs rose from 1968 to 1971 in 13 of the areas. In all 14 of these areas combined, suburban jobs increased by 974,000 while central city employment declined by 345,000.

In terms of newly created jobs, from 1950 to 1970 80 percent of the new jobs created in large metropolitan areas were located in the suburbs.[9]

By the early 1970s total suburban jobs outnumbered central city jobs in many areas. The 14 metropolitan area study showed suburban jobs outnumbering central city jobs in 10 of the areas, with two others rapidly approaching that point.[10] A second study indicated that by 1970 almost half of the employment in the 15 largest metropolitan areas was located outside of the central city's boundaries. In 1960 the suburbs of these areas had seven million jobs, while the central cities contained approximately 12 million jobs. A decade later, the suburbs had gained about three million jobs, while the central cities lost 836,000.[11]

Manufacturing jobs, which provide substantial opportunities for low- and moderate-income workers, have led the exodus from the central cities. The trend was clearly evident even in the 1950s. During the 1954–63 period, the 24 largest cities sustained an absolute loss of 605,000 manufacturing jobs, while 442,000 such jobs were created in suburban parts of the metropolitan areas.[12]

The New York region provides a dramatic example of the continuation of this trend in manufacturing. Between 1959 and 1967 New York City lost 70,000 manufacturing jobs, while outside the city jobs in factories increased by 140,000.[13] By 1968 the suburbs had acquired over half (57 percent) of all blue collar jobs in the region. New York's Regional Plan Association projected that "[t]he City will continue to lose blue collar jobs—about 130,000 of them between 1968 and 1985—while outside the City, blue collar jobs will increase by 320,000.[14]

In New Jersey, although the state as a whole gained over 75,000 new manufacturing jobs between 1960 and 1968, five counties lost jobs in this sector.[15] Three of these counties are either core areas or contain the major core areas of their respective metropolitan areas. (The other two counties that lost manufacturing jobs had far less manufacturing employment.) In contrast, over two-thirds of the state's manufacturing employment growth was concentrated within four suburban counties in the New York region.

The Push from the City and the Pull to the Suburbs. Several factors are involved in the dramatic moveout of jobs. Central cities have little remaining vacant land for industrial-commercial development and expansion. Traffic congestion and vandalism encourage corporate movement out of the city. Recruitment of high-skilled workers, particularly women, is difficult in many central city neighborhoods.

On the "pull" side, production, transportation and communication developments have made suburbia increasingly attractive to employers. Modern assemblyline production and warehousing operations call for spacious, single story facilities. Land for construction of these plants is readily available on the suburban fringes at relatively inexpensive prices. This abundance of land also provides room for employee parking, truck storage and future plant expansion.

The vastly expanded suburban road system is a twofold attraction for employers. Increasingly, corporate executives and other relatively high level

employees live in the suburbs and these roads permit them easy access to
suburban job sites. Secondly, a growing proportion of firms relies primarily
on truck transport. Thus, companies which had been tied to central locations
in order to be near ports or railroad terminals now find that they can reduce
transport costs by locating near an interchange on the expressway system.

For a number of reasons, then, most metropolitan areas have
experienced a dramatic redistribution of jobs from the central city to the
suburbs.

Impact of the Mismatch on Workers

Job Information Gap.   The physical separation of the place of
residence of unemployed and underemployed workers from prospective places
of work is making it more difficult for these potential employees even to learn
of available jobs.[16] Job vacancy information for low-skilled employment
is conveyed primarily through informal means, such as help wanted signs at the
job site and contacts with friends and relatives, rather than through newspaper
advertisements or employment offices.[17] Inner city residents, especially
minorities, have few opportunities to make the contacts necessary to receive
timely information on suburban job vacancies. Informal methods of job search
are largely limited to the ghetto, since central city job seekers tend to have few
contacts in the relatively affluent, largely white suburbs, and since few of their
friends either work in the suburbs or travel there frequently. Even if jobs are
plentiful in suburbia, city residents may know little or nothing of these opportunities.

Reverse Commuting: An Inadequate Solution.   Central city workers
who manage to locate available suburban jobs still face extreme hardships in
securing and retaining employment. Commuting costs, both in dollars and time,
are likely to be excessive in relation to overall income. These costs force residents of the inner city to forego suburban employment or to compete for these
jobs at a tremendous economic disadvantage.

Commuting by Car. [18]   Because of the expense of purchase and
operation, many lower-income families do not own cars. In 1967 only 57 percent of families with incomes of less than $5,000 a year owned cars. For families
with incomes below $3,000 the situation was still worse; little more than two
of every five such families owned automobiles.

A large proportion of the cars owned by lower-income families are
old, in poor repair and unfit for highway use. Only one in four families with an
income under $5,000 a year owned a car less than five years old and fewer
than one in ten owned one less than two years old. Only 15 percent of the families with income below $3,000 per year owned cars five years old or less. The

age and condition of these vehicles increases the chances that their owners will arrive at work late, if at all, thus giving the appearance of undependability and making job retention difficult. Reverse commuting does not generally lend itself to car pool and drop-off arrangements because of the geographic diversity of both places of residence and employment. The "energy crisis" of the 1970s makes reverse commuting even more burdensome than before. Those relying on cars to get to work pay an extra penalty in increasing fuel costs for each mile they drive. Rationing of gasoline could make commuting by car to suburban job sites impossible.

Use of Mass Transit. The dispersal of suburban job locations results in relatively few people traveling to any one location. For those without cars, reaching suburban jobs may be even more difficult, if not a practical impossibility. Most suburban rail and bus lines are not oriented toward the reverse commuter. For example, in the New York region commuting from the city to a suburban blue collar job generally requires a car. Few suburban factories, warehouses and construction sites are reachable from the city by public transportation.[19] Similarly, in the St. Louis area many suburban job centers cannot be reached by public transportation. A person wishing to commute from any one of the several black ghettos in San Francisco or the East Bay to jobs opening up in South San Francisco, Martinez, Livermore or Point Richmond would find it almost impossible if he had to rely on public transportation.[20]

Where public transportation to suburban job centers does exist it is often inordinately expensive. In fact, central city residents who use public transportation to commute to suburban jobs generally spend more to reach their jobs than those commuting into the city from the suburbs.[21] Those wanting jobs at a substantial distance, or beyond bus or rapid transit lines, pay an especially high price.

In New York it would cost a worker living in Harlem an estimated $40 a month to commute by public transportation to work in an aircraft plant in Farmingdale (Long Island), in a parts plant in Yonkers or Portchester (Westchester), or in a basic chemical plant or shipyard on Staten Island. The public transit cost for a Bedford Stuyvesant resident to work in the same places would be nearly $50 a month.[22]

A Philadelphia ghetto resident commuting to neighboring Montgomery County would have to change buses three times and spend about $6.60 each week for commuter tickets.

In Baltimore, the trip by public transportation from the inner core to a suburban job ranges from approximately $4.00 to $15.00 per week (to Annapolis).

In St. Louis, the trip to sites such as McDonnell Aircraft Corporation from the inner city would cost approximately $6.50 each week.

To commute from the ghetto of Hunter's Point in San Francisco to a job in Contra Costa County in the East Bay area would require from three to four transfers and a cost of $15.00 each week. Commuting from Alameda or West Oakland to jobs in Contra Costa County would cost about $11.50 per week.[23]

In addition to the out-of-pocket costs, commuting to the suburbs by public transportation is often excessively time-consuming for the inner-city resident. The National Alliance of Businessmen, a consortium of local and national industries organized to hire unemployed minority persons, suggests that commuting time should be no more than one hour each way.[24] However, many inner city residents who commute to suburban job sites are forced to travel far more than two hours per day on their round trip.

The San Francisco to Contra Costa County round trip takes four to five hours each day.

McDonnell Aircraft employees living in St. Louis must travel from three to four hours each day.

A Philadelphia to Montgomery County rush-hour commute requires about an hour and a half each way.[25]

The Growth of Reverse Commuting.   In spite of the difficulty of reverse commuting, this practice has grown significantly because of the sheer numbers of jobs which have moved to the suburbs and the continued unavailability of housing within the means of many of the employees. Reverse commuters numbered 845,000 nationwide in 1960 and 1,460,000 in 1970, an increase of 72.7 percent.[26] Individual metropolitan areas show dramatic changes during that decade:

Detroit went from 97,000 reverse commuters to 161,000.

Baltimore reverse commuters nearly doubled, from 37,000 to 73,000.

In Cleveland, reverse commuting more than tripled, going from 24,000 in 1960 to 81,000 in 1970.[27]

However, the central city to suburb commuters remain a relatively small portion of the people who journey to work. The costs of commuting continue to prevent larger numbers of inner-city residents from commuting to higher-paying jobs in the suburbs. For example, in 1970 only 16 percent of all Chicago blacks living in low-income neighborhoods worked in the suburbs, although these black suburban employees earned, on the average, nine dollars a week more than their black neighbors working in the city.[28]

Suburban Jobs and Central City Unemployment. The jobs-housing mismatch is one of the major causes of high unemployment among inner-city residents. Since their jobs are disappearing in the city, unemployment rates are high. Unemployment rates are higher in the cities than in the suburbs, generally, and highest among central city blacks. In the 20 largest metropolitan areas in 1968, the unemployment rate was almost one and a half times greater in the central cities than the suburbs.[29] Historically, black unemployment rates have been at least double those of whites for all worker groups.[30]

Impact of the Mismatch on Employers

Suburban employers must also pay a high price for the lack of low- and moderate-income housing in their area. They are having substantial difficulties finding and keeping employees. Job vacancy rates are generally higher in the suburbs than in central cities. Some suburban employers seeking to expand plants or other facilities have been unable to do so because of a lack of available manpower to fill the jobs. According to the National Association of Manufacturers, 250,000 manufacturing jobs alone were unfilled in suburban areas in 1968 for lack of adequate manpower.[31]

Suburban employers will have an even greater need for relatively low-paid workers over time. In the 1960s much of this need was met through the employment of suburban women who had never worked before. This source of labor cannot be expanded as rapidly in the future because the proportion of suburban women working is now at a record high. Already, there have been acute shortages of low-paid workers in many suburban areas, especially when the overall unemployment rate has been low. The situation for the employers will worsen as future growth pushes suburban job sites farther out from older central city areas where potential applicants for such jobs now live.[32]

Employers have begun to express this concern for meeting their labor needs. In 1970 Governor Cahill of New Jersey pointed out that the problem was a serious one in parts of the state.

> Morris County Planning Board found that a major housing related problem is the inability of local industry to fill an increasing number of job vacancies. The root of the problem is that people who could fill these positions are unable to find housing within a reasonable commuting distance. Somerset County Planning Board confirms this by finding that 45% of the major industrial employers and more than 50% of all other employers surveyed felt that continuation of present zoning policies, which restrict housing to large lots and expensive homes, would not satisfy their present labor needs.[33]

In addition, a survey of employers in an industrial corridor of suburban Montgomery County, Maryland and a nationwide survey of 150 leading corporate employers indicate that large organizations are becoming concerned with housing as a problem for their employees. The surveys showed that:

> As organization size increases with a corresponding increase in the need for unskilled or semi-skilled labor, local housing patterns become more important in the recruitment and retention of personnel. Adequate housing as a factor in absenteeism and labor turnover is much more important to the larger firms than the smaller firms, as indicated in the following charts:[34]

Employees Live So Far Away As To Increase Absenteeism

| | | Montgomery County Firms by Size (No. of Employees) | | |
	Nationwide	Under 25	25-99	100 or more
Yes	35%	21%	30%	35%
No	59%	72%	56%	50%
No Answer	5%	7%	14%	15%

Employees Live So Far Away As To Increase Turnover

| | | Montgomery County Firms by Size (No. of Employees) | | |
	Nationwide	Under 25	25-99	100 or more
Yes	41%	25%	19%	55%
No	52%	68%	59%	30%
No Answer	6%	7%	22%	15%

The Ford assembly plant in Mahwah, New Jersey employs 5,000 workers, only two percent of whom live in the immediate area. The company organized car pools to bring people from Newark and Jersey City and even from Harlem and Bedford Stuyvesant in New York. Still, absenteeism runs as high as 13 percent and the annual job turnover rate is 20 percent.[35]

Overcoming the Mismatch

Although improved mass transit from the central city may be helpful, any long term solution to the jobs-housing mismatch requires housing for suburban workers in suburbia. Because of the dispersal of suburban jobs, no mass transit system could successfully provide access for all those who need suburban jobs. The public resources required for a transit system that would even approach this goal would far exceed the expense of providing housing to overcome the jobs-housing mismatch.

Availability of Land for Housing

Not only are the available jobs increasingly in the suburbs, the land needed for new housing development is there as well. The vast majority of vacant land in metropolitan areas lies outside the central city. Development of lower-income housing on a large scale inside central cities would entail tremendous costs in time and money for demolition, relocation and redevelopment. Thus, the vacant land in the suburbs is an essential resource, immediately available to tackle this housing problem.

Potential for Central City Housing Development. Most of the land within central cities is developed. The supply of vacant land has fallen sharply in central cities in recent years and few large, vacant parcels now remain. In Washington, D.C. the proportion of land which was vacant dropped from 22 percent in 1928 to four percent in 1955. In Detroit the drop was from 22 percent in 1943 to eight percent in 1954. Even in the relatively new city of Los Angeles, the percentage of vacant land decreased from 64 percent in 1940 to 31 percent in 1960.[36] In the 1970s even less vacant land is available in these cities, in spite of increasing housing abandonment.

Sites for lower-income housing can be made available through redevelopment of central city areas which are currently developed. However, practical constraints limit the utility of this approach. The time and cost involved in acquiring and clearing existing structures and constructing housing on the site insure that redevelopments will remain a partial solution, at best. The clearance and renewal process takes six to nine years to complete. It requires immense administrative and waiting costs as compared to building on vacant land. The cost of the land itself is also high.

> Land prices in central city urban renewal areas have been rising even more rapidly than have suburban land prices. Moreover, the level of land prices in urban renewal areas is significantly higher than the level of land prices in suburban areas. This is true not only of acquisition values but, more importantly, of resale (reuse) values as well.[37]

The redevelopment process may also have very substantial personal costs. If the structures cleared are residential, families are displaced into a tight housing market. It is likely that those displaced will be lower-income people who will have an extremely difficult time finding decent relocation housing. In this situation, redevelopment of urban land simply defers the problem by compelling poor people to move somewhere else. Because urban renewal has had the net effect of reducing the lower-income housing supply, it is difficult politically to destroy existing housing no matter what the plans and promises for redevelopment may be.

The central city potential for lower-income housing development is generally limited to small amounts of vacant land and obsolete commercial and industrial areas. Other major land resources are necessary to carry out a significant lower-income housing program in a metropolitan area.[38]

Suburban Development Potential. In the metropolitan areas the vacant land is almost entirely in the suburbs. In the country's 20 largest urban areas, 99 percent of the vacant land lies outside of the central cities.[39] Unlike the central cities, the amount of vacant buildable land in the suburbs continues to expand as highways and mass transit systems bring more land into the urban complex. It has been suggested that:

> There is an ample supply of vacant land suitable for housing low-income families in a ten mile wide belt around just about every one of our cities, except possibly New York and Los Angeles, where it may be necessary to go 20 miles or farther.[40]

One study concluded that "utilization of the suburban vacant land supply to develop substantial low- and moderate-cost, job-linked housing units offers the only hope of securing the necessary vacant land base to deal with the substandard housing problems and with the unemployment and under-employment problems of the nation's largest cities."[41] In 1968 Congress adopted a ten year goal of providing six million housing units for low- and moderate-income people. To approach this objective, the vacant land supply in the suburbs will have to be utilized as well as the land resources of the central cities.

Educational Opportunity:
City-Suburban Disparities

In addition to the costs implicit in the jobs-housing mismatch, the lack of lower-income housing in suburbia deprives the poor, particularly minorities, of basic educational benefits. Within our metropolitan areas, equal educational opportunity remains a promise rather than a reality. In 1967 the Advisory Commission on Intergovernmental Relations concluded that "on the educational front, the central cities are falling further behind their suburban neighbors with each passing year . . . urban children who need education the most are receiving the least."[42]

Although there is much debate about the changes necessary to meet the educational needs of urban children, it appears that increasing the available resources and providing racially integrated environments may substantially increase educational opportunities. Developing housing for lower-income families in the suburbs serves these dual purposes and therefore may be a significant step toward equal educational opportunity.

Educational Resources: City v. Suburbs. Nationally, suburban spending levels on education, in terms of percentage of local revenues and on a per pupil basis, exceed central city efforts. Suburbs spend a higher percentage of their revenues for education than central city schools, in part because they have fewer noneducational costs, such as welfare and security, than the central cities. Suburbs spend an average of 53 percent of their local budgets on education while only 31 percent of central city expenditures are used for education.[43]

One study concluded that the amount spent per pupil is frequently a significant predictor of pupil performance. This finding holds particularly for large urban districts containing relatively large proportions of disadvantaged students. The relationship of expenditure to performance in large urban districts was quite strong, with an additional $100 of expenditures being associated with 2.6 months of achievement at the beginning of the expenditure range and 1.4 months at the end of the range.[44] However, there is a substantial dispute among people who have studied the question as to the effect of expenditures on performance. Some have even argued that student performance seems to decline as more resources are injected into the system. Whatever the real impact of dollars, the perception of parents and school administrators seems to be generally that the students benefit from higher levels of spending. For example, in lawsuits challenging disparities among school districts in levels of spending, the wealthy districts have struggled to retain their right to spend more for their schools than the poorer districts.

In addition to salary differentials which often attract better teachers to suburban schools, the suburban school environment is more conducive to learning than that of central city schools. Central city schools tend to experience more violence, student turnover and absenteeism, and to have more pupils with significant behavior problems than do suburban schools.

The resources available in a school system are reflected, in part, in the number of pupils per teacher in the system. The Report of the Commission on the Cities in the 70s asserted that education will not improve unless, among other things, student-teacher ratios decline. However, "in secondary education, there are 7 more students per classroom in the core schools than in the fringe schools in the Northeast, in the Midwest there are 21 more students per classroom."[45]

Not only are class sizes smaller in suburban districts, but these school systems have significantly more specialized personnel, such as guidance counselors and psychologists, as well as library books, audio-visual materials and special laboratories. A number of studies indicate that the level of services in a school district has a significant impact on educational outcomes:

> A relationship exists between the quality of school services provided to a pupil and his academic achievement, and that relationship is such that higher quality school services are associated with higher levels of achievement.[46]

Higher achievement in school seems to be associated with high post-school success and low achievement is associated with lack of success. Since achievement potentials tend to be greatest in the suburban schools, the greatest post-school success opportunities are generally afforded those who attend the better suburban schools.[47]

Desegregation and Educational Opportunity.   It is not merely the differential levels of resources which result in the widespread perception that suburban school children generally receive higher quality education than central city pupils. One major study, the Coleman Report, concluded that the racial composition of the school is a significant determinant of pupil achievement, so that "as the proportion of whites increases, the achievement of students in each racial group increases."[48] Although this study has been challenged vigorously, its general conclusions remain rather widely accepted. It has also been argued that:

> If the children of the poor are placed in environments which reflect hope—schools where children aspire and feel assured of success— they seem to respond positively to this peer influence. Test scores in achievement, self-concept and aspiration have indicated significant improvement in these areas.[49]

If racial composition of school populations is significant, the urban schools generally are providing inferior education in comparison to suburban schools. Central city public school populations are becoming increasingly black, as many white families have moved to the suburbs and others have taken their children out of the public school system. As a result, desegregation of schools within the boundaries of the central cities is becoming increasingly impractical. Federal courts in Detroit and Indianapolis have concluded that in these cities desegregation of schools is feasible only on a metropolitan basis.

Alternatives for Equalizing Educational Opportunity.   To the extent that disparities in city-suburban educational quality are based on resource differences, several solutions are possible. One approach is a direct equalization of resources among school districts. Momentum in this direction is being provided by a series of lawsuits which attack the existing disparities in per pupil expenditures as violative of the constitutional principle of equal protection. Although the Supreme Court rejected this proposition relative to the U.S. Constitution in the *Rodriguez* case, state courts may continue to be receptive to claims based on state constitutional grounds.[50] However, redistributing resources to inner-city schools deals with only a portion of the problem.

To the extent that inequality of opportunity results from segregated schools, a number of "educational" solutions have been put forth. Bussing is one of the major alternatives considered to date. However, in many cities the proportion of blacks in the public school population is so large that desegregation through bussing or other means within the city is not feasible.

Bussing of central city students to suburbs may be feasible on a limited basis, but it is expensive and time-consuming and requires central city-suburban cooperation or a court order. Thus, although bussing may be useful in some situations, it is not a panacea. The problem is so complex that both educational and housing alternatives are called for. Providing suburban housing alternatives for lower-income urban families, especially minorities, can provide access to school systems with high levels of resources in an integrated setting. This seems to be an important step toward increasing the educational opportunity of these children. The hope that is necessary to educational success is most likely to be achieved by living in a community where people have this kind of aspiration and expectation, rather than merely commuting in on a bus.

Fiscal-Social Costs of
Metropolitan Separation

Finally, the pattern of relatively affluent and white suburbs surrounding increasingly poor and black central cities poses a serious threat to the viability of the core cities. As industry and relatively affluent families leave the city, they take with them a signficant share of the city's tax base and leave behind the tax burdens. Costs of city services are increased, as those most in need of police, welfare and other services are forced to remain in the central city. At the same time, the resources necessary to supply the services dwindle. The central city continues to decline, services must be cut back and, as a snowball effect, more commercial establishments and middle-income families move to the suburbs.

The Advisory Commission on Intergovernmental Relations, a bipartisan body established by Congress, concluded in a 1967 study:

> Regardless of the level of the analysis, national totals or individual area, there is a growing concentration of the "high cost" citizen in the central city. There is every reason to believe this trend will continue. . . . For example, 27 percent of Maryland's population is located in Baltimore, yet 71 percent of Maryland's AFDC case load is to be found in that city. By the same token, Boston, with 14 percent of Massachusetts' population, accounts for 38 percent of that State's AFDC case load. . . .
> The large central cities are in the throes of a deepening fiscal crisis. On the one hand, they are confronted with the need to satisfy rapidly growing expenditure requirements triggered by the rising number of "high cost" citizens. On the other hand, their tax resources are growing at a decreasing rate (and in some cases actually declining), a reflection of the exodus of middle and high income

families and business firms from the central city to suburbia. . . .

A clear disparity in tax burden is evident between central city and outside central city. Local taxes in the central cities average 7.6 percent of the personal income of their residents; outside the central cities they equal only 5.6 percent of income. . . . The central cities increased their relative tax effort during a period when their property tax base either showed a deceleration in the rate of growth or an absolute decline. . . . The central city tax development contrasts sharply with trends on the outside where high income and a continuation of the growth of the property tax base mitigated tax pressures. . . .

On the municipal service or custodial front, the presence of "high cost" citizens, greater population density, and the need to service commuters force central cities to spend far more than most of their suburban neighbors for police and fire protection and sanitation services. The 37 largest central cities had a non-educational (municipal) outlay of $232 per capita in 1965—$100 greater than their suburban counterparts.[51]

In addition to the fiscal problems, the social costs of concentrating lower-income families in the inner city are very substantial. Those areas are characterized by high crime rates, youth gangs, drug addiction, unemployment and underemployment, poor quality housing and low health standards. As long as the poor and the black are forced to live in such areas, severe social problems will persist. Society will continue to pay high costs for coping with the problems associated with concentrating these families. Beyond that, society fails to benefit from the potential positive contributions of these people.

Development of low- and moderate-income housing on a metropolitanwide basis would help to relieve overcrowding in inner-city neighborhoods, thus reducing social tension and pathology and facilitating demolition of decaying buildings and redevelopment. At the same time, the reality of racial and economic integration in the suburbs could change the perceptions of middle-income whites. These families might begin to view the central city as a relatively more attractive option for residence and investment.

Suburban Housing: The Intersection of Justice and Necessity

Only small parts of metropolitan areas are accessible to lower-income Americans. If increasing their freedom of movement and housing choice were the sole justification for providing lower-income housing in suburbia, that would surely be enough. In addition, however, this housing would help overcome the growing jobs-housing mismatch, bringing people closer to potential jobs and stability to the employers' work force. It would increase the educational opportunities of lower-income students, particularly blacks, by giving them access to generally high quality schools in an integrated setting. Finally, by reducing the service needs, as well as attracting revenue sources to remain in, or return to, the city, suburbanizing lower-income housing will help the central cities remain viable. In sum, the benefits of providing suburban housing for low- and moderate-income people are enormous. The costs of not doing so are intolerable.

Chapter Two

The Suburban Obstacle Course:
Barriers to Building Housing
for Lower-Income People

In spite of the critical need to provide suburban housing opportunities for low-
and moderate-income people, this choice remains the exception rather than
the rule. Suburban communities control the kind of development that takes
place within their boundaries, primarily through land use controls. The powers
to control the use of land are established at the state level. In most states the
legislature has delegated the power to regulate land use to local communities.
For a variety of reasons, localities frequently use these regulartory powers to
prevent construction of housing that would serve lower-income families. The
most important land use control, in terms of its exclusionary effect, is the
zoning power. Local zoning ordinances are enacted pursuant to state zoning
enabling laws. Most state enabling statutes resemble the original Standard
Zoning Enabling Act which was drafted fifty years ago and authorized local
governments

> . . . to regulate and restrict the height, number of stories, and size
> of building and other structures, the percentage of lot that may
> be occupied, the size of yards, courts, and other open spaces,
> the density of population, and the location and use of build-
> ings, structures and land for trade, industry, residence, or other
> purposes.[1]

Communities are to exercise these powers for the broad purposes
of "health, safety, morals or the general welfare."[2] Armed with this vague
and broad authority, tens of thousands of localities have adopted increasingly
complex and wideranging zoning measures in order to advance purely local
interests. Local communities have generally determined land use policies without supervision or intervention by any other governmental body. Suburbs
have regulated development to further their own "general welfare."

All too often suburbs regulate development in ways that amount to exclusionary zoning. Exclusionary zoning is the array of zoning ordinances and practices which results in keeping out housing within the means of low- and moderate-income families.

Zoning and related regulations can increase the cost of the structure itself, the land on which the structure sits and the improvements that are required along the streets in front of the house. By excluding relatively low-cost forms of development, these regulations raise housing costs above the level at which low- and moderate-income families can afford to buy or rent. In recent years the land use controls which affect the kinds of construction and its cost in the suburbs have become increasingly restrictive.

In addition to the barriers imposed locally, the federal housing subsidy programs have had built-in constraints which prevent or inhibit their use in suburbia. Some of these programs can only be used in communities where the local governing body has taken affirmative steps to indicate acceptance of subsidized housing. Other federal programs have a maximum cost per unit in the legislation. Cost ceilings enable localities to use cost-inflating zoning devices to exclude subsidized housing. Given the political power of suburban constituencies in Congress, it is likely that future subsidy programs will also contain provisions permitting communities to prevent the use of the program within their borders.

Motives and Justifications for Exclusionary Practices

A community's motives for erecting barriers to lower-income housing are often difficult to ascertain. Racial and class prejudice may well be behind many of these practices, but they are mentioned openly only by the least sophisticated public officials. On the other hand, justifications for exclusionary practices are legion. These are the arguments used to defend a community's actions against legal and other challenges. They are almost always cast in terms purported to be neutral. And as courts begin to declare certain justifications nonneutral, others are put forth.

Fiscal Zoning.   A commonly articulated justification for exclusionary land use regulations is "fiscal zoning." The concept relates to the fact that the property tax is local government's primary source of revenue. It is collected on the basis of the value of real property within the jurisdiction. As a result, the use of a community's land is integrally related to its ability to provide quality education, police, fire and other services.

The National Commission on Urban Problems described the process:

> The game of "fiscal zoning" requires the players—i.e., zoning jurisdictions—to attract uses which add more in property taxes or

local sales taxes than they require in expensive public services and to exclude uses which do not pay their own way. In essence, this means that jurisdictions are influenced to seek industrial and commercial uses and luxury housing and discourage or prohibit such uses as housing for low- and moderate-income persons.[3]

It is commonly assumed, then, that the fiscal incentives are to exclude housing that would attract low- and moderate-income families, especially those with children. The theory argues that these families contribute little in property taxes because of the low assessed value of their houses or apartments, but they require relatively high municipal expenditures, particularly for education. However, recent cost-benefit analyses of low- and moderate-income housing, and of apartments in general, indicate that these units can produce more revenues than they cost in terms of governmental services. That is, this housing can be a fiscal winner for a community. For example, apartment developments averaging two bedrooms are likely to produce more in property taxes for schools than the cost of educating the children in the development. On the other hand, single family homes, which are usually built with three or more bedrooms, generally produce less in property taxes than the amount needed to educate the children. The local fisc may be in better shape from the construction of multifamily units than from developing single family housing on the same site.

Local finances may not really determine exclusionary policies. It is likely that the desire to fill the local coffers is the primary reason why communities attempt to attract industry. Localities compete aggressively to attract the good tax ratables. However, it does not follow that the motive for excluding lower-income housing is to keep out the fiscal losers. Indeed, critics of the fiscal argument have long maintained that it is merely a convenient smokescreen for motives which could not be presented openly. One study examined variations in concentrations of the poor within 30 metropolitan areas and the degree to which the variations were correlated with factors related to fiscal motives for land use controls.[4] This study found that the degree to which exclusionary policies are adopted seems to be unrelated to the local fiscal realities. For example, state programs of aid to education may attempt to equalize expenditures throughout the state. In states where state aid is strongly equalizing, local jurisdictions are less dependent on local property tax revenues to finance the public schools. In such instances, there should be less incentive to engage in fiscal zoning. However, the state equalization formulas seem to have no significant impact on the concentration of the poor within metropolitan areas. Other fiscal variables, such as local property tax as a percentage of personal income and local property tax as a percentage of local revenues, were also unrelated to the presence or absence of low-income people within particular jurisdictions. The study found "no substantial relationship between residential patterns and fiscal incentives for imposition of controls."[5]

Other recent studies also indicate that in spite of the rhetoric of fiscal zoning, finances have relatively little impact on local exclusionary practices. At the same time, several courts have undercut the fiscal rationale by declaring protection of the local purse to be an impermissible purpose for excluding low- and moderate-income people.

Protecting the Environment and Excluding the Poor.   With the coming of the environmental movement in the late 1960s many suburbs began to use the rhetoric of ecology to justify zoning practices having an exclusionary impact. There are clearly important environmental questions involved in suburban land development, but there are also communities willing to justify their exclusionary actions in whatever way will hold up in court. Perhaps the best way to test the motives at work is to see if the community is willing to try to reconcile the need for housing and the legitimate environmental values at stake.

For example, a locality's justifications often relate to the supposedly inevitable consequences of middle- and high-density development: open space and recreational areas will be lost; there will be aesthetic damage to the area; pedestrian and vehicular congestion will result; sewage treatment and water ecosystems will be overburdened; and areas of ecological importance will be destroyed. In most cases, these negative impacts can be reduced significantly or avoided entirely by sensitive site selection and design. Unwillingness on the part of a community to even attempt this reconciliation indicates that other motives are probably operating. If the community permits lower-density housing, which could have similar negative effects, in those areas, this is even more compelling evidence that environmental concerns are not the primary reason for exclusion.

Social Motives: Excluding Undesirables.   Legitimate environmental concerns are probably the real basis for exclusion in some cases, but it is likely that racial and economic class discrimination are the most powerful motives in shaping suburban land use policies.

> "Undesireable" people—minority groups and the poor—would not "fit in." Indeed, for many suburban dwellers it was just such "undesireable" aspects of the city that drove them out.[6]

The study which indicates the apparent irrelevance of fiscal factors supports the contention that race is a significant factor in shaping local land use policies:

> It is possible that the racial factor . . . affects the incidence only of *private* covenants restricting land use, and that public controls

are motivated by *neither* fiscal nor racial considerations but are
rather motivated by such "neutral" concerns as health, safety,
aesthetics and the like. But this seems to us unlikely; public controls and private covenants have nearly identical effects and are
commonly viewed as interchangeable; that the two devices are
animated by totally distinct motives is implausible.[7]

Many commonly used justifications for exclusionary devices mask
only slightly the racial and class motives involved: preservation of the social
character of the community; maintaining property values; avoiding behavioral
patterns which residents' children should not be exposed to; maintaining the
quality of the school system.

Exclusionary Devices

Just as the justifications for excluding lower-income housing are
numerous and varied, so are the techniques used which have exclusionary
effects. Zoning ordinances have received the most public attention. Although
it is more subtle, the administration of the zoning process may be even more
effective in keeping out the poor. Other devices which may have an exclusionary impact include subdivision regulations, building permit requirements,
slow growth or no growth ordinances and other local prerogatives which appear
neutral when taken at face value. Finally, the United States Congress is a
frequent, and not unconscious, ally of the exclusionary suburbs. The federal
housing subsidy programs come equipped with constraints which permit the
local community to prevent the use of the programs within its borders.

Zoning Ordinances. The zoning of vacant, developable land in
the suburbs has become a major factor in the perpetuation of the residential
segregation of individuals in our society by income. Communities use their
zoning ordinances to raise the price of residential access to a particular area,
thus barring the influx of people unable to pay the high costs. To the extent
that a community restricts multifamily structures, controls the size of buildings,
imposes density requirements or otherwise elevates land and building costs, it
precludes construction of housing which can accommodate the nonaffluent.

Prohibition of Apartments. Many suburbs prohibit apartments
entirely, often by not providing for multifamily developments in the zoning
ordinance. Exclusion of apartments is very effective in preventing the entry
into the community of lower-income people. It keeps out the kind of housing
which, along with mobile homes, is most accessible to those of modest means.
By spreading land costs over a larger number of units, apartment developments reduce costs. In addition, tenants are not required to accumulate the
substantial down payment needed for purchasing a home. As a result, apart-

ments may be affordable to those who could not buy a new single family house. Finally, many federal subsidy programs which have enabled lower-income families to secure new housing contemplate development of multi-family units.

Prohibition of apartments is common. For example, 99.2 percent of the undeveloped land in the New York area which is residentially zoned is restricted to single family dwellings.[8] In the suburbs of Newark, only one-half of one percent of the developable land is zoned to permit any form of multifamily dwelling.[9]

Restrictions on Apartment Development.   Even communities that permit construction of apartments often add restrictions that tend to make the developments inaccessible to lower-income families. Density limitations on apartment developments are commonplace. Minimum lot area requirements for multiple family dwellings have taken several forms, such as a minimum number of square feet of lot area for each unit or a minimum lot size for the development, with a minimum lot area for each unit. For example, the total lot area might be set at a minimum of 7,000 feet, with the lot area for the first unit exceeding 2,000 square feet, and for each unit after that at least 1,000 square feet of land.

Other ordinances require a certain minimum lot area based on the number of bedrooms in a unit, such as 1,000 square feet for a one bedroom unit, 1,500 square feet for a two bedroom unit, and 3,000 square feet for a three bedroom unit. This discourages development of units for families by forcing up the cost of apartments with three bedrooms.

Still more restrictive is the provision which limits the number of bedrooms permitted in apartments. The purpose is to keep down the number of children. This frequently used device has been called "vasectomy zoning." In the Newark, New Jersey suburbs, for example, 83 percent of the minute amount of land with multifamily zoning is subject to ordinances requiring that between 65 percent and 90 percent of the units have only one bedroom.[10] One community is even less subtle. It prohibits families with school age children from living in apartments and allows only one preschool age child per dwelling unit.[11]

The Newark area is not unique. It is common for suburbs that permit multifamily units to require that at least 80 percent of the units in a development have only one bedroom (or less), with up to 20 percent permitted to have two bedrooms.

Minimum Building Size Requirements.   Space enclosed by walls is much more expensive than land, so stiff minimum building size floor area requirements have perhaps the most direct effect on raising the cost of housing. There is an almost one to one correlation between floor size and cost of the unit. And as building costs climb, size minimums have an even greater exclusionary effect. Usually, the rationale given for minimum building size regulations is the need for a minimum amount of living space for health purposes. However, the minimum square footage required is almost never related to the number of people who will occupy the unit.

Perhaps the most common minimum floor area is 1,200 square feet.[12] In the Newark suburbs over 80 percent of the land is zoned in this way.[13] With average building costs of $20 per square foot for single family detached housing (probably a low estimate), a 1,200 square foot minimum floor space ordinance would translate into a price for the house itself of $24,000. Adding the cost of the land and improvements would make the cost of the package about $30,000, well beyond the range of low- and moderate-income people.

The impact of minimum building size requirements is particularly devastating in combination with a large minimum lot size. The size of a house, directly affected by minimum building size requirements and indirectly influenced by minimum lot size regulations, is the most important factor in establishing the price of the house. For example, in Madison, New Jersey a typical one acre minimum lot size and floor space requirement of 1,500 feet would price the house at a minimum of $45,000.[14]

Exclusion of Mobile Homes.   Mobile homes now constitute more than one-quarter of the new home market each year. Ordinances which prohibit mobile homes exclude the one form of new housing available to lower-income people without public subsidies. In most suburbs, however, mobile homes are either prohibited entirely or limited to industrial and commercial areas. A 1964 study in New York reviewed 237 local zoning ordinances and found that over half excluded mobile homes either explicitly or through height or floor area requirements which mobile homes could not meet. Only 82 communities permitted mobile homes on individual lots, as opposed to mobile home parks. Only 12 permitted mobile homes in residential areas. Most communities in the Boston region also prohibit mobile homes. Less than 10 percent of the cities and towns have any provision for their permanent location.[15]

In many states, mobile homes are defined legally as personal property, rather than real property. The units themselves provide no real property taxes to the municipality. For this reason, mobile homes are a fiscal liability. However, in New York State mobile homes are taxable as real property, so the fiscal incentive to exclude them appears to be less than in other states. Nevertheless, exclusion is the dominant pattern.

Mobile homes have also suffered from a negative image in terms of the aesthetics of the units themselves, as well as common prejudices about the occupants. These stereotypes, which portray mobile home dwellers as unconcerned about their homes and their neighborhoods, are often reinforced by the presence of these neighborhoods in the midst of industrial areas.

Large Lot Zoning.   In many residential districts, a certain minimum area must be provided for each dwelling unit. These minimum lot size requirements significantly affect the price of housing. Minimum lot size requirements become large lot zoning when the jurisdiction permits only single family residences on large lots. The community might prohibit building a house on a piece of land smaller than one, or even four acres.

Zoning out lower-income housing does not require four or even one acre minimum lot size. Given the cost of land in suburban areas, quarter-acre lot minimums would effectively price out lower-income housing. Thus, a challenge that succeeds in reducing the minimum lot size from two acres to a half acre will merely serve to line the pockets of developers who can build houses at four times the density. Reducing the lot size to a half acre will not advance the cause of lower-income people because the housing built will still be well beyond their means.

Large lot zoning can raise the cost of housing in several ways. If there is substantial large lot zoning, the total amount of housing that could be built in the area is significantly reduced. When there is a heavy demand for new housing, decreasing the number of buildable sites will inflate the prices of these sites. The number of sites which can accommodate small lots or multifamily units is also reduced by large lot zoning. Prices will rise to reflect the limited supply of these smaller sites. Beyond the price of the land itself, large lot zoning usually results in builders constructing larger, more expensive structures. Many builders believe that it is necessary, for marketing purposes, to build a larger house on a larger lot. Some will even apply a rule of thumb to relate the price of the lot to the total price of the house and lot, e.g., 20 percent. With this guideline, any increase in the land price would be reflected in a fivefold increase in the price of the total package.

In addition to the cost of the land and the house, large lots usually force up the costs of improvements. Because larger lots require greater frontage, the amount and cost of streets, sidewalks, gutters and water lines may be increased significantly. Improvement costs may be two or three times greater for a one acre lot than for a 6,000 square foot lot.[16]

Large lot zoning is prevalent in many metropolitan areas. For example, in four Newark, New Jersey suburbs 60 percent of the area is zoned for a minimum lot size of one acre or more, and only one percent of the land is zoned to permit construction of housing on more modest lots, 50–75 feet wide.[17] In Connecticut over 70 percent of the land zoned for residential use has a minimum lot size requirement of one acre or more.[18] In the New York metropolitan area as a whole 90 percent of the vacant land zoned for single family residences calls for lots of one-fourth acre or more, and two-thirds of this land is zoned for lots of at least one-half acre.[19]

Other Zoning Devices. Additional zoning requirements which may have an exclusionary impact include: limitations on number of stories in single family houses; maximum height restrictions; minimum floor areas for particular rooms; provision of mandatory parking facilities and other amenities; minimum frontages; landscaping requirements; architectural standards; setting aside land for industrial use; overzoning for commercial purposes; and referendum provisions for subsidized housing and zoning changes. Many of these are neutral in intent, but still may be exclusionary in effect.

Prevalence of Exclusionary Zoning Ordinances. Although exclusionary provisions are clearly widespread, there is little systematic information on the extent of various practices. To begin to collect this data, the New Jersey Department of Community Affairs studied land use patterns in the outer suburban ring of the northeastern part of the state. The analysis measured the amount of land suitable and/or available for residential development, the extent to which that land was subject to potentially exclusionary controls and the impact of the controls on the availability of low- and moderate-income housing.[20] Results from the four most rapidly growing counties showed a great deal of land available for continued expansion. In the four counties, about 400,000 acres (625 square miles) of developable vacant land were zoned for residential use. Of this acreage, a little over 2,000 acres, or one-half of one percent of the total, were zoned for multifamily dwellings. This represents a miniscule amount of land available for the kind of housing most available to low- and moderate-income people. Multiple dwelling units were also being built through rezonings, variances or special permits. Notwithstanding this exception, exclusion of apartments prevailed throughout most of the four county area. Of the small amount of land available for apartments, 83 percent was encumbered with restrictions on the number of bedrooms. These restrictions usually required that at least 80 percent of the units have only one bedroom and up to 20 percent may have two bedrooms.

Not only were restrictions on apartments prevalent in the four New Jersey counties, mobile homes also were excluded from all but three communities. These exceptions were insignificant, and for all intents and purposes mobile homes were excluded from the four counties.

An additional critical test of the potential for developing lower-income housing is the minimum building size provisions. In the New Jersey counties only about 10 percent of the land is subject to minimums under 1,000 square feet.

An additional critical test of the potential for developing lower-income housing is the minimum building size provisions. In the New Jersey counties only about 10 percent of the land is subject to minimums under

1,000 square feet. Even this provision puts the minimum cost of new housing well over $20,000. In addition, over three-fourths of the land was covered by 1,200 square feet or larger minimums.

Finally, there was little provision for small single family houses on small lots. About three-fourths of the developable land was zoned for large houses and large lots.

Thus, the state study found that the whole range of exclusionary practices was prevalent in northeastern New Jersey. Indications are that the New Jersey pattern is fairly typical, although it may be somewhat more extreme than in other parts of the country.

Subdivision Regulations

In addition to the zoning vehicle, municipalities use subdivision regulations to control the use of land within their borders. The zoning ordinance allocates land for different uses and building types throughout the municipality. It assumes that the land has already been divided into separate lots or parcels for purposes of development. In contrast, subdivision regulations

> (1) control the spatial arrangement of land subdivisions in terms of street patterns, block sizes and shapes; and (2) impose certain requirements as to construction of necessary physical improvements and dedication of land to public use within land subdivisions.[21]

The exclusionary effects of subdivision requirements are somewhat limited and quite subtle. They do not have as much impact on price as zoning regulations. The additional costs attributable to subdivision regulations include site-improvement costs for streets, alignments, grades, curbs, intersections, alleys, sewage and drainage facilities, street lighting and sidewalks, extension of utility services, and tie-ins with existing streets.

Because subdivision regulations are often vague, the municipality can sometimes extract substantial commitments from the developer as the price of approval. Developers have been required to undertake costly uprooting and enlarging of surrounding sewer mains. In addition to fulfilling his own development's needs, the developer may have to supply facilities for outlying potential growth areas, without financial assistance from the community or area property owners.

Subdivision regulations also require mandatory dedication of land (or fees in lieu of this) for schools, parks, and other community facilities. Relating potential population density of the area to be developed to corresponding park and school requirements is a reasonable way of deciding what the developer should provide, but often communities choose their own, more arbitrary methods, of reaching this decision. In so doing, the municipality may impose excessive costs on the developer, which are likely to be passed on to the occupants.

Fees are required of developers for administrative functions of subdivision regulation such as checking, filing and recording plats, and carrying out inspections. These fees, usually computed on a per foot basis, vary dramatically from community to community. Local governments have even forced developers to pay fees where none were legally required.

In sum, the cost-escalating impact of subdivision regulations are not of the same magnitude as the zoning devices, but they have the same tendency to price out of the community housing for lower-income families.

Building Codes. Building codes, almost by definition, are restrictive. They increase the cost of housing by specifying the materials and building techniques that must be used. All too often these requirements exceed what is necessary to insure that buildings can be safely occupied.

Many of the suburban building codes require on-site inspections. This prevents less expensive assembly of units at an off-site factory. Other codes require the use of certain types of electrical wiring and cast iron pipes, despite evidence that cheaper materials are equally serviceable. Another factor which increases costs is the lack of uniformity of building codes from community to community, preventing standardized construction approaches.

Slow Growth, No Growth, Controlled Growth and Managed Growth

As suburbanites have begun to face the negative consequences of rapid growth, they have moved in increasing numbers to control the pace and direction of growth or to stop it entirely. Here again, environmental concerns seem to be at the base of many antigrowth efforts. The techniques used have varied. Efforts to stop or slow growth have included water and sewer bond referenda defeated and hookups denied; phased, slowed or fixed growth chartered; or building moratoria debated or announced. In Livermore and Pleasonton, California the communities voted to prohibit issuing building permits when schools are overcrowded or water and sewer facilities are inadequate. In Florida the Dade County Commisson banned most new buildings in the eastern half of Key Biscayne and several other communities approved building and rezoning moratoria.[22]

The controlled growth movement received a major boost in 1972, when the highest court in New York State upheld the community of Ramapo's "development timing" ordinance.[23] Ramapo is in Rockland County, one of the wealthiest counties in the United States. Ramapo had amended its zoning ordinance to prevent the development of land for new housing unless the developer received a special permit, regardless of the existing residential zoning of his land. This permit is granted only if the land is located in an area which will be served by a specified minimum level of community services and facilities. Installation of these facilities is scheduled in accordance with the town's capital improvement program. This capital improvement program (CIP) covers sewerage, drainage, parks and recreation areas, roads, and firehouses. The Capital Improvement Program spans an 18-year period. Generally, land which will not be served with such facilities for as long as 18 years may not be developed for residential purposes in the interim.

Because of the Ramapo court decision, many localities are considering adopting similar ordinances. These ordinances have significant potential for exclusion, particularly if they are widespread within a region. For example, if every urbanizing jurisdiction in the New York region adopted a controlled growth ordinance, the possibility of adequately housing the region's lower-income population would become even more remote than it now appears. It would withdraw a great deal of land from potential development, and thus would tend to drive up the price of land that is more immediately developable.

In Ramapo, the timed development ordinance serves to increase the exclusionary impact of the pre-existing zoning pattern. When the timing controls were adopted in 1969, the zoning ordinance effectively kept out all but middle- and upper-income families. What the development plan and timing controls added to the burden already carried by lower-income groups seeking entry was the increase in cost of more immediately developable land and the foreclosing of clustered development by the capital improvement program.

Exclusionary Administrative Practices

Some of the most exclusionary devices cannot be discerned from a reading of the local ordinances. The ordinances may be administered in ways that are more discriminatory than the language of the ordinance would indicate. Local administrators interpret and implement the ordinances. They decide how the ordinances are to be enforced, how the various requirements are applied to encourage or discourage various types of development.

One planner has suggested that:

It is not zoning so much that is a restraint within our area [Dayton, Ohio] as it is the [in]consistent or inaccurate or arbitrary administration thereof.

We find that many times a rezoning application will be treated differently if it is for a luxury apartment than if it is for a 236 project. In other words, there are other factors that are weighed when there are low- and moderate-income or minority people involved.[24]

Rezoning and Special Exception.   The administrative device most
frequently used to prevent development of low- or moderate-income housing
is the rezoning process. A rezoning is a change in the use classification of a
particular piece of land. In most communities, developers need a rezoning of
land from the local zoning body in order to build at feasible densities. This
gives local officials the opportunity to determine the precise nature of the
development before approving its construction. Questions concerning the
income groups to be served and the numbers of bedrooms must be answered
by the developer in a way that is acceptable to the community. Otherwise, the
result may be outright denial, long delays or unreasonably burdensome conditions related to dedications of land or provision of facilities.

Seeking a rezoning is risky and costly. Since every local government has its own zoning requirements and procedures, developers are confronted with a new set of rules every time they move from one community to
another. Often the procedural rules are not clearly set out. Some requirements
may necessitate a significant capital outlay. The developer must prepare site
designs and architectural renderings. He also has to pay for the preparation
and presentation of evidence at the rezoning hearings. These costs cannot be
recovered if the rezoning is denied.

If a rezoning is denied, the developer can go to court, but the
litigation is likely to be costly and time-consuming. An action in a trial court
can take as long as a year, and in the appellate court two years or more. Few
developers can afford to wait that long. Options to buy land generally run
from six months to a year, after which they must be renewed at added expense.

Other Exclusionary Administrative Practices.   Even if a lawsuit
is successful and the local government is forced to rezone a site, the developer
may find it difficult to obtain various other permits needed for construction.

> As any experienced zoning lawyer will tell you, a victory at the
> appellate level may be of limited utility if a town wishes to frus-
> trate a developer. There are so many points during the process
> where local officials can cause delay and hamper a builder that a
> developer armed with a stunning victory at the appellate level
> has only begun the fight.[25]

The community has a whole range of apparently neutral regulatory devices which can be used to delay or prevent construction of "undesir-
able" projects:

> The number of review agencies that a developer has to go through
> increases the likelihood of administrative delays. At a minimum
> he is likely to face the planning board, the commission, and the

board of zoning appeals or adjustment—plus the zoning enforcement officer, the building inspector, and the health department.
He is probably at the mercy of the fire department, water and
sewer authorities or a public works department, the engineering
department, the school board, the traffic department or state highway department, the park and recreational department or park
authority, the redevelopment and housing authority, and so on.
He may also be subject to review by a design or architectural review committee, a conservation department, and a PUD or site
plan review committee. In other words, if the administration
should find delay an enticing form of exclusion, it would be difficult to avoid.[26]

Thus, even if the developer is victorious in his court challenge, he
must overcome many more hurdles before he can build the housing. Each of
these administrative devices permits the community, at the very least, to delay
the commencement of construction. Delay may be tantamount to exclusion.
It results in higher costs for the developer, including increased interest on loans,
payments for options, and rising costs of materials and labor. The developer
may not be able to build the project at all, if delays are so great that the
development becomes financially infeasible.

Evaluating Local Land Use Patterns:
Ordinances and Practices

In determining whether, or to what extent, a suburban community
is exclusionary, it is important to look at the ordinances, the administrative
practices and the question of mapping. Historically, zoning ordinances have
identified the uses permitted within particular kinds of zones and then charted
those zones on the map of the community. When this type of premapping,
or Euclidean zoning, is used, the mapping may be as important as the ordinance
in determining whether a community is exclusionary. For example, the issue
is not simply whether there are areas zoned for minimum lots of one or two
acres or larger. If there is adequate land in the community zoned to permit
moderately priced housing, large lot zoning is not of great significance. Large
lot zoning has increasingly exclusionary effects as the extent of its mapping
expands. In communities which have no zoning of higher density than one or
two acre zoning, exclusion of low- and moderate-income families is complete.
Mapping can be used to exclude lower-income housing in subtle
ways. Apartments may be permitted in a particular kind of zone, but that
zone may be mapped for only a minute percentage of the community's land.
The ordinance may permit mobile homes, but the only zone which includes
mobile homes may be located in a flood plain. The local board of health would
not permit a mobile home park on such a site. Or high-density apartments may
be mapped only for a zone which also permits office buildings. If it proves

much more profitable to build office space, the mapping for housing may turn
out to be illusory. Commercial developers can bid up the price of land and
make lower-income housing development financially unfeasible. Finally, "overzoning" for commerce and industry reduces the amount of land available
for residential development. As a result, the price of residential land goes up
and it is difficult or impossible to build lower-income housing.

Complicating the issue of whether a community is exclusionary
still further is the tendency toward non-Euclidean zoning. Increasingly, communities are zoning to insure that anyone who wishes to build will have to
seek a rezoning or some kind of special permit.

> Regulations are frequently written so that each apartment devel-
> oper has to negotiate with the community in order to get in at all.
> He negotiates either to get a zoning amendment because there is
> no permitted area zoned for apartments in the community, or
> he negotiates in order to get a special exception because the zoning
> ordinance does not permit apartments outright. In both cases the
> negotiation process is one of trying to bid up the price or cost of
> the apartment structure in order to limit the number of people
> who can come in at lower cost.[27]

Rather than have the zoning ordinance and the map determine the
permissible uses of a site, each developer must negotiate separately with the
responsible public body. The trend away from mapping is particularly strong
for apartments. There is relatively little suburban land on which apartments
can be built without a developer first obtaining a rezoning or special permit.
This scarcity of land premapped for apartment development creates additional
problems in terms of building low- and moderate-income housing. Because
there is so little vacant land zoned for apartment development, these sites are
likely to be extremely expensive (unless they are swamps or rock quarries).
The land cost is often too high to permit development of low- and moderate-
income housing even if high densities are permitted. Ironically, the existence
of large lot zoning and the negotiation process can provide a way out of this
dilemma. If the only land zoned for apartments is too expensive to permit
development of lower-income housing, the developer might instead purchase
a site zoned for single family houses on large lots. The price of the land will
reflect the current low density zoning. For example, under existing zoning
a one acre parcel might cost $15,000 and hold one house. The developer would
then seek a rezoning to permit apartment construction. If he could secure a
rezoning permitting development at a density of 10 units per acre, this would
reduce the land cost to $1,500 per unit and make it feasible to build lower-
income housing.

In short, the assessment of a community's land use policies is a
complex matter. Given the scarcity and cost of land zoned for relatively high

density development, the most crucial factor may be a community's willingness to change zoning to higher densities at the request of lower-income housing developers. The ordinance and the map may be important indicators of exclusion, but the real proof is in the actions of each locality in taking the necessary steps to either permit or prohibit construction of lower-income housing developments.

Federal Housing Programs:
Exclusionary Provisions

In addition to local roadblocks to lower-income housing, the federal government has built constraints into housing subsidy programs which supplement a community's exclusionary tools. Congress has provided a direct local veto over the use of some of these programs. Other programs carry statutory cost ceilings, which help communities wishing to exclude subsidized housing through the use of cost-escalating practices. Of the four major subsidy programs of the early 1970s, two provided the local governing body with a direct veto power, and the other two provided indirect assistance from the Congress in this endeavor.

Public Housing.   The oldest of the direct subsidy programs is low-rent public housing. This program serves low-income families and elderly people, including those with no income whatsoever, in both new and existing housing. Public housing continues to provide the greatest subsidy per unit of any subsidy program, making decent housing available for those who cannot afford standard housing in the private, unsubsidized market. In metropolitan areas the public housing program has provided housing increasingly for central city blacks. Sites have generally been located in the most segregated and deteriorated neighborhoods of the central city. Not until the late 1960s did HUD press for development of desegregated public housing in white areas of cities. Even these efforts were often at the prodding of the federal courts.

Suburbia has very little public housing. Even this minute amount is occupied almost entirely by elderly people rather than families. The act which established the public housing program provided that specified steps must be taken by the local community before the program could be used in the jurisdiction. As a result, inaction by the municipality serves to keep out public housing. The community may choose not to create a local housing authority, the agency which administers the public housing program. Even if a housing authority exists, it cannot operate within the boundaries of any municipality without the consent of the local governing body. A locality's refusal to provide this agreement means that there can be no public housing program in the community.

Rent Supplement Program.   A similar local veto exists in the Rent Supplement program. This program was enacted by Congress in 1965. It serves low-income families (much like public housing) in accommodations which are privately developed and owned.

When the Rent Supplement program was enacted, HUD considered using it as a means of providing integrated housing opportunities in the suburbs. When Congress was informed of these plans, it responded by approving only a small appropriation for the program. Congress also placed a condition on these funds, prohibiting their use in any community without the express approval of the local governing body. Inaction by a community is thus sufficient to keep out rent supplement units.

Moderate-Income Programs. Congress has clearly made the low-income housing programs a matter of local option. A similar result is achieved in the moderate-income subsidy programs through the cost ceilings written into the law. In the Housing Act of 1968, Congress created the section 235 program which provides for home ownership for moderate-income families, and the section 236 program which subsidizes rental housing for the same income group. Under each of these programs, an eligible sponsor applies to HUD for the subsidies which reduce the cost for moderate-income families. The total development cost of section 235 and 236 units may not exceed approximately $24,000. Through the use of exclusionary devices, a suburb can price this housing out of town.

In 1972 Congress considered a bill granting local communities a direct veto power over the use of all federally subsidized housing. Had it not been for strong lobbying by pro-housing forces and an election year rush to adjourn, the bill might well have passed.

Federal Housing Programs: An Uncertain Future. Even more basic, however, than the impediments present in specific subsidy programs is the question of the continued existence and funding of federal subsidized housing programs in any form. The future of federal housing programs was placed in serious doubt in January 1973. Outgoing HUD Secretary George Romney announced that HUD was halting virtually all new commitments to subsidize low- and moderate-income housing construction for an indefinite period. The programs were to be evaluated to see if they should be "improved, replaced or terminated."

In the fall of 1973 the administration announced its plans to phase out most of the subsidy programs, with the exception of one form of public housing called section 23 leasing. The leasing program had hardly been used in suburbia because of the local veto provision in the program. In addition, the administration proposed a "direct cash assistance" program which contemplated providing lower-income people with the money necessary to secure housing in the private market. Previous experiments with this approach showed neither expansion of housing choice nor new housing construction resulting from the program.

In addition to the questions raised by administration housing actions, subsidy programs are subject to the annual uncertainties of the congressional appropriation process. Thus, even if administration support continued for some form of housing subsidy programs, there is no assurance of continued congressional appropriations. Without federal subsidies, access to new suburban housing for low- and moderate-income people could only be through mobile home development.

Developer Inertia

The suburbs have an additional ally, in the form of inertia. Housing for the poor is built in the suburbs only if sponsors and developers take the initiative. They must overcome the obstacles and endure the red tape involved in the federal subsidy programs. Such community-minded developers risk coming out with a clear conscience and an empty wallet. Not surprisingly, most developers of subsidized housing prefer to take the path of least resistance and build where they are welcomed with open arms.

Suburban Exclusion: The Intersection of Injustice and Power

For 50 years states have delegated to localities the power to control the use of the land within their borders. Suburban communities have used this authority in ways that keep out housing for lower-income people. Zoning ordinances and subdivision regulations raise the cost of housing. These ordinances are usually administered to force developers to negotiate the character of each development with local officials. The community can thus prohibit any project it finds unacceptable. All too often, suburbs have employed their land use powers to deny access to lower-income people.

Part II

Public Sector Strategies for Suburban Access

Chapter Three

Introduction to Public Strategies

This country faces a difficult and potentially disastrous dilemma. It is both just and necessary for lower-income people to have access to suburban housing. At the same time, suburban communities have long had the power to maintain an unjust, costly practice of economic exclusion. The log jam must be broken. Suburbs must not be able to keep people from living there because of their income. The question which the rest of this book addresses is how to open the doors of suburbia. What governmental and private strategies can succeed in overcoming the barriers to building low- and moderate-income housing in the suburbs?

First, what role can public bodies play in opening the suburbs? County governments, regional bodies, state governments and the federal government cannot be neutral on the question of suburban access. They are inextricably involved in the metropolitan development process. They encourage or carry out planning, provide resources to local communities, and undertake related regulation. In the past, governments at all levels have been part of the problem. They have presided over an exclusionary system. Federal, state and local laws, policies and practices have contributed to the exclusion of lower-income people from suburbia. While our articulated goals emphasize adequate housing supply and choice for all Americans, the actions and inactions of government at all levels have impeded the achievement of those goals. Land use controls obstruct or prevent development of housing for lower-income people outside the central city. Federal laws help to raise the wall still higher by granting localities veto power over subsidized developments.

Not only has government helped to exclude the poor from suburbia, it financed the development of the suburbs for affluent white Americans. While suburban FHA and VA mortgage guarantees, highways, schools, and water and sewer facilities were paid for by everyone's tax dollars, the benefits were maldistributed. Government at all levels has a responsibility to redress the balance. Public bodies must redress the past practice of taxing all for suburban development, while only the relatively well-to-do gain access to the benefits.

It would be folly to expect large numbers of individual communities to open their doors voluntarily to lower-income people. Localities perceive themselves as having strong incentives to maintain their exclusionary posture. They have had the power to keep out the poor for 50 years. Since the U.S. Supreme Court upheld zoning as a legitimate exercise of the police power in *Euclid* v. *Ambler Realty,* the use of land has been a matter of almost exclusively local control.[1] It is clear that suburban communities, given continued free rein, would persist in closing their doors to low- and moderate-income people. Local autonomy is an important value, but it cannot be used to justify derogation of the rights of all Americans to choose where they wish to live. The independence of local communities needs to be limited to the extent necessary to guarantee free access to the suburbs.

In short, most suburban jurisdictions will keep doing their best to keep out housing for low- and moderate-income people. It is up to county and regional bodies, states, and the federal government to reverse this pattern. Changes require affirmative policies and programs at higher levels to provide lower-income groups the opportunity to live in suburbia. In the late 1960s public bodies began to take steps in that direction. In one part of the country, county governments passed ordinances requiring builders to include low- and moderate-income components in their housing developments. Although one of these promising ordinances was invalidated by the courts, the other still may be implemented. Moving to a larger geographical area, a number of metropolitan and regional agencies adopted housing allocation plans to facilitate suburban development of lower-income housing. These plans identify places where needed subsidized housing should be located. Several of the agencies have worked aggressively to implement these plans, to convert them from paper to real housing opportunities.

State governments have also tried to facilitate development of low- and moderate-income housing in suburbia. Many states have created housing finance agencies. These agencies sell tax-exempt bonds so they can make mortgage money available to housing developers. Because they are providing the financing, the agencies have a great voice in where the housing is to be located. A few housing finance agencies have focused on financing economically integrated suburban housing. However, none of these agencies has a mandate to build in the suburbs or authorization to eliminate or ignore the barriers suburbs have erected.

States have also reclaimed some of the power over land use that they have delegated for so long to localities. Increasingly, state legislatures are deciding that local governments should not be permitted to act totally autonomously in matters of regional and statewide concern. Although these laws generally emphasize environmental protection, one state has zeroed in on the problem of local exclusionary practices. The Massachusetts "anti-snob zoning" law sets limits on a locality's ability to deny necessary approvals for subsidized housing. Connecticut and Wisconsin have considered similar legislation.

Additional leverage is available to states (as well as to the federal government) through the "carrot and stick" process. State governments bestow benefits on local communities in many forms, including grants, loans and construction of state facilities. States can set particular kinds of actions by a locality as conditions for allocating these resources. For example, a state could give grants only to communities which eliminate the barriers to building low- and moderate-income housing. The Pennsylvania Department of Community Affairs has used this approach and has withheld grants to several suburbs which the department concluded were exclusionary. The state informed these communities that the state funds would be released when the localities had taken appropriate action to include lower-income housing.

Pennsylvania was also the first state to try litigation as a tool to open its suburban "creatures." The state joined a lawsuit against a large number of Philadelphia suburbs. The plaintiffs argued that these communities excluded housing for low- and moderate-income people and urged the court to require affirmative inclusionary actions by the localities.

Initial efforts to increase suburban access have not been confined to the county, regional and state levels. Even the slumbering federal giant has shown some signs of awakening to the problem. The "feds" have taken isolated actions which by no means amount to coherent policy in support of opening the suburbs to low- and moderate-income people. In fact, the president's 1971 Equal Housing Message placed the federal government in opposition to racial discrimination but abdicated all responsibility for dealing with economic exclusion. In two cases, the Justice Department sued suburban communities which refused to permit development of subsidized housing projects, but the suits alleged that racial discrimination was involved. The Justice Department made clear that it was acting pursuant to the president's message. Given this posture, the Justice Department is likely to sue only when a suburb practices blatant racial discrimination in keeping out lower-income housing.

In addition to litigation, the federal government has on occasion used its administrative authority to press for greater suburban housing opportunities. For example, HUD provides funds to metropolitan and regional planning agencies. In at least one instance, HUD conditioned a planning grant on the regional agency's commitment to develop a housing allocation plan of the kind described earlier. In several other cases, HUD used its "carrots" available to suburbs, such as open space and water and sewer grants, to encourage applicants for these funds to accept low- and moderate-income housing.

Perhaps the most visible federal effort in the early 1970s involved the administration of the subsidized housing programs. Early in 1972 HUD adopted regulations which encouraged development of subsidized housing outside of the inner city. These "project selection criteria" gave priority for the limited HUD funds to applicants who could open up new housing opportunities, including options in suburbia. In some areas, housing sponsors shifted their efforts to the suburbs. However, these regulations had only a short test, as the subsidy programs became the subject of first, a moratorium, and later, a planned phase-out.

Public strategies at all levels have taken one of two paths. Some approaches have focused on specific instances of exclusion or exclusionary practices. For example, the Massachusetts law provides a state review process which enables developers denied permits locally to seek state permission to build the housing. The suits brought by the state of Pennsylvania and the federal government have challenged specific suburban obstacles. Pennsylvania's suit related to a whole range of specific exclusionary practices, while the federal suits have dealt with the exclusion of individual subsidized housing projects.

Other governmental efforts have attempted to provide an "inclusionary" context or framework, rather than challenging particular local ordinances or practices. For example, housing allocation plans do not change zoning ordinances or practices directly, but their existence and widespread support for them may facilitate land use changes throughout individual communities or for particular subsidized housing projects.

The Potential of Public Strategies

The efforts by public bodies outlined above represent cautious first steps to solve the problem of suburban exclusion. Government has far greater leverage to increase suburban access than has been tapped. The potential governmental influence is enormous, through regulation, litigation, financing of housing, planning, and conditioning funding to local communities.

State and federal regulatory powers which might be employed to increase suburban access, such as civil rights provisions, have scarcely been used. For example, enforcement of employment discrimination laws could include requirements that suburban employers see to it that housing is available for lower-income employees near the job site.

States could also reclaim more of their land use control powers. They could require, for example, that localities plan and zone affirmatively to provide for lower-income housing.

In addition, some of the regulatory approaches that have been used by one level of government could also be used by others. As states moved to carve out a role for themselves relative to land use, the Congress considered a number of national land use policy bills. These bills contemplate encouraging additional state involvement in regulating the use of land. Meanwhile, existing federal policy required areawide comprehensive planning, including housing planning, as a precondition for a variety of federal grants. It was up to the responsible federal agencies to administer their planning grants and require- ments to assure that there were ongoing efforts to open the suburbs before federal funds would flow.

Beyond expanding the scope of regulatory activities, public agencies have other mechanisms at their disposal. First, states and the federal govern- ment could pursue litigation strategies being used by private organizations (see Chapters 17 and 18). Second, although a couple of states have created subsidy programs on a limited scale, this area remains largely the domain of the federal government. More states could create subsidy programs and use these programs to increase suburban access. Third, although regional agencies have been the prime initiators of allocation plans, states could also do this job. Alternatively, states could require that metropolitan or regional agencies develop and implement allocation plans. Finally, the carrot and stick approach could be used aggressively by state and federal agencies to condition benefits bestowed on inclusionary actions taken by localities. This approach could be expanded in terms of the state and federal agencies involved and should em- phasize the grants and facilities which have the most appeal for suburbanites.

In sum, the last few years have witnessed the development and implementation of a wide variety of public strategies for overcoming suburban hurdles to low- and moderate-income housing. Most of these activities are at an embryonic state. Many of the victories to date have been symbolic. Other efforts have met with defeat, at least temporarily. The resistance of the suburbs shows no sign of fading away. However, more public bodies are making efforts to increase suburban access each year.

The approaches discussed in the following chapters have been tried in only a few places. Many have potential for replication not only in different parts of the country, but at different levels of government as well.

Chapter Four

Inclusionary Zoning at the County Level

The county is generally the first governmental unit above the municipality. In states where counties retain substantial authority the county governments have significant opportunities to influence local housing patterns. Perhaps the most important steps counties can take are in the area of regulating development practices within their jurisdictions. Two suburban counties in the Washington, D.C. area passed such regulatory ordinances. Fairfax County, Virginia and Montgomery County, Maryland enacted legislation requiring residential builders to include a proportion of low- and moderate-income housing in their developments. The workability of these "inclusionary" ordinances remains untested. Virginia courts found the Fairfax ordinance to be illegal.[1] The more recent Montgomery County ordinance faced a similar challenge in the Maryland courts.

Fairfax County, Virginia:
Affluent Suburbia

Fairfax County, Virginia is directly in the path of the white, middle-income exodus from Washington, D.C. By 1970 it had surpassed Montgomery County, Maryland as the area's wealthiest county and was among the most affluent in the country. The county has an average family income of almost $16,000.[2] The median price of a new single family home is $35,000–$40,000.[3] The rise in housing costs has taken new single family dwellings beyond the reach of the county's employees as well as most blacks who live either in the county or in the District of Columbia. Apartment production has spurted as builders have switched from detached houses to multi-family projects. But even the apartment units are beyond the reach of low- and moderate-income people.

Developing Political Support for Lower-Income Housing. In the 1960s, citizens' groups such as the Fairfax County Federation of Citizens and the League of Women Voters carried out active programs against housing discrimination. As Fairfax has become an attractive destination for migrants from Washington, county racial patterns have changed dramatically. In 1940, 15.9 percent of the county's 40,929 inhabitants were black.[4] Thirty years later blacks constituted only three percent of the Fairfax County population. The citizens' groups attempted to insure that the county's housing stock was available to any blacks who could afford to move there.

By 1970 the thrust was shifting. The Fairfax Redevelopment and Housing Authority attempted to secure approval for sites for low-income public housing.[5] The public housing struggle provided an initial opportunity for airing the issue of developing lower-income housing in Fairfax County. The following year the Coalition for Housing Action began to organize support for zoning amendments to facilitate provision of new housing for low- and moderate-income people. This coalition of church groups viewed the proposed ordinance on lower-income housing as an economic approach to the race issue. Fairfax was the only Washington area jurisdiction with a decrease in its black population. It was an area where blacks needed housing. The coalition developed a 12-point program, related primarily to racial justice. The housing ordinance was the first item on this agenda.

As part of a countywide educational process, the Coalition for Housing Action presented a slide-tape show to demonstrate that low- and moderate-income housing can be aesthetically attractive. This presentation was given to a variety of interested groups before the ordinance was submitted formally.

An eight week drive produced 34,000 signatures on a petition supporting the proposed ordinance.[6] At the two public hearings held before the county supervisors, almost all of the testimony in support of the ordinance came from county residents who needed subsidized housing—local police, firemen, schoolteachers—mainly the white working class. Little support was forthcoming from builders. Having faced the public housing site selection problem, county board members were aware of the need for lower-income housing in the county. Several members favored the scattered-site approach and viewed the proposed ordinance as a means of implementing it. The Board of Supervisors passed the ordinance in August of 1971.

The Substance of the Ordinance. The Fairfax ordinance attempted to regulate development in precisely the opposite way from the general suburban pattern. Rather than excluding low- and moderate-income housing through zoning requirements, the ordinance provided for the mandatory inclusion of low- and moderate-income housing. For any residential development of 50 or more units (with the exception of single family housing and high rise apartments):

An applicant for PDH (Planned Development Housing) zoning or for an amended development thereunder . . . shall provide or cause others to provide, under the development plan, low-income units which shall not be less (and may be more) than six percent (6%) of the total number of units (other than detached single family dwelling units) specified in the development plan. The applicant shall also provide, or cause others to provide, the number of moderate-income dwelling units which, when added to the number of low-income dwelling units, shall not be less (and may be more) than fifteen percent (15%) of the total number of dwelling units (other than detached single family dwelling units) specified in the development plan.[7]

Every development covered by the ordinance must provide at least 15 percent of the dwelling units for low- and moderate-income families. At least six percent of the units must be for low-income families. Developers may meet this requirement by using federal subsidy programs, but they are only obligated to provide the housing to the extent that they can secure federal funds.[8] Developers may proceed without subsidy funds if they can provide housing at the same rentals and prices as would be available under government programs.

The percentages for low- and moderate-income dwelling units must be applied separately to each category of housing in a development, including one family, semidetached, two family, townhouses, and garden apartments.[9] The average number of bedrooms in the low- and moderate-income component must be consistent with the mix of units in the total development.

The developer may fulfill his low-income responsibilities by selling land or dwelling units to the redevelopment and housing authority under the public housing program.[10] With the approval of the redevelopment and housing authority and the county board, the applicant may substitute land or dwellings outside the proposed development, provided that undue concentration of low- and moderate-income housing does not result. Or he may arrange for subsidies under the rent supplement or any other available program which will bring the cost of housing within the means of low-income families. To meet the moderate-income requirement, the developer may apply to HUD or any other source of subsidy funds. He may forego the use of subsidies if he can build housing within the means of families whose incomes are moderate.[11]

If government subsidies are not available, the developer may be excused from providing a low- and moderate-income component, but he must satisfy the county executive that he is "making persistent efforts in good faith to obtain the proposed subsidies and provide such dwelling units."[12] The applicant's efforts are to be judged according to "the normal processing time and procedures required to obtain the various subsidies applied for. . . ."[13]

The amendments specify how long the developer must wait for an answer
from the relevant government agency. Unless he gets a tentative commitment
(e.g., an FHA "feasibility letter") within 180 days from the date he applies
for funds or has his development plan approved, his obligation to provide
subsidized housing is terminated.[14] If he gets a tentative commitment
within the 180 days his obligation is extended for another 180 days. If he
does not receive a final federal commitment within that period, the obligation
is terminated. These 180 day periods reflect the normal processing time for
government housing programs. They were included to assure that the developer
is not unduly delayed by red tape.

    If at any time before expiration of the relevant 180 day period a
responsible official notifies the developer that his project is not feasible (for
reasons other than cost limitations), or that funds will not be available, his
obligation to the county is terminated.[15] He is not required to shift to
another lower-income housing proposal if his initial proposal falls through.

    The county executive may authorize withholding building permits
and other necessary approvals for the development until the applicant complies with these requirements.[16] In such a case, the developer may appeal
to the planning commission and then to the board of supervisors.

    The Challenge in Court.   Shortly after the enactment of the Fair-
fax County zoning amendment, 11 lawsuits were filed to enjoin its operation.
Ten of the suits were initiated by one developer. The challenges argued that
the ordinance: (1) was not authorized under the Virginia Zoning Enabling Act;
(2) was arbitrary and capricious; (3) constituted an unconstitutional "taking"
of private property, without "just compensation"; (4) represented an unlawful
delegation of zoning authority to HUD or county administrators that should
be retained in the county board; (5) was unconstitutionally vague and therefore void; and (6) constituted unlawful "conditional zoning."

    In *De Groff Enterprises, Inc.* v. *Board of County Supervisors of
Fairfax County, Virginia, et al.*, the Circuit Court of Fairfax County nullified
the ordinance on grounds 1, 2, and 4.[17] The trial court did not address
the constitutional questions raised. The Supreme Court of Virginia sustained
the lower court opinion, ruling that the ordinance was unconstitutional as
well as being beyond the state enabling act.[18]

Implementation of a Fairfax-Type Ordinance

    As a result of the court decision, the workability of the Fairfax-
type ordinance remains untested. A number of questions must be addressed
with respect to such a mandatory ordinance.

    HUD Role.   HUD's cooperation is a key element in the viability
of this type of ordinance. If federal subsidy funds are available, HUD must

provide these funds promptly and apply cost, site and other requirements
flexibly. First, it is important that HUD provide priority funding for inclusionary efforts like Fairfax County's. Beyond making subsidy funds generally
available for the area, HUD's cooperation is needed in responding promptly to
specific subsidized housing applications from an area like Fairfax County.
The developer should be funded or relieved of his obligation. The development can then proceed without undue delay. HUD's red tape should not
be an excuse for political pressure from builders against adopting and enforcing
inclusionary ordinances.

To meet the need for efficient processing of applications, HUD
and Fairfax County formed a working group to adopt common development
standards. This eliminated the need for separate reviews of site plans. HUD
used the county's building code instead of its "minimum property standards,"
and relied on the county's inspectors for enforcement.

Cost Problems.   With the high cost of land and site development
in Fairfax and other suburban areas, there is a serious question of financial
feasibility in developing lower-income housing. HUD's moderate-income
subsidy programs are encumbered with statutory cost ceilings of $21,000 for
units with three or fewer bedrooms and $24,000 for units with four bed-
rooms or more. Within this total, HUD permits a land cost of about $1,500
per lot for townhouse development. But the cost of such a lot in Fairfax
County would be around $2,500. Thus, an additional subsidy is necessary to
make some suburban projects financially feasible.

If an inclusionary ordinance results in a financial deprivation
to the developer, it becomes additionally vulnerable to legal attack. The developer would have a claim that the requirements resulted in an unconstitutional taking of private property without just compensation. An ordinance
which imposed disproportionate burdens on the developer would be question-
able public policy even if it survived a legal challenge.

Site Selection.   HUD's administration of its site requirements is
important to the success of a Fairfax-type ordinance. HUD requires that there
be supportive services and facilities such as schools, recreation, shopping and
public transportation within a reasonable distance of a proposed site for subsidized housing. HUD could determine that a site is inadequately served for
low- and moderate-income families, while the local zoning and the economic
realities dictate use of the site for middle-income housing. However, since
many lower-income families do not own cars, proximity to shopping and public transportation may be more important to them than to affluent households.
In this sense, a particular site might be appropriate for middle-income families
and inappropriate for the less affluent. An accommodation is necessary, so
that HUD could provide subsidy funds to components of larger developments.

Otherwise, builders could not meet their obligation to provide low-income units and would have great difficulty building moderate-income units.

In sum, Fairfax-type legislation is closely tied to federal subsidy programs. Success is heavily dependent upon the availability of subsidies and the vagaries of the related administrative process.

Potential Response of Developers.   Continued operation of developers in the jurisdiction is also critical to the success of a Fairfax-type ordinance. It is impossible to predict the reaction of developers. Some may move their operations to other parts of the region or leave the region entirely, preferring to build elsewhere rather than get involved in the complexities of the federal programs.

Others may continue to build under the new requirements. Those who know the territory might be reluctant to start over in another area, searching for the good sites and finding out how to get local approvals. Some of them will also have had success with subsidized projects.

Alternative locations for development in the region might also be limited. For example, in the Washington, D.C. area, Montgomery County, Maryland imposed a sewer moratorium.[19] Alexandria, Virginia was already developed and Loudoun County had established controls to slow growth. Thus, developers seeking to leave Fairfax County would have some difficulty finding other rapidly developing parts of the region where they could set up shop.

In addition, the Fairfax County ordinance included provisions to lessen the burden on developers caused by the ordinance. First, the ordinance gave developers a density bonus.[20] It permitted them to build one additional higher-income unit for every two low- and moderate-income units included in the development. This enabled developers to build at higher densities than would ordinarily be permitted, thus increasing profits on the overall development. In addition, the county established (but did not finance) a fund to provide subsidies on top of other subsidy funds.[21] In order to obtain this local subsidy, the developer would have to show that he was unable to meet HUD's requirements for financial feasibility. Sponsors would then be eligible for grants up to $500 per unit for moderate-income housing and $1,000 for low-income units. However, this subsidy would not always be sufficient to bridge the gap between the level of HUD subsidies and the developer's actual costs.

An additional reason why developers might keep building in an area with a Fairfax-type ordinance is the flexibility permitted in designing developments. Federal subsidy programs do not limit the type of housing which can be built. Every type of structure from high-rise to single family detached units is permitted. A developer can physically integrate the subsidized units into his development.

The reaction of developers will be determined largely by their experience under an inclusionary ordinance. Economically integrated housing developments have been financially and socially successful in Massachusetts, Illinois and other parts of the country.[22] If the initial projects under a Fairfax-type ordinance succeeded, the chances of continued participation by developers would be greatly enhanced.

Loopholes for Developers.   The Fairfax ordinance exempted single family developments from its coverage. Unless such developments are included, developers could build single family housing to avoid the intent of the ordinance. In Fairfax County, however, it appeared that developers would continue to build multifamily housing in spite of the housing mix requirement, because of the strength of the lower-middle-income apartment housing market.

The ordinance also enables developers to avoid its impact by building developments of less than 50 units. A developer could subdivide a piece of land into two 49-unit developments instead of one 98-unit project, thus getting out from under the housing mix requirements. However, the recalcitrant developer must pay a price for this exercise. He would have to spend time and money on multiple rezonings. He would also risk denial of his request as his purpose became apparent.

The Formula.   The Fairfax ordinance provides clear standards of conduct for the developer. The county can fairly evaluate his plan and implementation efforts. However, legislation which sets out a specific formula may be vulnerable to political and legal attack on the grounds of arbitrariness. There is no magic in the numbers selected in Fairfax County or any other numbers which might have been chosen. The 15 percent low- and moderate-income figure was a political compromise, largely unrelated to any determination of the county's need. However, the six percent low-income requirement is rationally related to the 15 percent figure. Federal law permits piggybacking of low-income rent supplement funds onto 40 percent of the units in moderate-income projects. Fairfax adopted this proportion (six percent is 40 percent of 15 percent) in its formula.

In spite of the arguably arbitrary character of the percentages, the public debates concerning the Fairfax ordinance did not focus on the validity of the formula. Similarly, the courts' review did not focus on the justifications for the particular set of figures.

Updating the Numbers.   If a formula becomes outdated, it should be changed. What looks like a progressive figure when an ordinance is adopted might become unduly restrictive a decade later and actually impede access of the poor to suburbia. In Fairfax County, applying the ordinance to the construction rates of the early 1970s would produce 600 to 900 units of low-

and moderate-income housing per year. A major influx of industry, for example, could make the appropriate figure many times this amount. In that event, the political battle would have to be fought to raise the quota. Potential allies would include the newly arrived corporations and companies contemplating moving into the county and seeking housing for their employees within easy access to the job site.

Racial Impact of an Inclusionary Ordinance. In many suburban areas there is a substantial market for subsidized housing among whites already residing in the area. The inclusionary ordinance therefore has the potential to solidify the racially segregated housing patterns of a metropolitan area. Opportunities for in-migration must be provided, to increase housing choice for inner-city residents as the suburban housing supply grows. Although the zoning ordinance cannot be written in terms of racial mix, the implementation of the ordinance should emphasize providing housing choice for minorities. Developing more housing than is needed by current county residents would help. In addition, marketing should focus on attracting inner-city blacks.

Montgomery County, Maryland
In late 1973, in suburban Maryland, the Montgomery County Council enacted a zoning amendment similar to Fairfax County's.[23] Proposed legislation was submitted in August of 1971. The impetus came from citizens' organizations, with drafting by the Washington law firm which had been instrumental in developing the Fairfax County ordinance. In March 1972 public hearings were held on the proposal, followed by months of work sessions involving interested parties including representatives of the suburban Maryland homebuilders association, the local chapter of the American Institute of Architects and the County Bar Association. The county attorney rendered an opinion that the proposed ordinance would violate the Constitution, since the requirements imposed upon the developers would constitute a taking of private property, without just compensation.[24] In addition to the county attorney's opinion, a sewer moratorium complicated matters in Montgomery County. Development is limited until 1976, so an inclusionary ordinance might have little practical effect until that time. Nevertheless, the seven-member county council voted unanimously to require most large new housing developments to provide some housing for low- and moderate-income families. The ordinance is similar to Fairfax County's, but the Montgomery County requirements are unrelated to the availability of HUD funds and apply to all residential developments. The Montgomery County ordinance was expected to face a court challenge.

Under the Montgomery County zoning amendment, anyone applying for a building permit for 50 or more dwelling units at one location would be required to submit to the Department of Environmental Protection a statement agreeing that not less than 15 percent of the units would be moderately priced.[25] "Moderately priced dwelling units" were defined in alternative ways. They could be constructed, sold or rented under any of the federal low- or moderate-income housing programs. Or, the sales price or rental was not to exceed a maximum established by the planning commission, taking into account HUD ceilings and the incomes of residents and potential residents of Montgomery County. The sales price or rent of these units was to be controlled for a five year period, to insure occupancy by moderate-income people.[26] The developer's agreement to provide 15 percent moderately priced dwelling units must also include a commitment on the number, type and location of the units, as well as a plan for staging their construction.

Los Angeles Proposed Ordinance

In January 1973 the Los Angeles City Planning Commission approved a proposed ordinance that would "require that on property rezoned or approved for conditional use, 15 percent of any dwelling units built should be made available to low and moderate income households."[27] This ordinance resembled the Fairfax and Montgomery County zoning amendments in many respects. It required at least six percent low-income units and 15 percent low- and moderate-income units. It relied heavily on federal subsidy programs. Developers could appeal from adverse decisions to the governing body, in this case the city council.

The Los Angeles proposal also had significant unique features. For example, while Fairfax excluded high rises and developments with less than 50 units from coverage, the Los Angeles version specifically included all developments of five units or more in the categories of: apartment houses, apartment hotels, multiple or group dwellings, residential or condominium developments, cooperative apartments and residential planned developments. [28] The city's housing authority would administer the ordinance. The authority was to review residential applications and certify compliance with the housing requirement prior to issuance of a certificate of occupancy. Although the Fairfax ordinance envisioned a significant subsidiary role for the housing authority, it retained primary administrative responsibility in the county executive.

Finally, the Los Angeles approach closes an important loophole in the Fairfax ordinance. Rather than terminating the low-income responsibility if subsidies are not available, the Los Angeles proposal merely defers compliance. Obligations are deferred if the developer agrees to give the housing authority indefinite rights of first refusal on rentals and resales when subsidies become available.[29]

Status of the Proposed Ordinance. The Los Angeles City Attorney gave a legal opinion that the proposed ordinance was invalid as a taking of private property for public purposes without just compensation.[30] The opinion was similar to that of the Montgomery County Attorney. The planning commission approved the proposed ordinance anyway and recommended that the city council enact the ordinance. The council postponed action until well beyond the local elections.[31]

This ordinance was to be citywide rather than countywide, but its passage could still provide a test of the workability of such an inclusionary mechanism.

The Potential of Mandatory Inclusionary Legislation

In addition to questions of effectiveness and political feasibility generally facing suburban strategies, the mandatory ordinance is vulnerable to legal challenge. With two counties having enacted these provisions, it appears possible to build the broad base of support necessary to pass such legislation. This may be particularly true in places where there is great employment growth which provides moderate-income jobs in the public and private sectors.

Even if Fairfax-type ordinances can be passed elsewhere, they obviously will not yield concrete results unless they can withstand a challenge in court. Some of the legal problems may be dealt with by careful drafting which attempts to insure consistency with the state enabling legislation. The purpose of the ordinance should be clearly tied to health and welfare considerations such as providing "decent, safe and sanitary" housing for all people in the jurisdiction. The format should be regulatory rather than prohibitory, i.e., following the accepted traditional pattern. Definitions, such as "low- and moderate-income," should be internal to the ordinance rather than depending on definitions by HUD or some other outside agency.

Thoughtful drafting of the legislation can help it survive in the courts, but what is perhaps the thorniest problem—the "taking" issue—goes beyond drafting. It would be unconstitutional for a public body to literally take private property without reasonable compensation. Preventing the owner from using the property in any way at all would also constitute an unconstitutional taking. Somewhere short of that point, legitimate regulation begins. And it is not entirely clear how far regulation of the use of land can go without stepping over into a taking. If a Fairfax-type ordinance ended up either prohibiting development or making projects completely unfeasible economically, most courts would probably find the ordinance unconstitutional. There is sound public policy involved in that position. Communities should not be able to exact unreasonable tolls from developers seeking to come into town. If public bodies can impose these burdens for inclusionary purposes, they can mount up the costs for exclusionary purposes as well. And that is what communities do all the time, as indicated in Chapter 2.

It is crucial, therefore, to structure an inclusionary ordinance to avoid placing undue burdens on the developer. The density bonus is one mechanism. It should be substantial. A second approach would be to waive other requirements, such as dedication of land for parks or schools. The developer's lower-income housing obligation might even be placed in the alternative. He could supply the housing *or* dedicate the land. In either case, he should not have to make all the other dedications which would otherwise be required. Dedication of land for housing would be especially attractive because it would be, in effect, a 100 percent writedown, a very helpful subsidy.

Chapter Five

Allocating Housing on a Regional Basis

Moving from the county upward on the governmental ladder, the next level is the state. The country has not generally accepted the concept of metropolitan or regional units of government, but there is a growing recognition that many problems must be dealt with on a multijurisdictional basis because they do not stop at municipal boundaries. As a result, the decade of the 1960s witnessed the creation of hundreds of metropolitan and regional bodies. By 1970 almost all of the 233 Standard Metropolitan Statistical Areas (SMSAs) had some type of regional entity.

Regional bodies have taken a variety of forms. Councils of Government (COGs) are voluntary organizations of public officials and local governments. By 1970 the number of COGs had grown to 220. The other most common multijurisdictional entity is the regional planning commission. These agencies are created by state legislatures to carry out comprehensive areawide planning. In a particular region, either a COG or a regional planning commission might be charged with areawide planning responsibilities.

Until the middle and late 1960s, areawide organizations served limited functions such as providing information exchange or advisory comments to local governments. Then federal planning funds and the A-95 review process (discussed later in this chapter and in Chapter 13) served to enlarge the numbers and functions of metropolitan and regional bodies. At the same time, the formal legal authority of these agencies expanded little. COGs continued to be purely voluntary organizations, with their legal authority based on general interlocal agreement legislation or state enabling legislation. Regional planning commissions had limited authority from state legislatures. Constituent jurisdictions were not about to give up governmental powers to a regional body. State legislatures were not willing to hand over to these unaccountable agencies the power to implement their plans. For most agencies, their real

power as well as their formal authority was limited by their need to be sensitive to the wishes of the municipalities within their jurisdiction. This dependence
on the political and perhaps financial support of local governments continued
to provide a serious constraint on the ability of regional agencies to deal
with difficult social questions from a regional perspective. Given this set of
constraints, it is no wonder that for years regional agencies avoided controversial questions such as opening the suburbs to lower-income housing.
Further, it is not surprising that housing planning was divorced from implementation.

In spite of the constraints on metropolitan and regional bodies,
it has become generally accepted that planning for housing is comprehended
within their overall regional planning responsibility. The Department of
Housing and Urban Development, which provides financial support to most
of these agencies, requires that part of an agency's work program be related
to housing. Although regional housing planning is now an accepted and relatively widespread practice, this planning remains for the most part unrelated
to actual development of housing. Many planning agencies carry out statistical
analyses to determine the need for housing in the region as a whole, the
number of existing substandard units, or the cost of housing. They analyze
the existing situation and perhaps identify problems growing out of that analysis. But they can do more.

In spite of the constraints imposed by local governments, the
political sensitivity of the housing issue and the limited tools available for
implementation, regional bodies have significant potential for dealing with
the housing problem. Regional agencies have already begun to carry out regional
housing strategies. In 1970 the Miami Valley Regional Planning Commission
(MVRPC) in the Dayton, Ohio area, adopted the first regional allocation plan
for low- and moderate-income housing.[1] The plan proposed to distribute
geographically new housing necessary to accommodate all of the five county
region's low- and moderate-income residents in standard units. The aim of the
Dayton plan and its progeny is to provide for distribution of lower-income
housing throughout an entire metropolitan area or region in a way that is
equitable to the recipient communities while providing potential occupants
with wide geographical choice, as well as access to the full range of community
services and facilities.

Since the adoption of the original Miami Valley plan, a number of
other organizations have developed housing allocation plans, including the
Metropolitan Council of the Twin Cities, Minnesota area; San Bernardino
County, California Planning Department; Southeastern Wisconsin Regional
Planning Commission; Washington, D.C. Council of Governments; and the
Denver Regional Council of Governments.[2] Other agencies which have con-
sidered, or are in the process of developing, some form of housing allocation
plan include the Delaware Valley Regional Planning Commission, in the Phila-

delphia area; the East-West Gateway Coordinating Council in the St. Louis, Missouri area; the Mid-America Regional Council, based in Kansas City, Missouri; and the Sacramento, California Regional Area Planning Commission. Any such listing becomes outdated as soon as it is compiled, because planning agencies increasingly believe that they should be carrying out this kind of undertaking. National organizations of planners have indicated strong support for these plans.[3] Support for the development of allocation plans also comes from outside the planning profession—the United States Civil Rights Commission as well as the Department of Housing and Urban Development have strongly urged the creation of areawide housing plans.[4]

An Overview of the Allocation Planning Process

Although housing allocation plans differ significantly, they have certain features in common. They seek to facilitate development of housing on a rational basis throughout an area rather than continuing concentration in the central city. They identify criteria for locating the new housing. The criteria generally attempt to increase the housing choices of potential occupants and consider the needs and capacities of local communities involved. The plans either quantify the amount of housing desired for specific localities or designate priority areas to receive the needed housing. Generally, allocation plans propose a distribution of housing development within fairly large sub-areas of the region but do not identify specific sites for lower-income housing. This avoids the political problems involved in selecting sites at that early stage, as well as resulting inflation of the price of the proposed sites which might make subsidized development economically infeasible.

In short, a housing allocation plan is a statement by a regional body to its constituent communities that they have a responsibility to accept a reasonable amount of new housing for low- and moderate-income families. Complete realization of an allocation plan would result in a significant change in a region's housing patterns; many communities which had previously excluded lower-income housing would be pushed to open their doors. Given the magnitude of the changes that housing allocation plans contemplate, and their voluntary nature, the planning agency must have a broad base of political support to get a plan adopted, much less implemented. Thus the first order of business is to undertake a continuing program to develop community support among organizations, citizens and public officials. If the first stage of this campaign is successful, it should be possible for the policy-making board to adopt the plan once it is developed.

Then comes the even more difficult job of implementation. Plans are worthless without implementation. They may even be counterproductive, having raised expectations without delivering. Too much of the history of regional planning is recorded in plans filed on shelves and forgotten. Through an unstated pact, the planning agencies and the political structure have been divorced from each other. The plans have not reflected political realities, and the planners have abdicated any role in working with the politicians to get the plans implemented.

Since planners have historically abdicated any role in implementation it might be possible for planning agencies to write and adopt housing allocation plans, rest on their laurels and receive plaudits from the profession. However, the plans are not self-executing. The current generation of activist planners recognizes the history of plans not acted on and the political realities and knows that even more effort is needed to implement a plan than to develop it and get it adopted. As the first agency to produce a plan, the Dayton planners could have gotten their national recognition and stopped. Recognizing planning as a political process and housing as the goal, they set out to get the housing produced. Other regional bodies have begun to follow suit.

As regional housing planners have developed political skills, they have found that they have considerable power to see to it that their plans become a reality. The limits on their legal authority do not define the limits of their ability to implement plans. Implementation requires leverage. The best lever to date is the agency's handle on federal funds, through federal planning requirements such as the A–95 review process. The regional body reviews a local community's applications to federal agencies for water and sewer, open space and a multitude of other grants. The review is to determine the consistency with overall areawide planning, which includes the housing allocation plan. The regional body can seek local cooperation in accepting lower-income housing as a price for favorable comment on the community's application for federal funds. Regional agencies are learning to use this and other tools to bring about the housing their plans envision.

Impetus for Allocation Plans

Usually, the public body, through its staff or policy-making board, takes the initiative in developing an allocation plan. However, citizen groups and the federal government have also stimulated development of allocation plans. States could do likewise.

In the Dayton area, the planning commission staff proposed the concept of the housing plan to the commission, which eventually adopted the plan. The planners also took the lead in identifying the need for an allocation plan in San Bernardino. They saw that subsidized housing projects were concentrated in certain parts of their jurisdiction, causing overcrowding of schools and strains on local resources. Distributing subsidized housing throughout the area seemed to be an appropriate way to deal with this problem.

In the Denver area, the regional council of governments established a citizens' task force to study the region's housing problem. Representation on the task force was private and public, local, regional, state and federal. Members were from the COG, "housing consumers" (e.g., church groups,

League of Women Voters, state civil rights commission, Legal Aid, civic organizations related to housing), and "housing providers" (e.g., financing institutions, home builders, construction trades, state and federal housing agencies, chamber of commerce). Out of this broad-based group came support for the COG to develop a regional housing allocation plan.

Most of the allocation plans have come about as a result of the initiatives of the regional organizations. However, this has not always been the case. Outside forces can and should bring pressure to bear on reluctant regional bodies. For example, the Delaware Valley Regional Planning Commission (DVRPC) undertook its housing plan as a result of prodding by representatives of the Philadelphia area's poor people. In the latter half of 1971, the Bucks County Legal Aid Society and other legal services offices in metropolitan Philadelphia filed a petition with DVRPC on behalf of lower-income persons. [5] The petition challenged the commission's lack of an adequate mechanism to provide systematically for the low- and moderate-income housing needs of the region. The petitioners asserted that the commission was in violation of federal requirements to develop a "housing element," with "particular attention to the housing problems and lack of opportunities for housing of low-income and minority groups."[6] (See Chapter 13 for a detailed discussion of the federal requirements.) As a result of the petition and subsequent negotiations, DVRPC began gathering and processing data for a housing allocation model for the nine county Philadelphia metropolitan area.

In addition, in at least one instance HUD stimulated the development of an areawide housing allocation model. Early in 1971 HUD withheld $185,000 in planning funds from the Southeastern Wisconsin Regional Planning Commission (SEWRPC) because SEWRPC had failed to adopt a short-term action plan for the regional allocation of low- and moderate-income housing units. Faced with the loss of all open space funds for the seven county region because of the lack of a certified planning agency, SEWRPC capitulated to HUD's demands. By May 1971 SEWRPC and HUD had contracted for a short-term plan which allocated 2,000 units of low- and moderate-income housing throughout the region. (See Chapter 13 for a full description of the HUD-SEWRPC controversy.)

Community Support
Whether the impetus for the allocation plan is internal or external to the planning agency, developing widespread community support is an essential task for the agency from the outset of the project. A continuing program is necessary to secure the adoption of an allocation plan and assistance in its implementation.

Citizen Advisory Groups.
The Miami Valley Regional Planning Commission enlisted the support of key elements in the Dayton area community. In the earliest stages of the process, the planning staff helped form a housing

advisory group. The group consisted of representatives of public agencies and private organizations in the area, such as the Dayton Community Development Department, the Urban League and the community action agency of the antipoverty program, as well as the local organizations of homebuilders and realtors. Because of their continuous involvement from the outset, many of the participating organizations gave early endorsement to the plan.

The Washington COG also set up advisory groups. In the development of the housing report, the planning staff enlisted the advice of elected officials on the Community Resources Policy Committee, local public and quasi-public staff representatives on the Housing Technical Committee, and interested citizens, who served on the Housing Committee of the Metropolitan Congress of Citizens. Seeking the advice of key actors in the region on an ongoing basis is an extremely useful way of getting political support for the plan, as well as getting assistance in eliminating unnecessary objectionable features.

Voluntary Organizations.   In addition to the advisory group, the Miami Valley Regional Planning Commission sought and received the support of a variety of citizens' organizations and interest groups. The Greater Dayton League of Women Voters and a number of local church groups supported the effort. The area's business community provided significant backing through the Dayton Chamber of Commerce, as well as a group of top business executives. The corporate leaders were brought together by a former board chairman of a major national industrial firm based in Dayton. The Homebuilders Association of Metropolitan Dayton, seeing the potential for increased housing construction, brought together a coalition of local builders and developers to lend support to the plan and aid in the construction of subsidized housing units. Other regional bodies have sought the support of a similar range of groups for their plans.

Public Officials.   The Dayton planners also worked closely with public officials in the five county region, to secure their endorsement of the plan and pledges of continued cooperation in the implementation stage. MVRPC recognized the necessity for understanding, involvement and commitment on the part of elected officials. Other agencies have followed this lead.

The Public.   Beyond public officials, voluntary organizations and housing-related interest groups, the planning agency should attempt to gain the support of the general public. For example, the Miami Valley Regional Planning Commission presented its plan at public meetings of local suburban residents.[7] Commission staff introduced the subject to their audiences through a slide show, with taped narration. Slides dramatized the dimensions of the housing need in the region and presented the agency's plan to meet those needs. The commission staff then responded to citizen concerns, such as fears about the overcrowding of schools and the burden on taxpayers which could result from building lower-income housing. The planners emphasized that while local communities have little control over the yield of children from housing developed by the private market, the allocation plan would assess the absorption capacity of schools and the numbers of additional pupils predicted and include these as factors in the distribution plan. Thus, the costs of lower-income housing would be shared more equitably than those related to nonsubsidized housing. In addition, the planners explained the concept of scattered-site housing and the flexibility available in designing subsidized housing, to combat the commonly held stereotype of mammoth, crime-ridden projects. The Washington COG carried out a similar public education campaign, with a slide presentation available on request to community groups.

Washington COG and Dayton planners also worked with the mass media to promote favorable coverage of the "fair share" plan and its potential impact on the regional housing crisis. The media played a particularly supportive role in the Dayton area. Both Dayton newspapers provided early support for the allocation idea through extensive, sympathetic coverage and enthusiastic editorials. Similarly, the Denver Post gave the Denver Regional COG immediate editorial praise after it adopted the plan.[8]

Adoption of the Plan

An allocation plan becomes the official position of a council of governments or a planning agency through its adoption by the organization's policy-making board or commission. Getting the support of these policy-makers may be difficult because they usually represent the local communities and reflect the concerns of their constituents. Several features of the planning process as well as the plan itself may help persuade the decision-makers to adopt the allocation plan. First, the staff should involve the commission members from the outset, explaining and documenting the need for the plan. The planning staff should make complete and polished presentations to the commission, which reflect the thoroughness of the planning process. Some of the Dayton commissioners approved the original plan because of the highly competent way it was presented to them throughout the planning process. In addition, the Dayton planners presented a draft plan to the commissioners and requested that they consider it for 90 days before acting on it, thus providing an opportunity for wide discussion before the time for decision.

The decision-makers take responsibility for an allocation plan when they adopt it. They must be educated to the need for the plan and to the rationale of the particular plan. They must be convinced that it is a reasonable plan that can be defended against questions and criticisms of the regional community.

Of course, the substance of the plan is also important in securing the support of the commissioners. In Dayton and other cases, the stipulation that the allocations represented a ceiling on the local responsibility reassured many of the commissioners. No jurisdiction would be asked to accept an amount of subsidized housing in excess of its "fair share" allocation. Thus, for some communities the plan represented protection against what they perceived as potential inundation. Ideally, lower-income housing should not be viewed as a burden to be accepted grudgingly. However, the political realities are otherwise. In some cases there are fiscal realities at stake, too. A community which accepted an unlimited amount of subsidized housing might have great difficulty providing quality public services with the taxes it could raise. Whatever the fiscal impact, the political impact is clear. Allocation plans are likely to arouse great opposition, even with the best of public education efforts and with the utmost sensitivity to suburban concerns. These plans have received a good deal of criticism for placing a ceiling on a community's obligations. In principle, this is a legitimate objection. If there is to be real equality of housing opportunity, no community should be able to limit the number of lower-income people who can live there. Making the community's allocation or fair share the maximum number of units it is expected to accept creates legitimate exclusion at a certain point. Unfortunately, however, it is just this ceiling feature of the plan that makes it palatable to many suburban constituencies. The ceiling makes for worse policy but better politics. It is a difficult tradeoff.

The ceiling will not be a practical constraint in many communities. Most suburbs have very little lower-income housing relative to their reasonable share of a region's needs. Thus, while the objection to a lid, a limited responsibility of communities, is powerful in principle, it has limited practical consequences. Eliminating the ceiling would probably make allocation plans less viable politically and would do little to convince suburbanites that they have an indefinite responsibility to accept lower-income housing. The plan seeks to change the suburban attitude from no responsibility to some significant level of responsibility.

Ironically, the scale of the plan may bring support of some who are not sympathetic with the objection. In Dayton, for example, it appeared that some commissioners felt that there was little to lose in voting for the plan, since they believed that it was utopian and would never be implemented. At the same time, they could avoid a negative vote which might be interpreted as a sign of bigotry.

Support may also result from what is omitted from the plan. A key to adoption of the Dayton plan may have been the deletion of a highly controversial policy statement. The draft document authorized the staff to seek state legislation granting the commission the power to override local zoning ordinances to carry out the plan. In the negotiations leading to adoption, eliminating this politically charged provision reduced the opposition. It is likely that the planners had viewed the section as a "throwaway" from the outset, not expecting it to be approved.

Finally, some commissions favor adoption of allocation plans because they believe it is the morally correct position. In Dayton, where there were no votes in opposition to the plan, several commissioners voted for adoption even though it was clear that the majority of their communities opposed the plan. They voted their consciences.

Local Endorsements. After COGs or planning commissions adopt housing plans, they often seek adoption of the plan by the governing bodies of the local jurisdictions. The Washington COG plan was quickly endorsed by most of the large suburban jurisdictions in the area. Similarly, the San Bernardino County housing plan was endorsed by the three advisory planning agencies in the county. HUD agreed to accept and help implement the San Bernardino plan if a majority of the 14 cities and the county adopted it as a formal policy statement.[9] Nine of the 15 jurisdictions had adopted the model by the spring of 1972. In the Denver area, three cities in the region had formally adopted the COG's housing plan by May of 1973.[10] Their resolutions accepted the jurisdiction's numerical allocation as well as the responsibility for implementing the plan. Localities were asked to prepare and adopt plans for implementation by the end of 1973.

The Elements of Allocation Plans

The methodology used in developing models for distributing lower-income housing is extremely varied—plans use different methods for creating geographical divisions of the region, different criteria for allocating units, and widely different mathematical formulae for allocating units. (See Appendix for a detailed discussion of methodology.) Moreover, some plans quantify and then allocate all the region's "needed" units of low- and moderate-income housing; some plans allocate only the projected number of subsidized units the region would obtain; while a third approach is to establish priority areas for the development of lower-income units and measure proposed projects against these priorities.

Definition of the Region. In developing an allocation plan the region must first be defined. It should follow political boundaries and the public's definition of the region. The area should be large enough to permit complete fulfillment of the goals of the plan and to demonstrate to each jurisdiction that many others will share in meeting the overall housing responsibility.

Defining the region has not presented much difficulty. Generally, agencies have used their own jurisdictional areas for their housing planning areas. San Bernardino County Planning Department is the only agency which

has not allocated housing throughout its jurisdiction. It chose instead to exclude certain sparsely populated desert portions because of their differences
from the remainder of the area.[11]

Housing to be Allocated.   The planning agency must define the
units of housing it will distribute. Generally, the agency allocates the overall
amount of low- and moderate-income housing needed in the region or the subsidized units which HUD will make available for the area in a particular time
period.

The Miami Valley Regional Planning Commission took the first
course. It identified the number of additional sound housing units needed so
that every low- and moderate-income person in the region could have decent
housing within his means.[12] The need was determined by subtracting the
supply of useable units from the total need. Total need included the number of
households, the need to eliminate overcrowding and the desirability of providing a minimum vacancy rate. The planning commission concluded that
14,000 low- and moderate-income units were needed in the region and developed its allocation plan based on that level of need. Several other plans followed
similar approaches.

An advantage of starting with a housing needs analysis is that it
provides credibility for the housing plan. A statistical analysis gives public
officials and the community at large concrete evidence of the dimensions
of the housing need. The plan has the objectivity that comes with the use of
generally accepted indicators of housing need. In most metropolitan areas the
unfilled housing need is so great that quantifying the need will help generate
support for some kind of a plan.

If the plan is based on the overall regional need, the ultimate obligation of individual communities is clear. However, a focus on overall need
means that the numerical goals rarely will be met. Even if the plan is having a
major impact on the amount and location of low- and moderate-income housing built, it will still be subject to attack on the ground that its goals have not
been achieved, since the development of all the needed units over any reasonable time frame is not feasible. The subsidy funds are too limited, the constraints too great, to solve an area's housing problem in a relatively short period.
When the plan defines its objectives in quantitative terms which are likely to
be unattainable, it is all too easy for detractors and opponents to label the
plan a failure. This may undercut support for the plan and impede further
implementation. In contrast, the Metropolitan Washington Council of Governments plan apportioned only the available HUD subsidized units among the
local jurisdictions in the region:

> This formula presents fewer data problems and can be immediately
> and directly implemented as soon as it is adopted. Implementa-
> tion would be accomplished by HUD decisions about publicly and

privately proposed subsidized housing projects, with the advice of COG through the "A-95" Federal-Aid Review Process.[13]

Since the number of subsidized units which would be available was unknown at the outset, the Washington COG plan specified percentages of the units for the jurisdictions. When the allotment from HUD was determined, these proportions were converted into numbers of housing units. Similarly, the San Bernardino, California model allocates a percentage of the HUD-subsidized units available during a given fiscal year.

Focusing on the number of units for which funds will be available is realistic in terms of achieving stated objectives within a defined time period. The volume of housing which communities can expect is relatively small and the public opposition to the plan may be reduced from that which could be expected under a plan which divides up a very large need.

Perhaps the most effective approach would provide an ultimate allocation based on overall need, to reflect the region's real needs, with an annual allocation, based on a realistic appraisal of anticipated subsidy funds. This approach would permit the planning agency to build political support based on the magnitude of the overall need. At the same time, the concrete goals would reflect the subsidy funds expected for the region. These goals would be attainable. A subarea would thus receive a long-term allocation, with an unstated time period, as well as an annual allocation which would generally be a much smaller number of units.

Subareas. Whatever the means for determining the amount of housing to be distributed, these units are usually apportioned among areas of the region, or subareas. Most of the plans have designated municipalities, groups of municipalities, or counties as planning districts. This provides clear political responsibility for implementation of the plan. In addition, subareas should be relatively homogeneous in their developmental patterns. Intra-unit variations (e.g., heavily urbanized areas and rural ones in the same planning unit) should be relatively small compared to the differences among districts. While making these districts small enough to retain a degree of homogeneity, the agency should limit the number of subareas in order to make implementation manageable. If the agency is to coordinate and assist in the process of developing the needed housing, it should not have to focus on a large number of planning districts.

In sum, municipalities or groups of municipalities provide the optimum mix of attributes for subareas. Political responsibility is easily ascertainable and a good data base is obtainable.

Allocation Criteria. Perhaps the most difficult task in developing an allocation model is the selection of criteria to allocate the housing units to subareas. The criteria are used to provide an equitable distribution of housing among parts of the region. Criteria should address the real need of the potential occupants as well as the concerns of suburbanites to maximize the chances of widespread political support for the plan. Generally, these criteria relate to: (1) expanded choice in location for potential occupants of the housing; (2) capacity of the planning subarea to absorb additional units of low- and moderate-income housing and provide necessary facilities and services; and (3) need for low- and moderate-income housing in the particular subarea. However, criteria vary significantly among plans. Each allocation plan has utilized criteria based on local conditions and considerations.

Choice: Criteria related to choice channel housing for low- and moderate-income households into areas where housing within their means did not exist previously. Several plans have used a subarea's relative affluence as a choice factor. This has been accomplished by placing more units of housing in areas in which a proportionately large share of the region's families earn more than $15,000 or conversely placing fewer units of housing in subareas with proportionately large existing concentrations of low- and moderate-income families. To increase locational choice for low- and moderate-income people, allocation plans have also attempted to direct development toward areas of concentrations of jobs.

Capacity: In determining the relative capacity of planning districts to absorb additional low- and moderate-income housing, allocation plans have also generally focused on utilization of the local schools, compared to their capacity; tax base, as a measure of the potential financial resources available for providing facilities and services; and availability of vacant land for development of subsidized housing.

Determining the relative ability of different subareas to absorb additional pupils requires identification of a factor that indicates the utilization of the school system. The Miami Valley Regional Planning Commission used "pupils in excess of normal capacity," the number of students in attendance over and above the stated normal capacity.[14] Under this criterion, the most overcrowded districts were allocated the fewest additional units. Similarly, the San Bernardino model used "existing additional school capacity" to direct new pupils into the least saturated schools in the planning units in order not to adversely affect educational quality.[15]

Local governments must absorb a number of costs involved in serving new residents, including schools, police and fire protection. They continue to raise much of the necessary revenue through the property tax. Several plans therefore allocate housing to areas based on the tax base available to finance the additional facilities and services. Tax base can be measured in a variety of ways—assessed valuation per capita or assessed valuation per pupil are among the more frequently used methods. Where sales tax revenues are important sources of funds these too should be included in any formula testing a subarea's fiscal ability to absorb new low- and moderate-income housing units.

Ideally, it would be appropriate to determine the amount of vacant land suitable for residential development available in a planning unit as a measure of the ability to absorb additional low- and moderate-income housing. Because it is so difficult to arrive at precise figures, several plans have used rough indicators to approximate the quantity of vacant land available.

Needs: A number of criteria which have been employed relate to the existing housing needs within a planning subarea. The underlying policy is to locate part of the housing where lower-income families currently reside, to provide needed replacement housing for people who want to continue to live in those areas. The MVRPC plan and Denver plan are two examples of such an approach. The Dayton planners used as a factor "proportionate share of households with income less than $10,000." The greater the number of lower-income households residing in a planning unit, the greater the number of units assigned on this basis.

Denver COG focused on the amount of deficient housing in a jurisdiction as an indicator of its current need for subsidized housing. A unit which was physically substandard or overcrowded was considered deficient. Denver COG used a second criterion related to needs. Units are assigned based on the low-income housing needs. COG measured the number of low-income households against the number of units appropriately priced and available to these households. The COG determined the need of each jurisdiction as a percentage of the region's overall housing need. A third criterion focused on the need of moderate-income households.

Allocation Formulas.   The final step in the formulation of an allocation plan is the creation of a mathematical formula for translating the data related to distribution criteria into numbers of units to be allocated to each planning subarea. The number of housing units ultimately assigned to a subarea may be determined by averaging the results using individual allocation criteria. A weighted formula might also be used, to emphasize the relative importance of various criteria. The plans adopted to date have created diverse mathematical models to allocate the housing units.

Priority Areas Approach
The Metropolitan Council of the Twin Cities area is unique among regional bodies. Unlike other regional agencies, the Metro Council has important governmental powers. It was created by the Minnesota legislature in 1967 to coordinate orderly growth. The Metro Council has planning and operating authority over a regionwide sewage and solid waste disposal system. It reviews

plans and projects of single purpose bodies such as highway and transit commissions and can suspend proposed projects which are inconsistent with the
council's guidelines. In short, while the Metro Council seeks support and assistance from local jurisdictions in developing and implementing plans, it is not
subject to the control of localities. The council's jurisdiction covers seven
counties and 1.9 million people. The area contains about 50 percent of the
state's population but only five percent of the land area.

The Metro Council adopted a unique housing plan. Instead of
allocating numbers of units to subareas, the agency defined four degrees of
priority areas for development of subsidized housing. The Metro Council designated higher priorities for more developed areas to maximize the use of existing
services such as sewers, shopping centers, major highways, public transit
and employment opportunities, as well as to promote systematic metropolitan
growth.[16] A municipality's priority is based on the percentage of vacant
and agricultural land within its borders.

When evaluating competing proposals for housing projects within
the same priority category, the planning staff gives preference to the development that would provide greater locational choice to low- and moderate-income
persons, where there are few concentrations of subsidized housing.

The council felt that avoiding numerical allocations in the interim
plan would facilitate housing development without unnecessary political
fights, when funding is too minimal to meet a municipality's fair share of units.
[17] In addition, the identification of priority areas was designed to give clear
direction to subsidized housing developers in determining locations for their
proposed developments.

The priority area approach sets no limits on the amount of housing
in a particular area and thus risks concentrations of subsidized units in high
priority municipalities. There is little focus on public responsibility for implementation, since the plan does not quantify the local responsibility. Without
concrete standards, monitoring and evaluation of compliance become more
difficult.

However, numerical plans do not favor any particular subarea at
the outset; developers will tend to go where land costs are lowest and there is
little political resistance. These more receptive areas may or may not be the
most appropriate places to begin construction, in terms of the objectives of
the plan.

Regional agencies could also combine the numerical allocation
and priority area approaches. Subareas would be assigned specific numbers of
housing units. Each subarea would also be designated as a specific priority
based on the existing infrastructure. The regional agency could then encourage
development in the most appropriate areas first, while still emphasizing distribution of housing among planning districts.

Plan Revision. Since the allocation plan is a short-range device, revision and updating of data are necessities. The characteristics of the planning units may change significantly as housing needs change, subsidized construction takes place, data related to allocation criteria change and the criteria themselves require modification. The plan should be revised or redone frequently.

The Miami Valley Regional Planning Commission adopted a significantly modified plan early in 1973, less than three years after the adoption of its original plan.[18] The Metro Council intends to update both the priority areas and the numerical guidelines every two years.[19] In San Bernardino planners contemplate an annual analysis to update the formula and take into consideration changed conditions within the region.[20]

Implementation

A regional housing allocation plan establishes a framework for developing low- and moderate-income housing on a wide geographical basis. It does not provide the housing. It is far from a self-executing document. The implementation may be furthered by a variety of strategies, many of which involve the regional body. The planning agency is not impotent to carry out its plans, as is often claimed by the agencies themselves as well as their detractors. The planning body can and should play a significant role in seeing to it that housing is built consistent with the plan.

Unlike many earlier planning efforts, several planning agencies have become heavily involved in attempting to make their housing allocation plans a reality. Since regional bodies do not have the legal authority to eliminate exclusionary barriers or direct development to particular places, they must rely on their leverage and their persuasive skills to facilitate implementation of the allocation plan. As a catalyst in the development process, regional bodies must bring together the key actors, the local communities, the housing developers (private and public) and the federal funding agency. The regional agencies must proceed persistently and patiently, community by community, project by project. They must seek acceptance by individual communities of low- and moderate-income housing, seek the participation of housing sponsors and facilitate the flow of federal subsidy funds for the developments.

Gaining Community Acceptance of Housing Developments. Regional agencies should encourage local communities to accept specific housing developments. Some communities are receptive to subsidized housing once the allocation plan framework has been established. In other cases, the regional body must use whatever leverage it has to overcome suburban resistance to particular projects.

In the Twin Cities area, in the first months under the plan, several municipalities passed rent supplement resolutions, thus facilitating development of low-income housing by private developers under the rent supplement program. In addition, two suburban communities with no previous low rent public housing approved public housing programs. In general, responsiveness to the provision of subsidized housing in the suburbs increased substantially. In the Washington, D.C. area local jurisdictions also took the initiative in meeting the agency's fair share objectives. Arlington, Falls Church, and Bowie approved their first HUD-assisted housing projects. Fairfax, Montgomery, and Prince George's Counties applied for additional subsidized housing projects.

Where suburban cooperation is not readily forthcoming, the regional body should use its leverage to bring about openness. The A-95 review process is perhaps the best lever available to regional agencies. The A-95 review process was established by the Federal Office of Management and Budget (OMB) to coordinate the federal funds going into a region under various categorical grant programs. (See Chapter 13 for a detailed discussion of the A-95 review process). Under OMB Circular A-95 areawide planning organizations review applications for federal funds under a wide variety of programs before they are forwarded to the relevant federal agency. The regional body comments on the application's consistency or inconsistency with regional plans. The review process carries with it no veto power. The federal funding agency is not bound by the comments. The weight the agency gives to the comments is within its own discretion.

The Dayton planners indicated in early meetings with local officials that it would give weight to a community's progress on low- and moderate-income housing in doing A-95 reviews of applications for federal grant programs. The planning commission would comment negatively on applications for open space, water and sewer and other grants if the applicant community had not permitted development of lower-income housing. For this carrot and stick approach to be effective, there must be federal grant programs, the funds must be appropriated for the programs, and there must be suburban communities eager to get a piece of this federal pie. These suburbs may then be willing to pay a price for these grants in the form of facilitating construction of lower-income housing.

Unfortunately, few areawide agencies have been strong and decisive enough to use the A-95 process to challenge suburban barriers. Most agencies have not begun to tap the potential leverage available in this process. Nor has the federal government actively encouraged them to do so. In fact, many federal agencies pay little attention to A-95 comments when they are made. Regional and federal agencies must both act affirmatively for the A-95 process to be a useful tool for implementing allocation plans.

Soliciting Participation of Housing Sponsors. As communities take steps to permit construction of housing, there must be sponsors willing, ready and able to build the needed housing. The regional agency can help attract existing developers as well as assist in the formation of nonprofit sponsors. For example, the Miami Valley Regional Planning Commission has attempted to interest local builders, as well as developers from other parts of the country, in building subsidized projects in the Dayton area. The MVRPC staff provided technical assistance to housing sponsors on request, thus stimulating the formation of more than 30 nonprofit corporations, which consisted of development coalitions of bankers, builders, and packagers. Seed money was gathered to assist these developers to meet high front-end construction costs.

MVRPC also worked closely with the Dayton Metropolitan Housing Authority, whose jurisdiction includes virtually all of Montgomery County, and helped in the extension of the jurisdiction of the Yellow Springs Housing Authority throughout Greene County. These public housing authorities then attempted to negotiate agreements with local communities so that construction could follow.

In the Washington area, the COG has encouraged public agencies and private builders to find sites in areas where unused allocations remain. In southeastern Wisconsin, implementation was to include placing the information about each site in the hands of interested developers and lenders and assisting communities as well as developers in collecting information necessary for development, including assistance in preliminary development design and design review.

Facilitating the Flow of Federal Funds. Once a housing allocation plan is developed, the regional agency should seek "bonus" federal funds to assist in the implementation phase. HUD has repeatedly expressed its support for allocation plans. The regional bodies should ask that HUD put its money where its mouth is. Several agencies have done so. The Dayton planners requested and received a bonus allocation of subsidized housing units for use in the planning commission's five county jurisdiction. In response to the Washington COG Fair Share Plan, HUD authorized funding for 6,274 subsidized housing units for that metropolitan area during fiscal year 1973. This figure included a "bonus" of 1,783 units to assist in implementing COG's plan.

The regional agency should also help to expedite the processing of applications for federal subsidies. The agency should provide technical assistance to developers in selecting appropriate sites and in weaving their way through the federal processing maze. At the same time, the planners should seek the cooperation of HUD in cutting through red tape for housing projects in the region.

The regional agency should also try to get priority funding for community development grants (e.g., water and sewer facilities, open space) to reward cooperating communities. The Miami Valley Regional Planning Commission requested a facility grant bonus giving priority to suburban communities requesting project funds who are cooperating and providing their share of low- and moderate-income housing units in accordance with the plan. HUD agreed to do so.

Finally, the regional agency should request an increased planning grant from HUD to provide the resources for an aggressive implementation program. MVRPC applied for and received a substantially larger basic grant than it had received before the adoption of the plan. In addition, it received funds to carry out special projects. This added funding permits the agency to carry out the implementation activities described above, to develop a housing staff to coordinate activities throughout the region, to create nonprofit sponsors for subsidized housing and to continue educational efforts to broaden the base of support for the plan. In short, resources are required for the agency to act as the region's housing catalyst.

Impact of Housing Allocation Plans.   It is difficult to evaluate the impact of the efforts to implement housing allocation plans. The most concrete measure is the number of subsidized housing units built in the region. In most cases, the numbers increased around the time of the preparation of the plan and thereafter. However, the largest subsidy programs (except for public housing) were created in 1968 and were beginning to result in large numbers of housing starts just as the allocation plans were being developed. Thus, it is impossible to determine how many of the projects constructed in a region would have been built in the absence of the allocation plan. In most of these areas, the number of units built during the early 1970s would have jumped even without a plan and vigorous efforts at its implementation. The differences caused by the plan probably relate to the size of the increase, the proportion of suburban units constructed and the number and diversity of suburban jurisdictions receiving subsidized housing for the first time.

Again, the Dayton area is a case in point. Although it is difficult to attribute particular developments to MVRPC's efforts, it is clear that a substantial volume of subsidized housing has been built and planned, particularly in the suburbs, since the adoption of the plan, as compared to the period before the plan was in effect. About 10 percent of the 14,000 needed units had been provided by early 1973. More than 4,300 units of lower-income housing were either planned or under construction at that time. In spite of this progress, MVRPC was destined to fall substantially short of its five year goals. Some have declared the plan a failure based on this disparity. However, the plan itself indicates that the numbers were designed to provide guidance and that the political problems in implementation would be severe. All of the housing developed after mid-1970 is consistent with the plan; developments have not been built in excess of any planning unit's allocation.

Low- and Moderate-Income Units in the Miami Valley Area

	1969 (Before Plan)	1972 (Cumulative)	Proposed Units
In Dayton	95% (2,979)	81% (4,914)	22% (726)
Outside Dayton	5% (158)	19% (973)	78% (2,605)

The major political struggle has occurred in overwhelmingly white suburban Montgomery County. Especially in the affluent suburbs south of Dayton, it has been difficult to obtain zoning changes and local approval for rent supplements. MVRPC believes that a key to implementation is the development of a sound project south of Dayton to demonstrate to the region's residents and local officials that subsidized housing can work.

In sum, it is impossible to determine how much subsidized housing would have been built in the five county region or where the housing would have been located within the Dayton region in the absence of the Miami Valley plan. However, the evidence indicates a substantially accelerated pace in the dispersed development of low- and moderate-income housing as a result of MVRPC's development, adoption, and implementation of the plan.

The Metropolitan Council of the Twin Cities Area found that its plan was surprisingly well received.[21] Eighty-five percent of the subsidized housing proposals submitted since the adoption of the plan have been located in first or second priority areas. About half of the proposals made in 1971 were in suburban locations. Since the allocation plan has been in effect, 70 percent of all subsidized proposals have been in the suburbs. Many of these projects have been in suburban municipalities with little existing low- and moderate-income housing.

The Potential of Allocation Plans. Allocation plans are political documents. Their utility should be judged in terms of their ability to change people's minds and stimulate changes in housing patterns. These plans can be invaluable in creating a favorable climate for development of lower-income housing. They can help build momentum to break down suburban barriers, enlist the participation of developers and sponsors, and gain necessary support of federal agencies.

The development and implementation of an allocation plan is one of those human endeavors that is five percent inspiration and 95 percent perspiration. From the outset, a great deal of citizen input, participation and education is required. A systematic analysis of the region's housing need can be of great assistance in this process of persuasion. The needs analysis will demonstrate that there is a housing problem, that it affects large numbers of people and that it is not going to go away by itself.

The political-planning process should begin, therefore, with a demonstration of the magnitude of the region's housing problem. The planners should then proceed to distribute the housing among defined subareas based on allocation criteria. The criteria should reflect a sensitivity to suburbanites' concerns as well as the need to maximize housing choice. The planners should recognize that the criteria are ultimately arbitrary. The criteria and the overall plan should be simple and understandable, so they can be explained easily to the policy makers and the citizens of the region. In addition to its sensitivity and simplicity, the plan should be equitable and sensible. The disparities among subareas' allocations should seem reasonable to the casual observer. Communities without vacant land should not receive large allocations.

Once the allocation plan is adopted, the real job begins for the planning agency. The planners were only selling a relatively nonthreatening principle before; now they must convince communities to accept actual housing developments. They can argue that the plan contemplates a cooperative effort. All communities will accept some subsidized housing. None will be asked to accept a disproportionate share. If this and other persuasive techniques are not successful, the planning agency must be prepared to use its leverage, such as blocking federal grants through the A-95 review process.

In addition to overcoming community resistance, the planning agency must stimulate the interest of existing housing sponsors and assist in the formation of new ones. The planners must also knock on HUD's doors, seeking extra funds and accelerated processing. In short, the planners cannot dream their dreams and leave it to the politicians to make them into a reality. The planners must stay in the kitchen and take the political heat if the numbers in the plan are to become houses for people to live in. They must bring about "success stories," suburban lower-income housing developments that fit in with the surrounding community, are pleasant and secure places to live, and are financially viable.

Chapter Six

State Regulation of Land Use

Like the regional agencies, states are becoming involved in opening their suburban "creatures" to lower-income people. A number of approaches have been tried, ranging from creating state housing agencies which finance low- and moderate-income housing, to administrative intervention in the zoning process, to suing exclusionary suburbs. The number of states which have ventured into these politically hazardous waters is increasing.

While the metropolitan and regional bodies that have entered the housing struggle have had little authority to work with, the states have enormous legal power to influence local actions. The states created local communities and have the authority to regulate their "creatures." A crucial power which resides in the states is the regulation of land use. For the most part, they have given away this authority to local governments. They have passed zoning and planning enabling laws which delegate virtually total authority to local jurisdictions. This 50-year trend is reversing, however. The re-entry of the states into the regulation of land development has been called a "quiet revolution." As states have become more active, these changes have become less quiet. On the other hand, the results have been less than revolutionary, particularly in terms of housing patterns. Most of the state legislation has been motivated by environmental and broad planning concerns. A few states, however, have begun to recognize the important state interests at stake in the specific problem of suburban housing exclusion. Massachusetts has passed legislation in this area and several other states have considered bringing their legal authority to bear to overcome exclusionary practices.

State Review of Local Zoning Decisions

To reclaim some of their power to regulate the use of land, a number of states have enacted or considered legislation providing for state review of specified local zoning decisions. These laws retain the basic pattern of local

autonomy but define an area of state interest where local desires may be super-
seded. The Massachusetts Zoning Appeals Law is the only statute which establishes a state review process specifically for proposed low- and moderate-
income housing developments.[1] It establishes standards under which a locality
must grant a comprehensive permit to a developer of low- or moderate-income
housing despite local zoning, building or other codes which would otherwise
prevent the construction of such housing. The statute also establishes a state
review mechanism to insure that localities fulfill these obligations. Other
states, including Connecticut and Wisconsin, have considered similar legislation.[2] A related bill was proposed in Illinois. In addition, the legal profession's American Law Institute has prepared several drafts of a Model Land
Development Code for consideration by state legislatures.[3] The draft code
provides for state intervention in several types of land use decisions. Overcoming
exclusionary zoning is not the focus of the state machinery, but the state
could become involved in housing development through the code framework.
The Florida Land and Water Management Act, enacted in 1972, is based
largely on the model code's concept.

The Origin of the Massachusetts Statute

In 1967 the Massachusetts Senate directed the Legislative Research
Council to "undertake a study and investigation relative to the feasibility and
implications of restricting the zoning power to cities and county governments
with particular emphasis on the possibility that the smaller communities are
utilizing the zoning power in an unjust manner with respect to minority
groups."[4] The report of the research council found widespread exclusionary
practices throughout the state.[5] It concluded that:

> . . . to the extent that inner suburban communities prohibit multi-
> family and apartment housing, or attach height or other restrictions
> which made such housing feasible only on a "luxury" basis, the
> modest income housing problems of the entire metropolitan area
> are aggravated.[6]

In addition, subsidized housing is concentrated in a relatively small
number of Massachusetts communities. In 1972, 193 of the commonwealth's
cities and towns had no subsidized housing, while nearly 13 percent of Boston's
housing units are publicly assisted. Only 21 communities have more than the
state average of 4.66 percent subsidized units.[7] At the same time, housing
needs for low- and moderate-income families are very large, especially in
suburban areas where employment opportunities are increasing. The state's
Department of Community Affairs established a statewide five year target of
110,000 subsidized housing units, with 64,000 units in the low-income range
and 46,000 for moderate-income people.[8]

Because of this acute shortage of low- and moderate-income housing and the widespread impediments to meeting this need, the Massachusetts Legislature passed the Massachusetts Zoning Appeals Act in 1969. The statute's objective was not to allow

> ... cities or towns to unreasonably obstruct the construction of a limited amount of adequate low cost housing [and to] encourage such communities to establish conditions on such housing which will be consistent with local needs.[9]

It was understood at the time that the primary impact of the statute would be in suburban areas. Most suburban legislators opposed the act. Many central city legislators supported the act to force the suburbs to respond to the housing problem.

Inclusionary Requirements

The law establishes a maximum number of low- and moderate-income housing units which each community in the state must accept. Once federally- or state-subsidized housing constitutes 10 percent of a locality's total dwelling units, the community may deny any subsequent request to permit development of such housing.[10] The community has the same discretion if, at any point, low- and moderate-income housing occupies 1.5 percent of the land zoned for residential, commercial or industrial uses. Finally, the law places annual limits on the number of units a locality must accept until the overall limits are reached. The locality can refuse a proposal if "the application before the board would result in the commencement of construction of such housing on sites comprising more than three-tenths of one percent of such land area or ten acres, whichever is larger, in any one calendar year."[11]

If a locality has not met its quota, it may still be entitled to deny an application for subsidized housing. First, if the proposed project is "not consistent with local needs," the community may reject it.[12] Second, projects can be turned down because of valid planning considerations, including "the need to protect the health or safety of the occupants of the proposed housing or of the residents of the city or town, to promote better site and building design in relation to the surroundings, or to preserve open spaces. ..."[13] The community must apply these criteria consistently, regardless of whether the proposed project is subsidized. Therefore, a local board must grant a comprehensive permit unless the town has fulfilled its overall or annual quota of low- or moderate-income housing or unless the particular development does not meet the specified planning standards.

The Procedural Framework

Under the Massachusetts statute, a developer may secure permission to build low- and moderate-income housing by applying to the local zoning board of appeals for a "comprehensive permit."[14] This one step mechanism incorporates all aspects of local and state approval which a developer must obtain in order to build housing, including those related to health, sanitation, planning and building codes. The zoning board of appeals may grant a comprehensive permit by a majority vote. This is in contrast to the two-thirds vote of a city council or town meeting which is necessary for a rezoning.

If a local zoning board of appeals rejects an application for subsidized housing or imposes conditions unacceptable to the developer, he may appeal to the state's Housing Appeals Committee.[15] The Housing Appeals Committee is lodged in the Department of Community Affairs. This five member committee is composed of three appointees of the Commissioner of the Department of Community Affairs, one of whom must be an officer or employee of the department, and two members appointed by the governor. One of the governor's appointees must be a member of a board of selectmen (the governing body of a town) and one a member of a city council (or other governing body of a city).

In reviewing a denial of a permit, the Housing Appeals Committee evaluates whether the local decision was "reasonable" and "consistent with local needs." If the local board placed conditions on its approval, review is limited to the question of whether these conditions are "consistent with local needs" or "uneconomic."[16] The committee must determine whether these conditions would result in a nonprofit or public sponsor incurring a financial loss or a limited dividend developer failing to make a reasonable profit from the development. If the committee finds that the denial of the permit or the conditions attached are invalid, it can order the local board to issue the necessary permit without unreasonable conditions.[17] This one step permit eliminates the need to obtain separate local approvals and health certificates. Thus, a reversal by the state committee prevents the locality from using regulatory powers other than zoning to exclude subsidized housing.

Judicial Review

This administrative appeal process does not preclude additional review by the courts. Instead, the law adds a level of decision-making between the local zoning board and the state judiciary. The statute provides for an appeal to the state court by anyone who is "aggrieved" by the issuance of a comprehensive permit.[18] In addition, the Housing Appeals Committee and the housing sponsor are authorized to enforce the orders of the committee in the state court.

Upholding the Constitutionality
of the Law

It was not until four years after its enactment that the constitutionality of the Massachusetts Zoning Appeals Law was established. The state's highest court upheld the validity of the law in affirming the decision of the Housing Appeals Committee in cases involving Hanover and Concord.[19] In reaching its decision, the court faced issues of statutory interpretation, as well as constitutional questions. First, the towns which were challenging the law contended that the legislature never intended that the law be used to review and reverse local zoning decisions but merely wished to provide a stream-lined procedure for processing applications for the necessary local approvals. The court rejected this claim and held that:

> . . . chapter 774 confers on boards of appeals and the Housing Appeals Committee the power to override local "requirements and regulations," including zoning ordinances or by-laws, which are not consistent with local needs.[20]

Second, the towns claimed that the statute violated the home rule amendment in the state constitution. The court found that:

> . . . municipalities can pass zoning ordinances or bylaws as an exercise of their independent police powers but these powers cannot be exercised in a manner which frustrates the purpose or implementation of a general or special law enacted by the Legislature. The adoption of the Home Rule Amendment has not altered the Legislature's supreme power in zoning matters as long as the Legislature acts in accordance with § 8. Chapter 774 is a proper exercise of the powers reserved to the Legislature.[21]

Finally, in considering whether the statute was unconstitutionally vague, the court held that it contained adequately detailed and clear definitions of the factors to be considered throughout the administrative process. The court went a step further and strengthened the hand of the Housing Appeals Committee in scrutinizing local decisions. In describing the administrative balancing process between the region's needs and the locality's planning objections to a low- and moderate-income housing project, the court set as a standard that:

> . . . the municipality's failure to meet its minimum housing obligations, as defined in § 20, will provide compelling evidence that the regional need for housing does in fact outweigh the objections to the proposal.[22]

In addition to affirming the validity of the law, the court's decision clarified several ambiguous provisions of the statute which had hindered implementation. First, the act does not specifically grant local zoning boards of appeals the authority to grant permits for uses which violate the town's zoning ordinance. The act states that the local board of appeals shall have "the same power to issue permits or approvals as any local board or official who would otherwise act with respect to such application."[23] In appealing the state committee's decisions, the towns of Hanover and Concord argued that this language grants the local board authority to issue comprehensive permits only within the context of the town's zoning ordinance, i.e., for otherwise permissible uses. The Supreme Judicial Court interpreted the law to provide that both local boards and the state committee have the power to issue permits for housing meeting the objectives of the statute, whether or not provided for in the local zoning ordinance.[24]

Second, the court held that the local boards were to apply the same standards as the state committee in determining whether to grant a permit.[25] The law did not explicitly require local boards to consider regional needs, although the zoning act was placed in a section of the statutes dealing with regional planning. Since local boards had not traditionally considered regional issues, the absence of a specific directive in this regard in the statute seemed to permit them to apply their local standards. The court held to the contrary.

Impact of the Law

Although the Massachusetts act is a significant expression of a state's "inclusionary" policy, it facilitated very little suburban housing development in its first few years. The principle knocked heads with difficult realities. Some problems arose from defects in the statute itself while others involved the politics of suburban housing development. Only six communities had issued comprehensive permits by early 1973.[26] Two of these projects were stalled in court, while the other four proceeded to construction. These four, which comprise about 400 dwelling units, were all designed for the elderly; no family housing was underway under the statute's procedure.

Developers had appealed more than 25 cases to the Housing Appeals Committee.[27] The number of appeals roughly doubled each year since the law became effective at the end of 1969. Twenty of the cases remained active as of early 1973, with five having been withdrawn or not pursued by the developers. The Housing Appeals Committee had rendered decisions in only two of these cases. In each, the committee reversed the local board's decision and ordered that permits be issued. The towns appealed to the state superior court, which reported the cases to the state's judicial court in what emerged as the test of the validity of the statute. Pending the court's decision, communities, as well as the state committee, were reluctant to act based on the law. Local boards did not want to grant comprehensive permits under a statute that might be declared unconstitutional, nor did the Housing Appeals Committee wish to proceed with hearings and decisions until this cloud was removed. In its first actions since the law was upheld, the Housing Appeals Committee approved subsidized projects in Lexington, Bedford and Dartmouth. In each case, it reversed the decision of the local appeals board. The Dartmouth attorney indicated that the town would appeal in court.[28] By late 1973 the Housing Appeals Committee had before it requests to overrule zoning in eight communities, to permit construction of over 1,400 low- and moderate-income housing units.

Statutory Ambiguities and Gaps

Although the supreme court resolved several of the ambiguities in upholding the statute, others remained. First, the standards for denial of a permit are vague—"reasonable" and "consistent with local needs." The latter phrase related to (1) the degree to which the town has provided its share of the region's need for low- and moderate-income housing; and (2) the fulfillment of planning standards the locality has designated.[29] In the absence of a statutory definition of regional need, the Department of Community Affairs defined it as "the shortage of housing for families and individuals with incomes within the eligibility limits of the State or Federal program subsidizing the proposed housing."[30] However, the statutory quotas bear no direct relation to this regional shortage. In fact, the shortage is likely to be so great that a program which fulfilled every community's obligations under the law would fall far short of meeting the regional needs. Far more than 10 percent of the households in the state would be eligible for subsidies. The quotas contained in the statute do not mesh with the objective of meeting regional needs.

In addition to built in uncertainties in the standards to be applied, the statute has defects in its coverage. First, the law does not apply to all of the federal subsidy programs. It appears that housing covered by the act must be built by a public agency or a nonprofit or limited dividend organization.[31] As a result, two of the recently developed forms of the public housing program, "turnkey" and "leasing," do not seem to be covered by the statute. Under these programs, private developers may build housing which they sell and lease, respectively, to the local housing authority. The builder is not a nonprofit or limited dividend organization. As a result, the Massachusetts statute does not cover much of the housing subsidized through the public housing program.

Another defect in the law is the failure to distinguish between elderly housing and accommodations for families. It appears that a community could meet its legal obligation by granting rezonings for subsidized housing for the elderly that would occupy 1.5 percent of the jurisdiction's land. It would then have no responsibility to permit housing for lower-income families. In this context, lower-income housing for the elderly would not serve as an opening wedge into suburbia, as is sometimes advocated, but instead would legitimate a community's total exclusion of low- and moderate-income families. The community could accept politically safe elderly housing while continuing its exclusionary practices with regard to families. The state has indicated administratively that it will seek to cut off the flow of funds for elderly housing unless a community is also attempting to meet the need for family housing.[32]

A final gap in the statute is that the submission requirements for a comprehensive permit are not spelled out. This makes it possible for local communities to impose undue burdens on developers seeking these permits. It may cost a developer more to prepare the submission for one comprehensive permit than to prepare a series of submissions to different local agencies, following the conventional approval process. Since the zoning board of appeals must represent the interest of all the town's boards—health, building, survey, subdivision control, fire, sewer, traffic, etc.—the applicant must justify his project under the standards of all these boards. Under traditional procedures, a developer might do initial, limited planning and apply for a zoning change. If the rezoning is denied, the expense of more extensive planning to obtain health, fire, building and other permits is obviated. Under the comprehensive permit procedure, all these planning expenses must be risked before an application can be made.

Opposition to the Law

Suburban opponents of low- and moderate-income housing have used the vagueness of the law's standards to frustrate the operation of the statute. The best example of the exploitation of the ambiguities of the law involves a development proposed for the Boston suburb of Newton. The Newton Community Development Foundation planned to build several hundred units of subsidized housing for families on six sites in the town. The foundation requested a comprehensive permit from the Newton Zoning Board of Appeals. The application was denied and the foundation appealed to the Housing Appeals Committee.

Two years later, the committee had not decided the issue. The developers had presented their case in two hours, arguing tht the project was consistent with local needs. The opposition made use of the statutory standards to delay the matter indefinitely. Lawyers representing the town of Newton and residents who lived near the proposed sites presented numerous witnesses and prolonged the hearings through more than 50 sessions. In defense of this protracted presentation, the lawyers argued that the law did not define "reasonableness."[33] It was their objective to interpret the term for the benefit of the Housing Appeals Committee.

Meanwhile, the delay forced the Newton Community Development Foundation to renew several options on sites, necessitating additional expenses. Construction costs continued to rise and the expense involved in this delay could ultimately make the development economically infeasible.

Several towns besides Newton have attempted to block implementation of the law. For example, the town of Chelmsford used its eminent domain power to condemn a piece of land which had been identified as a potential site for low- and moderate-income housing.[34] The town then designated the site for conservation. The local board of appeals refused to grant a comprehensive permit. The developer appealed.

The town of Lexington changed its zoning regulations under the inducement of the state law.[35] It established a new zoning classification, which set a maximum density of 18 units per acre and required that 40 percent of the units built in the zone be for low- or moderate-income people. However, the town meeting did not apply the new zone to any parcel of land. The town had created a "floating zone." To apply the classification, it would have to rezone an area. A rezoning application requires a two-thirds vote. In spite of having created this zone, the town meeting continued to reject applications for rezonings to the new classification.[36] Even the threat of state review was not a sufficient threat to induce affirmative responses by the town meeting.

A number of other communities formed study commissions to evaluate the local need for low- and moderate-income housing and to make proposals. Local initiative stopped there in the first few years of the statute's operations. Communities recognized the housing problem, which they had previously ignored, but they were able to continue avoiding the development of lower-income housing projects in their back yards.

In addition to the opposition of particular communities to the operation of the law, there has been generalized opposition since its inception. Given the power of suburbs and towns in the state legislature, the law will always be in some degree of jeopardy. Each year since its passage has seen the submission of proposals to repeal the act. In 1973 the Massachusetts House defeated three proposals aimed at killing or crippling the law.[37]

The Need for Developers

If the Massachusetts law is to be effective, it is critical that there be developers willing to make use of the state review process. The law is not self-executing; housing does not appear automatically. As a practical matter, the antiexclusionary provisions operate on a case by case basis as developers seek the necessary local approval to build subsidized housing in a particular community. Developers have not come rushing into the fray, probably because attempting to take advantage of the law and enter into an unwilling locality may have significant costs for them.

If an appeal becomes necessary, the hearings may be lengthy and expensive. This delay, like any other, is costly for a developer and may mean the loss of his option on the land or his financing. His decision to fight the battle in the first place may make him very unpopular with local officials in the area. As a result, he may find obstacles in his path on other developments he undertakes in that community or others. The good will which the developer needs to weave his way through the local administrative maze may all but disappear.

In addition, as the Metropolitan Area (Boston) Planning Council has cautioned:

> . . . the law merely creates a new method . . . for relief from re-
> strictive provisions in local zoning and building codes. The initiative
> remains with these developers to find a site, to obtain financing
> and to develop a low- or moderate-income housing proposal. The
> law has no ameliorating effect on the availability of sites, the
> high cost of land, or the scarcity of federal and state funds for
> housing, each of which has a significant effect on the production
> of housing.[38]

Favorable decisions from the appeals committee do not necessarily
end the matter. At this point, the spectre of the loss of local control becomes
more of a reality for local residents and the issue may be joined again in court.
Suburbanites are likely to have the resources to exhaust judicial remedies, and
their incentive is to do so.

In the face of these obstacles, it appears that the developer most
willing and able to test the utility of the state law is the state itself, through
the Massachusetts Housing Finance Agency. (See Chapter 7 for a discussion of
state housing finance agencies.) This agency finances the development of
mixed-income housing. The law establishing the agency requires that all of
their developments contain low- and moderate-income components. MHFA
has made use of the state appeals process when it has been unable to secure
the necessary zoning changes at the local level. Other developers with the time
and money to fight the fight must also come forward and make use of the
state machinery.

Proposals in Other States

The Massachusetts act has prompted preparation of similar legislative proposals in several other states. A Connecticut version is entitled "An Act
Concerning Provision of Sites for the Construction of Low or Moderate Income
Housing, and Assistance to Municipalities."[39] The bill limits the occasions
on which municipalities may restrict the construction of such housing: "(1)
the builder has not proven that appropriate state or federal officials have
determined that the project meets federal or state applicable design standards;
(2) the town has met its quota; or (3) construction of the project would constitute a serious threat to the health or physical safety of the municipal residents
and no feasible method exists to eliminate such threat."[40]

The act establishes local quotas for low- and moderate-income
housing. If the town has not met its quota, and it fails to meet the standards
cited above, the act would make it illegal for a town or city to prevent development of lower-income housing. As in Massachusetts, the Connecticut bill would
create an appeals board, with powers to override local zoning decisions.

Unlike the Massachusetts law, the Connecticut bill defines regional
housing needs.[41] The relevant factors include: (1) the amount of substandard
housing in the region; (2) the availability of jobs for low- and moderate-income

people; (3) regional population projections; and (4) projected available financing for subsidized housing. These criteria are similar to many of those used by regional planning agencies in their housing allocation plans. Each of the factors in this section would receive equal weight in determining the regional housing need.

Finally, the Connecticut bill includes an incentive for the localities to cooperate. The state would provide grants-in-aid to communities which permit development of low- and moderate-income housing. These include annual general assistance grants of $200 per dwelling unit constructed. The payments could continue for five years after the initial occupancy of a unit. The bill also provides for state matching funds, if construction of the housing necessitated provision of municipal sewerage and water facilities. Finally, educational assistance grants would be made, based on the number of pupils residing in low- and moderate-income housing built under the statute. These provisions are subject to the objection that they reward localities for doing what they are required by law to do. They do provide such a reward, but political realities may necessitate providing carrots like these for there to be a real chance of enacting and implementing this type of legislation. Even with these provisions, the Connecticut bill died in committee.[42]

In Wisconsin, a legislative subcommittee has recommended that a state zoning appeals board be created.[43] The board would have the power to override local zoning ordinances where it was determined that their effect was exclusionary. As in Connecticut, the subcommittee's report recognized the need for financial incentives for cooperative communities:

> At the same time, recognizing that local communities have legitimate concerns about local costs and revenues, the state should investigate the use of state shared taxes, school aids and federal revenue sharing funds to provide incentives for local economic integration and should insure that state policies regarding such revenues neither penalize the community which contains low and moderate housing or inure to the benefit of communities which remain exclusive.[44]

A bill was prepared for introduction in the Wisconsin Assembly in mid-1973.[45] The bill did not go as far as the Massachusetts and Connecticut approaches in modifying traditional approval processes. The comprehensive permit could not be obtained at the local level. Only the state appeals board could grant such a permit. The permit did not relieve the developer from compliance with the local building code unless it specifically so stated. Before an appeal to the state board was available, the developer would have to seek approval from the local governing body as well as the local zoning or other administrative agency. Thus, the path to the appeals board is cluttered with red tape. Grounds for local rejection of a proposal relate to needs and plan-

ning considerations. The needs test is clearly a regional one, a strong point
of the bill. A community must accept "a fair and equitable share of the housing needs of low- and moderate-income persons and families, [in] a regional
market area."[46] The planning test is stricter than Massachusetts' but not
as difficult for the locality as in the Connecticut bill. If it finds that the proposed
development may reasonably be expected to cause serious harm to potential
occupants or neighbors, the locality can reject the application. The Connecticut bill required in addition that there be no feasible method of eliminating the
danger.

Once the issue came to the state board, it would be subject to a "de
novo" review. Rather than simply reviewing the record at the local level, the state
board would start the process from scratch. This means more time and expense
for the developer and a greater chance for a determined locality to keep out
the development. The process is further complicated by the long list of factors
the board is to consider in making its decision. The board is even authorized
to consider factors beyond the 12 enumerated in the bill. In sum, the bill
creates red tape, rather than cutting through it. It provides recalcitrant communities with numerous vehicles for delay, as well as ambiguous standards
for the appellate decision. Few developers would take advantage of this process.

Strengthening the Zoning
Appeals Statutes
In order to increase the chances for effectiveness, state zoning
appeals should include a number of provisions:

1. The local board of appeals should be specifically authorized to override
   local zoning laws when application is made for a comprehensive permit.
2. A clause providing for application for a conditional permit should be inserted
   so that developers are not faced with all the problems of producing advanced
   design proposals initially. Also, the requirements for a developer's submissions should be explicit.
3. The local board of appeals should base its decisions on the same regional
   factors as the state board.
4. A definition of regional need must be provided.
5. Coverage of the bill must be explicitly stated to include all low- and
   moderate-income housing programs.
6. Separate minimums should be developed for elderly and family housing,
   so that a town may not fill its overall quota with housing for the elderly.

The Workers' Residential Rights Act
In Illinois, state legislation has been proposed which attempts to
ensure that housing for low- and moderate-income workers is built in areas
of expanding employment opportunities. The Workers' Residential Rights

Act would obligate communities that receive the benefits of business growth to assume the responsibility for accepting housing for the workers at this new facility. All communities in which jobs have been created since 1967 would be affected. These communities are subject to a system similar to the Massachusetts Zoning Appeals Act. They cannot exclude low- and moderate-income housing unless annual and overall quotas are reached. In this case, however, the quotas are directly related to the growth of jobs. Communities may also zone to control low- and moderate-income housing under the bill, so long as they adopt a plan which meets the needs of the workers. As in Massachusetts, the initiative for developing the housing remains with the sponsors that normally undertake this kind of construction. The community must refrain from excluding the needed housing.

The Workers' Residential Rights Act recognizes the growing mismatch between jobs and housing. It also acknowledged the role of suburban communities in encouraging employers to develop employment facilities. All too often, these communities make no effort to accommodate the housing needs of low- and moderate-income workers. The bill declares "that all persons must be given the fullest opportunity to seek work wherever they may find it and to live in reasonable proximity to their place of employment."[47]

A community may not deny zoning, building or other local approvals necessary for construction of any qualified mixed-income development, regardless of local regulations, unless the community has met the minimum housing needs of low- and moderate-income workers. Although the locality's regulations can be overridden, the law provides a set of standards for the housing to protect the locality and prospective occupants. The development must meet the requirements of the public program under which it is financed. The site must not be in an area declared environmentally unsuitable by the state and federal environmental protection agencies. The housing must contain three, four and five bedroom units at least in proportion to the community's overall pattern. Finally, if the locality has adopted a low- and moderate-income housing plan, the development must be consistent with that plan. The plan may designate districts on the zoning map in which the housing can be built; require that all developments contain a specified percentage of low- and moderate-income housing; or enact floating zone or planned unit development ordinances or locally developed approaches to meeting the housing needs of low- and moderate-income workers. With these standards the community has a high degree of protection but it is not permitted to stand in the way of sound, necessary mixed-income developments.

The community's zoning and other regulations go into effect again once subsidized housing construction reaches 15 percent of the total new jobs created locally since 1967 (the last time before 1973 that the census bureau took job censuses, thereby insuring that statistics on job increases will be available). For example, the act would not apply to a community which has had an increase of 1,000 jobs in its employment base since 1967 but which has had built within it 150 or more low- and moderate-income housing units since 1967. The local obligation is also fulfilled if either 15 percent or 5,000 (whichever is less) of the community's housing units are low- and moderate-income housing units built since 1967. Finally, the law includes an annual ceiling of two percent of the total housing units in the community. A locality can reject a mixed-income development if it would mean construction of low- and moderate-income housing in excess of two percent of the community's housing units.

The bill is intended to be self-executing. Unlike the Massachusetts statute, there is no state agency to designate covered communities or to review local plans or disapprovals of specific projects. The initiative lies with those adversely affected by local actions, primarily developers and potential occupants. They must convince a court that the community has violated statutory requirements by rejecting a proposed project. For the most part, the bill defines standards clearly enough so that developers and communities can understand their rights and obligations. Communities can determine how many low- and moderate-income units are protected by the act by counting their employment increase in the specified time period. Their obligation to accept low- and moderate-income housing is measured by the numerical formulas written into the bill. The 15 percent figure represents the approximate percentage of low- and moderate-income people in the work force in the Chicago metropolitan area.

However, standards for the community low- and moderate-income housing plans are not clear. The community can adopt any of a number of specified approaches to providing sites to meet the minimum housing needs of low- and moderate-income workers, or it can create its own. It may not impose restrictions on sites it designates that would make them uneconomic for mixed-income developments. Nor can the community select sites that are unsuitable in terms of facilities and services. Aside from these limitations, which are fairly general, the bill provides little assistance for courts which would have to rule on the adequacy of a local plan or a project's consistency with the plan. In this respect, the bill is subject to the criticism which has been made of the Massachusetts law. It is even more critical here, since there is no administrative agency to interpret the law based on its practical experience. Instead, the courts would have to interpret the law in the first instance. Communities would engage in all manner of game-playing, as illustrated by the efforts of Newton before the Massachusetts Housing Appeals Committee. For example, what happens if the community designates sufficient sites for low- and moderate-income units, but the sites are all used for luxury apartment developments? Does the override provision cease to be effective because there are no more sites consistent with the community's plan? If a community is permitted to develop a local plan, it must be judged in terms of its ability to achieve the goal of the minimum housing needs. It must be clear that designated sites may not be used for other purposes or that if such sites are used, other equally appropriate sites must be identified until the minimum housing needs are met.

The bill requires clearer standards for the local plans. If this were done, it might be well to let the courts apply these standards in the first instance. In Massachusetts, most communities which lose before the state housing appeals body go to court anyway, and the developer may incur greater costs with an administrative review system than he would face by going directly to court.

The Workers' Residential Rights Act has great political and practical advantages in linking housing so directly to jobs. It is difficult for a community which is reaping the financial benefits of industrial or commercial growth to deny any responsibility for housing the workers. In addition, the have nots outnumber the haves in this context. Most communities do not have a major influx of jobs and would vote to insure that the selected localities that experience economic growth also assume responsibility for housing the workers. Employers might also support such a bill, since it would help them have a labor supply readily available.

The political viability of the Workers' Residential Rights Act was put to a test in Illinois. It was submitted to the House of Representatives early in 1973 and received a majority vote. However, the speaker of the house determined that the bill infringed on home rule powers granted in the recently adopted Illinois Constitution and therefore required a three-fifths vote of the entire membership for passage.

In spite of the mechanical problems referred to earlier, the bill is a highly practical approach. It identifies clearly which communities are to accept low- and moderate-income housing and virtually assures that there will be a market for the housing because of the proximity of jobs. This bill would thus operate on a relatively small scale, providing housing for new workers in selected communities, but it would have a good chance for broad support in many states and a real opportunity to achieve its objectives.

The Model Land Development Code

Although generalized state involvement in land use decisions does not insure attention to low- and moderate-income housing, such an approach has some potential for overcoming exclusionary barriers. The legal profession has developed a draft Model Land Development Code which provides for a state role in major land use decisions. In 1972, the Florida legislature passed a law patterned on the model code. Although the focus of the law is environmental protection, it may serve as a foot in the door towards suburban exclusionary practices.

The American Law Institute, or ALI, is a research organization representing established segments of the legal profession, including appeals court judges, law school faculty and large city law firms. In the area of land

development, the ALI has been working on a Model Land Development Code
for several years. The purpose of the draftsmen is to provide legislation that
would take the place of existing state enabling acts for zoning, planning and
subdivision control.

As originally conceived, the ALI effort viewed the land use system
as an essentially local one. However, by the time that the third tentative draft
was issued in 1971, the ALI had moved significantly toward identifying a state
role and a regional perspective.[48] This change reflected the increasing visi-
bility of environmental questions which could not be resolved within a single
municipality. The ALI draft does not provide a specific state role in the housing
area, as in Massachusetts, but instead creates a general mechanism for state
involvement in land use control. Local control remains the rule; it is sacrificed
where important state or regional interests clearly require it, and then only
to the degree necessary to achieve the state or regional goal.

Organizational Structure.   Under the ALI code, the local land
development agency makes the initial decision on all development proposals.
Article 7 of the draft code—"State Land Development Regulation"—identifies
development questions which are of state or regional concern. When these
broader interests are involved, the local agency is directed to base its decision
on whether state or regional standards are met.[49] The local agency must
apply the state standards even if doing so is contrary to the applicable local
ordinance. A "State Land Planning Agency" sets up the standards with which
the local agency must comply.[50] The state land planning agency may also
participate in hearings before the local agency if a development will have a
state or regional impact. If the decision is unfavorable, the state planning agency
may appeal.

The "State Land Adjudicatory Board" decides appeals from decisions of local agencies, where a statewide interest is involved.[51] In addition
to the state planning agency, the developer and any other party to the local
hearing have a right of appeal.

Matters of State Concern.   The code assumes that 90 percent of
land use decisions are best left entirely in local hands, because they have no
significant effect on state or national interest and local officials are most
knowledgeable about local conditions and therefore best equipped to make
the decisions. In attempting to strike a balance between retention of local control in the vast majority of cases and expanding state participation in matters
of broader concern, the code defined three ways of identifying matters of
state or regional interest. First, "Districts of Critical State Concern" are to be
designated by the state due to their natural resources or past development. This
section may relate to forests, tidelands or highway interchanges and fringes of
airports, but it does not seem useful as a spur to providing housing.

Second, the code provides that some types of development, by their very nature, are of statewide concern. These include airports and major highways. If a developer asserts that the proposed development is a matter of statewide concern, the local agency is required to apply the state's standards to determine whether it is a "development of state or regional benefit" and the "probable net benefit from the development exceeds the probable net detriment. . . ." [52] If the local agency finds that these tests have been met, it is to grant permission even if the development is not authorized by the local ordinance. An appeal to the state board is available. Again, it is not clear that subsidized housing sponsors would benefit from this scheme. The project must constitute a "development of state or regional benefit" to warrant special treatment. Small projects, which have been encouraged by HUD in recent years, might be considered to have little impact beyond the jurisdiction in which they are located. However, the "state or regional benefit" definition includes one category which could advance subsidized housing:

> (4) development by any person receiving state or federal aid designed to facilitate a type of development specified by the State Land Planning Agency by rule.[53]

Under this section, the state planning agency could issue a rule designating subsidized housing as being of "state or regional benefit." Decisions concerning this housing would then be made using statewide standards and would be appealable to the state land adjudicatory board.

Should a development pass the "state or regional benefit" test, it still must survive the cost-benefit analysis. Unfortunately, the array of factors to be considered may make it possible for the local agency to rationalize excluding low- and moderate-income housing. These factors include impact on municipal services, burden on taxpayers, immediate cost burdens on the local government and environmental impact, all of which have been used by municipalities to justify exclusionary zoning. Of the 10 factors identified, the only one which clearly has an inclusionary slant relates to the effect of the development on "the ability of people to find adequate housing reasonably accessible to their place of employment." [54]

The third type of development of statewide concern is unrelated to its location or its nature, but depends solely on its size. Some developments may be of sufficient scale that they are deemed to have regional or statewide significance. These developments must be consistent with the local ordinance unless:

> . . . the departure from the ordinance is reasonably necessary to enable a substantial segment of the population of a larger community of which the local government is a part to obtain reasonable access to housing, employment, educational or recreational opportunities.[55]

A developer of a large-scale mixed-income housing development could argue that the shortage of housing opportunities in the area for lower-income families justified development inconsistent with the local ordinance. If the local board denied the application, an appeal to the state board would be available.

Additional requirements are imposed on those large scale developments which substantially increase employment opportunities within the jurisdiction:

(1)   adequate and reasonably accessible housing for prospective employees is available within or without the jurisdiction of the local government; or

(2)   the local government has adopted a Land Development Plan designed to make available adequate and reasonably accessible housing within a reasonable time; or

(3)   a State Land Development Plan shows that the proposed location is a desirable location for the proposed employment source.[56]

Although this provision relates more directly to subsidized housing than any other in the draft code, it still does not assure the development of such housing. First, the jobs created by the development may be largely in the middle-income range or above. Second, a somewhat general plan, rather than either actual construction of housing or a concrete plan with timetables, may be sufficient to fulfill the code's requirement. Third, a state plan is presumed conclusively to be adequate, even though it may totally ignore the housing question. Finally, responsibility for the housing is diffused. It need not be within the jurisdiction where the development is to take place but must be reasonably accessible to the job sites. This standard may be reasonable from a planning standpoint, but it makes the identification of local responsibility for including the housing very difficult.

The overall impact of the Model Land Development Code on low- and moderate-income housing development is uncertain. It provides no specific remedy for developers of such housing who are excluded at the local level but relies on general standards applicable to a variety of land uses. The focus is procedural, rather than substantive. For example, it is hoped that providing an administrative review process will reduce costs for developers, compared to the alternative judicial forum. However, as in Massachusetts, the state board could merely serve as an additional step in the review process rather than a substitute for the courts. The administrative appeal, cheaper in itself than the courts, could become part of an even more time-consuming, financially burdensome process than now exists for the subsidized developer. To deal with this problem, the draft sets up a narrow standard of judicial review. The court must find that the state agency's action was arbitrary and capricious in order to reverse the decision. Even with this limitation, the developer may lose time, money, and even the project by pursuing the review process to its conclusion.

In sum, the reporters for the Model Land Development Code appear to have used an indirect approach to low- and moderate-income housing. Rather than defining such housing as a matter of statewide interest, they have focused on general types of development with impact beyond the locality. Their hope lies in the assumption that state officials would not have the parochial concerns of individual municipalities. There is little evidence that a procedural approach lacking policy goals would have a favorable impact on the substantive question of development of low- and moderate-income housing. The answer would seem to lie more in the politics of selection of the state board than in any broad perspective presumably inherent in state officials. Passage of the apparently neutral model code provisions, followed by the appointment of a strong prohousing board could be a significant strategy for change. Otherwise, elevating land use decisions of statewide concern to the state level is not likely to alter housing patterns significantly.

The Model Land Development Code as a Model: The Florida Case

In 1972, Florida enacted a law based largely on the ALI Model Land Development Code.[57] The Florida law adopts the premise of the model code that certain land use decisions should be elevated to the state level. The state becomes involved in decisions which will have a significant impact outside the locality where the land is located. The state designates "areas of critical concern," and establishes principles to guide the development of such areas. Areas covered by the act include those with environmental, historical, natural or archeological resources of regional or statewide importance; a proposed area of major development potential; or an existing or proposed major public facility.

The statute also involves the state in regulating "developments of regional impact." These are developments which would have a substantial effect on the health, welfare and safety of the residents of more than one county because of the nature, size or location of the development. The legislature designated "developments presumed to be of regional impact," such as airports, shopping centers and large residential developments.

For "areas of critical state concern," the local government is authorized to write land development regulations for submission to the Division of State Planning. If the locality fails to develop suitable regulations, the state agency is to undertake this task itself. After approval at the state level, the local government administers these regulations.

For "developments of regional impact," the locality must consider regional and state effects in deciding whether to issue permits. This determination is to be based in part on an analysis by the designated regional planning agency of the regional effect of the proposed project. It is at this point that housing considerations are made explicit. The regional planning agency is required to consider a number of factors in preparing its reports and recommendations, including the extent to which "the development will favorably or adversely affect the ability of people to find adequate housing reasonably accessible to their places of employment. . . ."[58]

Finally, the law provides for an administrative review at the state level of local decisions. The Land and Water Adjudicatory Commission, made up of the governor and the cabinet, is to hear and decide appeals from local decisions involving both "areas of critical state concern" and "developments of regional impact."

The Florida statute follows closely the pattern of the model code. Its direct references to housing are limited. Its thrust is environmental. In Florida, where there are major environmental battles to be fought over the preservation of valuable land and water resources, it is unlikely that this law will significantly advance the housing cause. Administrative efforts will probably focus on the more traditionally defined physical environmental issues, rather than the right of people to live in a decent environment near their work.

Hackensack Meadowlands. The state of New Jersey picked up on the notion of an "area of critical state concern." The legislature created the Hackensack Meadowlands Commission, a state agency, to plan and regulate development in this 20,000 acre area across the Hudson River from New York City. The Meadowlands served as a garbage dump for New York City. The Army Corps of Engineers agreed to recommend reclamation to Congress if the state would guarantee that development of the area would not be left in the hands of the 14 municipalities and two counties that had jurisdiction over land development. In 1967 the state passed legislation creating a seven person commission to preside over development of the area.

The state became involved in the Hackensack Meadowlands for broader reasons than the achievement of economic integration in housing. However, the regulatory framework the state established permitted the inclusion of housing mix as an objective of development of this vast area. In fact, the draft development regulations for the Meadowlands required a balanced housing supply. Developers were to provide:

> . . . housing that will result in a community with a mix and balance of income levels that shall reflect regional housing needs and the range of job opportunities available in the Hackensack Meadowlands District.[59]

State Zoning Enabling Legislation
In addition to involving themselves in specific land use decisions related to housing, states can change their planning and zoning enabling laws.

States gave land use powers to localities in the first place, and states can take away or restrict these powers. States can redefine the purposes for which local communities are permitted to zone. As indicated in Chapter 2, state enabling laws have traditionally given localities virtually free rein to zone. States could make several kinds of changes in these laws which would retain the basic principle of local autonomy while moving communities toward an inclusionary posture relative to lower-income housing. First, the state law could prohibit zoning that has the purpose or effect of excluding any economic or racial group. A 1969 New Jersey bill provided that:

> [t]he powers of land use planning and control delegated by this act shall not be used for the purpose of excluding any economic, racial, religious or ethnic group from the enjoyment of residence, land ownership, tenancy or land uses anywhere in the state.[60]

This bill would have been even stronger even if it had focused on the effect of local practices rather than the purpose. An effect test would be likely to have an even more significant impact on local practices. In addition, it would provide an excellent basis for lawsuits where exclusionary suburbs did not change their zoning patterns. Plaintiffs would only have to show that the effect of the local practices was to keep them out, rather than demonstrating that exclusion was the locality's purpose.

Another useful revision of the state zoning enabling legislation would be a requirement that a locality consider the regional implications in making land use decisions. The "general welfare" would mean more than the welfare of the locality; it would extend to the region in which the community is located. For example, the New Jersey bill would have required that local zoning ordinances reflect:

> ... the need for various types of housing for all economic and social groups in the municipality, and in the surrounding region including but not limited to housing for families or persons employed within the municipality and persons whose displacement is caused by public projects within the region and adjoining regions.[61]

In 1967, Vermont took a step in this regional direction. It amended the municipal planning and enabling law to require urban communities to pay attention to housing and regional considerations.[62] Again, this law may influence local practices directly as well as providing a basis for lawsuits by those excluded from communities (see Chapter 17 for a discussion of regional litigation strategies).

State enabling legislation might also be revised, as California has done, to require municipalities to include a "housing element" in local plans.[63] The local plans are to provide for all economic groups. This legislation regulates local planning rather than zoning, so the impact may be limited. However, even this legislation may provide a useful rationale in exclusionary zoning lawsuits.

The Potential of State Involvement in
Land Use Regulation

It is clear that states are reclaiming many of their powers to regulate the use of land within their borders. After 50 years of leaving it to localities, states have begun to recognize that some land use decisions are so critical to state interests that there must be state involvement. There will probably be more state land use agencies created to review these local decisions. Although only Massachusetts has focused on low- and moderate-income housing as a specific area of state review, other states are getting their feet in the land use door. Generalized state review processes, such as those outlined in the Model Land Development Code, are not likely to have much impact on opening the suburbs. Instead, the real potential lies in pressing the states to expand their role in the land use area. Once a state is back in the land use ball game, proponents of open suburbs must push the state to focus in on lower-income housing as a land use issue of critical state concern. The Massachusetts Zoning Appeals law, the Illinois Workers' Residential Rights Act, and the redefinition of the purposes of local zoning through enabling legislation represent promising approaches. Any of these statutory strategies, as they are being refined, provides a state with an important tool for opening the suburbs. The potential is particularly great if the regulatory legislation is combined with direct state involvement in the financing and development of subsidized housing.

Chapter Seven

State Financing and Development of Housing

The Massachusetts Zoning Appeals law and other state land use regulations depend on housing sponsors and developers to challenge local decisions. Often the developer most capable of taking this initiative is the state itself, through a housing finance agency (HFA). With or without a state land use review process, financing and developing subsidized housing is perhaps the most direct means for states to influence the location of low- and moderate-income housing.

      States have been creating housing finance agencies since the early 1960s.[1] The number of state finance agencies has grown rapidly, from 13 in 1971 to 24 by early 1973.[2] At that time, legislation was pending in several other states.[3] The growth of SHFAs indicates a recognition by the states that the private housing market cannot meet the needs of low- and moderate-income families. Although the responsibilities and authorities of state housing agencies vary substantially, they have some functions in common.[4]

Mortgage Lending

      First, housing finance agencies act as mortgage lenders. They make available construction loans and long-term financing for housing developments, much as a private mortgagee would do. The agencies sell bonds to get the money that they lend to developers. The revenues from the projects are then used to pay the principal and interest on the bonds. The HFAs can make mortgage loans at lower interest rates than private lending institutions. Their revenue bonds, being tax-exempt, can be sold at rates below those in the conventional market. Purchasers of the bonds are willing to accept a rate of return which is less than they could get from other investments because they do not have to pay income tax on income from these bonds. If the state guarantees the bonds, the interest rate the agency must pay is even lower and

it is easier to find buyers for these securities. When the taxing power of the
state is available to make up losses that may occur through mortgage defaults,
the interest rate is about 1.5 percentage points lower than on bonds that do
not have the state's backing. These lower interest costs are direclty reflected
in rents. For example, a $25,000 mortgage financed over 40 years at six percent
interest implies a monthly debt service charge of $137.56 while the same
mortgage financed at five percent would only require $120.55 a month. There-
fore, providing effective guarantees to bondholders results in lower interest
costs which can be passed on to tenants in the form of reduced rents.

Program Administration

A second common function of HFAs is to administer housing
programs. They often arrange subsidies for a portion of the units in a development. HFAs can thus provide housing for families with incomes ranging from
over $16,000 per year (for the unsubsidized portion), to under $5,000 (for
the portion assisted by section 236 and rent supplements) in a single development.[5]

State Agencies as Developers

Generally, state housing agencies do not have broad development
and condemnation powers. However, at least 10 agencies have power to acquire
land for housing development.[6] With this authority an agency can assemble
parcels for development, manage them until the assembly is complete, provide relocation services, and then sell or lease the package to a qualified
developer. The HFA's advantage over a private developer in this activity is
the lower price it pays for its money, both short- and long-term.

A few agencies, such as the New York Urban Development Corporation and the Connecticut Housing Finance Authority, have the power to
develop the housing themselves. State legislatures have been reluctant to
provide related development powers such as eminent domain and local zoning
overrides. For example, the Maryland agency can exercise eminent domain
over a particular piece of property only on request of the local government.[7]
New York's Urban Development Corporation is the only state agency ever
authorized to override local zoning decisions.[8]

Overriding Local Zoning:
The UDC Experience

The New York state legislature created the Urban Development
Corporation, or UDC, in the aftermath of the April 1968 assassination of
Dr. Martin Luther King, Jr. Like so much social legislation, its passage was
precipitated by the occurrence of a tragic event. Even so, the UDC bill failed
initially in the state assembly. New York Governor Nelson Rockefeller, who
was attending the King funeral in Atlanta, applied his clout and the bill passed

the legislature.[9] UDC was given a wide range of powers to assist in the redevelopment process in the stae as well as in the development of subsidized housing. It can use state and federal programs if it wishes. The agency is authorized to operate in any community in the state, to purchase, lease or condemn property and redevelop the property with industrial, commercial or civic buildings or low-, moderate- or middle-income housing.[10]

Uniquely, UDC was authorized to override "the requirements of local laws, ordinances, codes, charters, or regulations applicable to such construction, reconstruction, rehabilitation, alteration or improvement . . . when, in the discretion of the corporation, such compliance is not feasible or practicable."[11] If a locality opposed a UDC project, the corporation could proceed anyway, on a six to three vote by its board of directors. The legislature also gave UDC certain exemptions from state and local taxes. UDC usually pays around 10 percent of the shelter rent in lieu of local real estate taxes. UDC also has the power to condemn property for its projects.

After UDC threatened to use its most powerful took, the zoning override, in suburban Westchester County, the legislature repealed that provision. [12] This 1973 amendment also permitted towns and incorporated villages to veto UDC housing developments even if they complied with local zoning and building codes.

Use of the Override. For its first several years, UDC did not rely on its override power. Instead, the agency responded to invitations from local officials to assist in the development of needed low- and moderate-income housing.[13] In 1969 the governor sent letters to all the mayors in New York state asking them what projects they would like UDC to do for them. UDCs policy was to use the zoning override sparingly. It was usually used with the consent of local officials to cut through local red tape. It was not necessary to go through the usual channels for a zoning variance or other approvals. For example, in the Rochester suburb of Pittsford the UDC began construction on a 300 unit development in 1970 without local zoning changes. It built the project over some opposition from the community and local legislators. Strong support from business leaders, including Kodak and Xerox, provided much of the needed impetus for the project.

UDC received its first real challenge from a community in Amherst, outside of Buffalo. The state university was building the new campus of the University of Buffalo on a site in Amherst and it was decided that a new town would go well with it. Amherst is sparsely populated. Much of the housing there is for upper-income families.

Amherst feared that the combination of a great many nontaxable subsidized housing units proposed by UDC plus other tax breaks which UDC could claim for itself might serve to wreak havoc upon Amherst's economy. When UDC's response failed to allay these fears, Amherst took UDC to court.

The issue was resolved with an out-of-court settlement embodied in a contract between UDC and the town of Amherst. This marked the first time UDC had entered into an agreement any more binding than the usual memorandum of understanding which it signs with most communities. The resolution provided for 1,000 fewer total residential units than were originally planned; 50 percent fewer (1,870) partially taxed (subsidized) units, and 800 more fully taxed units.

In Amherst, UDC acceded to the community's wishes in ways that had not been necessary in their prior projects. The new town, of course, was started as a UDC initiative rather than on invitation from local officials. In addition, the scale of development contemplated was far greater than UDC's typical projects and therefore was a significant threat to the character of the existing community. The result was a demand for local participation in the planning process, a negotiation between the parties, and an accommodation of the diverse interests represented.

Early Efforts to Repeal the Override.   Even in its early days, legislative attacks were mounted against UDC. About a dozen bills curtailing the agency's power were introduced in 1969, two of which passed the assembly but were killed in senate committee. Still more such bills were submitted in 1970; again, they did not survive in the senate. In spite of this extremely limited use of the override power in the agency's early years, its very existence was sufficiently threatening for the legislature to pass a bill rescinding the power in 1971. Only a veto by Governor Rockefeller preserved the power for UDC.[14]

The "Nine Towns Program".   Having survived the legislature's attack on its powers, UDC President Edward Logue announced on June 20, 1972 that the agency was going to develop a series of subsidized housing projects in nine relatively rural communities in Westchester County, adjacent to New York City.[15]

UDC concluded that housing at moderate prices was needed for current residents as well as nonresident employees of local industry.[16] First, 53,000 Westchester families spent more than the commonly accepted maximum of 25 percent of their income for housing. In addition, the county had 17,500 substandard housing units. And the county was being invaded by industry. It already contained the headquarters of 27 firms, and 47 firms listed on the New York and American stock exchanges operated facilities in Westchester. In 1971, 53 other firms announced plans to expand into Westchester. At that time, there were 116,000 persons commuting into the county to work. Eighty percent of them earned less than $12,000 per year. There was a clear need for subsidized housing in Westchester County.

UDC had built housing in Westchester before at the invitation of the county executive. The agency had already constructed or started work on 1,500 units of housing in the larger cities of Yonkers, Ossining, White Plains and Peekskill, but additional housing sites were not readily available around these cities. UDC decided to go to the smaller outlying towns. The Nine Towns Program contemplated building 100 units of housing in each of nine towns in northern Westchester. The towns contained mostly upper-income housing.

The Nine Towns Program was based on a fair share principle similar to that used by the Miami Valley Regional Planning Commission and other such agencies. One hundred units of low- and moderate-income housing—town houses and garden apartments—would be built in each of the towns: Bedford, Cortlandt, Greenburgh, Harrison, Lewisboro, New Castle, North Castle, Somers and Yorktown. In each case, the usual UDC ratio was to be employed: 70 apartments would be for moderate-income families, 20 for low-income families and 10 for the elderly.[17] In accordance with UDC's general practice, 20 percent of the units would be made available for minority group families.

The plan was designed to have minimum impact on the recipient communities. The new units would average less than four percent of the existing housing stock. No more than one site would be in any one school district. Priority in occupancy was to be: first, those displaced by urban renewal or other government projects; second, Vietnam war veterans and their families; third, residents of the town; fourth, persons employed by the town regardless of place of residence; fifth, persons living anywhere in the county; sixth, people working elsewhere in the county.[18]

In order to build the Westchester projects major zoning changes were necessary, either through local action or exercise of the override power. Approximately 99 percent of the residentially zoned land in the county permitted only single family homes—no apartments.[19] All but one of the sites proposed by UDC were zoned for single family homes, with minimum lot sizes as high as four acres. UDC announced that it would seek the cooperation of the towns involved, but that it would build the projects even if such cooperation was not forthcoming.[20] The override authority was the stick designed to induce local public officials to negotiate about the proposed sites or provide substitute sites.

Opposition to the Nine Towns Program. Opposition mounted quickly. The "United Towns for Home Rule" was established, to oppose "the absolute and unfettered power of a state superagency to come uninvited into a community to override its zoning and to unilaterally impose its will upon that community."[21] The organization challenged the UDC program on a number of grounds, including lack of public facilities and services, poor site selection, incomplete tax impact studies, nonconformity to master plans, a contradiction of home rule, and impact on marginal home owners.[22]

The potential benefits of the program were not understood in the county. Many people who were eligible for the proposed housing were among

UDC's most vehement opponents. These people may have been unaware that
they had first priority on these units. Alternatively, their racial feelings may
have been so strong that they opposed the plan in order to exclude the blacks
who would be involved.

United Towns for Home Rule demanded consultation with the
UDC and made opposition to UDC a campaign issue in the fall elections of
1972. In August 1972 Governor Rockefeller declared a moratorium on the
Nine Towns Program until January 15, 1973.[23] The time was to be spent in
consultation with local officials and in finding agreeable sites.

It appeared that some of the opposition to the Nine Towns Plan
was directed at UDC rather than at subsidized housing per se. A survey conducted by Oliver Quayle for the UDC concluded that the majority of Westchester County residents would support the construction of subsidized housing
in their own towns if the initiative were local.[24] About 60 percent of those
polled opposed such developments if the UDC was to be the sponsor. The poll,
which was based on hour-long interviews with 505 people in 101 locations in
the county, showed little differences in attitude between people living in the
nine towns slated for UDC housing and residents of other parts of the county.

Support for the Nine Towns Program.   The UDC Nine Towns
Plan received immediate and widely publicized support as well as opposition.
The League of Women Voters, the Northeast Westchester Council on Equality
and the builders association provided early and vocal support.[25] In addition, blacks organized the Coalition of Black Westchester Residents to support
the UDC plan. A total of over 20 citizens groups expressed support for the
effort.[26] In addition, the *New York Times* gave editorial support to the Nine
Towns Program:

> . . . the UDC plan could best be criticized as being too modest . . .
> Mr. Logue and the UDC have made mistakes in their four years, but
> the Westchester undertaking is not one of them. It represents a
> reasonable and realistic step toward healthy suburban develop-
> ment.[27]

The *White Plains Reporter Dispatch* also supported UDC editorially.

After the Rockefeller Moratorium.   In mid-January 1973, Edward
Logue announced that the moratorium had concluded in Westchester, but he
indicated that he hoped persuasion would be sufficient and that it would not
be necessary to use the override power.[28] The reactions of the nine towns
were mixed. Bedford's housing study group concluded that the UDC was
the entity most capable of providing needed housing in the community.
Bedford and Greenburgh both indicated that agency projects, with modifica-

tions, would be acceptable. At the other extreme, the supervisor of New Castle, which did not reply to the governor's request for an alternative plan, indicated that the town would sue if the state agency tried to develop housing there. In between, Somers, Lewisboro and North Castle replied that they wished to discuss specific, privately financed developments with UDC. Harrison indicated that it was trying to develop a plan using federal subsidies. Yorktown asserted that it was already providing enough multifamily housing on its own, and Cortlandt did not reply.[29]

One reason for at least partial compliance may be the fact that Suburban Action Institute had announced plans to build several thousand units of low- and moderate-income housing on 600 acres in Lewisboro, New York.[30] It planned to build a mixed-income community of 13,800 residents in a town whose population was 6,700. In comparison to the 4,600 units proposed by Suburban Action, the 100 unit UDC plan seemed to many Lewisboro residents to be very reasonable.

If the Lewisboro Town Board rejected Suburban Action's request for a zoning change the town would probably have to defend this action in court. Aside from a small area zoned for commercial development, the town permits only single family housing, mostly on two acre lots. This pattern might make the town vulnerable in a lawsuit. The possibility of a legal setback gave the town an incentive to cooperate with UDC in developing a smaller subsidized project, the existence of which might provide a defense in a subsequent Suburban Action lawsuit. The town supervisor predicted that the multifamily housing would be under construction in Lewisboro by the end of 1973.[31]

Repeal of the Override. Prior to the Westchester effort, a commentator had suggested that the override was "like having the H-bomb. It's good to have in reserve in negotiations, but it's just too much power to use without all hell breaking loose."[32] Although not profound, the statement was prophetic. The political realities had been clear from the outset. By the summer of 1973, the UDC had been stripped of its power to develop housing in suburban areas without permission of the locality. The legislature enacted a measure which made UDC subject to greater local control than private developers. It provided that any town or incorporated village could veto UDC residential developments even if they met local zoning and building regulations. The statute goes beyond a repeal of the override to providing an express veto power to these localities:

> Notwithstanding any inconsistent provision of this act or of any general or special law, no plan for a proposed residential project in a town or incorporated village which has not been affirmed by the corporation prior to May first, ninetten hundred seventy-

three, shall be affirmed if, within thirty days after the public hearing held pursuant to subdivision two of section sixteen of this act or within thirty days after June first, nineteen hundred seventy-three, whichever date is later, the local governing body of such town or village submits in writing to the corporation formal objections to the proposed residential project, unless and until such objections are withdrawn. . . .[33]

In granting the veto authority to towns and villages, the legislature provided suburbia with a new tool for exclusion. This statute gives them a means of excluding UDC development without even having to justify this action.

In approving this measure, Governor Rockefeller acknowledged the political strength of the opposition to the Westchester Nine Towns Program.[34] He indicated that it was necessary to cut back on UDC's powers to obtain legislative approval of financing for the agency. Without this support, UDC could not have continued to develop housing. The new law gave UDC an additional $500 million in bonding capacity.

Shortly after the legislature established the local veto power over UDC projects, the Town Board of Babylon rejected a UDC proposal for 182 moderate-income units in the black area of Wyandanch. The American Civil Liberties Union planned to file a suit challenging the local veto as racially discriminatory. The ACLU also intended to challenge the legality of the state law which created the local veto power.

Arguments are likely to focus on the legislative debates, which included a number of references to the racially discriminatory effect of the local veto law.

Limitations of the Override

The repeal of the UDC override authority indicates a fundamental weakness in the strategy. UDC's plan in Westchester was a modest one. It provided for only 100 units in each of nine towns, or 900 units spread throughout a large portion of the county. Many of the units would be for the elderly. More would be occupied by moderate-income families. Few would house low-income families. But even this small-scale effort aroused sufficient opposition to bring about removal of the override authority. UDC's override power was thus a delicate commodity. Its value lay in its existence, not its use. But if UDC could not use it without losing it, localities did not have to take the threat seriously. The agency's credibility was limited because of the widespread potential legislative opposition. UDC had to walk a difficult tightrope, trying to achieve its objectives while avoiding stirring up so much opposition that the legislature would clip its wings and strip the agency of the override and other powers. This turned out to be impossible.

The question remains as to whether or not the concept of UDC and the zoning override can be generalized to other states. Around 25–30 states have studied this posibility. Few governors have the political pull to get such a provision through their legislatures, even if they support the principle. A weaker version of the UDC bill was defeated in the Maryland legislature in 1969. In 1970 Governor Cahill of New Jersey proposed a modified UDC approach, which would permit the existing Housing Finance Agency, "after consultation by appropriate state officials with municipal officials . . . to overcome abusive application of local zoning laws."[35] To provide safeguards for the municipalities, the governor suggested that:

> . . . the H.F.A. could be required to consider the effect of the proposed housing on the local planning scheme and to thoroughly consult with local officials prior to making its final decision. Additional limitations on the percentage of land, or the number of units which could be approved for construction in any single muncipality could also be incorporated into this approach. Further, an incentive in the form of State aid in lieu of taxes, or State aid for schools would be highly desireable.[36]

The governor pointed out that the exemption from local regulations was already available for state facilities such as highways, prisons, state buildings and colleges. In addition, public utilities may be granted similar exemptions if the state's Public Utilities Commission finds that the utility is reasonably necessary for the public good.

The governor was trying to alter the UDC concept in ways that might make the approach more politically palatable to local officials. Their maximum obligations would be specified and the state would provide a financial incentive for the community to accept the housing. Nevertheless, the proposal gained little legislative support.

In Colorado, a legislative committee proposed a bill to create a state housing finance agency, with a provision for court challenges of local practices that prevent development of low-income housing.[37]

In Illinois, a bill was submitted to create an "Illinois Community Development Corporation."[38] It is modeled on New York State's Urban Development Corporation in that the corporation can finance, develop and manage a variety of projects, including housing, industrial and multipurpose developments. The corporation is required to work cooperatively with the local municipality, although in certain circumstances it can override the wishes of the locality. Although this bill will surely be opposed because of its section 11, "Cooperation With Local Government," it does provide significant safeguards for local prerogatives. The local planning agency has the opportunity to review each project plan, and if it recommends disapproval or modification, the state corporation may proceed with the plan only if two-thirds of its board of directors votes to do so. In addition, the corporation must comply with local ordinances and codes (e.g., zoning ordinance, building code) unless it "makes a specific finding that such compliance is not feasible or practicable." Thus local prerogatives are respected, except when they must give way to geographically broader purposes. This bill also received little immediate support.

Production Record of Housing Agencies

By early 1973, state housing agencies had financed construction of approximately 150,000 units of housing.[39] Obligations and reservations under federal subsidy programs amounted to 71,929 units and almost $100 million. The vast bulk of construction starts and subsidy commitments belong to a few agencies. Almost half of the agencies have made no contributions to the total number. In most cases, this is because a lead time of two years is needed before a new agency's efforts bear fruit. An agency's bonds, which are used to finance the housing, are not marketable until the courts have affirmed the constitutionality of the law creating the agency. Once that is done, purchasers of bonds will be willing to buy the agency's bonds and it can begin to finance housing development. Only approximately a half-dozen agencies have been in existence long enough to have put the constitutional test far behind them and moved deeply into financing housing. After the creation of the New York financing agency in 1961, the next wave of legislation did not begin until 1966. Massachusetts, Illinois, New Jersey, and Michigan established agencies in the late 1960s. New York created a second agency, UDC, in this period. These states have produced most of the state-financed housing.

Suburban Development

Much of the focus of state housing agency programs has been on the suburbs.[40] A study of three major state agencies showed that 65 percent of their units went into the suburbs.[41] Twenty percent of the units were for middle-income households and only six percent for low-income families. Many of these developments are economically and racially integrated, with low-, moderate- and middle-income people living in the same development. In fact, the Massachusetts law requires the Housing Finance Agency (MHFA) to build in this fashion. Although MHFA has encountered resistance on some developments, the mixed-income character of the developments serves to reduce local opposition. For housing agencies to build mixed-income housing, subsidies are necessary beyond the reduced interest rate resulting from the sale of tax-exempt bonds.

With the uncertainties that constantly surround the future of federal subsidy programs, states should create their own subsidy programs. In the absence of federal or state subsidies, all that housing agencies can do is provide housing to middle-income people at somewhat reduced rentals. Instead of providing access to the suburbs for lower-income people, HFAs would then probably just perpetuate metropolitan economic segregation. They would be providing an additional vehicle for the flight of the affluent to suburbia. Some housing agencies are already traveling down this counterproductive path, especially with the slowdown and apparent phasing out of federal programs.

At least two states have begun to recognize the need to use state resources to subsidize housing for lower-income occupants. Massachusetts and New York have created their own subsidy programs. Most of the funds go to the state housing agency. In Massachusetts the program provides interest subsidies like the federal section 236 program. New York provides assistance to low-income families so they can afford to rent units financed by the state's financing agency or the UDC. In both cases, the state assistance is designed to complement federal programs. The state programs were funded on a limited scale. If the housing finance agencies are to reach their potential for increasing suburban access for lower-income people, then state subsidy programs will have to be expanded and others created.

State housing agencies can provide quality mixed-income housing. They can also challenge communities which do not want their housing. If they have the money and political support from the legislatures and the will to do the job, HFAs can make some large holes in the suburban wall. An HFA that is unwilling to accept this challenge, as well as the challenge of rebuilding central city neighborhoods, ought not exist.

Chapter Eight

The State's Carrots and Sticks

In addition to regulating the use of suburban land directly and financing development of housing on that land, states can use other leverage to influence local development patterns. For example, states make funds available to local communities under a variety of programs. They can condition these grants on specified local actions.

The Theory of the Carrot
and the Stick

In the housing context, the state might deny program funds to communities which have little or no low- and moderate-income housing. State funds could be used both to reward communities which have such housing and to induce other communities to provide the housing. As it provides such housing, or makes sufficient progress that performance can be evaluated favorably, the community would become eligible for various state funds.

Conditions for the receipt of assistance should be stated in terms of result, or effect, rather than in terms of particular method or steps to be taken to achieve the desired result. This approach serves the needs of the local communities, which retain flexibility to act based on their knowledge of their own terrain. It also prevents backfire; if the state dictates the precise course of action to be taken, the state is out of luck if the community complies but still does not arrive at the result the state contemplated.

The conditions which are attached to a grant might have little programmatic relation to the program's statutory purpose. The state might attach housing conditions to grants related to parks, schools or other projects not directly involving housing. If possible, the conditions should be binding upon the same local entity which seeks state assistance. State influence will diminish if, for example, a park district is requesting state funds but an independent housing authority is the agency subject to the conditions on the grant.

119

Finally, the state needs to be able to enforce its conditions. Ideally, all of the actions promised by the locality would be completed before state funds begin to flow. This may be politically, or practically, extremely difficult. Housing requires a substantial lead time for development. However, it should be possible to hold back state funds until enough reliable progress has been made toward providing housing to release funds. A midstream cutoff of funds may also be possible if conditions are violated in the course of the program. However, there are programmatic benefits to be gained in keeping the state assistance flowing. For this reason, the state might choose to continue to fund that particular program and withhold future assistance for other projects desired by the locality. This approach is particularly useful if the locality relies on the state regularly for assistance. The locality would then be notified that its performance in complying with conditions under one program would determine its eligibility for future assistance under a variety of other programs.

The Practice of the Carrot and the Stick
In order to employ a carrot and stick approach at the state level to increase housing opportunities, basic requirements include carrots and a fundamental interest in promoting housing opportunities. Theoretically, the best place to find this combination is in the state-level departments of community affairs (DCAs) which were spawned in response to the urban riots of the 1960s. More than 30 states have created these departments to focus on housing and other concerns of the states' urban areas. They generally provide technical assistance to municipalities and assist in the administration of federal grants. However, these departments tend to have budgets and staffs which are among the smallest for state agencies. Few DCAs have significant funds to distribute. Their carrots are limited. In spite of these constraints, a few DCAs have had a major impact, including agencies in New Jersey, Connecticut and Pennsylvania.

To date, the Pennsylvania Department of Community Affairs is the only such state agency which has both the authority over grants and the interest in housing to become actively involved in overcoming suburban exclusionary barriers. In 1972 the Pennsylvania Department of Community Affairs began to use state recreational funds, under programs it administered, as a carrot to influence suburbs to remove the barriers to low- and moderate-income housing.

Conditional Recreational Funds
The Project 500 Act, passed by the Pennsylvania legislature in 1968, provides matching grants to localities which pay up to 50 percent of the cost of acquiring land and developing county and municipal park and recreation land.[1] The program was financed by a $500 million bond issue.

Secretary William Wilcox, of the Department of Community Affairs, requested two opinions from the attorney general of the commonwealth relative to the administration of the Project 500 Act. The first dealt with the "authority of the Department of Community Affairs to prescribe to municipalities controls over who may be admitted to recreational facilities and what fees may be charged for use of such facilities."[2] The attorney general ruled that the Department of Community Affairs was not merely to act as a "pass through" of state funds to the localities, but was authorized by the legislature to administer or supervise state grant programs, including establishing rules and regulations to carry out the purposes of the law. The attorney general concluded that this administrative authority applied to the Project 500 Act, even though it was enacted after the department's enabling act, since this program was specifically given to the department to administer.

The department was also given specific authority in the Project 500 Act to obtain information from localities. The act requires that "development projects shall be submitted to the Department of Community Affairs by the political subdivision in an application which contains information as may be required by the Department of Community Affairs. . . ."[3] The Attorney General interpreted this provision as sufficiently expansive to permit inquiry into whether the particular project would be consistent with other statutory and Constitutional provisions.

Having concluded that the legislature "did intend to give the Department reasonable discretion to inquire as to whether any proposed 'Project 500' project will violate state or federal law. . .", the Attorney General illustrated the point by reference to the civil rights issue.[4] Before funding a project, the Department of Community Affairs was to be assured that the applicant would operate the facility, including admissions and fees policies, in conformity with state and federal civil rights laws. To fail to do so could put the department in the position of spending public funds illegally or unconstitutionally:

> . . . the Department of Community Affairs is under a statutory duty not to disperse funds that will be used in an unconstitutional manner and to take whatever regulatory steps necessary in order to be reasonably certain that no project receiving funds will unconstitutionally restrict admission to facilities. . . .
> There can be no other conclusion, therefore, other than that municipal admission restrictions or fees may very well raise constitutional questions of the highest gravity. That conclusion not only necessitates appropriate scrutiny by the Department of Community Affairs under its statutory authority outlined in the previous section, but also requires the Department to consider whether the *funding* of a project that will be unconstitutionally administered by a Pennsylvania municipality is itself an unconstitutional state act.[5]

Subsequently, the Department of Community Affairs requested the attorney general's opinion on the applicability of this January 13 opinion to "communities having exclusionary development policies." Exclusionary development policies were defined as "zoning and other land-use control practices that effectively preclude construction of dwelling units that could house minority, and low-income and (in some cases) middle-income families, either by direct exclusion or by raising the price of residential development."[6] This opinion built on the foundation of the earlier one and provided the Department of Community Affairs with substantial leverage in dealing with exclusionary communities. The attorney general concluded that the earlier opinion did apply to exclusionary communities because carrying out exclusionary policies may result in low-income and minority persons being denied access to facilities developed with Project 500 funds. Where residence requirements are imposed for use of Project 500 facilities, the presence of exclusionary zoning almost automatically denies low-income people and minorities access to the facility, since they cannot become residents. Even where there were no residence requirements, the attorney general found that the department had an obligation to make an independent determination of accessibility. If transportation costs or other factors result in practical inaccessibility, the effect may be the same as if there were residence requirements: restriction of access to state-assisted recreational facilities. If a community's policies would have that result, it would be illegal for the Department of Community Affairs to approve a recreation grant for the locality.

The attorney general concluded that:

> The Department must look carefully at the effect of such exclusionary development practices on the use of and access to recreational facilities. Any restriction that has the effect of restricting the use of a State funded facility by race or wealth, must receive the Department's closest scrutiny. The existence of such restrictions will be a reason for denial of such funds in appropriate circumstances, for example, if no affirmative programs are established to ameliorate or eliminate the effect of such restrictions on racial minorities or low-income people.[7]

Upper St. Clair Township.   Based on these rulings of the attorney general, the Department of Community Affairs reviewed Project 500 applications against this standard of exclusionary development policies. In several instances, the department made initial determinations that communities which were otherwise eligible for grants could not receive the funds, because of their exclusionary policies. In May 1972 Secretary Wilcox announced that he was withholding a $54,000 recreation grant to the affluent Pittsburgh suburb of Upper St. Clair Township, because the community maintained exclusionary zoning ordinances.[8] Wilcox cited the attorney general's opinion as the authority for this action.

Upper St. Clair Township is a bedroom suburb in the southern part of Allegheny County. The dominant feature of the community is single family homes, with virtually no multifamily units and no mobile homes. The great majority of these homes are valued at $25,000 or more, with many in the $50,000 plus category. The median house value and median rent are twice as high in Upper St. Clair as in the Pittsburgh metropolitan area as a whole. New single family housing starts at about $40,000. This housing is thus well beyond the range of low- and moderate-income families. That fact is reflected in the median income in the community, which is about $20,000 as compared to $8,800 for the whole metropolitan area and $10,132 for the Pittsburgh suburbs generally.

The land use policies and practices of Upper St. Clair are exclusionary in several ways. Very little land is zoned for multifamily use, a total of 75 acres out of the community's 2,800 acres (as of 1965) of undeveloped land. Maximum density permitted on these sites is 10 units per acre, thus providing for 750 multifamily units if all of the land was developed at the maximum possible density. Even on this land, multifamily housing is not permitted as of right. Developers of multifamily housing must submit detailed plans and supporting documentation to the planning commission and the board of commissoners to receive the necessary approval to build. Single family developers of the same sites are not required to follow these procedures.

Most of the township's land is zoned for single family residences, with the minimum lot size either 13,000 or 26,000 square feet, and virtually no land is zoned for smaller lot sizes. Finally, a conservation district covers approximately one-fourth of the land. Two acre lots are required for development in this district. Estimates of maximum future population, given current zoning, are in the 27,000 to 28,000 range. This represents a density of four and two-third persons per acre, a vastly lower density than in the central city and many other Pittsburgh suburbs.

The population of Upper St. Clair is thus predominantly middle- and upper-income, with the land use policies insuring the continuation of this pattern. Even the township's employees cannot afford to reside there. Based on these facts and the attorney general's interpretation of the law, the Department of Community Affairs stopped the grant for a park in Upper St. Clair. Local officials requested a hearing in order to argue that they should not be denied the state funds.

In December 1972 a two day administrative hearing was held. A panel of three outside urban experts was appointed by Secretary Wilcox. The panel was to recommend a course of action, which would not be binding on the parties but would hopefully enable them to reconcile their differences without a court fight. In challenging the state's action, the township made

several arguments. First, Upper St. Clair was no more exclusionary than any
other community. High land and housing costs resulted from location, land
availability and patterns of population rather than any exclusionary policy.
In fact, the township commissioners had recently approved the construction
of two townhouse apartment complexes, over the opposition of many residents.
The chairman of the township's planning commission, a planner by profession,
claimed that the community was unsuitable for lower-income housing because
of its distance from the metropolitan area's job centers. He suggested that it
would be extremely difficult for lower-income workers to find transportation
from this strictly bedroom suburb to their jobs in other suburbs or the central
city.

Second, the township argued that the Department of Community
Affairs did not have the right to subject recreation grants to these kinds of
conditions. The legislature did not impose the requirements that the department was asserting were applicable. Moreover, the township claimed that it
was being discriminated against because the Department of Community Affairs
did not issue regulations on a statewide basis, but selected Upper St. Clair
for special treatment. Finally, the town asserted that the ruling was retroactive,
since it was issued after the state had already released funds to cover 50 percent of the cost of property acquisition for the park.

In response, the state argued that the exclusion of lower-income
people from Upper St. Clair was real. Although the ordinance provided for
some multifamily dwellings, no moderately priced units had been approved.
Of the 285 homes sold in the township in 1972, 97 went for $50,000 to
$75,000 and most were priced from $32,000 to $50,000. The state also argued
that it had notified the community that the application did not meet the
guidelines for Project 500 at the initial "letter of intent" stage, before the
state was formally committed to funding the project.

Finally, the state argued that Upper St. Clair had received $350,000
in state grants under the Project 500 program, and that given its exclusionary
character the township should be given low priority for future funds. The
state did not intend to impose its development policies on communities, but
asserted that exclusionary communities should be prepared to pay their own
way in providing local facilities and services.

In May 1973 the panel upheld the denial of state funds to Upper
St. Clair. The panel concluded that the regulations of the Department of
Community Affairs permitted the rejection because the township had pursued and was continuing to pursue exclusionary land development policies.
After finding that the makeup of the population was exclusive and the zoning
ordinance exclusionary, the panel suggested the steps that Upper St. Clair
might take to become inclusionary:

> The panel recognizes that even the adoption of less restrictive zoning
> provisions, which would enable cheaper development cost, will not

open Upper St. Clair Township to the lower income persons of the
Pittsburgh metropolitan region, such as those shown in the lower
three (or perhaps four) quintiles of income distribution. The only
manner in which that sizeable portion of the Pittsburgh metropolitan population will obtain access to the Township, and other Townships like it, in this period of extraordinary housing cost is by the
Township, or a metropolitan body affirmatively undertaking to
provide housing that is subsidized. Families with incomes of less
than $12,000 cannot afford to buy even a modest priced home or
apartment at today's lowest development cost. Consequently, any
community which has not established a government agency or a
government-related nonprofit agency to develop housing under the
federal subsidy programs has, in our view, effectively excluded
major portions of populations such as those in the Pittsburgh metropolitan region from its boundaries. Because of the sizeable vacant
developable land in the Township, there is ample opportunity to
allow housing for a more representative population to develop
there.[9]

Upper St. Clair indicated that it would challenge the state's withholding of funds in the courts. On the other hand, Southampton, in Bucks
County, agreed that it would plan to provide housing for low- and moderate-
income housing. The carrot in the latter case was $380,000 for a park.[10]

Tredyffrin Township. In still another instance of the carrot and
stick approach, the Pennsylvania Department of Community Affairs denied
a $150,000 grant to Tredyffrin Township in Chester County in eastern Penn-
sylvania.[11] The grant was intended for use in the development of a $300,000
arboretum. The department found the application consistent with recreation
and conservation objectives of the state but inconsistent with the department's
policy on exclusionary development policies because: (1) Tredyffrin has the
second highest average house value (for owner-occupied units—$40,499) and
average contract rent ($178.00) in the Philadelphia region; (2) median income
as of 1960 was $10,579, as compared to the state's $5,719; (3) 60 percent of
the available land is zoned for minimum lot sizes of 100,000 square feet (more
than two acres); (4) of the 2,650 units which could be developed under present
zoning, only 200 units could be developed on lots smaller than 30,000 square
feet. In addition to the large lot sizes precluding development of low- and
moderate-income housing in those districts, the two acre minimum used up so
much land that prices of remaining acreage were inflated. As a result, the only
multifamily structures which were financially feasible were luxury apartments.

The negotiations between state and local officials to change these
patterns and make the community eligible for the grant revolved around a
proposed planned unit development called Chesterbrook. Chesterbrook was
an 865 acre development which contemplated the construction of 5,200 dwelling units. The developer made a

specific commitment to provide housing opportunities for a broad
range of income groups. Plan of development for Chesterbrook
proposed a range of housing for sale which provides significant
opportunities for families with moderate incomes. Condominium
apartment units will be sold in a price range from $18,000 to
$28,000. Single family attached townhouses will be sold in a
price range from $28,000 to $35,000. . . . Both the condominium
apartment and single family attached townhouses will provide housing opportunities for moderate income families which are presently
not available within Tredyffrin Township.

   In addition, when Federal or state housing programs are available
which provide an opportunity to sell housing to lower income
families on an individual basis, we will, where feasible, utilize these
programs to provide housing for lower income families within the
Chesterbrook community.[12]

After these commitments were made by the developer, the township supervisors reversed their previous position and approved the zoning
change necessary to permit construction of Chesterbrook. The Department
of Community Affairs considered this rezoning a sufficient step away from
prior discriminatory zoning policies and released the recreation funds without
waiting for the issuance of a building permit.

   Opposition formed on both sides. The Bucks County Legal Aid
Society was not satisfied that the developer's plans would provide housing
opportunities for low-income people. On the other hand, CORC, Citizens Opposed to Rezoning Chesterbrook, threatened a lawsuit to halt the development
in any form. In addition, they sought state legislation to provide for acquisition of the site for Valley Forge State Park. The parties faced a long, drawn
out struggle to decide the issues.

Department of Community Affairs
Overall Policy

The Pennsylvania Attorney General's opinions have implications
beyond Upper St. Clair and Tredyffrin Township and beyond the Project 500
program. If the Department of Community Affairs is required to scrutinize
carefully the development policies of applicants for recreation funds, it
appears to be under a similar obligation relative to the other grant programs
it administers, unless the legislature has specified otherwise. In fact, the
department interpreted the opinion as giving it "a clear cut mandate to review all program applications to make sure that they are nondiscriminatory
in every respect."[13] The secretary of the Department of Community Affairs
stated his intention to administer the programs on a consistent basis:

   . . . no edict has been or will be issued by me with respect to the
   provision of housing as a condition of grants administered by this

department . . . all grant programs of this department, where
there are no statutory mandates to the contrary, will be administered in a fashion to discourage exclusionary zoning. Communities
which exclude all but the rich or near rich will be placed at the
end of the line for grants.

   In short, we think that first priority for the disbursement of tax
dollars provided by the citizens of Pennsylvania should go to
those communities which are themselves open to all citizens.[14]

Secretary Wilcox also pointed out that his department was not
alone in administering its programs to increase housing opportunities. The
Pennsylvania Industrial Development Authority, which gives low-interest loans
to private industry, adopted a resolution on November 3, 1971:

   RESOLVED, that in considering future applications for loans this
   Authority should be mindful of the availability of moderate and
   low cost housing in the project area, and that criteria should be
   developed for future guidelines for the authority relating to the
   availability of such housing.[15]

Wilcox also sought support at the federal level. He requested that
federal agencies participate in a withholding of federal funds from exclusionary
communities in Pennsylvania.[16] No reply was forthcoming.

Refining the Carrot and Stick Strategy

   If a policy of conditioning grants on inclusionary policies was
applied strictly, it could bring all DCA programs to a screeching halt because
so many communities are exclusionary. Even though it is rational and consistent to apply the same standard to all applicants under all assistance programs,
it may not be politically feasible. Uniform application might stimulate a unified
opposition which could force the legislature to strip the department of the
authority to condition grants, or eliminate the carrots themselves, the grant
programs. The department must strike a delicate balance in the use of its
leverage.

   The Pennsylvania Department of Community Affairs position looks
toward this type of flexible approach. Although the attorney general's opinion
speaks in terms of eligibility and illegal expenditures of state funds, Wilcox
speaks in terms of priorities. In almost any grant program, the demand for
funds is greater than the supply. The funds then must be allocated, either on
a first-come first-served basis or on some kind of a priority system. If the
latter is used, as Wilcox suggests, the state does not need to define local communities as ineligible. The agency merely assigns a lower priority to communities which have no low- and moderate-income housing and no plans to provide
such housing. Communities which have low priority at the time of application

for funds, i.e., exclusionary communities, can increase their chances for funding by taking affirmative actions to increase housing opportunities for low- and moderate-income people. In this framework, the state is not imposing its will on local communities but making rational decisions about the expenditure of its limited resources. Communities can remain exclusionary and take their chances on securing some of the funds, or they can take steps in the housing area to move closer to the front of the line.

In addition to providing flexibility, a priority approach to the carrot and stick technique eliminates the need to demonstrate that a community is guilty of wrongdoing. Labeling a community as discriminatory not only generates political opposition but increases the likelihood of litigation. State funds may be tied up, and exclusionary practices will probably not be changed during this time-consuming process. The carrot and stick approach is an administrative strategy. If the state is forced to justify its action in court, much of the advantage of the strategy, and the lawsuit as well, may be lost.

In this regard, it often may be advantageous for a state agency to proceed without a specific opinion of an attorney general but to rely instead on its general administrative responsibility to establish criteria for the expenditure of state funds. Labeling the question as an administrative one rather than a legal one reduces the chances of the matter getting into court and also may limit the degree of intervention should the issue reach the judicial arena. Courts generally defer to administrative agencies when they are acting within delegated authority. A "clear abuse of discretion" is difficult to prove, and any community asserting that a state's denial of a grant constitutes such an abuse would have to bear a heavy burden of proof. Of course, the agency must be sure that its actions are within its general statutory mandates, so that it can defend its actions politically, as well as legally, if necessary.

In sum, the state agency must have flexibility in administering its programs to increase housing opportunities. Such flexibility is often furthered by using a priority system for approving grants and identifying the issue as an administrative rather than a legal one. This may eliminate the need for proving local wrongdoing and permit casting the issue in terms of affirmative action as a means of increasing the likelihood of securing a grant. If a community is told that it is eligible but its application has a low priority for limited funds, it is unlikely to get help from the courts to obtain the funds. A legal opinion making the community ineligible for a grant, however, may serve to precipitate lawsuits by communities which have been alleged to discriminate.

Maximizing the State's Leverage: Tactics

The use by a state of its financial leverage raises the question of the adequacy of the leverage. Is the carrot sufficiently enticing that the community will take steps it would otherwise not be willing to take in order to secure the program funds? This issue is particularly difficult in the area of suburban access, because many of the communities involved can afford to opt out of the program rather than meet the state's conditions.

The state can maximize its leverage through several tactics. First, it should notify an applicant at the earliest opportunity that there is an important housing issue which requires resolution before a grant can be approved. The state agency should be on record with the locality early, so that the locality cannot make legitimate claims of surprise.

Second, the state's position should be clear. If possible, the state should define the objective of providing a significant amount of low- and moderate-income housing in the community and leave the identification of the means of reaching that end to the locality. The state agency's posture should be positive toward resolving the issues, perhaps providing suggestions of specific steps which might be taken as well as inviting the community to propose other initiatives.

Third, the state should wait until as many local actions as possible have been accomplished before releasing the grant. For example, in Tredyffrin Township, the development of Chesterbrook was to be the sine qua non for the state recreation grant. Ideally, the grant would be released when the development was completed. As a practical matter, this was impossible. However, funds were released in this case before all necessary local approvals (e.g., building permit) were given. Although the rezoning had been granted, the development might still have been prevented through impediments established locally. Unless a continuing grantor-grantee relationship exists between the state and the specific locality, releasing the initial grant too early might mean that the housing is never actually developed in the community. In Tredyffrin, the state's leverage may have been dissipated when the recreation funds were released.

Limitations of the Carrot and Stick Strategy

There are important limitations on the carrot and stick in the suburban housing context. First, this approach is reactive. The state cannot take the initiative and identify exclusionary communities but must respond to requests for assistance from local communities. The opportunities to use leverage are random. The state cannot plan a comprehensive approach to a metropolitan area and implement it systematically through financial inducements, although it could establish conditions based on the local obligations established by a regional housing allocation plan. Second, affluent suburbs may opt out of the process rather than meet conditions unless the grants are large and for facilities fundamental to their development, such as schools, and water and sewer facilities. Finally, the political problems may be very serious in using park programs and the like to achieve seemingly unrelated social objectives.

The carrot and stick strategy depends on relative levels of resources between state and localities, and the extent of local opposition to low- and moderate-income housing, as well as the skill and flexibility with which this strategy is implemented by state officials. Pennsylvania's Department of Community Affairs has taken significant first steps in using state assistance programs to increase suburban housing opportunities. This approach should be transferable, in varying degrees, to other states. As the level and variety of state programs increases, opportunities expand for the states to use the distribution of these funds for inducing localities to eliminate exclusionary practices.

Chapter Nine

Allocation Planning at the State Level

States as well as the regional bodies can establish the planning framework for rational development of housing in metropolitan areas. A state planning agency or department of community affairs could pursue this policy administratively. Alternatively, the state could enact legislation providing for planning the distribution of housing among localities.

Massachusetts: The Administrative Approach

In Massachusetts, the Department of Community Affairs proposed a fair share formula for distributing low- and moderate-income housing among the cities and towns of the state.[1] Early in 1973, the department published a Regional Housing Planning Circular to provide guidance for regional planning agencies in setting housing production targets for localities.[2] The circular laid out a timetable for state, regional and local agencies to arrive at allocations of specific numbers of housing units by mid-1973. The circular also outlined suggested allocation criteria including availability of vacant or buildable land, proximity to jobs, and recent subsidized housing efforts. Finally, the circular discussed timing. Targets were to be set for each of five years, 1973 through 1977. Criteria for dividing a town's total allocation among the five years included general public facilities and services; fiscal and administrative capacity of the community; and lead time required to secure policy commitments in light of prior local attitudes towards subsidized housing. These factors would indicate whether reduced targets were necessary in the early years to permit a community to gear up.

The planning process was completed on schedule. By May 1973 the Department of Community Affairs produced a study providing for specific targets for the state's communities. The difficult job of implementation lay ahead.

131

New Jersey: Proposed Legislation

In New Jersey, legislation was developed which would involve the state in housing allocation planning. In 1972 Governor Cahill proposed the Balanced Housing Plan Act, which was to apply the fair share principle to the entire state. The governor began to lay the groundwork for this approach two years earlier. In a special message to the legislature in 1970 Governor Cahill analyzed the problem. After citing zoning abuses as a barrier to constructing low- and moderate-income housing and the increasing intervention of the courts in the exclusionary zoning area, Governor Cahill said:

> Whatever the reasons for the perversion of zoning and planning laws that exists today, I am convinced that we cannot afford the luxury of continuing the status quo in this area. My purpose today is not to condemn the "home rule" concept in relation to land use. My purpose is to warn you that the system is failing. It is failing because it is not meeting the needs of all our people. Its failure is demonstrated continually by the court deicisons which are becoming increasingly more aggressive and rapid in striking the abuses presently existing in zoning and planning fields.
>
> . . . These decisions and others presently pending in the courts of this State and Nation have led knowledgeable attorneys to freely predict that large acreage and large square foot requirements, along with absolute prohibition against apartment construction, will soon be held to be violative of the Constitution and outside the scope of planning and zoning officials. It seems to me, therefore, that the message should be loud and clear! We must undertake corrective measures now if we are to insure the maintenance of controls in the hands of local officials . . . some way must be found . . . to overcome abusive application of local zoning laws.[3]

The governor proposed that the primary power to zone and plan remain at the local level. He also urged providing housing opportunities for all of the state's people by insuring that municipalities "strike a more realistic balance in distributing available land and in assigning the restrictions that will govern it . . . it is clear that today with 82 percent of the remaining developable land in the eight counties studied [in northern New Jersey] having minimum lot sizes ranging from a half-acre on up, we do not have anything that resembles a reasonable balance."[4] Although Governor Cahill did not propose specific legislation in 1970 to achieve this balance, he discussed alternative approaches for the legislature's consideration. He included as possible models for action the Massachusetts Zoning Law and the New York Urban Development Corporation Act.

In March 1972 Governor Cahill delivered a second special message on housing to the legislature. He again raised the spectre of the judiciary taking control of local land use decisions and cited several cases moving in this direction which had been decided since his previous message. He presented to the legislature proposals "designed to relieve the housing crisis, guide the municipalities in the elimination of abuses in the zoning and planning areas, and insure the continuation of control in the hands of our local officials."[5] The major proposal in this package was the Balanced Housing Plan Act. This bill was designed to encourage expansion of the supply of low- and moderate-income housing, distributed fairly throughout the state:

> In essence, what we must achieve is a balance in housing; low, moderate and expensive, single and multi-family. I am not suggesting that the balance should be equal or that every community should be the same. . . . What I am suggesting is that a mixture of housing opportunities must be afforded to our citizens. It should be emphasized that this is a purely voluntary plan; no municipality is mandated or forced to comply. It is, however, an orderly approach and a reasonable alternative to probable judicial action that may well require construction in areas not especially suited under county and municipal planning for this kind of development.[6]

The Balanced Housing Plan Act contemplates a determination by the state every two years of the additional need for low- and moderate-income housing. This analysis would take into account the existence of housing for low- and moderate-income families, the availability and location of low- and moderate-income jobs, population and employment projections, the existence of substandard housing and projected substandard housing, housing vacancy rates, present and projected financing available for housing for low- and moderate-income families, and such other factors as the Commissioner shall determine to be relevant.[7]

After this state housing goal was calculated, the state would allocate these units among the counties. It would consider the above factors, as well as the state development plan, available land, and the impact on public services. The allocation would be made "to the maximum extent possible in conformance with existing zoning."[8] The bill requires intergovernmental consultation and public hearings throughout the state before designation of the state goal and the county allocations.

The county planning boards would then have six months within which to allocate their units among the municipalities, based on availability of sites, access to jobs, tax base, number of low- and moderate-income households, substandard housing, county and state plans and federal policies. Again, this determination would be made after a public hearing. If counties did not do the necessary planning, the state would step in and calculate municipal allocations. Communities could, on a voluntary basis, either designate areas where low- and moderate-income housing could be constructed or develop policies that would assure that suitable land would be made available. Municipalities would not be required to comply with the plan or to participate in any way.

Municipalities could also request that the county board certify their plans as being in accordance with municipal housing goals. Certification would mean that sufficient sites had been made available to accommodate the locality's allocation. Once a municipality is certified, the state's attorney general is authorized to intervene in cases where that locality's zoning practices are at issue and defend the integrity of the state housing goal and the county and municipal allocations.

The Balanced Housing Plan bill was introduced in the legislature in November 1972. The state's Community Affairs Department retained a consulting firm to investigate questions which were likely to be raised in discussions concerning this measure. Potential inquiries involved methods of calculating goals.

Although New Jersey legislative leaders indicated that it was unlikely that the bill would pass, similar bills could receive serious consideration in the future if the New Jersey or other state courts place severe limits on local exclusionary practices. The incentive for localities to support this bill is that they would participate in defining their responsibilities, rather than facing the possibility that a state judge would perform this task and pre-empt the local decision-making process. Local participation might prevent the lawsuits, or at least limit the relief ordered by the courts.

Chapter Ten

The State as Plaintiff

If the politics permit it, states can confront their exclusionary "creatures" directly. They can take suburban communities to court to vindicate the constitution and the zoning enabling act. To date, one state has moved on this front. The Commonwealth of Pennsylvania sued a number of suburbs after concluding that the land use practices of these communities were in violation of the state's zoning enabling act and otherwise illegal. In 1971 the state and a number of private parties filed suit in state court against Bucks County and all of its constituent municipalities.[1] The plaintiffs sought to eliminate exclusionary zoning and open up these Philadelphia suburbs to low- and moderate-income housing.

In addition to serving as a plaintiff in the case, the state, through the Welfare Department, had previously provided a $50,000 grant to the Bucks County Legal Aid Society to work on housing matters involving low-income persons. The Legal Aid Society was an important participant in the case, representing the class of low-income plaintiffs.

The complaint in *Commonwealth of Pennsylvania* v. *County of Bucks* alleged that the county and the individual municipalities had used their zoning powers to keep out low- and moderate-income housing. The plaintiffs asserted that this violated the 14th Amendment of the United States Constitution, the Pennsylvania Constitution and federal and state statutes. The complaint alleged that these municipalities zoned areas for moderate and higher densities only when a developer requested a rezoning for luxury housing.

Pennsylvania argued that it is entitled to make use of the judicial process to challenge exclusionary practices, that it has "standing" to sue on two grounds: (1) the general powers inherent in the concept of sovereignty and (2) statutory and procedural authority.[2] First, states have a general right to file suit, independent of any statutory provision. Because of its status as a sovereign entity and its corporate rights, a state can sue to protect its financial interests or promote the general welfare.

135

Beyond the inherent capacity of a state to sue, Pennsylvania law confers a specific authority in the state in this regard. The Pennsylvania Administrative Code and the Rules of Civil Procedure specifically provide that the state's Justice Department and the attorney general have the power to sue. With the approval of the governor, they may file suit in the name of the Commonwealth to enforce the state law. The state argued that it had a responsibility, under U.S. Supreme Court decisions, to insure that functions which it delegates to others are not carried out in a discriminatory manner.

The trial court dismissed the complaint, without a trial on the merits of the case. The state and the other plaintiffs appealed.

The Potential of Litigation by States

It is unlikely that many states will volunteer to face the political heat of suing their constituent communities, particularly on such a sensitive issue as lower-income housing. The Pennsylvania Attorney General's office has a community advocate unit which has gone out on a number of limbs.

If states can be convinced to take initiatives in litigation, there are many strategies and remedies available (see Chapter 17 for a discussion of the approaches being used by private litigants). In addition, the states have great resources, in staff and money, to bring to bear in these cases, as well as significant leverage in negotiating settlements with local communities.

There are perhaps three routes towards state initiative in suburban housing litigation. First, an aggressive, concerned state executive branch may be willing to face the political problems involved. This seems to be the case in Pennsylvania. Second, private litigants may give the state a choice of joining the suit as a plaintiff or being joined as a defendant. The state may decide in some cases that being sued is more costly politically than suing. Third, business interests, labor unions and other powerful interest groups who are harmed by exclusionary practices may bring pressure to bear on the state to open its suburbs.

Chapter Eleven

Administration of Federal Housing Programs

To increase suburban housing opportunities states can regulate land use, finance and develop housing, use the leverage of grant programs, develop plans for allocating housing, and even sue their suburbs. The federal government can do all this, and more, if it chooses to. Perhaps the most important additional tool the federal government has had is the subsidized housing programs themselves. Through these programs, the federal government has had its most direct role in determining the location of low- and moderate-income housing. Couple these programs with the government's array of laws, executive orders, grant programs, resources, regulations and administrative discretion, and the federal government comes out with an even greater potential than the state governments for opening the suburbs. This potential remains largely untapped. In terms of increasing suburban access, federal policy has been bad. Federal practice has been even worse.

The Stated Federal Policy

On June 11, 1971 the White House issued a statement by the president on "Federal Policies Relative to Equal Housing Opportunity." This statement represented the resolution of internal differences within the administration which had begun to surface in 1970. The disagreement was between HUD and the Justice Department over the role the federal government should play in increasing housing opportunities for the poor and the black, particularly in the suburbs. HUD was advocating a somewhat more aggressive stance than the Justice Department and the White House. Discussions touched on a number of issues, including HUD's efforts to increase housing opportunities in suburban Warren, Michigan; HUD's proposed project selection criteria for subsidized housing programs; and a possible Justice Department discrimination lawsuit in Black Jack, Missouri. Policy development, or clarification, required many months.

Finally, in mid-1971, the federal policy was articulated. The statement purported to make no new policy, but rather to "define and explain" the existing policy as codified in various laws, executive orders and other administrative pronouncements. The statement indicated the nature and scope of future federal actions, as well as areas of inaction. In general terms, the statement asserted that the federal government had a mandate to prevent racial discrimination in housing, but did not have any responsibility to promote increased housing opportunity for lower-income people.

One of the most significant directions pointed to in the president's statement involved the administration of federal housing programs. (Other aspects of the statement will be discussed in Chapters 12–15.) According to the president, the law required that these programs be administered to further racially equal housing opportunity on a metropolitan basis. Several months later, HUD followed the president's lead and issued project selection criteria for subsidized housing programs. These criteria enabled HUD to select subsidized projects for funding from the large number of applications submitted to the agency. The criteria reflected a number of federal objectives, particularly increasing locational opportunities for racial minorities. In addition, HUD established "affirmative marketing" regulations which applied to unsubsidized as well as subsidized programs. Housing sponsors were required to plan and carry out a marketing program to attract minorities to their developments.

At the same time, HUD initiated a housing allowance experiment. Selected families in a few cities who could not afford decent housing received cash subsidies which enabled them to secure standard housing of their own choice in the private market. The difference between the market cost of the housing and the amount the family could afford to pay was subsidized by HUD. An expanded housing allowance, under the name direct cash assistance program, was the central feature of the president's 1973 housing message. At the beginning of 1973, the administration became so disenchanted with the federal programs that it announced an indefinite moratorium on funding new developments. During the moratorium, HUD reviewed the programs and proposed alternatives which were incorporated into the president's housing message. The result of the HUD evaluation was a proposal for phasing in a vastly expanded direct cash assistance program, retaining the leased public housing program and phasing out the other construction subsidy programs. The administration proposals faced a long, uphill struggle in Congress. Meanwhile, the prior programs, described in Chapter 2, proceeded at a reduced rate.

Whatever programs are developed for assisting lower-income families to secure decent housing, locational choice will remain a central question. Whatever their form, subsidies are critical to increasing suburban access, because lower economic groups cannot afford new housing built solely by the private market. Opening the door to suburbia for the poor and minorities is a fundamental federal responsibility. Achieving this goal obviously requires assistance from many quarters, but the federal government cannot delegate away this responsibility.

Project Selection Criteria

At the time of the president's 1971 statement, HUD had had drafts of project selection criteria ready for months. After the statement, approval finally came from the White House to make these proposed regulations public. Until that point, HUD abided by the locational decisions of housing sponsors. Subsidized housing programs were administered essentially on a first-come first-served basis. Applications for subsidy funds far exceeded congressional appropriations. There was almost always a waiting list for funds, or a "pipeline." Of the proposed projects which met basic eligibility requirements, those which were received first were funded first. Projects were not evaluated or compared in terms of their ability to further national objectives.

The project selection criteria were developed to enable HUD to select from among eligible applications those which would go the farthest towards meeting equal opportunity and other national goals. These criteria were to be applied to all subsidized housing programs.

Impetus for Developing Selection Criteria. The project selection criteria were developed in part as a response to the tremendous increase in federally subsidized housing by 1971.

> In 1969 only 12% of all new construction was federally assisted. By 1970 that percentage had more than doubled to 25% where it has remained ever since. Moreover, the substantial gain in the number of federally assisted housing starts was accompanied by a considerably larger backlog of project applications. First-come, first-served may have been a satisfactory method of deciding which projects to fund in 1969, but when HUD offices became deluged with applications, it appeared clearly irrational.[1]

Impetus for the project selection criteria also came from federal court decisions. Several cases required HUD to examine the socio-economic impact of housing projects before approving them for funding. In *Shannon* v. *United States Department of Housing and Urban Development*, black plaintiffs in a black neighborhood of Philadelphia sued to enjoin HUD from subsidizing a low-income housing development in their area.[2] They claimed that building the project on the proposed site would increase the already high concentration of low-income black residents in that neighborhood. The plaintiffs also argued that HUD had no procedures for considering (and did not in fact consider) the effect of this project on racial concentration in that neighborhood or in the city as a whole. The contested development was a rent supplement project, built for low-income tenants. The court concluded that the development was the "functional equivalent" of public housing projects nearby, thereby adding to racial concentration represented by earlier public housing projects in the area. The court decided that:

> ... the Agency must utilize some institutionalized method whereby, in considering site selection or type selection, it has before it the relevant racial and socio-economic information necessary for compliance with its duties under the 1964 and 1968 Civil Rights Acts.[3]

The opinion left room for HUD to approve proposed projects which would add to racial concentration in "instances where a pressing case may be made for rebuilding of a racial ghetto." But HUD may not do so without weighing the socio-economic implications:

> We hold only that the agency's judgment must be an informed one; óne which weighs the alternatives and finds that the need for physical rehabilitation or additional minority housing at the site in question clearly outweighs the disadvantage of increasing or perpetuating racial concentration.[4]

The president's statement of June 11, 1971 reflected the principle articulated in the *Shannon* case with regard to approval of sites for federally subsidized housing:

> Based on careful review of the legislative history of the 1964 and 1968 Civil Rights Acts, and also of the program context within which the law has developed, I interpret the "affirmative action" mandate of the 1968 act to mean that the administrator of a housing program should include, among the various criteria by which applications for assistance are judged, the extent to which a proposed project, or the overall development plan of which it is a part, will in fact open up new, nonsegregated housing opportunities that will contribute to decreasing the effects of past housing discrimination. This does not mean that no federally assisted low- and moderate-income housing may be built within areas of minority concentration. It does not mean that housing officials in Federal agencies should dictate local land use policies. It does mean that in choosing among the various applications for Federal aid, consideration should be given to their impact on patterns of racial concentration.
> In furtherance of this policy, not only the Department of Housing and Urban Development but also the other departments and agencies administering housing programs—the Veterans Administration, the Farmers Home Administration and the Department of Defense—will administer their programs in a way which will advance

equal housing opportunity for people of all income levels on a metropolitan areawide basis.[5]

Three days after the president's statement, HUD published proposed project selection criteria. While HUD was still accepting comments from the public on this draft, a second federal court decision was rendered against the department. The U.S. Court of Appeals for the Seventh Circuit held, in *Gautreaux* v. *Romney*, that HUD had violated the Constitution and the 1964 Civil Rights Act by funding the discriminatory public housing program in the City of Chicago.[6] The specific provisions violated were the due process clause of the Fifth Amendment and section 601 of the 1964 Civil Rights Act, barring discrimination in the administration of federal programs. The court acknowledged that HUD had urged the Chicago Housing Authority (CHA) to locate public housing in white areas of the city. However, the court decided that neither these efforts nor the recognized need for housing in the city justified HUD's continued funding of a segregated housing system.

From *Shannon*, *Gautreaux*, and the presidential policy statement, HUD distilled several principles governing its site approval decisions:

1. HUD must have an institutionalized method to weigh socio-economic factors in considering housing proposals.
2. HUD should include, among the various criteria by which applications for housing assistance are judged, the extent to which a proposed project, or the overall development plan of which it is a part, will in fact open up new, nonsegregated housing opportunities that will contribute to decreasing the effects of past housing discrimination. This means that HUD should consider the impact of proposals on patterns of racial concentration.
3. Involuntary racial concentration leads to urban blight; it is therefore contrary to national housing policy for HUD to reinforce racial concentration in making its housing site decisions.
4. HUD may approve housing proposals in areas of racial concentration when its informed judgment is that the need for physical rehabilitation or additional minority housing at the site in question clearly outweighs the disadvantage of increasing or perpetuating racial concentration.
5. HUD may not knowingly acquiesce in a racially discriminatory housing program or proposal.
6. Community opposition to sites outside areas of minority concentration does not justify HUD's funding of a racially discriminatory housing program or proposal.[7]

HUD then attempted to incorporate these principles into criteria for evaluating and funding housing proposals. In January 1972 HUD formally published these regulations. They became effective the following month. The criteria place great weight on the location of the proposed project, but also consider other factors in selecting applications for assistance. Of the eight criteria, three relate directly to increasing locational choice, although none refer specifically to the suburbs:

1. Criterion No. 2, Minority Housing Opportunities. The stated objectives here are: "to provide minority families with opportunities for housing in a wide range of locations" and "to open up nonsegregated housing opportunities that will contribute to decreasing the effects of past housing discrimination."

2. Criterion No. 3, Improved Location for Low[er] Income Families. Objectives include: "to avoid concentrating subsidized housing in any one section of a metropolitan area or town" and "to locate subsidized housing in areas reasonably accessible to job opportunities."

3. Criterion No. 4, Relationship to Orderly Growth and Development. Objectives include: "to develop housing consistent with officially approved state or multijurisdictional plans" and "to encourage formulation of areawide plans which include a housing element relative to needs and goals for low- and moderate-income housing as well as balanced production throughout a metropolitan area." This criterion envisions the implementation of regional or metropolitan allocation plans to encourage housing choice, as well as the use of the criterion itself as an inducement to develop allocation plans. [8]

Other selection criteria include the need for low-income housing in the area, environmental factors, ability of the sponsor to complete the project, potential to provide job and business opportunities for minorities, and provision for sound management (for multifamily projects). Applications are rated under each of the criteria as superior, adequate or poor. A poor rating on any criterion disqualifies the project for funding. Proposals are then ranked according to the number of superior and adequate ratings they receive and priority for funding given to the projects with the highest ratings.

The thrust of the criteria is towards development of subsidized housing in white areas of the cities and the suburbs. The criteria do not deal directly with local exclusionary practices or the local approval requirements and cost ceilings built into the federal programs. They do not insure that the housing will be built in places which have previously rejected it. However, the criteria may induce developers to build in the suburbs, by giving them a preference for the limited subsidy funds if they can obtain the necessary approvals.

The selection criteria are subject to widely varying interpretations by the several dozen HUD area and insuring offices which administer them. The criteria were designed to be general and flexible, but the cost of pursuing that course may be that all of the projects in some metropolitan areas will be in black areas of the central city while in other metropolitan areas all projects will be in suburbs and none in the black community. The criteria are general enough for

most sites to be either approved or disapproved. With general criteria and no
overall plan or direction (projects are evaluated on a case by case basis, generally), the outcome is unpredictable. Because of these ambiguities and the fear
that no subsidy funds would be available for the inner city, black organizations
raised a storm of protest.

To respond to this concern and to provide a balanced approach to
project selection, one HUD area office (Chicago) administratively adopted a
matching system. For each project approved in a predominantly minority
area, the office approves a similar project located in a predominantly nonminority area (less than 30 percent minority). The type of project and the number of units are matched as closely as possible. For example, two projects in a
suburb have been matched with a similar but larger project in the inner city.
Therefore, even if a project receives a poor rating under criterion 2 (minority
housing opportunities), the rating may be upgraded to adequate if there is a
project in a nonminority area to match it with.

Over a year after the project selection criteria took effect, HUD had
not made public systematic nationwide data on their locational impact. As of this
writing it is impossible to determine whether the adoption of the project selection criteria has changed the locational patterns of subsidized housing.

Affirmative Marketing Requirements

To complement the project selection criteria, HUD adopted affirmative fair housing marketing regulations. These requirements apply to both
unsubsidized and subsidized housing assisted by FHA. Local housing authorities, the sponsors of low-rent public housing, are subject to separate requirements
on tenant assignment. In explaining these requirements to the Congress, George
Romney, former HUD secretary, said in 1972:

> We have developed in tandem with the Project Selection Criteria,
> new Affirmative Marketing Regulations which will require, effective
> February 25, that users of our housing programs take affirmative
> steps to make minority citizens aware of the availability of that
> housing. To the extent the criteria operate to open up new housing
> opportunities for minorities, we believe it is self-evident that affir-
> mative steps should be taken to make the intended beneficiaries
> aware of these opportunities:
> (a) Carry out an affirmative program to attract buyers or tenants
>   of all minority and majority groups to the housing for initial
>   sale or rental. An affirmative marketing program shall be in
>   effect for each multifamily project throughout the life of the
>   mortgage. Such a program shall typically involve publicizing
>   to minority persons the availability of housing opportunities
>   through the type of media customarily utilized by the appli-
>   cant, including minority publications or other minority outlets

which are available in the housing market area. All advertising shall include either the Department-approved Equal
Housing Opportunity logo or slogan or statement and all advertising depicting persons shall depict persons of majority and
minority groups.

(b)   Maintain a nondiscriminatory hiring policy in recruiting from
both minority and majority groups for staff engaged in the
sale or rental of properties.

(c)   Instruct all employees and agents in writing and orally in the
policy of nondiscrimination and fair housing.

(d)   Specifically solicit eligible buyers or tenants reported to the
applicant by the Area or Insuring Office.

(e)   Prominently display in all offices in which sale or rental activity pertaining to the project or subdivision takes place the
Department-approved Fair Housing Poster and include in any
printed material used in connection with sales or rentals, the
Department-approved Equal Housing Opportunity logo or
slogan or statement.

(f)   Post in a conspicuous position on all FHA project sites a sign
displaying prominently either the Department-approved Equal
Housing Opportunity logo or slogan or statement.[9]

Applicant housing sponsors must submit an affirmative fair housing
marketing plan for approval by HUD. The plan describes how the sponsor
intends to attract minority (as well as majority) buyers or tenants to the housing
for initial sale or rental. Affirmative fair housing marketing plan forms request
that the applicant include information concerning the direction of marketing
activity, the marketing program, staffing, solicitation of those referred by HUD,
and other efforts planned as part of the outreach program. These forms are
submitted and reviewed before the initial approval of a project, i.e., issuance of a
feasibility letter. If the form is not approved, it is sent back to the sponsor along
with a letter stating why his plan was not approved. The plan must be improved
and resubmitted before approval can be issued. The project is not approved unless
the plan is resubmitted with acceptable modifications. If the affirmative marketing requirements were followed to the letter, it is likely that few plans would
be approved. Information provided by the sponsor is often general. It may contain little more than the names of area newspapers, with no indication of the
content, frequency, size or timing of the advertising. HUD's instructions require
this kind of detailed description of the marketing program.

In spite of the low quality of the affirmative marketing plans, HUD
generally approves them. When HUD approves a plan, it sends a letter to the
sponsor notifying him that his affirmative marketing plan has been approved and
requesting that he forward to HUD copies of advertisements, other promotional
material, and correspondence with community groups, as well as the monthly

sale or rental reports. HUD keeps a folder on each project that has been approved. Copies of materials and reports from the sponsor are supposed to be included in the folders. For example, monthly sale or rental reports include information on applications for the month and cumulative total sales, and also a breakdown by racial/ethnic group. These reports also include a percentage breakdown of minority groups for the estimated number of visitors. Each of the project folders is supposed to be reviewed monthly by HUD to see if requirements are being complied with. However, it appears that these reviews are rarely made. In fact, many of the folders have not been looked at since they were put into the files. Generally, plans are reviewed only when an applicant submits a plan for another project, or when there are many complaints of discrimination. Moreover, review at the project site is a rare event.

HUD's regulations contemplated that the agency would establish sanctions for housing sponsors who do not comply with the requirements:

> Applicants failing to comply with the requirements of this subpart will make themselves liable to sanctions authorized by regulations, rules or policies, governing the program pursuant to which the application was made, including but not limited to denial of further participation in departmental programs and referral to the Department of Justice for suit by the United States for injunctive or other appropriate relief.[10]

HUD has not developed rules and regulations providing for sanctions. Sanctions which could be applied by HUD in cases of noncompliance include: (1) suspension or termination of HUD assistance to the development, whether it be insurance, direct subsidy or both; (2) declaring that the sponsor would be ineligible for future participation in HUD programs; or (3) determination, perhaps through negotiations with the sponsor, of a specific number of units to be reserved as a minimum for minority occupancy. The last approach would be analogous to the "Philadelphia Plan" used in the employment field by the Labor Department to increase opportunities for minorities on federally contracted construction jobs. This approach may be most promising because it focuses on the effect of the marketing efforts rather than the process. If compliance is based only on the sponsor having carried out certain actions, all-white suburban projects may be the result of the project selection criteria and the affirmative marketing requirements, operating together. A sponsor who has met the minimum requirements might not be penalized for such a result. In fact, he may receive funding for additional projects with segregated occupancy.

The Future of Federal Housing Programs

Further complicating the question of the ability of federal programs to assist in opening the suburbs is the uncertainty of future federal involvement in housing. The administration abruptly suspended all of the subsidy programs at the beginning of 1973. The stated grounds for impoundment of these congressionally-appropriated funds were waste and fraud in the building and lending industry, which received the bulk of the subsidies. In fact, some of the subsidy programs had not experienced widespread abuses. In addition, much of the corruption had taken place in inner-city mortgage insurance programs. These latter programs remained in force when the subsidized programs were suspended.

In short, by putting a hold on all the subsidized programs while some were providing much needed decent housing for low- and moderate-income people, the administration threw out the baby with the bathwater. At the same time, keeping all the insurance programs in effect, in spite of major problems in some of these programs, indicates that there were probably political purposes involved in the selective shutdown. First, the subsidy programs showed up on the federal budget; insurance programs did not. Second, subsidized programs involved the government very directly in the construction of new housing. This housing had to be built somewhere. As civil rights groups pressed for suburban development, the federal government was faced with legal pressures to finance suburban housing. This thrust aroused opposition among the administration's suburban constituents. The easy way out was to stop the programs. The courts cannot force the federal government to provide subsidies for suburban development if there are no construction subsidy programs.

Whatever the administration's motives in suspending the subsidy programs, HUD used the ensuing period to review the programs and develop alternatives. (Meanwhile, housing groups filed suit in opposition to the impoundment. The federal district court concluded that the administration did not have the authority to refuse to spend these appropriated funds, but the moratorium continued as the case became mired in the appeal process.) The product of the nine months of study was a set of housing policy recommendations from the White House. The proposal focused on direct cash assistance as the most promising approach to helping low-income families. According to the administration, this approach would maximize freedom of choice. However, in the tight housing market that characterizes many metropolitan areas, the supply of decent housing is limited. Recipients of direct cash assistance would have little choice if there is not enough decent housing to go around. In addition, the amount of subsidy per family would probably not be sufficient to enable lower-income families to move to newer suburban areas. These cost factors plus racial discrimination would probably result in many direct cash assistance recipients paying more money for the same quality housing they were already living in. Where there is too little decent housing and a dual housing market (one for whites, one for blacks), direct cash assistance may translate into inflated rents rather than better housing. The apparent failure of HUD's affirmative marketing requirements is one indication that the dual housing market continues to exist and that a direct cash program would bring great inflationary pressures and limited expansion of locational choice.

The administration's proposals paid passing recognition to the need for continuing subsidies of some housing units. The message recommended additional approval of 200,000 subsidized units, of which 150,000 would be new construction. This is a drop in the bucket compared to the 10 year goal of six million low- and moderate-income units adopted in the 1968 housing act. In short, the administration beat a hasty retreat. It proposed one half of a sound program. The direct cash assistance concept is useful, in combination with construction subsidies, to expand the supply and a range of efforts to open the suburbs. The administration backed off from subsidies needed to increase the supply of housing and showed little inclination to make aggressive use of the other tools available for opening the suburbs.

Chapter Twelve

Federal Carrot and Stick: HUD

In addition to its housing programs for low- and moderate-income people, HUD administers a number of other housing and categorical assistance programs. The distribution of these grants, guarantees and loans gives HUD opportunities for increasing the access of lower-income people to suburbia. When suburban communities seek assistance for community development activities, HUD can impose conditions relating to housing opportunities. HUD has not used this carrot and stick technique systematically. Most of the efforts in this area predated the president's 1971 statement which rejected any federal role in promoting economic integration. HUD's attempts to use the leverage of its funds to increase suburban housing opportunities usually involved either the water and sewer or the open space program. These programs are especially attractive to developing suburban communities.

In one case which received nationwide attention—Warren, Michigan—HUD used the Workable Program and the urban renewal program as carrots to secure equal housing opportunity. Although the exclusion in Warren was predominantly racial rather than economic, this experience illustrates the use of federal resources as leverage to increase suburban housing opportunities.

Workable Program

To be eligible for urban renewal and related grants, a community must have a Workable Program for Community Improvement approved by HUD. The president's statement on equal housing opportunity described the effect of this requirement of a two year action plan to deal with blight and other development problems:

> Where the "workable program" requirement—imposed on local communities by the Housing Act of 1949, as amended in 1954, in connection with urban renewal and related programs—is a condition

of eligibility, HUD may not make a grant in the absence of a HUD-certified workable program for community improvement. The program must make reasonable provision for low- and moderate-income housing, which must of course be available on a nondiscriminatory basis.[1]

Urban renewal and the related programs for which the Workable Program is a prerequisite to funding have been used primarily by central cities and small towns. Relatively few suburbs have reached the condition of deterioration necessary for participation in the urban renewal program. Even fewer have been willing to admit this state of affairs.

Warren, Michigan represents a dramatic exception to this general pattern. Early in 1969 this virtually all-white Detroit suburb became the first city in Michigan to qualify for assistance under the federal Neighborhood Development Program (NDP). The Neighborhood Development Program was a streamlined form of urban renewal, designed to make the redevelopment process more efficient. The older portions of Warren, adjacent to Detroit, consisted of modest houses, many of which were in need of rehabilitation. Studies had indicated that some 1,300 houses on Warren's older south side were in need of rehabilitation or clearance for new land usage. NDP appeared to be an appropriate vehicle to accomplish this task.

As a prerequisite to obtaining the NDP grant, Warren needed HUD's approval of the city's Workable Program. HUD expressed concern that equal opportunity in housing did not receive adequate attention in the Workable Program submission. Of 180,000 people in Warren, there were approximately 130 blacks, or .07 percent of the population. In contrast, blacks constituted about one-third of the population in neighboring Detroit. This disparity could not be explained to any large extent by economic factors. Warren's median family income was approximately $11,000. The need for an equal opportunity program was apparent. After receiving verbal assurances that the city would develop and implement such a program, HUD approved the Workable Program and NDP applications. The city received approximately $2 million in HUD assistance for the first year of its NDP. It did not develop an equal housing program.

When it came time to renew the NDP grant for the second year, the city's Workable Program had expired. Again, an approved Workable Program was needed before the NDP could be funded. HUD requested that the city develop a specific plan in writing to assure the availability of housing, particularly for low- and moderate-income families, on a desegregated basis. Although HUD insisted that Warren develop its own program, it provided the city with a list of actions in this area for its consideration. Some of these actions related to developing low- and moderate-income housing:

The City Council could proceed with the proposed 100 units of multifamily housing, for low- and moderate-income families in Area

3 of the NDP, which were cancelled in September, 1969.

A local housing authority could be established to seek assistance from HUD in providing for low-rent housing units.[2]

Many of the suggestions related to increasing access of blacks to the existing housing stock in Warren: passage of a fair housing ordinance and enforcement machinery; a study of minority workers' attitudes towards the community; and a public education campaign on open occupancy.

Warren's program evolved after several months of negotiations between HUD and city officials. It did not include immediate actions to develop low- and moderate-income housing. Instead, the city planned to focus on open occupancy by passing a fair housing ordinance and establishing an enforcement agency. While the details of Warren's program were being worked out, a major snag developed. On July 21, 1970 a Detroit newspaper announced that the "federal government intends to use its vast power to force integration of America's white suburbs—and it is using the Detroit suburbs as a key starting point."[3] Three successive front page stories announced that HUD had selected Warren as a "target" for its efforts to "force integration" in the suburbs. The articles quoted extensively from a HUD staff memorandum which proposed a "strategy for administering HUD programs to increase suburban minority housing opportunities."

Warren officials reacted to the furor created by these stories by threatening to drop the NDP and the equal housing program. Because of assurances by HUD that it did not have a policy of forced racial integration, the city council approved the NDP plan. It appeared that the issue was finally resolved. All that remained was for Warren to sign the HUD contract and name members to the fair housing board. However, continuation of the urban renewal program was placed on the ballot, through voter initiative, for a November 1970 referendum. The community voted decisively (57–43 percent) to terminate the program, which represented a potential $10 million in federal funds over the next several years. After the federal program was rejected, the referendum was challenged in court as being racially motivated. At the end of 1973, this case was still pending.

The referendum marked the end of any federally-induced efforts to increase housing opportunities in Warren, Michigan. The carrot of $2 million per year for several years was not sufficiently enticing to bring about a modest fair housing program. Several smaller suburbs in the Detroit area were not as recalcitrant as Warren. The redevelopment efforts involved a larger proportion of their community. Thus, there was widespread local support for taking steps necessary to secure federal funds. Officials in these communities had observed events in Warren very closely and wished to avoid similar confrontations. They developed housing plans which HUD found acceptable. Generally, their plans also related to fair housing efforts rather than development of low-and moderate-income housing. They included only limited first steps similar to those discussed in Warren.

Water and Sewer Grants

In addition to the Workable Program and urban renewal programs, HUD has used other community development programs to encourage the development of low- and moderate-income housing. For example, under the water and sewer program HUD awards grants to finance community water and sewer facilities.[4] The maximum grant in most cases is 50 percent of the land and construction costs. HUD has informed some applicants for water and sewer grants that in order to move their application high enough up the priority list to be funded, the community could develop a low- and moderate-income housing plan.

In one case, HUD refused to approve an application from Baltimore County, Maryland for $1.7 million in water and sewer and open space grants. HUD indicated that it would not fund these projects until the county submitted an adequate plan for housing for lower-income people. The county's first housing plan was found by HUD to be unacceptable.[5]

In another instance, the Cleveland suburb of Westlake applied for a $1,500,000 grant for a sanitary sewer system. The project was the second phase of a $30,000,000 proposed system. Because of limitations on the community's bonding power, Westlake had to seek outside assistance for the balance of the system. Although the project was technically eligible under the law and regulations, it did not score high under the rating system HUD used to allocate the program's limited funds among eligible applicants. Westlake lost points because the service area of the sewer system was predominantly white middle- and upper-income, and there was apparent financial feasibility without federal assistance.

Instead of rejecting the city's application, HUD informed Westlake that it could raise its priority and improve its chances for funding by undertaking significant low- and moderate-income housing development and assuring equal housing opportunities for minorities. HUD made suggestions for local actions, including: (1) entering into a cooperation agreement with the Cuyuhoga Metropolitan Housing Authority for the purpose of developing low rent public housing in Westlake; (2) contacting the FHA insuring office in Cleveland to: (a) determine requirements for FHA subsidized housing, (b) seek the names of developers involved in development of 235 and 236 housing, and (c) determine the steps necessary for the city to take to develop the housing; (3) remove legal impediments to developing low- and moderate-income housing.

More than three-fourths of all land available in Westlake was zoned for single family construction, with a minimum lot size of 15,000 square feet and a minimum floor space of 1500 square feet. This zoning made it economically infeasible to develop low- and moderate-income single family housing in

Westlake. Only about seven percent of the available land in the city was zoned for multifamily use, at densities which precluded development of subsidized housing.

Although the community expressed a willingness to permit development of one moderate-income housing development, it never actually made the necessary changes. A formal application for section 236 assistance was never submitted. In addition, the city took no steps to provide the approvals necessary for the development of low-income housing. It did not execute a cooperation agreement with the metropolitan housing authority nor did it entertain the resolution necessary for the rent supplement program. As a result, HUD did not approve the water and sewer application.

Open Space Grants

Open space grants assist communities with maintenance of open space.[6] The grants cover 50 percent of the cost of acquiring the land as well as specified development expenses. In response to an application for funds under the open space program from Kettering, Ohio, HUD indicated that:

> In carrying out HUD's responsibility to insure greater housing opportunities, we give priority to communities applying for Open Space and other financial assistance which undertake significant efforts to further the national policy of increasing the supply of low- and moderate-income housing. . . . HUD receives eligible requests for many more open space projects than HUD's appropriations will permit to be funded. Thus, priorities must be set according to the type of project for which assistance is requested, and to the financial, physical and social characteristics of the project and the project area.[7]

HUD then stated that Kettering could increase its priority for funding by developing a housing program for low- and moderate-income people. HUD suggested that the city consider proposing a low- and moderate-income development plan and timetable, among other actions. In response, Kettering strengthened its fair housing ordinance and accepted a moderate-income housing development for the elderly. HUD approved the open space application.

In this case, the major leverage was not the grant itself because the amount of money at stake was small and the community was sufficiently affluent to buy the land itself. Instead, it was public pressure that caused Kettering to act. The community did not want to be viewed as racist or exclusionary. Given this leverage, HUD should not have settled for a local commitment to build elderly housing. This development would not provide increased housing opportunities for lower-income Dayton area families.

Housing for the Elderly

Many suburbs are anxious to secure subsidized housing projects for the elderly under public housing or other programs. This permits long-time residents and parents of current residents to live in the community during retirement, when their reduced income would otherwise require that they move to a lower-cost area. Middle- and upper-middle income suburbs usually apply for elderly housing without any thought of providing housing for families in the same income group. HUD should use housing programs for the elderly as leverage to induce suburban communities to accept low- and moderate-income housing. Subsidies for housing for the elderly are scarce resources, and HUD has a responsibility to allocate these resources on a priority basis to communities which are actively working to provide housing for families.

Mortgage Insurance

HUD, through the Federal Housing Administration (FHA), insures mortgages for single family homes and apartment houses under a variety of programs. HUD could use mortgage insurance for middle-income people as a lever to encourage suburbs to provide housing for lower-income people. The cutoff of FHA insurance in a community is perhaps the most politically difficult card for HUD to play. It is also likely to be an effective one, particularly in times of tight money. If FHA-insured mortgages are the only ones available, suburbs might accept lower-income housing in order to make sure that mortgage money is available in their community.

Limited Leverage of Community
Development Programs

Since the president's 1971 statement on equal housing opportunity, HUD has not been aggressive in pursuing suburban housing objectives through the leverage of its programs. However, even if an administration pursued this suburban strategy aggressively, it would remain a limited one. HUD operates under constraints similar to those facing state grant-making agencies. First, the carrot must be a very enticing one to local communities relative to the political and other costs involved in meeting the conditions. Few suburbs go through the Workable Program process because the subsequent carrot of urban renewal is not very appealing. Even in Warren, where a significant portion of the community needed redevelopment, the majority of the citizens lived in newer, more affluent surroundings and were indifferent to the needs of the south end of town. When the conditions on the grant appeared too burdensome, they rejected the urban renewal program.

HUD's primary carrots in the suburbs have been the water and sewer program and the open space program. These programs have great appeal to suburban communities. The programs have long been oversubscribed. However, the Westlake example indicates that even if the community wants the grant badly, it may decide that accepting subsidized housing is too high a price to pay.

HUD's open space program suffers from an additional limitation. The dollar amount potentially available to an individual applicant is so small that it is not likely to induce substantial action on housing issues. While water and sewer grants may be in the neighborhood of a million dollars, open space grants are more likely to be $50,000 to $75,000.

Second, HUD is basically a reactive agency. It did not seek out Warren, Michigan or Westlake, Ohio. These communities applied for assistance. This reactive posture makes it difficult to develop a coherent, comprehensive strategy for a metropolitan area. The Detroit area provided perhaps the best opportunity in the country for HUD to take a consistent initiative, since a number of suburban communities were seeking urban renewal and other grants. Even in that area, however, the suburbs involved with HUD programs represented only a small fraction of the suburban ring.

HUD has some potential for taking initiative and soliciting applications. It has done so on occasion with the water and sewer and Neighborhood Development programs. Sometimes a program has been oversold as a result of solicitations, with the requests for funds far exceeding the congressional appropriations. With carefully planned solicitation, however, HUD could exercise some control over the flow of applications under the categorical aid programs.

As at the state level, the carrot and stick strategy also has timing problems built into it. Any one shot grant, as under the open space program, is likely to be approved before the agreed-upon housing is actually built. In this case, HUD has only persuasion and publicity available to bring about compliance with the city's commitment. If HUD and the community have an ongoing relationship, as under the annual funding arrangement of the Neighborhood Development Program, the agency has a greater chance of insuring local performance.

Finally, the president's statement indicated that the federal government would not force any community to accept subsidized housing. The statement did not reject the use of the carrot and the stick. HUD could still reward communities which accepted subsidized housing by giving them priority access to the limited amount of community development funds. Unfortunately, however, this statement seems to have had a "chilling" effect. HUD has been reluctant to use the leverage of its community development programs to seek increased suburban housing opportunities. A limited strategy evolved into a nonexistent strategy. Its disuse is not a result of a negative evaluation and adoption of an alternative approach. Instead, its demise relates to the political heat generated and an administration decision to make efforts only where racial discrimination is clearly evident.

Special Revenue Sharing

In 1971, the administration proposed that Congress enact special revenue sharing legislation. The purpose was to phase out a large number of categorical aid programs in favor of a few grants to localities which could be used for broad purposes. One of the grant packages would have provided funds for community development. Although special revenue sharing for community development was not passed by Congress initially, the concept was revitalized by the admiminstration in its proposed Better Communities Act of 1973. The bill would replace an array of HUD categorical programs: urban renewal (including neighborhood development programs, code enforcement, demolition grants, and interim assistance); model cities; neighborhood facilities; water and sewer grants; open space and historic preservation; rehabilitation loans; and public facility loans. Housing programs would not be replaced by the act.

The Better Communities Act would phase out all of the categorical aids which had been, or could be, used to induce suburban acceptance of subsidized housing. In addition, it would provide little opportunity for HUD to influence local actions. Communities would receive an annual "entitlement," on a formula basis. They would not be required to submit applications for federal approval. HUD's role would be limited to auditing local records to assure that funds were used for authorized purposes. In this postaudit process, HUD would determine whether any person was denied access to, or the benefits of, any facility, service or activity carried out with Better Communities funds because of race, color, national origin or sex.

As limited as federal leverage is with categorical grants, it would virtually disappear under anything like the proposed form of special revenue sharing. The objective of eliminating unnecessary strings is an admirable one, but federal programs should provide for furthering national policies, such as equal opportunity in housing. Communities should not be entitled to unrestricted funds unless they provide significant housing opportunities for all income and racial groups. This string is essential. It should be incorporated into any replacement for categorical aid programs. HUD should review and approve local housing programs before it releases community development funds in any form.

New Communities Program

Even if a special revenue program was adopted, it would not replace HUD's New Communities program. The 1968 and 1970 New Communities Acts authorized HUD to assist developers of large-scale new communities. The 1968 Act was limited to private developers. The 1970 law extended the coverage of the program to public agencies.

Several kinds of assistance are available to HUD-approved new community developers. First, HUD guarantees bonds, debentures, notes and other obligations issued by the new community developer to finance property acquisition and land development and to pay for the use of real property. Second, HUD can make direct loans to new community developers to enable them to pay interest on debts they have incurred in financing the development. Third, public service grants may be available to a state or local agency which provides necessary services, to cover these costs until permanent arrangements are made. Grants can be made for up to three years. (No such grants have been made.)

Finally, HUD can provide financial assistance up to two-thirds of the estimated cost of planning new community programs. (No loans or grants have been made under this provision.)

The guarantees for the developer's obligations are the core of the New Communities program. They facilitate the developer's securing the long term financing in the large amounts necessary for a new community. If the new community developer cannot make the required periodic payments, the federal government will make such payments or pay off the obligation entirely so the holders of the obligation will suffer no loss. The government thus removes the risk for those providing the financing. The 1968 act established a ceiling of $250 million in total guarantees, with a limit of $50 million for any one community. The 1970 amendments doubled the ceiling on total guarantees.

HUD specifies several types of developments which are eligible for these guarantees: new communities within metropolitan areas, serving as an alternative to urban sprawl; additions to existing towns and cities, which can be converted into growth centers to prevent decline and accommodate population increase; new-town-in-town developments in or adjacent to existing cities; free-standing new communities.

For developments to receive assistance under the program, they must meet statutory and administrative requirements, including: (1) economic feasibility; (2) contribution to orderly growth and development of the area; (3) acceptable plan for financing land acquisition; and (4) sound internal development plan. The development plan must include an assurance of "a proper balance of housing for families of low- and moderate-income." The law provides no definition of this balance. HUD's proposed regulations would provide some clarification. Developers are required to provide a housing "mix," a range of housing for sale and rental to all income groups, including a "substantial amount" of low- and moderate-income housing. The appropriate mix depends on the distribution, by income and size, of families in the region; the supply of, and demand for, housing, particularly for low- and moderate-income families; and the income and housing needs of people likely to be employed in the community.

Related regulations regarding equal opportunity prohibit discrimination relating to the use, sale, lease or disposition of land and require establishment of an affirmative action program for marketing and advertising. In addition, the "social element" of a proposal must assure that housing will be distributed to prevent racial or economic segregation and provide everyone with full access to services.

As of mid-1973, HUD had issued 15 commitments. Guarantee exposure, for developers' debentures, was $293 million, of which $197 million had been sold.[8] Many of these projects constitute suburbs of major cities. Park Forest South is within commuting distance of Chicago. Jonathan, Minnesota is in the metropolitan area of the Twin Cities. Riverton and Gananda, New York are both located within 12 miles of Rochester. Most of the communities are being built by private developers, but the Urban Development Corporation is the sponsor of two other projects in New York—Lysander and Roosevelt Island.

The "deal" between HUD and the developer is formalized in a "project agreement." The project agreement incorporates the developer's commitments relating to HUD's various requirements, including plans to provide low- and moderate-income housing and prohibit discrimination. For example, the Park Forest South document specifies that the developer will provide a scaled amount of low-and moderate-income housing based on the Chicago area demographic profile. Specifically, the long term development activities include the construction of low- and moderate-income housing units according to an agreed upon timetable:

1971-100	*1978-300	*1985-350
1972-200	*1979-300	*1986-350
1973-200	*1980-300	*1987-350
1974-200	*1981-300	*1988-350
1975-250	*1982-300	*1989-350
*1976-250	*1983-350	*1990-350
*1977-300	*1984-350	

*If, after 1973, the secretary of HUD determines that the housing goals should be increased to equal the proportions reflected in the metropolitan area, the developer is obligated to provide the additional housing. Before 1975, the developer must meet the 1971-75 goals in this schedule.

The developer's policy statement calls for integration of classes and races, avoidance of ghettoes or minority isolation, compliance with state and local antidiscrimination laws and encouragement of occupancy by minorities. The implementation strategy included mixing together houses of various types, with a range of rentals and sales prices. In addition, a village ordinance prohibits discrimination in the sale, rental or advertising of housing. A human relations commission was to hear complaints, act to eliminate unlawful real estate practices and otherwise enforce the ordinance.

The Park Forest South developers committeed themselves through these agreements to a racially and economically integrated community. Fifteen percent of the projected population of 110,000 were to live in 4,500 low- and moderate-income units.

Other HUD-approved new communities have also made substantial commitments to low- and moderate-income housing. The project agreements concluded to date indicate that these communities may provide a significant proportion of low- and moderate-income housing. However, obtaining adequate commitments from developers is only the first step. A more difficult task is insuring that these commitments are met. For example, Park Forest South did not break ground on its first subsidized development until 1973, although its schedule had projected completion of 300 units by the end of 1972. Park Forest South received a HUD commitment in June 1970. The project agreement was signed in March 1971. Two years later, the developers were two years behind the agreed-upon schedule for building low- and moderate-income housing. Other new community developers had also fallen behind their timetables.

Enforcing Housing Commitments

In implementing any carrot and stick strategy, enforcement of commitments is a difficult problem; it is a particularly thorny one in the New Communities program. If HUD applies sanctions it may increase the chances that the developer will not be able to pay off his obligations and the project will fail. In that case, HUD is left holding the bag, since it has guaranteed those financing the development against loss. HUD would have to pay off the bonds or other obligations. The HUD commitment on a new community is a very large one, as well as a long-term one, which gives the department a very basic interest in the project's financial success. Cutting off various kinds of assistance to the developer may move him to develop lower-income housing, but it may also increase the chances that the community will "go under." In this context, HUD would do well to impose sanctions by selective withholding of supplemental categorical grants. Combining this stick with the pressure of publicity may influence developers to meet their agreed-upon responsibilities. These developers must market an image of their community. They may be particularly vulnerable to adverse publicity, such as an announcement by HUD that the developer is not meeting contractual commitments.

The Potential of the New Communities Program

The New Communities program provides an illustration of the importance of federal housing subsidies, as emphasized in the preceding chapter. Without these subsidies a unique opportunity may be lost. With a new community there is little or no existing population to oppose construction of low- and moderate-income housing. At the same time, there is a specific federal requirement of economic mix. The developer's participation in the program indicates that he is willing to provide housing for a variety of income groups. He may be reluctant to do so because of a fear that economic integration efforts will hinder marketing to middle- and upper-income people. But he is bound to build housing at the lower ranges.

In short, the New Communities program provides a rare combination of ingredients: limited local opposition to lower-income housing, an attractive carrot in the form of financial guarantees, and an explicit statutory and administrative requirement of a balanced housing supply. But if there are no subsidies available, new community developers may not be able to meet their housing commitments even if they want to. The subsidies must be provided, so that this opportunity is not lost. HUD recognized the importance of keeping subsidy money flowing to new communities when it exempted projects slated for new communities from the 1973 moratorium. The subsidies must continue to flow. At the same time, HUD must use its leverage to assure that the developers meet their low- and moderate-income housing commitments.

Chapter Thirteen

Federal Planning Programs and Requirements

HUD can influence the actions of regional bodies as well as local communities. Most of these agencies receive funds from HUD under the Comprehensive Planning Assistance program, to engage in comprehensive planning as well as in specialized functional planning on an areawide basis.[1] Most regional agencies are also involved in HUD's certification process, under which HUD evaluates the agency's structure and activities. Under a number of grant programs, a community is eligible only if certain planning requirements are met for the particular region. The certification process is designed to assure that the planning requirements are met and the localities are eligible for these grants.

Regional planning agencies also participate in the federal government's A-95 review process. The Office of Management and Budget, through Circular A-95, requires that applications for a wide variety of federal grants be reviewed by a metropolitan or regional clearinghouse for consistency with the regional plan and other grants coming into the area.

The federal government thus has a wide range of relationships with planning agencies and substantial potential for influencing their activities, through section 701grants, the certification process and the A-95 review process. The "feds" can encourage planning agencies to undertake housing allocation plans and take other steps to facilitate development of suburban low- and moderate-income housing.

Comprehensive Planning
Assistance Program

Through the Comprehensive Planning Assistance, or section 701, program HUD provides a substantial portion of the operating funds of regional planning agencies, councils of governments, or whatever entity is designated as the areawide planning organization. The planning under the section 701 program may include matters such as land development patterns, provision of needs such as water and sewer, housing, transportation, recreation and community facilities. The HUD grant usually covers two-thirds of the cost of the planning project, although it may be for three-fourths of the cost in some cases.[2] The grants are for a one year period. Most of these agencies would not survive without the federal dollars. The planning grant is therefore not only an attractive carrot but a necessary one for the regional agencies.

In 1968 Congress added a requirement that the planning undertaken under this program include a "housing element." Section 601 of the Housing and Urban Development Act of 1968 provided, in part, that:

> Planning carried out with assistance under this section shall also include a housing element as part of the preparation of comprehensive land use plans and this consideration of the housing needs and land use requirements for housing in each comprehensive plan shall take into account all available evidence of the assumptions and statistical bases upon which the projections of zoning, community facilities, and population growth is based; so that the housing needs of both the region and the local communities studied in the planning will be adequately covered in terms of existing and prospective in-migrant population growth.[3]

In administering this provision, HUD imposes a requirement that the regional agency analyze the housing needs within its jurisdiction:

> The housing work program shall analyze the existing housing market in terms of supply and demand by user group. The work program shall further identify:
>
> (1)   Needs met by private market;
> (2)   Needs met with public assistance; and
> (3)   Needs not being met.[4]

In addition, planning agencies receiving assistance from HUD must "define strategies and specific steps by which housing needs, and its [sic] related public services and facilities, can be met through responsive governmental programs and private action."[5]

The Housing Element Requirement: SEWRPC.   Because most regional planning agencies could not exist without HUD's financial support, HUD is in a good position to employ the carrot and stick approach by conditioning planning funds on the development of an action-oriented "housing element" for low- and moderate-income families. For the most part, however, HUD has been content to fund long-term housing needs studies and projections which are unrelated to immediate or short-range actions to meet these needs.

An important exception to this trend, which provides a useful model, is HUD's actions relative to the Southeastern Wisconsin Regional Planning Commission (SEWRPC). SEWRPC is one of eight regional planning commissions in Wisconsin, and it contains the state's largest city, Milwaukee, as well as Racine and Kenosha.

Prior to 1968, SEWRPC was not directly involved in housing. In that year, both the city of Milwaukee and HUD requested SEWRPC to undertake a regional housing study. The commission prepared a prospectus to get the housing study rolling and to meet the housing element requirement. The housing prospectus was completed by the end of 1969 and was approved as the initial housing element by HUD early in 1970. The total cost of the three year housing study was expected to be about $500,000.

In early 1971, however, HUD informed SEWRPC that it was temporarily withholding authorization to initiate additional work on the regional housing study. HUD explained that the major deficiency in SEWRPC's housing plan was the lack of a short-term lower-income housing action plan. HUD stressed the need for active participation of SEWRPC in the decisions concerning the location of low- and moderate-income housing in the southeastern Wisconsin region.

HUD reserved the funds for SEWRPC's annual planning grant on the assumption that the differences would be resolved. The grant amounted to $309,882, of which $185,000 was targeted for the 1971 portion of the housing study. After two months of discussions failed to produce a housing action plan acceptable to HUD, the federal agency informed SEWRPC that "authority to expend funds for the Regional Housing Study is hereby suspended." [6] Because of the inadequacy of the housing element, approval of the 1971 planning grant was held up. In a letter of March 31, 1971 HUD reiterated that "our primary concern with the work program as it exists is its lack of a short term action plan or strategy," and proceeded to "offer an example of what might be done to meet that need." HUD then indicated what it thought should be the objectives of SEWRPC's housing plan, as well as some methods by which SEWRPC could achieve these objectives.

Objective I
Identification of specific areas where low- and moderate-income housing should be constructed.
Method
A number of units needed at the outset should be determined on a best estimate basis. HUD proposed that SEWRPC begin by planning for the location of the next 8,000 units. HUD thought more precise quantification would follow as SEWRPC's overall studies progressed.

Allocation of the units among areas within the region would be based on SEWRPC's Regional Development Objectives, the Regional Land Use Plan and the application of additional quickly identifiable preliminary criteria. The additional criteria might include: 1) ratio of jobs to residents; 2) availability of transportation; 3) school capacities; 4) tax base; 5) index of substandard housing; 6) absence of housing for low- and moderate-income families. Such criteria would be refined over time.

Objective II
Identification of sites within those areas appropriate for the construction of these units.
Method
The site survey would involve starting an inventory in the areas designated for units. Using preliminary criteria to evaluate specific geographic areas, it would be possible to have site information in a short time.

Objective III
Identification of obstacles to the construction of housing on these sites: e.g. cost, zoning, building codes, community resistance.
Method
The obstacles would be identified during the inventory in the course of determining land cost, zoning and code requirements for these areas.

Objective IV
Determination of various methods for the immediate removal of inappropriate obstacles, thus bringing the cost to a feasible level.
Method
Actions to overcome the obstacles would involve ascertaining the immediately available financial resources and finding ways to use them to lower land costs where necessary. For example, a commitment from a county to subsidize land acquisition might bring costs to a feasible level. It would also involve working directly with the communities or counties to remove zoning or code obstacles. Longer term approaches to these obstacles involving state legislation could be developed later in the year.

Objective V
Initiation of communications with the producers and financers of housing to get housing constructed on the sites.
Method
SEWRPC would need to contact private developers, the nonprofits, the counties, municipalities, some state government officials and HUD and become a catalyst for the development of an operational strategy for the immediate use of the identified sites.[7]

HUD urged SEWRPC either to submit a revised work program which followed

HUD's recommended outline or to develop some other approach that would place SEWRPC in an active position concerning low- and moderate-income housing.[8] Ultimately SEWRPC agreed to specify locations for 2,000 units as a "best estimate with the understanding that it will be adjusted as soon as SEWRPC is able to obtain a better quantified figure."[9] HUD gave SEWRPC six months to complete the short-term action plan and integrate it into the original regional housing study.

Throughout the discussions, HUD's position received substantial local support. The Milwaukee Tenants Union wrote to their congressman to express the belief that the decision to withhold funds from SEWRPC until the commission developed an action plan "was both a courageous and needed move on the part of HUD."[10] The tenants union also expressed the hope that the congressman would support HUD's actions. Milwaukee Mayor Henry Maier said that SEWRPC's housing proposal involved three to four years of "intermediate planning" which he called "obvious procrastination" on the housing issue and supported HUD's efforts to get the agency moving.[11]

As a result of this negotiation between SEWRPC and HUD, SEWRPC's staff conducted the short-range housing action program. The commission also recorded data on each available site, including site size, ownership, present zoning, availability of utilities, distance to essential services, neighborhood conditions and residential development potential. Obstacles to the immedate construction of housing on the sites were also recorded. This short-range action housing program was completed in the summer of 1972.

The experience with SEWRPC illustrates the kind of leverage HUD has available through the use of its planning funds and its housing element mandate. Unfortunately, this episode remains a virtually unused precedent. HUD should systematically require short-range lower-income housing action plans as a condition of approving section 701 grants. The planning agency should design its own housing work program, but it should not be funded unless the program meets this action standard.

Certification

While the section 701 program provides planning grants, the certification process involves planning requirements which are a condition of eligibility for various "hardware" grants. The president's statement of June 1971 summarized the relationship between planning grants and planning requirements:

> Where comprehensive planning is supported by a federal grant under the 1954 Act, as amended in 1968, the plan must include a "housing element" to insure that "the housing needs of both the region and the local communities studied in the planning will be

adequately covered in terms of existing and prospective in-migrant population growth." This provision has broad application, since such planning grants are often used to prepare the areawide plans which are a prerequisite for federal financial assistance under the water and sewer, open space and new communities programs.[12]

The president's statement refers to relationships among areawide planning organizations, planning assistance grants, plans, and a number of federal categorical grant programs. Central to this scheme is the certification process, an administrative device created by HUD. Before certification,"planning findings" had been made on an application by application basis. Any time a community applied for a grant under one of a number of programs, HUD would have to make positive "planning findings" for the region in which the applicant was located before it could approve the local grant. It was to short-cut this case by case approach that HUD created certification. Areawide planning organizations are certified for a one year period, eliminating the need for planning findings for individual applications during that time. Communities within the region know where they stand for the certification period. They know that they have a year to operate programs before meeting the planning requirement again.

There are three types of certification, with different requirements and implications.

Certification I: This concerns the acceptability to HUD of the regional planning body as an organization, particularly in regard to policy board composition (e.g., is there a sufficient number of elected officials?) and the adequacy of nonfederal financial support for the agency. In order to receive HUD's section 701 planning assistance funds, HUD generally requires that an organization have Certification I or is otherwise making adequate progress in the opinion of the federal agency.

Certification II: This is given by HUD if an areawide planning organization is carrying out adequate comprehensive planning, including a housing element which meets statutory and administrative requirements. Certification II is necessary for applicants within the region to be eligible for open space and water and sewer grants from HUD, as well as grants from the Environmental Protection Agency. Under an EPA-HUD agreement, EPA will not approve grants without a positive planning finding by HUD.

When HUD held up approval of a planning grant for the Southeastern Wisconsin Regional Planning Commission, it also withheld Certification II. This made it impossible for HUD to grant certain funds to any community in the region. HUD's inability to certify SEWRPC was dictated by HUD's regulations, under which Certification II requires a finding that the agency has an acceptable work program, including an acceptable housing element. HUD emphasized that its inability to certify was not a sanction, but was simply a matter of the department complying with its own regulations.

Certification III: This relates to functional planning. A separate certification is available for each functional area. Certification III is necessary for applicants within the jurisdiction to be eligible for federal funding for open space planning of any park of regional significance. If a park is not of regional significance Certifications I and II are needed, as well as adequate local open space planning.

Thus, the certification device is used by HUD to implement programmatic requirements that there be an acceptable areawide planning agency and an acceptable level of planning. In addition, many programs administered by HUD as well as other federal agencies require not only that there be an acceptable plan, but also that the particular application be consistent with that comprehensive plan.

The certification process gives HUD added leverage through the "consistency with the comprehensive plan" requirements built into many categorical grant programs. Without an acceptable planning organization and an acceptable plan the requirement of consistency with the plan cannot be met. The following federal programs require the existence of, and consistency with, a comprehensive metropolitan or regional plan:

1. HUD: Water and Sewer and Open Space Programs. The determination of the adequacy of the areawide plan is made through the certification process and a finding is made as to whether each application is consistent with that plan.
2. Environmental Protection Agency: Waste Treatment Facilities. HUD has an advisory role because of the agreement between the agencies mentioned earlier. Although there is no statutory requirement for this specific form of cooperation, EPA's legislation requires the coordination and consistency of planning activities.
3. Department of Transportation (DOT). The capital grant programs of the Urban Mass Transit Administration (UMTA) contain the planning requirement. Under the executive order shifting these programs from HUD to DOT, HUD retains an advisory role on the planning finding. HUD may employ the same standards here as in its own certification process in determining the adequacy of comprehensive planning. Although the consistency with the plan requirement is not involved here, the housing element requirement is thus incorporated into the UMTA planning review.

Potential Leverage in Certification
The certification process contains a good deal of potential leverage

with regard to both regional agencies and their constitutent communities. Without certification, entire metropolitan areas are denied eligibility for a variety of categorical programs, some of which are funded at high levels. As in the case of the 701 program, the potential for opening suburbs through this process is virtually untapped.

The A-95 Review Process

As federal categorical programs proliferated in the 1960s, the need for coordinating these grants at some level of government became more apparent. The Departments of Housing and Urban Development; Health, Education and Welfare; and Transportation; as well as the Environmental Protection Agency and other domestic agencies, were distributing large sums of money through their programs to assist states and localities in their community development efforts. However, there was no mechanism to insure that the projects carried out with these grants were consistent with a single comprehensive plan for the area or whether they were mutually supporting or at least not interfering with each other. In 1969 the federal Office of Management and Budget (OMB) moved to fill this void by issuing Circular A-95, which established a Project Notification Review System as an

> . . . attempt on the part of the Federal government to establish
> systematic procedures for program agencies and project applicants
> to consult with one another and with planning entities at the
> state, regional and local levels in order to coordinate their plans
> and render them more consistent.[13]

Statutory Basis for Circular A-95.   Circular A-95 implemented two statutory provisions relating to intergovernmental cooperation and co-ordination: (1) section 204 of the Demonstration Cities and Metropolitan Development Act of 1966 and (2) title IV of the Intergovernmental Coopera-tion Act of 1968.[14] Section 204 provides that all applications for federal assistance for specified public facilities in a metropolitan area must be screened by an areawide comprehensive planning agency. The agency is to forward comments to the federal government regarding the relationship of the proposed project to the overall development of the area.

The Intergovernmental Cooperation Act directs that (1) evalua-tion and review procedures pertaining to federal programs and projects which have a "significant impact on area and community development" be regularized; (2) that, as much as possible, national, state, regional and local points of view are to be considered during the planning process; and (3) that maximum con-gruence between national objectives and the objectives of state, regional and local planning occur.[15]

Clearinghouses. In order to coordinate federally-supported programs with local, regional, state and national development plans, Circular A-95 provides for the designation of clearinghouses to review and comment on applications for federal funding under a long list of grant programs. Three types of clearinghouses are provided for by A-95. The governor designates as the state clearinghouse the state agency which has comprehensive planning responsibilities. The governor also identifies regional clearinghouses, which are nonmetropolitan areawide agencies with a general planning capacity. Finally, metropolitan clearinghouses are recognized by OMB for purposes of the Demonstration Cities and Metropolitan Development Act of 1966. In almost half of the 233 metropolitan areas (SMSAs) in the country, councils of governments (COGs) were named as metropolitan clearinghouses for their area. In other areas, the metropolitan clearinghouse is the metropolitan or regional planning agency. A basic shortcoming in the A-95 process is that the clearinghouse is usually an arm of the communities whose applications it reviews. If the clearinghouse is a council of governments, it is made up of the public officials of constituent communities. If the clearinghouse is a regional planning agency, its board is likely to be made up of representatives of the communities. In addition, the nonfederal funding sometimes comes from voluntary contributions from localities. For clearinghouses to be effective reviewers, they must have a degree of independence from the localities. State support for the clearinghouses through a percentage of tax receipts would help provide this independence.

The Review Procedure. In 1971 OMB expanded the programs subject to the A-95 review process to include over 100 programs which it considers central to metropolitan development. Programs covered relate to matters such as open space, airport planning, new towns, highways, water supply and sewage treatment. Federal agencies which have programs covered are responsible for establishing procedures for implementing the review process. These agencies include the Departments of Housing and Urban Development; Health, Education and Welfare; Labor; Agriculture; Commerce; Interior; Justice; and Defense; as well as the Environmental Protection Agency and the Office of Economic Opportunity. HUD has more programs covered than any other federal agency.

A local or state agency or voluntary organization which plans to apply for a federal grant under a program covered by the circular is required to notify the appropriate clearinghouse of its intention. The notification includes a summary of the proposed project. The clearinghouse then reviews the application and comments on it in terms of its consistency with areawide planning. When the review process is completed the applicant submits the proposal to the federal funding agency, along with any comments made by the clearinghouse.

The federal agency involved then reviews the application and decides whether to approve it. The agency is obligated to notify the clearinghouse within seven days of any action taken. In spite of this requirement, federal agencies often do not notify the clearinghouses of their funding decisions. In evaluating an application, the federal agency is free to place whatever weight it deems appropriate on the comments of the clearinghouse. For example, even if the clearinghouse submits a strong negative review, with an explicit recommendation against funding, the funding agency may approve the application. Circular A-95 requires only "review and comment" by the clearinghouse and does not require the federal agency to do any more than consider this review in its decision-making. If the federal agency has confidence in the ability of a particular clearinghouse to evaluate applications, the reviews may have substantial impact. Practices vary widely among federal agencies and clearinghouses. In some metropolitan areas, a negative review of a water and sewer application, for example, virtually assures that HUD will disapprove the grant.

If a clearinghouse does not have the confidence of a particular federal agency, its reviews are likely to have little impact. It cannot appeal from an agency's decision to fund a project in spite of a negative review. Further, it cannot accomplish a "pocket veto" and prevent funding by refusing to comment at all. The comment requirement has been interpreted to mean that the clearinghouse must be given an opportunity to comment, which is lost if it is not used.

The Office of Management and Budget could put pressure on the executive agencies to take the clearinghouses' comments seriously. Congressionally appropriated funds flow through OMB before they get to the designated agencies. If OMB found that A-95 reviews were being consistently ignored by a particular federal agency, it could delay forwarding appropriations to that agency until it began to pay attention to the comments.

Civil Rights Concerns and Circular A-95. Until 1972, the A-95 process did not specifically require consideration of the civil rights impact of proposed projects. Early in that year OMB revised the circular in order to "provide for the consideration of civil rights implications in reviews of applications for assistance under Federal programs covered therein."[16] Accordingly, "public agencies charged with enforcing State and local civil rights laws [are provided] with an opportunity to participate in the review process established."[17] Comments could relate to "the extent to which the project contributes to more balanced patterns of settlement and delivery of services to all sectors of the area population, including minority groups."[18] The evaluations and recommendations of civil rights agencies were to be channeled through the appropriate clearinghouse.

In the San Francisco area, the state Fair Employment Practice Commission was designated as the responsible agency for implementing the civil rights provisions of A-95. The commission entered into an agreement with the National Committee Against Discrimination in Housing to carry out a pilot project in the Bay area to provide input into the A-95 process. The commission requested all applicants for federal funds to fill out a questionnaire on the civil rights impact of the proposed project. The questionnaire included questions on the current minority population of the area and the possible exclusionary effects of the project.

The state commission also made several important requests of the federal funding agencies.

> 1. Notify all applicants seeking funds from your agency that, in compliance with Revised Circular A-95, they are required to file a "notice of intent" well in advance of the submission of a formal proposal so that appropriate reviews of the impact of the proposed project can be made. 2. Inform all project applicants of the amendment to Circular A-95 (which authorizes comments on the civil rights impact of specific projects seeking federal funds) and urge them to cooperate fully with agencies and/or organizations seeking information on the potential civil rights impact of their proposed programs. 3. Develop procedures within your agency for evaluating and responding to the comments generated by clearinghouses, affected agencies and/or local community groups on the potential civil rights impact of specific projects. 4. Require modifications in proposals which will have a negative civil rights impact and encourage applicants to involve individuals, groups and agencies, with civil rights expertise and commitment, in the development and evaluation of proposals.[19]

In essence, the Fair Employment Practice Commission was asking the federal funding agencies to take the A-95 process and particularly the civil rights impact of projects seriously. Unlike many of the clearinghouses, state and private civil rights agencies have a degree of independence which enables them to criticize seriously applications for federal funds. The steps requested of the federal agencies by the California commission would significantly increase the chances for the A-95 process to have an important impact.

Civil rights concerns are germane to both housing and community development projects. Housing projects subject to the A-95 review include: (1) 50 or more lots involving any HUD home mortgage plan; (2) multifamily projects with 100 or more units under any HUD mortgage insurance program (subsidized or unsubsidized) or under the public housing program; (3) HUD-assisted mobile home courts with 100 or more spaces.

If there is a regional housing allocation plan, subsidized housing proposals can be reviewed against that plan. Whether or not such a plan exists, the review should relate primarily to the location of the project in terms of whether it expands locational choice of lower-income and minority families. If proposed projects do not provide for suburban housing opportunities, as well as central city sites, reviews should recommend more balanced development. The comment should also be used to discourage large concentrations of subsidized housing and to promote developments with an economic mix of families.

Equally significant is the opportunity for regional agencies to comment on community development projects such as water and sewer facilities and open space acquisition grants. Here, comments should relate to the nature of the community applying for the grant. If a community has little or no subsidized housing and few minorities living there the recommendation should be against federal approval of the application unless the community takes affirmative steps to provide such housing opportunities.

Since late 1971 there have been several challenges, through the A-95 review process, to applications for community development grants. These efforts, which have been in Connecticut, were designed to get towns to eliminate exclusionary zoning ordinances as a condition of obtaining federal assistance. The first Connecticut A-95 controversy involved the neighboring towns of Berlin and New Britain, communities of vastly different character. New Britain is an industrial city of 83,000 people, with a five percent minority population. It occupies 13 square miles of land. Of its residentially developed land, half is used for apartments. The community has 1,700 units of subsidized housing. Neighboring Berlin is a suburb with 14,000 people, only 50 of whom are minorities. Although Berlin has only about one-sixth the population of New Britain, it has double the area, 26 square miles. None of this land is zoned for apartments.

In 1971, Berlin applied to the federal Environmental Protection Agency for a $760,000 grant, as part of the $1.5 million total cost of a sanitary sewer line. New Britain objected to the application because Berlin had not provided its fair share of the region's low- and moderate-income housing. The New Britain planning chairman argued that:

> . . . a zoning and development policy which encourages industry
> to locate within a town's borders but discourages its employees
> from becoming residents unless they can afford to buy a home,
> only shifts the burden to New Britain and its already overtaxed
> housing, sewer, and other resources.[20]

Leaders of both communities recognized that it was in their self-interest to resolve the dispute. Berlin officials knew that the Environmental Protection Agency had limited funds and a backlog of applications. Thus, adverse comments on the A-95 review could result in a rejection of Berlin's application. At the same time, New Britain leaders realized that the sewer system was necessary to enable Berlin to absorb apartment development. Berlin had only septic tanks in use and could not support multifamily units even if it changed the zoning to permit them.

In the settlement, New Britain agreed that it would send the federal government only a copy of an "advisory comment to a neighboring community," rather than a formal negative A-95 review. This comment would state New Britain's position on the need for immediate development of low- and moderate-income housing in Berlin. While Berlin would be thus put on notice, it would still be in a position to secure its sewer grant.

In a second instance in Connecticut, the state Commission on Human Rights and Opportunities intervened in opposition to a sewer application. The commission objected that the town of Simsbury's building lot requirements and single family housing requirements were exclusionary. There was no outright prohibition of apartments, but the cumulative effect of the zoning ordinances was that only the relatively well-to-do could afford to live in Simsbury.

Again, the matter was resolved by negotiation, this time between the state commission and local public officials. The town made several commitments: (1) the sewer plant would be designed to allow for and maintain low- and moderate-income housing development; (2) the zoning code would be amended to provide for such housing; (3) the local planning commission would move toward a more open and balanced community by including new developments of moderate-income housing; and (4) the town would consider the adoption of a municipal ordinance for the formation of a local human rights commission.[21]

Realizing the Potential of
Circular A-95

Circular A-95 has been viewed by some civil rights strategists as "one of the most important single tools of federal policy identified in [our] two years of study of the metropolitan racial polarization issue."[22]

However, this potential remains largely unrealized. Changes are needed, at the regional as well as the federal level:

1. Many clearinghouses do not have fully developed regional plans against which to evaluate a specific application. This is particularly true in the housing area, where only a few agencies have developed allocation plans. As proposed earlier in this chapter, clearinghouses should be required to establish a comprehensive plan for regional development, including a plan for low- and moderate-income housing. This plan would be in fulfillment of the housing element requirement under HUD's planning assistance pro-

gram. Failure to meet this requirement would result in the clearinghouse not being funded or certified by HUD. The entire area would then be ineligible for specified federal programs.

2. Housing developments which are relatively small are exempt from the A-95 review. HUD has moved away from subsidizing large institutional-type projects and toward scatteration. In order for the clearinghouse to assist in the implementation of this policy it needs to participate even in the smaller developments. By the middle of 1973 OMB had recognized this problem and was considering changing the minimums for new construction applications to 25 lots for subdivisions and 50 units for multifamily projects. These proposals were stimulated by requests to OMB from the clearinghouses, which argued that a smaller project could have a significant impact on an area, particularly in combination with other projects.

3. The A-95 process contains no veto power for the clearinghouse. The only requirement A-95 imposes on the applicant is to make the appropriate contact with the clearinghouse. Without this opportunity for comment, the federal government is prohibited from approving the application. For A-95 to have teeth the clearinghouse must take it seriously and the federal agencies must support that effort. In order to insure that these comments are considered carefully, the federal agency involved should at least be required to document in writing its reasons for acting inconsistently with the clearinghouse recommendations when it does so. It must explain how its actions "increase program effectiveness" more than would action pursuant to the clearinghouse recommendations. The Office of Management and Budget has drafted requirements to this effect. The requirements should be promulgated.

4. In order to carry out the A-95 process, the clearinghouse need not be certified by HUD or be receiving planning assistance funds from HUD. Thus, HUD's leverage in its certification process and the 701 planning program cannot be expanded to the range of programs covered by A-95. Metropolitan areas lacking a certified or funded planning agency may still have an A-95 clearinghouse available, thus retaining eligibility, from OMB's perspective, for the covered grant programs. Therefore, OMB should require that the clearinghouse be an agency which is certified by HUD (Certifications I and II). Without such certification, there should be no clearinghouse for the area. The certification process would then take on far greater significance, since it would be a prerequisite to funding under all of the programs subject to Circular A-95.

5. The clearinghouses are given little guidance in how to identify active civil rights agencies which are capable of responding promptly and with sensitivity to civil rights issues. Similarly, there are no criteria for determining which applications may have civil rights implications and should be forwarded to these reviewers. The clearinghouse must determine, largely

without standards, which, if any, civil rights agencies to contact for assistance on particular applications. In order to insure that relevant civil rights
questions are raised, all applications should be referred to such agencies.
To guide the clearinghouses, OMB should establish general standards for
selecting the agencies. This would guarantee that organizations with commitment and capacity are called on for their input. Procedures should also
insure that notification of the pendency of the application is prompt and
that the federal agencies inform the civil rights agencies promptly of any
action taken. If the action is inconsistent with the organization's position,
the federal agency's reasons for so acting should be detailed. For example,
if HUD approved a sewer grant for a suburb after the civil rights agency
had recommended rejection due to the community's exclusionary practices,
HUD would have to provide a specific explanation for the approval of the
grant.

6. Coverage of A–95 should be expanded to include the social programs of
various agencies. This would permit active regional agencies to use their
leverage in relation to these programs. It would force less progressive
agencies to begin to address social issues. Draft revisions have been prepared
by OMB for expanding the coverage of A–95. The agency should adopt the
changes.

Land Use Policy Bill

In the early 1970s, Congress considered expanding the federal role
in land use planning. In 1973 the Senate Interior Committee completed its
third year of hearings on national land use policy. A number of bills had been
introduced on this subject. Like the American Law Institute's Model Land
Development Code, the Congressional bills focused on elevating certain land
use decisions from the local to the state level. Finally, in mid-1973, the Senate
passed the Land Use Policy and Planning Act, which would authorize grants
to states to develop and implement land use programs. The bill encourages
states to exercise control over large-scale developments which may be impacted
by key facilities such as airports, those which are to be located in areas of
critical environmental concern or those which have potential regional benefit.

As in the case of the ALI code, the thrust of the Senate bill is
procedural. It seeks to move the decision-making process to the state level
when issues are involved that relate to many municipalities. The substantive
policies that the bill advances relate primarily to protection of the environment; thus the origin of the bill in the Senate Interior Committee and the provision that the law would be administered by the Secretary of the Interior.

The Senate bill has some potential for advancing the housing cause.
For a state to remain eligible for grants after the initial five-year period it
would have to have an adequate land use program, including a means for
"assuring that local regulations do not arbitrarily or capriciously restrict or

exclude development of public facilities, housing, or utilities of regional benefit."[23]

Meanwhile, the House Committee on Interior and Insular Affairs was considering another land use bill which borrowed from the model code. Its definitions were broad enough to include housing, but there was little direct reference to the subject. State regulations would have to "assure that local regulations do not unreasonably restrict or exclude development and land use of regional or national benefit."[24] Such developments include "private development and land use for which there is a demonstrable need affecting the interests of constituents of more than one local government which outweighs the benefits of any applicable restrictive or exclusionary local regulations."[25] As with the ALI model code, it would be up to a prohousing state agency to interpret this general language in ways that would open up housing opportunities. In addition, the subcommittee print requires that the state planning process provide for adequate housing in proximity to employment centers.

Even if the generalized process in the land use bills was translated into a prohousing orientation, sanctions would be needed at the federal level. Legislation should provide for withholding of community development assistance where planning and implementation did not meet federal requirements, including elimination of local barriers to low- and moderate-income housing.

In the absence of a housing thrust and sanctions, federal land use legislation would be, at best, irrelevant to increasing housing choice and, at worst, could provide additional rationales and processes in support of exclusionary practices.

Chapter Fourteen

Federal Carrot and Stick: Location of Government Facilities

HUD is not the only federal agency with carrots to dispense to local communities and a mandate in the housing area. The federal government is constantly selecting locations for its facilities, either for construction or acquisition of federally-owned buildings or leasing of private space. Such a facility brings many benefits to a community: jobs are provided; spinoff businesses are created; and, if the facilities are leased, rental income and property taxes are generated. The community reaps the gains from receiving a federally owned or leased facility as surely as if it receives a water and sewer or urban renewal grant. As in the case of a categorical grant, the federal government can require that conditions related to federal policy be met before the community is selected as a recipient of the federal benefits. Federal agencies have come under a mandate to address the issue of low- and moderate-income housing in locating their facilities.

In the last two decades, many federal agencies have moved from central cities, particularly Washington, D.C., to the suburbs. Because of the lack of lower-income housing in those areas, employees have paid a heavy price in loss of jobs or excessive commuting costs. Instead of being part of the solution, the federal government has been part of the problem. The presence of federal facilities has done little to encourage doing away with suburban exclusionary practices. For example, although Arlington County, Virginia has 4.2 million square feet of federally leased space, there is no publicly assisted housing there. Voters and legislators have both turned it down.[1]

In effect, rather than using the leverage of its facilities, the federal government has rewarded exclusionary suburbs with substantial financial benefits. In selecting sites for facilities the General Services Administration, and the other agencies involved, should require that the locality provide housing for the low- and moderate-income employees of the federal facility, as well as other low-income workers in the area. Government owned or leased facilities should be located only in communities where the agency's employees can find decent shelter within their means.

Decentralization of Federal Facilities

Like private industry, the federal government has been decentralizing its facilities and relocating many agencies from the central cities to the suburban parts of metropolitan areas. Although the Washington area has been most affected, many moveouts have taken place in other areas as well.

Federal agency relocation had its beginnings in the 1950s. Moves were made because of the cold war fear that concentrating federal facilities would provide an easy target in case of a military attack. In 1958 the Atomic Energy Commission moved 27 miles from Washington to Germantown, Maryland with 2,000 employees, thus becoming the first major federal relocation in the D.C. area.[2] In subsequent moves the rationale has been economics. Because of the refusal of Congress to appropriate funds to build new structures in the city, agencies turned to rented office space in the suburbs, where the cost was one-half that of the central city. For example, by 1970 northern Virginia had more federally-leased space than Washington. The trend probably peaked in 1970 when the Navy Department transferred 12,500 employees to Arlington, Virginia and the Public Health Service shifted 5,500 workers to Rockville, Maryland.

General purpose public buildings, such as federal office buildings housing a number of federal agencies, continue to be located primarily in central cities. Buildings of a special purpose which house a single federal agency continue to reflect the trend toward suburban location.[3]

Impact of Suburbanizing Facilities

As in the case of private corporations migrating to suburbia, the movement of government operations has caused hardships for lower-income and minority group federal employees. Often these suburban locations ". . . are [in] areas in which the supply of housing within the means of low- and moderate-income employees is either inadequate or nonexistent. Many of these communities traditionally have excluded minority group families, regardless of income."[4] These workers must either give up their jobs or pay the cost in time, money and the inconvenience of extensive reverse commuting from the central city to the new suburban locations. These lower level employees are disproportionately black. The moveouts hit them hardest. When part of the Department of Health, Education and Welfare relocated out of Washington, D.C., an agency official predicted:

> . . . the move of the two HEW agencies to Rockville (in suburban Maryland) was "the Great Whitener." It would only be a matter of time until the balance would shift back to a nearly all-white

staff. Low-income black employees who cannot afford to move or the extra commuting costs lose. High income whites benefit.[5]

In several of these relocations to suburbia, the U.S. Civil Rights Commission has uncovered discrimination in hiring and housing practices. These include the National Bureau of Standards' move to suburban Montgomery County, Maryland and the Manned Spaceflight Centers to the suburbs of Houston, Texas. These moves were made in the early 1960s. The move of the Bureau of Standards resulted in a decrease of 73 black employees in the first four years. At the same time, overall employment at the agency increased by 125. The high cost of transportation and the lack of low- and moderate-income housing made it increasingly difficult for blacks to retain their jobs.[6] In the past, then, the federal government placed facilities regardless of the openness of the community, thus contributing to patterns of economic and racial segregation in metropolitan areas.

The General Services Administration
The General Services Administration (GSA) is responsible for acquiring, leasing and assigning office space for most federal departments and agencies. GSA acts as the government's landlord for over 10,000 facilities. Its jurisdiction does not include all federal facilities, however. In fact, some of the most controversial moves to suburban locations have been made by agencies which are responsible for their own locations and physical facilities.

GSA Initiatives on Housing
As a result of problems caused by federal agency relocation during the 1950s and 1960s, GSA adopted regulations in 1969 regarding housing opportunities and the acquisition of real property.

> GSA will avoid locations which will work hardships on employees because (1) there is a lack of adequate housing for low and moderate income employees within a reasonable proximity and (2) the location is not readily accessible from other areas of the urban center.[7]

This regulation is worded rather vaguely, with terms such as adequate and reasonable not defined. However, these directives were a step forward. Until that time, neither GSA nor any other federal agency had specifically considered the housing needs of lower-income or minority-group employees among criteria by which sites for federal facilities would be selected. The U.S. Civil Rights Commission commented on these changes:

> The attitude and policy of GSA have been changing over recent

years from one of bare recognition of any responsibility toward the housing problems of lower-income employees and minority group employees to at least partial recognition and acceptance of responsibility.[8]

Executive Order 11512

In February 1970 the president issued Executive Order 11512, which further defined federal site selection responsibilities. The executive order requires GSA, and other executive agencies, to consider the availability of low- and moderate-income housing as a factor in selecting sites for federal facilities.[9] However, it is not clear what weight is to be given to housing in relation to other locational considerations. The executive order states only that:

> The Administrator, and the heads of executive agencies, shall be guided by the following policies for the acquisition, assignment, reassignment, and utilization of office buildings and space in the United States: . . .
> . . . (6) The availability of adequate low and moderate income housing . . .

The housing provision is one of seven factors identified in the executive order, including healthful and safe working conditions; consistency with local and regional planning; preferences for agency consolidation; and use of permanent, government-owned space. Cost, agency needs and space availability still seem to be of primary concern. The Civil Rights Commission has raised the question in regard to these policies:

> While the order specifies that these [housing requirements] are among the policies by which departments and agencies are to be guided, it is not clear what priority is to be accorded them in relation to other, and perhaps conflicting, policies, such as "efficient performance" (Sec. 2 [a] [1]) and "adequacy of parking" (Sec. [2] [1]). Further, the order is silent on the matter of racial discrimination.[10]

HUD-GSA Memorandum of Understanding

The executive order was followed by the issuance, on June 14, 1971, of a memorandum of understanding between the Department of Housing and Urban Development and the General Services Administration. The memorandum was a first step towards implementation of the executive order. The memorandum provides that, in selecting sites for federal facilities, GSA will ". . . consider to the maximum possible extent the availability of low and moderate income housing without discrimination. . . ."[11] GSA was to rely on HUD's assessment of the availability of such housing. This procedure is applicable to both government-owned public building projects and to major lease actions. If GSA desires to build or lease where HUD finds that there is inadequate housing available, ". . . GSA and HUD will develop an affirmative action plan designed to insure that an adequate supply of such housing will be available before the building or space is to be occupied or within six months thereafter."[12] Commitments by local officials of the community in question should be in the plan. The agency which is to occupy the facility is also to participate in the plan.

HUD and GSA have each developed internal procedures to implement the memorandum. Minimum threshold levels for application of the procedures were set at 100 low- and moderate-income employees at a facility for both lease and new construction. Under these procedures HUD's general responsibilities include: (1) reporting findings of project development investigations to GSA on the availability of low- and moderate-income housing to federal employees on a nondiscriminatory basis; (2) developing jointly with GSA, the federal agency involved and the community an affirmative action plan where HUD has concluded that GSA's preferred location is not accessible to an adequate supply of low- and moderate-income housing on a nondiscriminatory basis; and (3) giving priority consideration to applications for assistance under HUD programs for housing proposed in accordance with the plan.

GSA's general responsibilities include: (1) providing HUD with necessary information it needs to investigate a survey area, such as the number of potential employees involved and pay grade distribution; (2) considering HUD's findings on the adequacy of survey area housing to the maximum possible extent in deciding the final site of new facilities; (3) participating with HUD and other parties on affirmative action plans; and (4) providing written explanation to HUD if GSA selects a site which HUD reported as inadequate.

The responsibilities of the federal agency involved include: (1) providing data to GSA and HUD; (2) considering housing availability to the maximum extent feasible when deciding its locational preferences; and (3) participating with HUD and GSA on affirmative action plans.

Defects in the Administrative Machinery

The site selection requirements of the executive order, the HUD-GSA memorandum and the implementing procedures have major weaknesses built into them. First, HUD is not required to provide funding for necessary low- and moderate-income housing but merely to give priority to these proposals. Presumably, if HUD fails to approve needed housing, because of supervening priorities or a freeze on housing funds, the federal facility may proceed without adequate housing in the community. Second, evaluation of available housing in the community is placed entirely in the hands of HUD and GSA, both of whom have incentives to make an affirmative finding in order to permit the facility to proceed. There is no provision made for an independent evaluation of the local housing situation which could discover inadequacies missed by the federal investigators. Third, there is no requirement of consultation with agency employees prior to selection of a site. Relocation is not a guaranteed subject of collective bargaining between the employee union and the agency. In fact, the move is often decided on without discussions with employees.

Finally, the responsibility of GSA and other agencies to deal with the overall housing needs of the community remains undefined. If their obligation was only to find housing for the agency's employees, this could be achieved in ways that actually worsened, rather than improved, the local housing situation. For example, an intensive search for existing vacant, sound units at reasonable prices might turn up enough dwellings for employees who wish to move into the community. However, if there was already a shortage of decent housing for this income group, sopping up available units would merely exacerbate the housing problem for prior residents. The federal employees win the game of "musical houses," but the community suffers a more serious housing shortage than previously. For this reason, the federal government must insure that the overall supply of low- and moderate-income housing in the community is increased. It is not enough that the federal agency's employees are housed adequately, if others are worse off as a result. In spite of the GSA administrator's protestations to the contrary, the agency's responsibility is not limited to the federal employees.

> Our job is providing buildings for the Federal Government. . . .
> We cannot . . . solve the total housing problems of an overall community. This is not GSA's job. It may be others' in Government, but it is not GSA's.[13]

Challenges to Location of Facilities

Private groups have challenged the selection of sites for several federal facilities. The earliest efforts predated the current administrative machinery. When the Navy Department and the Public Health Service announced their intention to move major operations out of the District of Columbia, lower-income black employees filed suit to enjoin these relocations. The plaintiffs charged that such shifts would discriminate against them because there was a shortage of low- and moderate-income housing in the suburbs to which the agencies were moving. Furthermore, the plaintiffs claimed that public transportation systems were inadequate and the impracticality of commuting would force many of them to give up their jobs.

The Public Health Service suit was terminated when a program was created to provide alternative government jobs to the employees who wished to stay in the city. (It was claimed later that many of these jobs were dead end jobs that could not have been filled otherwise.) The Navy Department argued successfully in court that they had to move from the dilapidated World War I temporary buildings on the Mall and that they were moving only two miles away. But crossing the Potomac River, which is included in the two mile distance, increases cost and travelling time from the city.

A third suit was filed by the Metropolitan Washington Planning and Housing Agency against GSA to prevent the move of U.S. Geological Survey (USGS) employees to Reston, Virginia. The complaint alleged that the new town developers, Gulf-Reston, had no firm commitment to provide housing for low- and moderate-income USGS employees. USGS has 2,200 employees; 20 percent are black, of whom 56 percent earn under $4,900 a year. The request for an injunction to prevent the move was denied. However, GSA did include in the contract with Gulf-Reston a provision that Reston will "offer . . . to construct a variety of housing units at reasonable prices. . . ." The USGS facility was due to open in spring 1974. Six months before that, it appeared that the agency might face a second challenge.

The county board was considering legal action to bar the agency from occupying the facility because there was not adequate housing in the area for employees. Although the agency and Reston claimed that there was sufficient housing to meet the needs, the county board contended that the freeze on subsidized housing funds had resulted in a housing shortage.[14]

As a result of such cases in the Washington, D.C. area, and the desire to avoid additional legal problems, GSA issued a temporary edict that no more agencies under its jurisdiction would be moved from Washington to the suburbs. Thus, GSA prevented the Government Printing Office, a largely black unit, from relocating out of the city.

The Brookhaven Case

A case involving an Internal Revenue Service data processing center in Brookhaven, New York has become the first major test of Executive Order 11512 and the HUD-GSA memorandum. This case has nationwide implications, since the objective is to force GSA to award facilities only to those suburban towns that are willing to provide needed low- and moderate-income housing.

Brookhaven is one of nine towns in Suffolk County. It is Long Island's largest town in area, and fastest growing in population. The 1960 population of Brookhaven was 109,900; the 1970 population was 226,000 and projected population for 1980 is 500,000. Three percent of the town is black.

The IRS center, which opened in the summer of 1972, provides 4,000 jobs, 2,500 year round and 1,500 more during tax season. A majority of the employees will be in lower-salaried positions; 75 percent will earn less than $7,320. The annual payroll will be $19 million. The Town of Brookhaven is the developer and owner of the building and will receive $3 million annual rent from the federal government for a 20 year lease period. The construction cost of the facility is $25 million.

The IRS Selection Process. In May 1969 IRS contracted with a private research organization to identify potential areas for three data processing centers in the U.S. Suffolk County was one of the areas recommended. In July of that year a survey made by the GSA regional office of an enlarged delineated area in western Suffolk produced 17 potential sites. In March 1970 GSA began to advertise requirements for the IRS site. They received 13 offers at the close of advertising in June. The New York regional GSA office recommended the Brookhaven site because the town's bid was the lowest (in terms of rental charged to the government), accessibility to the site was good (it was between two major east-west arteries) and there was a high concentration of low-income families and unemployed persons in Brookhaven and neighboring Islip. Brookhaven received the award in September 1970.

As part of its application, Brookhaven had submitted to GSA a socio-economic report on housing indicating that there would be adequate housing for employees when the facility opened. The report said that within a 20 mile radius of the site 4,000 homes were being sold each year for under $13,500 and 14,000 homes between $13,500 and $20,000. In spite of the incredibly low sale values listed, GSA never attempted to check the validity of the information before the site was approved. GSA relied entirely on the town's assurances and a 1967 FHA study.

Five months after Brookhaven received the award for the site GSA asked the town to document the statistics in its housing report. The town sent GSA about 500 deed transfer slips. Based on these slips, GSA had calculated the average cost of a single family home at $12,414.[15] However, in June 1971 *Newsday*, a Long Island daily newspaper, found that the town had duped federal officials. Its list of low-income houses included 53 seasonal homes, 16 vacant lots and nine commercial establishments, including a bowling alley. Town officials said that these were an oversight. A further check of the slips indicated that one out of every three did not include a mortgage value on the house, but only the cash that apparently changed hands as a down payment. Examples taken from the slips showed a home represented as costing $1,500 really cost $23,000 and a home represented as costing $14,500 actually cost $48,000.

The Bi-County Regional Planning Commission aslo found that Brookhaven's housing situation was very different from what the town had represented to GSA. It calculated the 1968 low- and moderate-income housing need to be 3,800 units. Sixteen percent of the town's housing, 50 percent greater than the county average, was substandard. There were 3,000 deteriorated or dilapidated housing units. Yet there were no publicly assisted housing units in the town.

The Brookhaven Town Board began to fear that it would not meet GSA housing requirements. The board passed a resolution stating that it would consider creating a public housing authority. The resolution was passed and forwarded to GSA in August of 1970. GSA responded that "our job in award- ing a federal facility is not to provide adequate housing for every person in the town, or wipe out substandard housing," and thus whether or not Brookhaven has a housing authority is a "purely local issue." [16] In December 1970, just three months after receiving the contract, the town board voted against creating a public housing authority. This action received no criticism or comment from GSA. In July 1971 the town board rejected a public housing authority for the second time.

Shortly before the award, two GSA investigators who had been assigned to gather information on the availability of low- and moderate-income housing in the environs of Brookhaven concluded that there was practically no low-income housing in these townships. GSA rejected these findings by its own staff and accepted at face value the housing report by Brookhaven.

The Legal Challenge. Following the town board's initial rejection of a housing authority, the Brookhaven Housing Coalition decided to sue. The coalition, which represents about 20 local religious and community groups, had been pressing the town for creation of a public housing authority and provision of lower-income housing for a year. The Coalition, joined by the National Committee Against Discrimination in Housing and the NAACP, filed suit in 1971 to enjoin the town from leasing the IRS center to the govern- ment unless the town agreed to provide an adequate supply of low-income housing. The suit alleged that the GSA violated Title VIII of the Civil Rights Act, Executive Order 11512 and its own site selection rules in selecting Brook- haven. The complaint also alleged that GSA "did not make an objective and meaningful investigation of the availability of housing . . . prior to the selection of the site," and that neither GSA nor IRS made any serious attempt to assure that Brookhaven would take affirmative action to open up housing opportunities. [17]

In April 1972 Federal District Judge Orrin G. Judd found that GSA had violated Executive Order 11512 and issued a preliminary injunction. He held that "the Executive Order was intended for the benefit of both em- ployees and nonemployee residents of the area," and that it "calls for affirma- tive action" by GSA to promote equal housing opportunities in conjunction with locating federal facilities. [18] As a partial remedy, the court ordered GSA to insure that certain federally-owned housing units at the former Suffolk Air Force Base be made available for low- and moderate-income families. These 220 units of housing were located 22 miles from the IRS center. Because of the advanced stage of construction, the judge refused to enjoin the govern- ment from occupying the IRS center.

Shortly after the decision, GSA requested the court to dissolve or modify the injunction because the government desired to sell the air force base housing to the town of Southampton. The town intended to sponsor a middle-income development with these units. The plaintiffs opposed this motion, arguing that GSA's proposal would not further housing opportunities for low-income families and that GSA had failed to come forth with a plan of affirmative action to insure minority access to these units. Most of these units have at least three bedrooms, making them very appropriate for use as low-income family housing. The district court denied GSA's request to change the earlier order. The judge stated that, with respect to the air force base units, GSA could "comply with legal requirements by including an affirmative action plan to assure that low-income and minority group families will in fact occupy an appropriate proportion of the units."[19] Furthermore, the court said "the assurances should be specific and not general." GSA appealed this denial to the U.S. Court of Appeals. GSA had still not undertaken an affirmative action plan as of the beginning of 1973.

If a suburb wants the benefits of the presence of a federal facility, it should be willing to supply low-income housing on an open occupancy basis. Brookhaven was not cooperative in doing so. GSA, the federal agency responsible, was not diligent in seeing that the town provided housing. GSA remained part of the problem.

GSA Potential

Senator Ribicoff's Government Facilities Location Act would help make GSA part of the solution. The bill prohibits federal agencies (and contractors) from locating in a town which does not have an acceptable plan for housing for low- and middle-income employees. When an agency must locate in a community which does not meet housing criteria, the government will provide the housing for current and potential lower- and middle-income employees. Community development grants would be offered to localities with acceptable housing plans. This would compensate the city for its expense in providing the extra services needed by additional population. Until the passage of such a law, pressure on the relevant agencies, including additional litigation, will be necessary to direct federal facilities into inclusionary communities. The government's economic leverage is one of its major tools for opening the suburbs. If the government fails to carry out its mandate, it should be forced to do so.

Chapter Fifteen

Federal Enforcement of Civil Rights Provisions

The federal government has a variety of civil rights laws and executive orders related to housing at its disposal. Federal policy prohibits discrimination in housing on the basis of race, color, religion, sex or national origin. Although these civil rights guarantees are not couched in terms of income, they relate to lower-income people because a disproportionate number of minorities are in this income group. Thus, equalizing the housing opportunities of blacks and other minorities often requires providing low- and moderate-income housing. For this reason, civil rights guarantees can be useful vehicles for opening up low- and moderate-income housing opportunities in suburbia.

Executive Order 11063

The federal role in assuring nondiscrimination in housing began on November 20, 1962 when President Kennedy issued Executive Order 11063. It directed

> all departments and agencies in the executive branch of the Federal Government, insofar as their functions relate to the provision, re-habilitation, or operation of housing and related facilities, to take all action necessary and appropriate to prevent discrimination because of race, color, creed or national origin.[1]

Two major areas of housing were not covered by the order: those financed by mortgage lending institutions whose deposits were insured by the federal government; and housing which had received federal aid before the order was issued. Housing covered by the order comprised only one percent of the nation's housing inventory. While the coverage of the order was rather limited, the sanctions provided were relatively strong. Enforcement was authorized through litigation. The federal government could also withdraw funds from those who did not comply with the order. These sanctions remain virtually unused. The executive order has had little impact.

Title VI of the 1964 Civil Rights Act
Title VI of the Civil Rights Act of 1964 enlarged the coverage of the guaranty of nondiscrimination.

> No person in the United States shall, on the ground of race, color, or national origin, be excluded from participation in, be denied the benefits of, or be subjected to discrimination under any program or activity receiving Federal financial assistance.[2]

Title VI applied to all public housing and urban renewal programs. However, it did not cover contracts of insurance or guaranty, or conventionally financed housing. The means of enforcement were essentially the same as those under the executive order. This law has also had little impact on housing patterns, in part because of the cumbersome procedures necessary before suspension or withholding of funds.

Title VIII of the 1968 Civil Rights Act
HUD and the Justice Department share the responsibility for enforcement of the federal fair housing law. The president's statement of June 1971 outlined the law and the enforcement responsibilities of these departments.

> In the Civil Rights Act of 1968, the Congress declared that 'It is the policy of the United States to provide, within constitutional limitations, for fair housing throughout the United States.'
> Title VIII of the 1968 act goes beyond the previous statutes (which in terms of housing, had dealt only with that which was federally assisted) to prohibit discrimination on account of race, color, religion or national origin in most private real estate actions, whether sale or rental and regardless of whether Federal assistance is involved or not. . . .
> Title VIII of the 1968 Civil Rights Act requires HUD to investigate complaints of housing discrimination and, where appropriate, to attempt to resolve such complaints through persuasion or conciliation. . . .
> Under the terms of Title VIII of the 1968 Civil Rights Act, the Attorney General is empowered to bring suits in Federal Court where he finds that racial discrimination in housing constitutes a 'pattern or practice,' or where housing discrimination cases raise issues of general public importance.[3]

Title VIII of the Civil Rights Act of 1968 expanded the prohibitions on discrimination in housing to include financing, advertising, brokerage, sale and rental of housing. HUD's enforcement powers are limited to investigation and voluntary conciliation. If HUD decides that litigation is necessary, it must recommend that course of action to the Justice Department and relinquish responsibility for the matter.

HUD's Implementation of the Fair Housing Law

To carry out its fair housing responsibilities, HUD established a system to handle complaints of discrimination. When a complaint is received HUD investigates it and, if warranted, attempts to conciliate it. During this process HUD cannot prevent the sale or rental of the property in question. It has no power to issue cease and desist orders. If conciliation efforts are successful, a settlement agreement is drawn up and signed by HUD, the complainant and the respondent. A typical agreement includes an offer of the housing sought or comparable housing and, sometimes, a monetary award. The latter would be compensation for the humiliation experienced and for extra expenses induced by the discrimination. The agreement might also include a commitment by the respondent to reform marketing practices with regard to minorities as well as to take affirmative steps to make the nondiscriminatory policy known to the public. If the conciliation conference is unsuccessful the complaint can be turned over to the Justice Department for possible prosecution.

While HUD set up a system to handle complaints of housing discrimination, and a number of people have secured housing and/or damages, the process has not significantly altered metropolitan housing patterns. The housing market available to minority groups has not widened significantly. Case by case investigation and resolution of complaints is a time-consuming process. A 1971 study by the U.S. Civil Rights Commission found that the average time for processing a complaint was five to six months and in some cases a year passed between the date of filing and the final conciliation. Initially, HUD projected that 10,000 complaints would be received in 1969. However, HUD received only 3,206 fair housing complaints nationwide in fiscal year 1973. This number represents a 19 percent increase over 1972. HUD closed 2,806 cases in fiscal year 1973.[4] In sum, the complaint process, which represents the bulk of title VIII enforcement, is a limited one. HUD's powers are limited. The staff is limited. The number of cases which can be handled is small relative to the dimensions of the problem. The institutional practices which keep blacks, particularly those of lower-income, out of the suburbs remain largely untouched by this process. HUD's fair housing enforcement efforts relate only randomly to suburban housing for lower-income families. Much of the enforcement effort involves discrimination against middle-income blacks, both in cities and suburbs, and relatively little relates to lower-income blacks seeking housing in suburbia.

Department of Justice

The primary fair housing responsibility of the Department of Justice is the implementation of section 813 of Title VIII. This section gives the attorney general responsibility for eliminating patterns and practices of discrimination in housing and acting against denials of equal housing opportunity which raise issues of general importance. As in the case of HUD, most of the Justice Department's efforts have involved purely racial discrimination with few implications for economic integration. Some of these suits have involved major defendants, including cases involving 21,000 housing units in New York City, 9,000 units in Los Angeles and 14 large real estate companies in Cleveland. Most of the litigation has resulted in consent decrees, entered voluntarily by the defendants and without judicial findings of discrimination. These decrees generally include permanent injunctions against future discrimination and provisions for affirmative relief, such as inclusion of fair housing statements in advertisements, advertising in minority media, other solicitation of purchasers in minority areas and supplying fair housing groups with vacancy lists. These steps are designed to correct the effects of past discrimination.

In addition to consent decrees, the Justice Department has achieved some court victories in fair housing litigation involving private discrimination. However, the department has played an extremely limited role in challenging communities, particularly suburbs, which discriminate by excluding low- and moderate-income housing. It has been involved in only three such lawsuits. In *Kennedy Park Homes* v. *Lackawanna,* the Justice Department intervened and obtained a court order requiring local approval of a subsidized housing development outside of the city's black ghetto.[5] In the first suit involving suburban exclusion, *United States* v. *City of Black Jack, Missouri,* the Justice Department alleged that this St. Louis suburb's conduct in blocking the construction of a subsidized housing project had "the purpose and effect of perpetuating racial segregation in housing," in violation of Title VIII.[6]

The Justice Department's role in moving against exclusionary communities was explained by the president's housing statement of 1971:

> The courts have also held that when its reasons for doing so are racial, a community may not rezone in order to exclude a federally assisted housing development. In such cases, where change in land use regulations are made for what turns out to be a racially discriminatory purpose, the Attorney General, in appropriate circumstances, will also bring legal proceedings.[7]

The federal government's policy, then, is that it will not sue exclusionary suburbs merely because they have no minority residents, even if the nearby central city has a large percentage of blacks and low-income people. The rationale is that the absence of minorities could be due to factors other than racial discrimination. The Justice Department will not initiate litigation unless there have been demonstrable acts by the municipality which strongly suggest that racial discrimination is the purpose behind exclusionary measures. Displays of discriminatory conduct will, of course, become increasingly rare as communities become more sophisticated and develop appropriate rhetoric to conceal discriminatory purposes.

Lackawanna, New York
In the cases filed against municipalities, the Justice Department identified overt actions of discrimination by the local communities. In *Lackawanna*, the vast majority of the city's black population lived in substandard housing in the first ward. The second and third wards were essentially white, with better housing than the black area. In response to community opposition to a proposed subsidized project in the third ward, the city council rezoned the area for park and recreational purposes. The council also imposed an indefinite moratorium on approval of subdivisions. After the developer sued, and the federal government intervened on the side of the developer, the council rescinded the rezoning and the moratorium. However, the mayor later refused to approve an extension of the sewer system necessary for the proposed subdivision.

Based on the facts presented in the trial, the district court concluded that the actions of the city officials were in response to the discriminatory attitudes of the community, which sought to continue the confinement of the city's low-income blacks to the first ward. The court of appeals affirmed this finding, declaring that "racial motivation resulting in invidious discrimination guided the actions of the city." [8] The Supreme Court declined to hear the case, so the court of appeals decision stood.

Black Jack, Missouri
The discriminatory actions of the community in the *Black Jack* case were perhaps even more blatant than in *Lackawanna*. In December 1969 Park View Heights Corporation, a nonprofit organization, contracted to buy a piece of land for a subsidized housing development. The site was in an unincorporated area of St. Louis County. County zoning permitted multifamily use of the type proposed by Park View Heights. As the plans for a racially integrated housing development received public attention, opposition arose in the area. Local citizens created the municipality of Black Jack, and the newly formed city council adopted a zoning ordinance which effectively prohibited multifamily construction in the city. Extensive evidence indicated that opponents of the project used racially-directed scare tactics to arouse community sentiment against the project. The Justice Department alleged that this ordinance violated Title VIII and requested the court to order the city to take the necessary steps to permit prompt construction of the subsidized development.

These allegations were made against a history of racial discrimination in Black Jack. The Justice Department had discovered evidence of discrimination in the private housing market, which was 98 percent white and only two percent black. This evidence of past discrimination allowed the Justice Department to argue that the present action prohibiting the multifamily development would freeze present discriminatory patterns and was therefore unconstitutional.

Even with clear evidence of racial discrimination, the Justice Department was reluctant to file suit in Black Jack. On November 11, 1969 HUD requested the attorney general to bring an action. It was not until a year and a half later (three days after the president's equal housing statement) that the suit was filed. By that time, the American Civil Liberties Union had already filed a suit against the city involving the same housing development.

Parma, Ohio

The *Black Jack* case does not seem to have set a pattern for Justice Department enforcement of title VIII. The Department did not file its next suit against an allegedly exclusionary community until April 27, 1973. The department sued the City of Parma, Ohio, the largest suburb of Cleveland. Parma has a population of 100,216, of whom 50 persons are black. As in *Black Jack*, a suit by a private organization preceded the Justice Department cases. This time the National Committee Against Discrimination in Housing brought the initial suit.

In November 1971 Parma voters passed two ordinances which are challenged in this lawsuit. One requires a majority referendum before city approval of any subsidized housing project. The second imposes a 35-foot height limit on all housing. The complaint alleged that the city had prevented the construction of section 236 housing on account of race and "adopted and implemented procedures which have the purpose and effect of preventing the construction of racially integrated housing for persons of low- and moderate-income, and of discouraging prospective sponsors of such housing from attempting to build it in Parma."[9] A developer of a 200 unit subsidized project for the elderly was barred from building the development by the city. The Justice Department alleged that these actions constituted a denial of housing to blacks in violation of Title VIII of the Civil Rights Act of 1968.

Consistent with the president's 1971 statement, the Justice Department indicated that the suit "is not to enforce economic integration but to insure that there are no artificial barriers to equal opportunity in housing for all persons regardless of race."[10] The relief requested was an injunction against:

    (a) Interfering with any person or group of persons seeking to exercise the right to equal housing opportunity with regard to race, color, religion or national origin, or the right to aid or encourage others in the exercise of those rights;

    (b) Discriminating against any person or group of persons on account of race, color, religion or national origin, in the planning, development, or implementation of any program or project relating to housing;

(c) Engaging in any conduct which has the purpose or effect of perpetuating or promoting racial residential segregation; and

(d) Failing or refusing to take all necessary and appropriate steps to correct the effects of its past unlawful practices.[11]

The Stance of the Justice Department

Even if the *Black Jack* and *Parma* cases resulted in important precedents as well as construction of the housing projects at issue, this volume of litigation would not reflect an aggressive federal posture. The Justice Department has set a pace of filing one suit every two years against an allegedly discriminatory community. There are certainly many other communities which have adopted zoning or referendum ordinances and which had racially discriminatory motives in so doing. The Justice Department should focus much of its Title VIII effort on these cases with potential for broad impact. However, the policy appears to be to continue the politically safer course of responding to complaints against landlords, developers and realtors where the victims are not necessarily poor and the housing not necessarily suburban.

Section 808 (e) (5)

Section 808 (e) (5) of Title VIII provides that "[t]he Secretary of Housing and Urban Development shall administer the programs and activities relating to housing and urban development in a manner affirmatively to further the policy of this title."[12] There is no legislative history to explain what Congress intended when it gave the Secretary of HUD this broad affirmative mandate. Hearings on Title VIII did not focus on this provision. It remained for HUD to interpret this general requirement. The project selection criteria and the affirmative marketing requirements for the subsidized housing programs are based in part on section 808 (e) (5). Although it was not always articulated by HUD, many of the carrot and stick approaches, such as the Warren, Michigan effort, used as part of their rationale HUD's affirmative fair housing responsibility.

Section 808 (e) (5) is probably a sufficiently broad mandate to provide HUD with the legal authority to take far-ranging steps, like imposing absolute conditions on all of its grant, insurance and other programs. HUD could render ineligible any applicant whose supply of low- and moderate-income housing, as well as other kinds of housing for minorities, proves inadequate.

Corporate Relocation as Employment Discrimination

Title VII of the 1964 Civil Rights Act prohibits discrimination in employment on grounds of race, sex, national origin, color and religion. The Equal Employment Opportunity Commission (EEOC) and the Justice Department are charged with enforcement of this law. Like the Justice Department, EEOC efforts have focused on individual complaints and traditional kinds of discrimination such as refusal to hire minorities, discriminatory testing procedures, or differential salaries and advancement opportunities. The EEOC should also direct its attention to moves by companies from a central city to suburbia. These relocations may constitute a violation of the Civil Rights Act.

As indicated in Chapter 1, corporate relocation to the suburbs may have a substantial detrimental impact on lower-income employees, particularly minorities. Often a company moves to an area where there is no housing for these employees currently available, under construction, or planned for the immediate future. The employees are forced to choose between giving up their jobs or commuting at great expense, assuming this trip is feasible. Thus, the move may eliminate a source of jobs for minority workers living in the inner city, while increasing opportunities for predominantly white management personnel already residing in the suburbs.

Interpreting Title VII

Because of the differential impact of corporate relocations, these moves may violate Title VII. Section 703 of the 1964 law makes it unlawful for an employer to engage in discriminatory employment practices. In 1971 the Supreme Court interpreted this provision to mean that any employment practice that has a disparate impact on minority workers is prima facie illegal. The employer then has the burden to prove that the practice was not discriminatory. The Supreme Court, in *Griggs* v. *Duke Power Company*, defined a two step approach for evaluating an employment practice.[13] First, does the practice discriminate against any person or group because of race? This includes "not only overt discrimination but also practices that are fair in form, but discriminatory in operation."[14] Second, does the practice bear a demonstrable relationship to successful performance on the job? "If an employment practice which operates to exclude Negroes (or other minority representatives) cannot be shown to be related to the job performance, the practice is prohibited."[15]

Under the act, discrimination is illegal with respect to the "compensation, terms, conditions and privileges of employment, because of such individual's race, color, religion, or national origin."[16] If an employer locates a facility in an area where blacks cannot obtain housing, he is effectively offering them jobs under different terms and conditions than those offered persons who are able to live nearby. A memorandum prepared by the EEOC general counsel's office supported this position:

> The transfer of an employer's facilities constitutes a *prima facie* violation of Title VII if (1) the community from which an employer moves has a higher percentage of minority workers than the community to which he moves, or (2) the transfer affects the employment situation of the employer's minority workers more adversely than it affects his remaining workers, and (3) the employer fails to take measures to correct such disparate effects.[17]

The memo suggested that once this prima facie violation is established, the offending company bears the burden of proving that his action served a valid business purpose. The employer must show that the relocation is vital to the operation of his business and that the advantages outweigh the discriminatory effect on the minority workforce. Second, he must prove that the move will effectively carry out the business purpose the move is intended to serve. Next, the employer must show that there is no acceptable alternative which would better accomplish the business purpose or achieve it equally well with less racial impact. Finally, he must also show that the relocation would improve the company's competitive position more than a move to an area where minority workers reside. Court decisions have set stringent standards where the violator claimed justification due to overriding business needs. In *Diaz* v. *Pan American Airways* the federal court said that a policy having a discriminatory impact is valid only when the essence or primary function of a business would be undermined by a contrary policy.[18]

In spite of the EEOC general counsel's memorandum and the commission chairman's public statement that "the physical removal of jobs beyond the reach of minority workers is . . . a violation of Title VII, by bringing about a forseeable discriminatory effect," the EEOC has still not taken formal action against any company on the issue.[19]

The EEOC should adopt its counsel's interpretation that

> a corporate relocation or proposed relocation to a suburban area where minority workers do not reside constitutes a violation of Title VII unless the corporation has taken steps to assure equal employment opportunity.[20]

Of course, the corporation could forego relocating, or meet its obligations by carrying out special minority recruitment programs or paying commuting expenses and offering continued employment to central city workers. Instead of concentrating on facilitating commuting, the employer could "use legal and commercial leverage to assure housing opportunities for minorities."[21] If commuting was impossible, the corporation could fulfill the legal requirements only by seeing to it that housing was provided for minority employees. Much of the housing needed would probably be for low- and moderate-income people.

To enforce the requirements, EEOC should systematically review proposed corporate relocations to suburbia. It should intervene in any instance where the move may have a disparate detrimental impact on minority employees. EEOC should not wait, as it generally does, for a complaint to be filed. Instead, it should use its authority to initiate proceedings on its own motion against the offending company. The commission would then investigate the proposed move further and either (1) dismiss it as not constituting a violation of the act, or (2) determine that there is reasonable cause to believe that the complaint is well-founded. A finding of illegal action is not necessary to trigger

EEOC efforts to provide relief. If a probable violation is found the commission can try to remedy the allegedly unlawful practice by informal methods of conciliation. The EEOC can seek agreement from the employer and the local community to take specified steps to increase the housing opportunities for minority and lower-income workers. This process would provide the corporation and the community with an incentive to move quickly to develop acceptable housing plans and secure the necessary approval and cooperation at the local level. Any delay on housing would impede the employer's move to a new facility. Although the administrative process can be a slow and tortuous one, it may be hastened by the fact that delay in resolving the housing issue may not be in the interest of any of the parties. In cases where the EEOC cannot obtain a satisfactory conciliation agreement, it can seek judicial enforcement. Should the commission be successful in court, failure to comply would then constitute contempt of court.

With its authority to conciliate and go to court, the EEOC has potential for influencing corporate relocations By seeking preliminary injunctive relief, the agency may be able to delay moves until adequate housing is provided. This potential should be tapped.

Executive Orders 11246 and 11375

The Department of Labor's Office of Federal Contract Compliance (OFCC) also has civil rights enforcement responsibilities. It implements Executive Orders 11246 and 11375, which regulate the employment practices of government contractors. All employers covered are required to take affirmative action to provide equal employment opportunity. The presence or absence of prior discrimination is irrelevant. The executive orders cover all facilities of a federal contractor even if only one of the contractor's facilities is engaged in work on a government contract. Noncompliance with federal contract requirements can result in contract cancellation and/or debarment from future federal contracts.

The federal contract compliance effort has significant potential since it is estimated that about one-third of the nation's labor force is employed by companies which are federal contractors and that there are more than 100,000 employment facilities where government contracts are involved.

In Philadelphia, the OFCC imposed goals and timetables for minority employment on federal and federally-assisted construction contractors. This "Philadelphia Plan" implemented the affirmative action requirement. The Court of Appeals for the Third Circuit, in *Contractors Ass'n* v. *Shultz*, upheld this interpretation of the executive orders.[22] Since these actions were based on the federal government's purchasing power rather than on civil rights authority, the court held that setting goals was justifiable in order to have available a pool of trained minority workers for the federal construction program. To the extent that government contractors are located in suburbia, the court's holding seems to support the imposition of housing requirements by OFCC to provide a minority employment pool. The Department of Labor could either proceed on a case by case basis or adopt regulations relating to housing obligations of government contractors relocating in the suburbs or already located there.

OFCC employs a compliance review to administer Executive Orders 11246 and 11375. Personnel of the contracting agency, supervised by the OFCC, evaluate the employer's affirmative action plan. The plan analyzes minority employment problems and provides goals and timetables for their resolution. Although the general requirement of an affirmative action plan was adopted in 1968, the Labor Department did not specify employer obligations until it issued Order Number 4 in 1970.[23] This regulation requests an analysis by the employer of his underutilization of minorities. Most of the factors to be considered relate to the area surrounding the facility. For a suburban operation minority residents and workers in the immediate area may be minimal, so these standards are not useful. However, the employer must also analyze "the availability of minorities having requisite skills in an area in which the contractor can reasonably recruit."[24] This provision puts the suburban employer on notice to consider central city minorities in establishing his goals for minority employment. Corrective action is to be taken if the analysis reveals, among other things, lack of access to suitable housing [which] inhibits employment of qualified minorities for professional and management positions. Thus, Order Number 4 contemplates, in part, the lack of access of central city minorities to suburban job sites and imposes an obligation on employer-contractors to take remedial action. However, the order deals with existing facilities and imposes no clear requirements on contractors seeking to relocate in suburbia. For this reason it has been suggested that:

> Order Number 4 should be amended to require explicitly that all government contractors adopt a plant location or removal policy which will force them to consider minority employment implications. Furthermore, they should be required to report proposed plant movements, their analysis of the probable effect upon minority employment, and their plans in detail including cost estimates, for meeting the problem. In this way, the administration of the executive order could assure that contractor-employers were not only cognizant of the problem but had taken all appropriate steps to deal with it.[25]

Part III

Private Sector Strategies for Suburban Access

Chapter Sixteen

Introduction to Private Sector Strategies

Even if public bodies were meeting their responsibilities and fulfilling their potential for increasing suburban access, there would still be a need for an open suburbs movement of private organizations. Public agencies are not doing this job, so private action is absolutely critical to achieving open suburbs. Private groups have stepped into this vacuum. They have challenged the communities directly. They have pressured the public bodies to carry out their responsibilities and they have worked to build political support for what has been an unpopular cause.

Efforts by private organizations to overcome suburban barriers reached a significant scale in the late 1960s. The open suburbs movement, as it has been called, has relied heavily on litigation as a strategy. Many lawsuits have challenged exclusionary local ordinances or practices. Some have attacked attempts by localities to block specific subsidized projects. Several recent cases have challenged the overall zoning patterns of a locality or a group of localities. These cases seek to establish an affirmative responsibility to provide for low- and moderate-income housing.

In addition to zoning lawsuits, other exclusionary practices, such as failure to approve the use of subsidy programs and refusal to issue building permits for low-income housing projects have also been challenged in court. Other suits attempt to pressure public agencies to observe their own requirements and guidelines. For example, the *Brookhaven* lawsuit was initiated because local groups felt that the General Services Administration had not fulfilled the requirements of the executive order in selecting a site for the Internal Revenue Service facility.

In addition to these and other housing cases, lawsuits involving public schools may have some impact on suburban barriers to low- and moderate-income housing. One set of cases involves efforts to desegregate schools on a metropolitan basis rather than solely within a central city. The school finance cases involve attempts to equalize expenditures for public education among school districts. Depending on their outcome, these cases could affect suburban incentives to exclude low- and moderate-income housing.

Choosing Litigation as a Strategy

The movement to open the suburbs is a minority movement; it does not have the support of the majority of the population. Most suburbanites want to continue keeping out low- and moderate-income people. Inner-city blacks and black leaders have not become deeply involved in opening the suburbs. Although surveys indicate that many lower-income blacks would like to move to the suburbs, it has not become a gut issue, like job discrimination or police brutality. Some black leaders oppose opening the suburbs because of the fear of eroding the black political base in the central city. Finally, the coalition of whites which supported the civil rights movement in the 1960s has not become active in opening the suburbs. Labor, the church and intellectuals have not been mobilized on this issue, perhaps in part because it hits too close to home.

The open suburbs movement thus does not have a broad base of public support. For this reason litigation has been viewed as a useful strategy. It does not require vast rallies or lobbying campaigns to bring about change. A second reason for the choice of a litigation strategy is that many of the organizations involved had previously been committed to using the courts as their vehicle for social change. In addition, many of these organizations must not engage in any substantial lobbying or they will lose their tax-exempt status. Most of the groups in the open suburbs movement pay no taxes on their income. Contributions made to them are tax-deductible for the donor. Loss of tax exemption would undoubtedly mean loss of foundation support. Many of the organizations could not survive without foundation support. Consequently, they generally steer clear of lobbying. Because of their historical thrust, litigation became a logical alternative.

Litigation is viewed as having a number of additional advantages. It can influence governmental policies and practices. As suggested in Chapter 11, the *Shannon* and *Gautreaux* cases helped bring about HUD's project selection criteria and affirmative marketing requirements. Courts are often willing to move on social issues before the legislature or the bureaucracy is ready. Litigation can also be useful in negotiating with local officials. Even the threat of a lawsuit, with its attendant costs and adverse publicity for the locality, may soften the official opposition to lower-income housing. The case need never be filed, or if it is filed it may be dropped, if the community agrees to take the requested actions.

In addition to the leverage that lawsuits provide, they can be a valuable vehicle for public education. They can dramatize publicly the inequities in the land use system and get the media attention necessary to increase public support for the movement.

Finally, litigation is used to establish legal precedents which apply beyond the case at issue. Courts may establish new rights for minority or poor plaintiffs or invalidate suburban exclusionary practices. They can, in short, change the rules of the game.

Building a Constituency

Another approach pursued by voluntary organizations is to attempt to build a political base of support for suburban low- and moderate-income housing. Sometimes this effort is initiated within a single community. In the Chicago area, a metropolitanwide coalition was formed, in addition to more localized groups, to generate areawide support. Rather than challenging specific exclusionary devices, this approach seeks to establish an inclusionary framework, a regional allocation plan.

The Actors

There is a wide range of private sector actors involved in the open suburbs movement. They range from organizations formed specifically for that purpose to corporations who find that suburban exclusion creates problems for them in operating their businesses. For example, Suburban Action Institute (SAI) is

> a unique nonprofit civil rights organization founded in 1969 by two urban planners. . . . SAI works to open the suburbs of America's metropolitan areas to jobs and housing for low and moderate income families and for members of minority groups.[1]

Suburban Action Institute has undertaken a range of strategies. It has carried out many of the major exclusionary zoning cases. SAI has also performed the watchdog function with a number of federal agencies. Its affiliate, Garden Cities Development Corporation, developed the broader strategy of planning large-scale developments on suburban sites, to be implemented by litigation, if necessary. The efforts of Suburban Action and Garden Cities are focused on the New York region.

No other national or regional organization focuses so exclusively on suburban development of low- and moderate-income housing. Perhaps the National Committee Against Discrimination in Housing (NCDH) comes closest. Its focus is entirely on housing; but it deals with racial discrimination, in urban as well as suburban areas, in existing housing as well as new housing and in high- and middle-income housing as well as in lower-income housing. NCDH has become increasingly involved in exclusionary zoning lawsuits.

Other participants in this movement include civil rights and civil liberties organizations like the American Civil Liberties Union and the NAACP Legal Defense Fund. These groups are involved in a whole range of civil rights issues but devote some of their resources to the problem of suburban access.

Finally, some corporations have become aware of the suburban housing problem. As indicated in Chapter 1, they have been hurt by absenteeism and turnover resulting from the lack of suburban housing for their employees. Few corporations have been willing to engage in the struggle as yet, but pressure is likely to mount, internally as well as externally, for them to do so.

Chapter Seventeen

Exclusionary Zoning Litigation

Since the late 1960s there have been an increasing number of lawsuits challenging suburban zoning barriers to low- and moderate-income housing. This effort has become the primary focus of the open suburbs movement. Public interest organizations, nonprofit housing sponsors and private developers have brought cases challenging a whole array of exclusionary devices. These groups have sued in both state and federal courts under a variety of legal theories. Significant legal precedents have been established, undercutting some of the basis for exclusionary zoning. However, the process has not gone far enough to permit identification of many trends in these decisions.

Lawsuits have challenged most of the ordinance provisions and administrative practices described in Chapter 2. The results have been mixed. In the federal courts, cases have usually involved allegations of racial discrimination. Where the courts have found such bias, they have declared the local practice invalid as a denial of equal protection of the law. State courts, in struggling with concepts such as the "police power," the "general welfare" and "due process", have reached varying conclusions as to the validity of different practices.

Even when the courts have held exclusionary zoning practices invalid, housing for excluded economic groups has not automatically appeared. The traditional remedies provided by the courts do not insure that low- and moderate-income housing will actually be built. To date, exclusionary zoning victories have had limited impact in terms of increasing the housing opportunities in the exclusionary communities. To be effective, remedies must take into account the realities of the housing development process, such as the need for multiple local preconstruction approvals in addition to a rezoning or variance. They must clear away as many of the obstacles to construction as are within the court's power. The focus here is primarily on the remedial question because it is the effectiveness of the remedies that determines whether housing opportunities are actually expanded.

Challenging Exclusionary Practices: Ordinances

Prohibition of Apartments. Zoning ordinances which do not permit apartments anywhere in the municipality have traditionally been upheld by
the courts. However, in *Appeal of Girsh*, the Pennsylvania Supreme Court held
that it was invalid for the zoning ordinance of a Philadelphia suburb to totally
prohibit apartments.[1] The court said that the exclusion did not promote
the general welfare and was not within the state's police power. In New Jersey,
the superior court held invalid an ordinance which essentially prohibited
apartments, in *Southern Burlington County NAACP* v. *Township of Mount
Laurel*.[2]

Minimum Building Size Requirements. Perhaps the best known
case involving minimum floor space requirements for single family units is
Lionshead Lake, Inc. v. *Township of Wayne*.[3] The New Jersey court upheld the
locality's ordinance. Since that time, courts in New Jersey and other states have
invalidated similar provisions.

Exclusion of Mobile Homes. The judicial response to localities' prohibiting mobile homes has also been mixed. In New Jersey the Supreme Court
sustained an exclusion of mobile homes from an entire township of 23 square
miles. *Vickers* v. *Township Committee of Gloucester Township* held that a
locality need not permit a use which it believes would be repugnant to its
planning scheme.[4] The Michigan courts, on the other hand, have consistently
struck down provisions excluding mobile homes. In *Bristow* v. *City of Woodhaven* the Michigan Court of Appeals even invalidated a provision limiting
trailer courts to general business districts.[5] The land in this classification was
very limited and mostly developed. Therefore, the court found that the zoning
ordinance effectively excluded mobile homes from the town. The court decided
that the town had not justified this exclusion.

In Pennsylvania the intermediate court placed the burden on the
locality to justify exclusion of a legitimate use such as mobile homes. In *Derry
Borough* v. *Shomo* the court found that the real purpose of a minimum floor
area provision was to regulate and restrict mobile homes.[6] The largest mobile
home permitted on the state's roads would be too small to meet the minimum
requirements of the ordinance. The court held that the community could not
enact this kind of total exclusion without proving that the use prohibited was
detrimental to the health, welfare, safety and morals of the community.

Minimum Lot Size Requirements. The Massachusetts Supreme
Court upheld a one acre minimum lot size that covered nearly half of the town
in *Simon* v. *Town of Needham*.[7] The court relied on health and safety factors
to justify the ordinance. Many later cases in other states used similar rationales

to uphold minimum lot requirements of various sizes. Then the Pennsylvania Supreme Court took the contrary position in two landmark cases. In *National Land and Investment Co.* v. *Easttown Township Board of Adjustment* the court decided the four acre minimums were unreasonable and were therefore unconstitutional on due process grounds.[8] In *Appeal of Concord Township (Kit-Mar Builders, Inc.)* the court found the town's two and three acre minimums to be no more reasonable than the four acre provision struck down in *National Land.*[9] In *Board of County Supervisors of Fairfax County* v. *Carper* the Virginia court struck down an ordinance establishing a two acre minimum lot size for the western two-thirds of the county.[10] Finally, in *Schere* v. *Township of Freehold* the New Jersey superior court rejected a 40,000 square foot minimum lot size in an area surrounded by much smaller lots.[11]

Challenges to the Overall Ordinance

In addition to the cases challenging specific devices, recent cases have sought to invalidate entire local ordinances as exclusionary. In *Oakwood at Madison, Inc.* v. *Township of Madison* the New Jersey Superior Court struck down an ordinance which contained many exclusionary provisions—virtual exclusion of apartments, high minimum floor space requirements, and large areas zoned for one or two acre minimum lot sizes. [12]

A second far reaching New Jersey division came in the *Mount Laurel* case.[13] The local ordinance had generally prohibited apartments since 1954. It also excluded mobile homes. The superior court found the entire ordinance invalid.

Challenging Exclusionary Administrative Practices

A number of cases have challenged the failure to provide rezoning or other local approvals for specific subsidized housing projects. Several of these decisions have found violations of the plaintiffs' constitutional rights.

The federal court of appeals upheld a district court finding of unconstitutionality in *Daily* v. *City of Lawton.*[14] The city had refused to grant a rezoning necessary for the development of a low- and moderate-income project. The site of the proposed development was zoned for public facilities and was being used as a parochial school. Most of the surrounding area was zoned for relatively high-density residential uses. When the sponsor of a subsidized housing project sought to have his parcel rezoned to the same classification as the surrounding area, the application was denied. The district court concluded that the purpose of the city's inaction was racial, to "keep a large concentration of Negroes and other minority groups from living" in the area.[15] Facts relied on by the court in finding racial motivation included anonymous calls to the developers, testimony of a dissenting zoning board commissioner, and the racial composition of the area.

In *Sisters of Providence* v. *City of Evanston*, the federal district court denied a motion to dismiss the case.[16] It held that the cause of action could be sustained under both the equal protection and due process clauses of the Constitution, as well as on statutory grounds. As in *Lawton*, the city had refused to rezone a parcel of land on which a developer proposed to build federally subsidized housing. The complaint alleged that the city's denial was based on racial discrimination and that there was a history of housing segregation in this racially-mixed suburb of Chicago. The court stated that "Evanston cannot deny a petition to rezone by relying on existing zoning, absent a valid land use reason, where the effect of this denial is to further racial discrimination."[17]

A similar type of case involves the rezoning of a site in order to prohibit a proposed subsidized project. In *Kennedy Park Homes Association* v. *City of Lackawanna* the court of appeals affirmed a district court holding that the refusal by the city to permit the development of a low-income subdivision in the all-white third ward was illegal. In Lackawanna, most of the city's black population lived in substandard housing in the first ward. In response to community opposition to the proposed third ward housing project, the city council rezoned the area for park and recreational purposes. The council also imposed an indefinite moratorium on approval of subdivisions. After the developer sued, and the federal government intervened, the council rescinded the rezoning and the moratorium. However, the mayor later refused to approve an extension of the sewer system necessary for the proposed subdivision. The court found that the actions of the city officials were invalid because they were in response to the discriminatory attitudes of the community, which sought to continue the confinement of the city's low-income blacks to the first ward.

Park View Heights Corp. v. *City of Black Jack* and *G. & D. Holland Construction Company* v. *City of Marysville* also involved changes in zoning to block construction of federally subsidized housing.[18] In the *Black Jack* case a subsidized development was announced for the unincorporated area of St. Louis County, Missouri. The residents of the area decided to incorporate into the municipality of Black Jack. The city council then adopted a zoning ordinance which prohibited multifamily housing on the proposed site. The plaintiffs claimed that the action by the city constituted a "taking" of property without due process, under the Fifth and 14th Amendments, and a violation of the right to travel, the equal protection clause and the 13th Amendment. The district court dismissed the case on technical grounds, but the court of appeals reversed and sent it back for trial.

In the *Holland Construction Company* case in California, a developer obtained a zoning change to permit construction of apartments. He then sold the land to another developer who wanted to build subsidized housing on the site. When the community got wind of these plans it rezoned the property for lower density development. The court found that the second rezoning was invalid because it was intended to discriminate against lower-income people.

Finally, in *Southern Alameda Spanish-Speaking Organization (SASSO)* v. *City of Union City*, a nonprofit sponsor of subsidized housing obtained a rezoning for its site in a middle-class area of Union City.[19] However, the project was blocked by a referendum which nullified the city council's action in rezoning the parcel. The district court refused to enjoin the referendum and after the referendum the court of appeals declined to overturn it.

The court of appeals made no decision on the equal protection issue, but remanded it to the district court, asserting that a substantial constitutional question was raised if the plan was discriminatory and denied "decent housing and an integrated environment to low-income residents of Union City."[20] The district court did not find that the zoning denial violated equal protection rights but did find that the housing problem for lower-income residents of Union City was so severe that failure by the city to take immediate action to alleviate the problem would result in a denial of equal protection. The court

> reserved the right . . . to grant plaintiffs relief in respect to rezoning . . . if and when it finds . . . that the housing situation has become such that the failure to rezone has become, in effect, denial of decent housing to low-income residents and denial of equal protection of the law.[21]

These cases all involve administration of the zoning process to bar particular lower-income housing developments. When the plaintiffs have demonstrated a racial motive or purpose, the federal courts have found the action unconstitutional. However, if the local purpose in blocking a project relates to economic exclusion, its validity remains an open question. The Supreme Court's decision in *James* v. *Valtierra* further muddies these waters.[22] In that case, the Supreme Court upheld the validity of a California law requiring local referenda for public housing projects. It emphasized the fundamental character of the suffrage and the historically widespread use of the referendum in California. Still, this leaves open the question of whether a community may refuse to rezone, or rezone, for the purpose of excluding lower-income housing. As one commentator has said:

> The *Lawton-SASSO-Lackawanna* rulings constituted an impressive first round of 14th Amendment challenges to exclusionary zoning. They set forth strong principles of law indicating that the Federal Courts were prepared to protect minorities and the poor from zoning and planning decisions which deprive them of equal housing opportunities. These victories, however, were followed by a setback in April, 1971, when the U.S. Supreme Court held in *James* v. *Valtierra* that a California constitutional provision requiring local voter referendum approval as a prerequisite for the construction

of public housing was constitutional. . . . Two post- *Valtierra* decisions (*Crow* v. *Brown, Sisters of Providence* v. *City of Evanston*) do indicate that the lower courts are still prepared to move boldly in ruling on Fourteenth Amendment challenges in this area.[23]

Remedies: Getting Housing Built

Even if the plaintiff secures a favorable decision in an exclusionary zoning case, the difficult task remains of designing and carrying out a remedy that will provide actual housing opportunities. Exclusionary zoning cases have not generally been successful by this measure. A number of cases have provided valuable precedents, but little housing has resulted. The traditional remedies have failed to recognize the scope of the locality's involvement in the development process. The courts have generally limited themselves to prohibitive and injunctive approaches, rather than flexible, affirmative ones which seek to facilitate housing development instead of merely removing a specific obstacle. The courts have usually stepped out of the picture after issuing a limited initial order, thus inviting evasion by the locality.

Winning in Court, Losing at the Site

Several Pennsylvania zoning cases illustrate the practical difficulties involved in converting a judicial victory into new housing opportunities. In these cases, the housing proposed was not even for low- and moderate-income people. The developers were seeking to use their land more intensively than the zoning permitted in order to make a greater profit in building housing for relatively affluent families. Still, the roadblocks were set up.

In *National Land and Investment Co.* v. *Easttown Township Board of Adjustment*, the developer challenged an ordinance which required a minimum lot size of four acres.[24] He had been denied a building permit to construct a single family home on a one acre lot. In *Appeal of Girsh*, the developer sought to build two nine-story luxury apartment houses on a tract of land zoned for single family dwellings. In the last of this Pennsylvania triumvirate, *Appeal of Concord Township* (*Kit-Mar Builders, Inc.*), the developer requested the right to build single family homes on one acre lots rather than the two and three acre lots which the township required.[25]

In each of these cases, the court found that the locality had acted illegally. However, the municipality was able to prevent the proposed developments from being built, while complying literally with the court order:

> None of the landmark decisions of the Supreme Court of Pennsylvania . . . resulted in a victory for the builder in the sense that the builder was able, as a result of litigation, to construct the development he proposed to build. Joseph Girsh never built his apartments. After the decision of the Supreme Court, *In re Girsh* . . . the

Township classified several properties other than that owned by
Girsh for apartment development. The present owners of the Girsh
property are still attempting to convince the Township and the
courts that apartments should be permitted on the tract involved in
the *Girsh* case. In fact, the Girsh property, possibly as a result of the
persistence demonstrated by the would-be developers, has now been
condemned as a public park. . . .
    Kit-Mar Builders . . . are still negotiating for subdivision approval.
. . . Finally, even after the Supreme Court invalidated the four-acre
zoning involved in *National Land and Investment Co.* v. *Easttown
Township Board of Adjustment* . . ., Easttown Township then
threatened to impose three-acre zoning. National Land finally aban-
doned its effort to build on one-acre lots, and the case was settled
at two-acre minimum lots.[26]

These cases illustrate the practical realties associated with limited
court orders. As indicated in Chapter 2, communities seeking to evade a court
order related to subsidized housing have even more devices at their command
than in the Pennsylvania cases, where the proposed developments were designed
for middle- and upper-income families.

The Courts' duty to Provide Effective Relief. Courts have a responsibility to provide effective relief once they have found a violation of the Constitution. This duty includes doing whatever is necessary to right the wrong.
The Supreme Court has stated this most clearly and frequently in the school
desegregation cases. For example, in *Green* v. *County School Board*, the
Supreme Court set as the standard of relief a decree "that promises to work,
and promises realistically to work, *now*."[27] The principle applies equally to
nonschool issues. In exclusionary zoning cases the measure of whether the
remedy is working should be actual production of low- and moderate-income
housing.

    Courts should be flexible and consider the use of all available tech-
niques. The administrative awkwardness or inconvenience involved cannot bar
the use of a particular form of relief. Finally, courts must continue supervision
of these cases until full relief has been provided. Supplemental orders, encompassing additional or different approaches from the original order, may be
necessary for this purpose.

The Beginnings of Affirmative Relief. In light of this duty to provide
effective relief, and the ineffectiveness of traditional remedies, both federal
and state courts have begun to provide affirmative kinds of relief in zoning
cases. In *Kennedy Park Homes* v. *Lackawanna*, a federal district court held that
Lackawanna has an "obligation to consider and plan for all of the citizens in

the community."[28] The court ordered the city to take whatever affirmative steps were necessary to allow the proposed subsidized housing project at issue to begin construction.

> 1. That . . . defendants shall immediately take whatever action is necessary to provide adequate sewage service to the K.P.H.A. subdivision.
> 2. That defendants affirmatively take whatever steps are necessary to allow the Kennedy Park Subdivision to begin construction.
> 3. That defendants be enjoined from issuing building permits for any construction in the second and third wards which will contribute additional sanitary sewage to the municipal system until Kennedy Park Subdivision has been granted permission to tap into the sewer system by the appropriate authority.[29]

In defining its remedial responsibility, the district court stated ". . . . the Court has not merely the power but the duty to render a decree which will so far as possible eliminate the discriminatory effects of the past as well as bar discrimination in the future."[30]

In *Southern Alameda Spanish-Speaking Organization (SASSO)* v. *City of Union City* the municipality was ordered by the court to take affirmative steps to insure equal availability of housing.[31] Union City was ordered to develop a plan for the construction of low- and moderate-income housing. The district court gave the town a ten month period to take action to remedy the plaintiffs' grievances:

> Such steps shall include, so far as necessary and reasonably feasible under the law, not only encouragement and, if possible, implementation of programs dependent on the initiative of private residential developers and upon the cooperation of private landowners or occupants, e. g., Section 235 and 236 programs, the so-called Section 23 Alameda County low-cost leasing program and housing rehabilitation grant and loan program (including, if possible, implementation of the SASSO housing Section 236 program either as now proposed or as modified) but also public housing programs requiring the exercise of the fiscal and eminent domain powers of the City if such be necessary and reasonably feasible under the law to accomplish the object of this order, in the event that private initiative and land owner cooperation (over which admittedly the City has no control) are insufficient to reasonably accommodate the housing needs of low income residents (e.g., public housing, public urban renewal programs and other similar public programs designed for that purpose).[32]

Pursuant to this order, the city rezoned 11 acres of the original

24 acre site. Construction was begun on a 140 unit subsidized housing development early in 1973.

In *Southern Burlington County NAACP* v. *Township of Mount
Laurel* the court held a zoning ordinance unconstitutional and ordered broad,
affirmative relief.[33] Mount Laurel was to prepare a plan which included identification of the housing needs of low- and moderate-income persons residing
in the township, those presently employed by the municipality or in commercial
and industrial uses in the township, and those expected to be employed by the
municipality or in commercial and industrial uses which could reasonably be
anticipated in the township.

The township was then to decide upon the estimated number of
both low- and moderate-income units which could be constructed each year to
provide for these needs. In addition, the court ordered the township to develop

> a plan of implementation . . . an affirmative program . . . to en-
> courage the satisfaction of the needs as set forth. Said plan should
> encompass the most effective and thorough means by which
> municipal action can be utilized to accomplish the goals as pre-
> viously set forth.[34]

As part of this implementation plan, the town was to consider any
problems which might interfere with the implementation of the plan. The
township was required to identify each and every said factor; the way in which
each factor interferes with or bars implementation of said plan; possible alternative plans or municipal action which could temporarily or permanently,
wholly or in part, eliminate said factors; and the reason why the alternative
plans were not'adopted.[35]

Refinement of Affirmative Remedies. Although the courts are
beginning to recognize the need for affirmative relief, they still must refine and
develop these approaches relative to: (1) remedies specific to a particular development or site; and (2) regional remedies which provide a generalized framework
for meeting what courts are increasingly identifying as a regional problem:
the need for decent housing for all families.

Single Site Cases

In the single site case, the court should remove all possible roadblocks in order to facilitate development of low- and moderate-income housing
on a particular suburban site. It would intervene at the request of a developer
or other plaintiff who had requested a rezoning to permit development of
housing for low- and moderate-income families. The requested change might be
from single family to multifamily use or from low-density multifamily to
higher-density development.

The developer must be able to proceed promptly if the project is to be successful. A court order limited to rezoning will not accomplish that objective if the community is intent on preventing construction. As indicated in Chapter 2, a municipality can throw up numerous obstructions, if it is so inclined. In response to local dilatory tactics, the court could borrow the principle of the comprehensive permit from the Massachusetts Zoning Appeals Act and apply to it the legal principle of the "set-aside." As a corollary to the duty to provide effective relief, courts may set aside state or local laws which impede complete relief, even when that law does not itself violate the Constitution. For example, the court may require local officials to ignore state law where necessary to remedy the effects of past discrimination. In *Gautreaux* v. *Chicago Housing Authority* the validity of the state law providing for city council approval of public housing sites was not at issue,[36] nor were the city council's reasons for its failure to approve sites. Indeed, in the absence of the prior constitutional violation, the city council's reasons for not approving the sites might have been valid. However, the court had already found that the plaintiff's constitutional rights had been violated by the discriminatory site and tenant selection policies of the housing authority. Thus, the court ordered relief to proceed, i.e., development of public housing, without adherence to the otherwise valid state requirement for city council site approval.

In order for the set-aside principle to apply, it is necessary only that the operation of a state or local law is frustrating constitutionally required relief. In the zoning context, the set-aside would allow the developer to bypass otherwise valid local regulations such as building code or subdivision requirements because the court has the power to set aside these requirements to get construction started. To obtain a local set-aside order, the developer would show that he made a good faith effort to obtain necessary local approvals, that these approvals were denied, and that the denial frustrates relief.

In *Metropolitan Housing Development Corporation* v. *Village of Arlington Heights* the plaintiffs requested a similar type of relief:

> Enjoin all defendants from enforcing any zoning ordinance or other restriction as to the subject property which would prohibit the proposed development and from refusing to take any affirmative steps necessary for plaintiff MHDC to begin and complete construction.[37]

As in *Lackawanna*, the plaintiffs recognized that the town might use other means to block construction of the subsidized project, even if the rezoning was granted. They requested that the court grant relief which would be effective and retain jurisdiction of the case until construction was completed. In this and other cases, the court might also require the community to provide any local approvals necessary for the use of federal subsidy programs. To insure that the site is used for low- amd moderate-income housing, even if ownership changes, the court should also make the rezoning conditional on the owner developing low- and moderate-income housing.

Large-Scale Single Site Relief. An illustration of the potential under the single site strategy is the approach of the Garden Cities Development Corporation. Garden Cities is a nonprofit housing developer affiliated with Suburban Action Institute. Early in 1972 Suburban Action announced plans to develop a 6,000-unit planned community in affluent Mahwah, New Jersey, designed to serve all income and racial groups.[38] Garden Cities Development Corporation had entered into a conditional sales contract to purchase a large piece of land in Mahwah. The site was zoned for a minimum lot size of two acres. The sale was conditional on Garden Cities obtaining a zoning amendment to permit development of townhouses and apartments according to an overall plan. In its application to the Township Committee of Mahwah and the Planning Board, requesting a zoning amendment, Garden Cities indicated its desire:

> . . . to develop a community of six thousand townhouse and garden apartment units on 720 acres of its land in Mahwah. The housing is intended to respond to the compelling local, regional and statewide need to house the elderly; young married couples and other young adults; those families of low, moderate and even middle income who cannot now afford housing on the private market; and particularly, employees of Mahwah's many commercial, industrial and educational facilities.[39]

The development would accommodate almost 19,000 people with annual incomes between $5,000 and $20,000. (The 1970 population of the 25.7 square mile town was under 11,000.) Forty percent of the dwelling units were to be subsidized. This would permit many of the 6,000 employees of Mahwah's Ford plant, as well as those of the town's Western Union, ABEX and other corporate facilities, to live in the community. Previously, only a few of these employees were able to live in Mahwah, with the remainder commuting from as far away as the ghettoes of New York City, one to two hours away.

The application for the zoning amendment was submitted in September 1972. The public hearing on the Garden Cities proposal was held in December 1972. Garden Cities Development Corporation indicated that it would challenge the town in court if the planning and zoning commission did not agree to rezone the land to accommodate the proposed development. By mid-1973, it appeared that litigation would be necessary. The Bergen County Board was considering rezoning Garden Cities' site for open space or recreational purposes.[40] If a court challenge was initiated, a favorable determination could facilitate implementation of the plan and development of an economically and racially integrated community of several thousand families.

In the year and a half after the Mahwah proposal was made public, Garden Cities Development Corporation announced plans for three additional economically and racially integrated communities. The first was a 600 acre development in Lewisboro, New York (one of the towns in the Urban Development Corporation's Nine Towns Program).[41] It was to consist of 4,600 units, housing 13,800 people. Forty percent of the units were to be for families with incomes under $10,000, 20 percent for families earning between $10,000 and $12,000, and 40 percent for households with incomes above that amount. As in the case of Mahwah, Lewisboro was a virtually all-white, affluent town. Ninety percent of its housing was single family units selling for an average of $50,000.

Garden Cities followed the Lewisboro announcement with plans for a 4,000–6,000 development in Centerport on Long Island and a $50 million community of 8,000 people in Lake Candlewood, Connecticut.[42] These proposals would almost surely face stiff resistance from the respective communities. Litigation would be needed to pave the way for actual construction.

Regional Remedies

Beyond relief related to a specific site, it is becoming apparent that in many situations housing for low- and moderate-income families must be provided on a regional basis for relief to be fully effective. The courts have recognized the regional nature of local zoning actions, particularly those related to housing.

Regional Impact of Local Zoning.   The United States Supreme Court decision which upheld the constitutionality of zoning almost 50 years ago foreshadowed the recent cases which recognize the regional impact of zoning decisions. In *Village of Euclid* v. *Ambler Realty Co.*, the Supreme Court acknowledged the "possibility of cases where the general public interest would so far outweigh the interest of the municipality that the municipality would not be allowed to stand in the way."[43]

Several zoning decisions, particularly in the courts of New Jersey and Pennsylvania, have considered whether local zoning is consistent not only with the needs of the individual community but also with the welfare of the larger region or metropolitan area. In 1949, in *Duffcon Concrete Products* v. *Borough of Cresskill*, the Supreme Court of New Jersey first indicated that local zoning decisions must consider regional impact.

> What may be the most appropriate use of any particular property depends not only on all the conditions, physical, economic and social, prevailing within the municipality and its needs present and reasonably prospective, but also on *the nature of the entire region* in which the municipality is located and the use to which the land in that region has been or may be put most advantageously. The effective development of a region should not and cannot

be made to depend upon the adventitious location of municipal boundaries, often prescribed decades or even centuries ago, and based in many instances on considerations of geography, of commerce, or of politics that are no longer significant to zoning. (Emphasis added.)[44]

Two decades later a New Jersey court reiterated this principle in invalidating a zoning amendment which had the effect of permitting only luxury apartments. The court, in *Molino* v. *Mayor and Council of the Borough of Glassboro*, said:

No municipality can isolate itself from the difficulties which are prevalent in all segments of society. When the general public interest is paramount to the limited interest of the municipality then the municipality cannot create road blocks.[45]

Local Responsibility and Regional Needs. Having required that localities consider the regional impact of certain zoning decisions, and having designated housing as a matter of regional concern, New Jersey and Pennsylvania courts have begun to indicate that local communities have a legal responsibility to accept their share of this housing. In *Oakwood at Madison, Inc.* v. *Township of Madison* the court found that housing was a use with regional impact, thus obligating each community to accept a proportionate share of the regional need.

Regional needs are a proper consideration in local zoning. . . . In pursuing the valid zoning purpose of a balanced community, a municipality must not ignore housing needs, that is, its fair proportion of the obligation to meet the housing needs of its own population and of the region. Housing needs are encompassed within the general welfare. The general welfare does not stop at each municipal boundary. Large areas of vacant and undeveloped land should not be zoned as Madison Township has, into such minimum lot sizes and with such other restrictions that regional as well as local housing needs are shunted aside.[46]

In three Pennsylvania cases invalidating exclusionary zoning ordinances, the court focused on the regional impact of these ordinances. The recognition given to the interests of nonresidents shows that the court regarded housing as a regional issue to be faced by all the region's communities. In *National Land and Investment Co.* v. *Easttown Township Board of Adjustment* the Pennsylvania Supreme Court concluded that a four acre minimum lot size ordinance was an unreasonable exercise of the police power since it attempted to prevent population growth in the community as a means of retaining its character:

Zoning provisions may not be used, however, to avoid the increased responsibilities and economic burdens which time and national growth invariably bring. . . . Four acre zoning represents Easttown's position that it does not choose to accommodate those who are pressing for admittance to the township unless such admittance will not create additional burdens upon governmental functions and services. The question posed is whether the township can stand in the way of the natural forces which send our growing population into hitherto undeveloped areas in search of a comfortable place to live. We have concluded not.[47]

Five years later, in *Appeal of Girsh*, the Pennsylvania Supreme Court invalidated a town's zoning ordinance because of its failure to provide for apartments.[48] The opinion emphasized that the challenged zoning ordinance significantly reduced the opportunities for those outside to move into the community.

Nether Providence Township may not permissibly choose to only take as many people as can live in single-family housing, in effect, freezing the population at near present levels. Obviously, if every municipality took that view, population spread would be completely frustrated. Municipal services must be provided *somewhere,* and if Nether Providence is a logical place for development to take place, *it should not be heard to say that it will* not bear its rightful part of the burden. (Emphasis added.) [49]

Similarly, in *Appeal of Concord Township* the Pennsylvania Supreme Court invalidated a minimum lot size ordinance, recognizing that the fundamental issue concerned the rights of nonresidents who sought housing in the area.

It is not for any given Township to say who may or may not live within its confines, while disregarding the interests of the entire area. If Concord Township is successful in unnaturally limiting its population growth through the use of exclusive zoning regulations, the people who would normally live there will inevitably have to live in another community, and the requirement that they do so is not a decision that Concord Township should alone be able to make.
. . . We fully realize that the overall solutions to these problems lies with greater regional planning; but until the time comes that we have such a system we must confront the situation as it is. *The power currently resides in the hands of each local governing unit, and we will not tolerate their abusing that power in attempting to zone out growth at the expense of neighboring communities.* (Emphasis added.)[50]

In viewing housing and zoning as matters of regional concern the New Jersey and Pennsylvania courts have recognized the realities of population growth and mobility, and have adopted a regional concept of the general welfare. Interests other than those of local inhabitants must be considered by zoning officials. Nonresidents have a substantial interest in the availability of housing in suburban areas.

Designing the Regional Remedy: Defining the Region

If the courts were to rely on the regional impact concept in designing remedies, they could specify the responsibility of the municipalities in terms of the amount of low- and moderate-income housing to be provided. Each community would be assigned a proportionate share of the low- and moderate-income housing needed in the region and would be required to take the necessary steps to facilitate development of the housing. The court would adopt mechanisms to insure implementation.

The first step would be to identify the region in which housing would be distributed. The court would make the selection from a number of possible regions. In *Commonwealth of Pennsylvania and Bucks County Interfaith Housing Corporation, et al.* v. *County of Bucks, et al.* the plaintiffs proposed the county as the relevant region.[51] Bucks County is adjacent to Philadelphia and contains 54 municipalities, each of which is a defendant in the suit. The plaintiffs "suggested the county as the suitable unit for consideration of regional influences" because:

> ... the legislature has designated the county as the appropriate planning unit by granting county planning commissions the authority to adopt comprehensive plans for counties. ... The municipalities are required to give such county comprehensive plan consideration in their own planning and zoning. ... Moreover, the Bucks County Planning Commission is presently preparing such a comprehensive plan, aided by a grant of federal funds. ... Therefore, the Bucks County Planning Commission is required to include the consideration of housing for low-income and moderate-income persons in its comprehensive plan.[52]

Sometimes, the appropriate region for providing low- and moderate-income housing remedies may include two or more counties. In the related area of school desegregation the district court, in *Bradley* v. *Milliken*, defined a multicounty region for purposes of relief.[53]

A third possible region is the Standard Metropolitan Statistical Area. The federal Office of Management and Budget recognizes SMSAs. Generally, an SMSA is a county or a group of contiguous counties which contains at least one city of 50,000 people. The urbanized portion of an SMSA might also be an appropriate region. Finally, HUD defines "housing market areas" throughout the country, which it determines represent coherent markets throughout which there is mobility. In many cases, these different definitions of the region will coincide. For example, the housing market area is generally identical to the SMSA, which is a county or multicounty area.

If alternative regions are available in a particular case, the determination of the appropriate one should be based on several factors. First, if there is a designated areawide planning agency, the geographical jurisdiction of that agency should be considered. Those boundary lines represent a legislative definition of an appropriate area for planning purposes. In addition to the deference due that assessment, use of the planning agency's jurisdiction insures the availability of an expert body capable of carrying out the planning necessary for the decree. If the planning agency was included among the named defendants, the court could then simply order the agency to carry out the appropriate planning tasks. Second, the area defined by the court should be perceived as a region by low- and moderate-income people. The area should be limited to places that this income group would consider moving to. It should not include rural or agricultural areas likely to retain that character indefinitely. Third, the region should be defined so as to simplify implementation of the decree by the court. A larger region may require additional judicial time in supervision through hearings and supplemental orders.

In sum, the appropriate region is likely to be either a county or multicounty area, perhaps coextensive with the SMSA and the housing market area. The choice should depend on the growth and mobility patterns in the particular area, the geographical authority of the appropriate planning agency, and judicial manageability of the case.

Adoption of an Allocation Plan.   Once the court has defined the region, it remains to determine the number of low- and moderate-income housing units each municipality is required to accept. The need for low- and moderate-income housing in the region as a whole should be assessed; the overall need should then be distributed among the municipalities. This would be an appropriate task for the planning agency or, if none is available, an outside expert appointed by the court. The court might identify the criteria to be used in allocating the needed housing, or leave this determination to the planners. The planners would submit to the court, for incorporation into the final order, an allocation plan, comparable to those discussed in Chapter 5, which would quantify the obligation of each defendant municipality. To facilitate construction according to the plan, the decree would include implementation provisions.

Implementation of the Allocation Plan.   In setting out how it will supervise the case after the order is issued the court should balance several potentially conflicting objectives. First, any approach should be within the competence of the court to administer. The court should not be confronted with a multitude of hearings and the resultant need to issue numerous, complex supplemental orders. Second, the court should attempt to insure efficient development of housing. It should provide relief as rapidly as possible. Unnecessary delay is a hardship for the potential occupants as well as the developers and may even make a project financially infeasible. Finally, the court's approach should seek maximum retention of local control of the planning and zoning process. It should see to it that valid local concerns, such as those clearly related to health and safety, are considered. Several alternatives are available to the courts for implementing the allocation plan. Some have already been proposed as requested relief in exclusionary zoning cases.

The "Set-Aside" in the Regional Context.   The set-aside principle discussed in relation to single site relief could be applied in a regional remedy. Any developer of subsidized housing whose project was consistent with the court-ordered allocation plan and who was denied any necessary local approvals could request the court to set aside the local requirements. The developer would have to demonstrate only that he had made a good faith effort to secure the local approvals, that the locality had denied the approvals, and that the denial frustrates relief, i.e., construction of housing. The reasons for the denial and the merits of those reasons would not be at issue, because local regulations may be set aside if they frustrate constitutionally required relief even if they are otherwise valid. The community would be enjoined from impeding the development in any way. The developer would be permitted to commence and complete construction of the project without making further efforts to obtain local approvals.

In addition to limiting judicial intervention, the set-aside technique facilitates rapid development of housing. The developer proceeds through the local administrative process in the same way as any other residential developer. If his plans are approved, he can build. If his good faith efforts are unsuccessful, a brief judicial process is initiated which results in court permission to build.

The municipality's interest in health, safety and other valid concerns would be protected in several ways within the set-aside framework. First, if the project was subsidized by HUD it would have to meet federal standards for construction and environmental quality, including the availability of supportive services and facilities. Second, the developer has the incentives provided by the market to build sound projects. Finally, the court could order municipalities receiving subsidized housing to make periodic status reports which could include explanation of any hardships the set-aside has caused them. This might lead the court to impose additional requirements on developers seeking set-asides. Although these protections do not assure that subsidized projects will comply literally with local administrative regulations, they should provide adequate protection against major deviations.

The Judicial Override.   The court could also use an override approach modeled on the original New York Urban Development Corporation legislation. Instead of a project by project set-aside, developers of low- and moderate-income housing would be granted a generalized authority to override local zoning and other codes, after making good faith efforts to comply with these requirements. The court could delegate this authority to all subsidized developers, or to a subgroup such as the state housing finance agency. The override would be in effect for a particular locality until its remedial obligation was fulfilled.

The override technique would minimize continuing judicial intervention. Once the court granted this authority, it would not be involved in individual projects but could merely monitor regional progress on a periodic basis.

Mandating Economic Mix. The court could require that developers building housing of any type in the relevant municipalities include a specified percentage of units for low- and moderate-income families within their development. The statutory analogs here are the Fairfax County, Virginia and Montgomery County, Maryland zoning ordinances, discussed in Chapter 4. The court might prohibit the municipalities from granting zoning or other approvals to residential developments unless they contain a specified percentage of low- and moderate-income housing units. For example, in *Planning for People Coalition* v. *County of Du Page* the plaintiffs' complaint requests that

> Du Page County be enjoined from giving any zoning approval
> or building permits for new residential developments for the
> relatively wealthy without, at the same time, making adequate
> provisions for housing for persons with low- and moderate-
> incomes.[54]

A remedial order should spell out the proportion of lower-income housing required and the kinds of developments covered.

The court's continuing role could be limited largely to periodic monitoring of the progress of development. If any community attempted to block all residential developments, the developer of an economically integrated project could seek a set-aside, after making good faith efforts to secure the necessary local approvals. Providing developers with this extra incentive to build low- and moderate-income housing may accelerate the provision of such housing. At the same time, local control of planning and zoning would remain largely intact. The community would continue to decide which areas should be residential, industrial and commercial.

Additional Remedial Provisions. To insure that relief is comprehensive and effective, the court might include additional provisions in the decree. First, the court could order municipalities to grant any approvals necessary for the utilization of federal subsidy programs. Second, the court could order any local housing authorities with jurisdiction in the suburban areas to develop low-rent public housing as rapidly as possible, in accordance with the allocation plan.

Requested Remedies in Recent Cases

In several recent cases the plaintiffs have sought relief similar to that discussed in this chapter. *Accion Hispana Inc.* v. *Town of New Canaan*, involves a challenge to the zoning scheme of an affluent suburb of New York.[55] The complaint attacks a whole range of land use practices, including two and four acre minimum lot sizes, extreme limitations on multifamily housing, and prohibition of mobile homes. The broad-scale relief requested includes invalidating the existing land use laws and ordering enactment of new laws which would include:

1. The reservation of not less than five sites of vacant, developable land to be used solely for the development of single and/or multi-family housing units for persons of low and moderate income, such sites to be:
    (a) Zoned for a density approximately equal to the average density of middle and upper-income multi-family housing now in New Canaan;
    (b) Of sufficient distance from one another so as to avoid ghettoization and provide prospective residents with a diversity of choice of surroundings similar to that enjoyed by existing white middle and upper-income residents of the town; and
    (c) Of sufficient land area so that, when developed as aforesaid, the proportion that New Canaan's minority residents bears to New Canaan's population as a whole will be approximately equal to such proportion in the State, region or nation, as the Court deems most appropriate;
2. Diversified sites throughout the Town for the development of significant numbers of housing units other than single-family detached dwellings;
3. Land for housing sufficient to meet the needs of all employees of business, industry and public service which enter New Canaan subsequent to the commencement of this suit;
4. The utilization of mobile homes as dwellings.[56]

Plaintiffs requested that the town be given 45 days to submit a new law for the court's approval. In the interim the town would not be permitted to grant rezonings or issue building permits. The town would be required to vote the necessary approval so that developers could make use of the federal rent supplement program. The court would retain jurisdiction, and the town would submit quarterly reports to the court on the status of the low- and moderate-income housing sites.

In *Cornwall Estates Co.* v. *Town of Cornwall* the plaintiffs include 10 low- and moderate-income black individuals from neighboring Newburgh, suing on behalf of all minority and lower-income persons excluded from residence in Cornwall.[57] Another plaintiff is the Cornwall Estates Company, which had tried unsuccessfully for more than six years to build townhouses in Cornwall for persons of moderate income. The company alleged that the town obstructed the development because the units were to have three or more bedrooms, thus bringing school children into the community.

The suit challenged the changes which had been made in the town's zoning ordinance since Cornwall Estates Company first proposed its development—the creation of a bedroom limitation for development in the multifamily zone and the rezoning of the company's land to preclude townhouse development. Plaintiffs also challenged the virtual prohibition of multifamily development in Cornwall and the one and two acre minimum lot size requirements. Plaintiffs asked that Cornwall be required to rezone substantial portions of its land for low- and moderate-income housing, and to take all steps necessary to permit the Cornwall Estates project to proceed.[58] Cornwall Estates pledged to construct federally subsidized housing on its site.

Finally, in the *Fair Housing Development Fund Corporation* v. *Burke* the plaintiffs charged that the zoning ordinances of the Town of Oyster Bay, Long Island, New York excluded low-income families.[59] Plaintiffs requested the court to declare the ordinance unconstitutional and to order the town to prepare and implement a plan to accommodate the housing needs of low-income families, both residents and nonresidents of the town. This was to:

> provide for and assure land-use opportunities for the construction of low and moderate income dwelling units within the Town to meet the needs of the Plaintiffs and the members of the class they represent, and will end existing racial segregation in housing therein.[60]

In seeking to vindicate the constitutional rights of low- and moderate-income families, courts cannot guarantee that such housing will actually be built. For example, the courts are dependent on Congress to enact subsidized housing programs and appropriate funds to carry them out. In spite of the fact that parts of the process may be outside their control, the courts' responsibility is to take all steps within their power to provide real remedies for those deprived of constitutional rights. In cases involving individual sites, courts must insure that the site is preserved for low- and moderate-income housing and that the locality's intransigence does not impede construction of the housing. Regional remedies should also be employed. The court's role is not to engage in areawide housing planning but to require that planners do so. Having adopted an allocation plan, the court should see to it that the plan is implemented.

Chapter Eighteen

Related Inclusionary Litigation

In addition to exclusionary zoning cases, open suburbs groups have initiated a variety of other lawsuits to facilitate development of lower-income housing. One type of suit has challenged the validity of the local approval requirements in federal subsidy programs. The plaintiffs have argued that it is invalid to apply requirements to lower-income housing that do not govern other residential developments.

A second kind of lawsuit which attempts to facilitate suburban access focuses on past instances of discrimination in the operation of housing and urban development programs. The plaintiffs seek areawide remedies as relief necessitated because of illegal actions by one or more communities. For example, discriminatory practices by local housing authorities have resulted in construction of public housing on a segregated basis in many cities. If a court finds this pattern illegal it has a duty to direct development on a desegregated basis. As a practical matter, relief for the plaintiffs may require building housing outside the central city.

A third type of case that has begun to appear asserts that a corporation move from a central city to a suburb is illegal unless there is adequate housing for the workers within reasonable distance of the job site. This kind of suit can be based on federal civil rights and employment discrimination laws. As indicated in Chapter 15, the general counsel of the Equal Employment Opportunity Commission has given his opinion that corporate relocations can constitute employment discrimination. Several complaints have been made to the EEOC on this basis and one lawsuit has challenged the move of an employer from a central city to a suburban area.

Finally, prohousing groups are beginning to file suits to force public agencies to meet their responsibilities to increase housing opportunities. The *Brookhaven* case, discussed in Chapter 14, is an illustration of this approach.

Inclusionary litigation has a very short track record. The record is mixed and, as in the zoning cases, the victories have been largely in the court-room. However, some of the lawsuits that have been filed or contemplated have a great deal of potential for facilitating suburban access for lower-income people.

Local Approval Requirements

As indicated in Chapter 2, one of the barriers to building low-income housing in the suburbs is the local approval requirements in the federal laws. The programs which serve the poorest people cannot be used in any community which does not officially express its acceptance of subsidized housing. Thus, housing built under the public housing and rent supplement programs is singled out for special local examination which is not imposed on any other housing built in the community. A challenge to the rent supplement program's local approval requirement was initiated in *Moody* v. *Bangor Township.*[1] In addition, the cooperation agreement requirement in the public housing program has been challenged in *Mahaley et al.* v. *Cuyahoga Metropolitan Housing Authority.*[2] The plaintiffs challenged the constitutionality of the federal law that requires a cooperation agreement between housing authorities and municipalities before public housing can be constructed.

A civic organization, PATH Association, sued on behalf of public housing residents in Cleveland. The association contended that the cooperation agreement was a device to keep public housing out of the suburbs and that the requirement was effectively keeping black public housing tenants confined in the central city. Only East Cleveland, Cleveland Heights, and Oakwood had entered cooperation agreements with the Cuyahoga Metropolitan Housing Authority (CMHA) for public housing. In spite of this pattern, a three-judge federal court decided early in 1973 that the plaintiffs had not shown that the requirement for cooperation agreements was "based on a suspect category or affects fundamental rights." The judges wrote that "it seems that this law is neutral on its face; however, it may have been manipulated improperly."[3] Thus, the federal court was unwilling to declare the cooperation agreement requirement unconstitutional.

Discrimination in Local Housing Programs

Although courts have been reluctant to declare local approval requirements enacted by Congress invalid, they have taken a hard look at the administration of the programs at the local level. In several cases courts have found that the programs have been carried out in a discriminatory manner. *Mahaley* is a case in point. In spite of the unwillingness of the three-judge court to invalidate the federal law, it recognized that illegal discrimination might have taken place. It returned the case to Judge Battisti, one of the two district judges on the panel. He was to resolve the question of whether the municipalities' actions or inactions were impermissible. Judge Battisti stated that:

... any municipal conduct which has the purpose or effect of discriminating against Negroes or perpetuating racial concentration or segregation in housing is violative of the civil rights of Negroes and a denial of equal protection, absent a showing by the municipality of a supervening and compelling necessity. . . . given a *prima facie* showing of discriminatory effect, the cities must come forward with a supervening necessity of compelling interest to overcome a finding of discrimination.[4]

The court found a *prima facie* discriminatory effect because of the concentration of blacks in the City of Cleveland and whites in the suburbs. It also pointed to the housing authority's unsuccessful efforts to secure cooperation agreements with the suburbs. The court found that the suburbs' refusal to make a determination of need for public housing was arbitrary and unreasonable in the face of the clear evidence of such a need in Cuyahoga county:

The suburban defendants offer no compelling reason to justify their failure to sign a Cooperation Agreement. The defendant suburbs made bald allegations that their failure to act or enter into Cooperation Agreements was not motivated by racially discriminatory reasons. They offered only allegations of no need for low-income housing and their fear of a property tax loss. Neither reason was supported by the evidence, and the latter should not be considered adequate or compelling even if proof had been offered.[5]

The court ordered the Cuyahoga Metropolitan Housing Authority:

to prepare a plan setting forth the number of scattered site units it intends to place in each of the defendant suburbs. In preparing the plan, CMHA should examine the needs of each suburban community in Cuyahoga County, recognizing that it can only be effectuated as to the defendant suburban cities. The plan is to be submitted within 90 days.[6]

The court urged the housing authority and the defendant suburbs to negotiate within the ensuing 180-day period to resolve the issues and prepare an allocation plan jointly. If the negotiations proved fruitless, hearings would be held to consider suburbs' objections to the housing authority's plan. If the court found that the suburbs' objections to taking the housing were not constitutionally permissible, it would find that the refusal to sign the cooperation agreement was for a constitutionally invalid reason. The court would then grant appropriate relief to permit the housing to proceed.

The CMHA Plan.   In June 1973 CMHA submitted to the court its plan for providing housing in all suburban municipalities of the county within its jurisdiction. The plan resembled in some ways the housing allocation plans discussed in Chapter 5. It analyzed the need for low-income housing in Cleveland and its suburbs. It then added to the suburban need an estimate of the number of eligible households living in the City of Cleveland who wished to move to the suburbs. The initial five year stage of the plan provided for the production (by construction, leasing or acquisition) of approximately 25 percent of the identified need, or 12,833 units. Three thousand units were to go in Cleveland and the other 9,833 in the suburbs. During the last year of the initial stage CMHA would prepare the next stage of the plan. The second stage would take into account population changes in the county and the effects of the first stage developments.

The needs analysis indicated that there were almost 48,000 households in the county who were eligible for public housing. More than two-thirds of those people lived in Cleveland. However, when the number of eligible households seeking to move out of the city was subtracted from the city total and added to the suburban total, the result was a 50–50 city-suburban split. CMHA then allocated the suburban units among municipalities:

> The allocation of units among suburban communities was first made based upon the difference between the number of eligibles who live in each community and the percentage of eligibles as a proportion of all households living in the suburbs. This distribution was then adjusted by CMHA to eliminate allocations which were impracticably small and those failing to meet locational standards; and to reflect local conditions, and to the extent practical, disperse units away from existing concentrations of public housing and low-income population.[7]

Pursuant to the court order, allocations were made for all communities within CMHA's jurisdiction. It was understood, however, that any remedial action would be limited to the five suburbs named as defendants in the lawsuit. For these, the plan allocated: Euclid, 1,000 units; Parma, 800; Garfield Heights, 300; and Westlake and Solon, 200 units each. These defendants appealed to the Sixth Circuit Court of Appeals.

Implementation of the Plan.   If a definitive judicial decision is made that these suburbs acted impermissibly, implementation of the plan still would lie ahead. The court's remedial powers would come into play here. First, the court should either order the communities to execute cooperation agreements with CMHA, or set aside the cooperation agreement requirement, using the rationale that the requirement impedes guaranteeing constitutional rights. The district court issued such a set-aside order relative to a state-imposed local approval requirement in the *Gautreaux* case.[8] The Seventh Circuit Court of Appeals affirmed that order.

Once having removed the impediment of the federal requirement for a local approval, the court in *Mahaley* would probably need to take other steps to insure that public housing was actually built. Remedial approaches discussed in the preceding chapter would apply here as well.

Creating and Activating Housing Authorities. A variation on the *Mahaley* theme would be a suit to require suburban localities to create local housing authorities or activate ones that are moribund. For example, the County Housing Authority in Du Page County, Illinois, west of Chicago, has not provided a single public housing unit in the approximately 25 years of its existence. It seems to have been created in order to pre-empt the field, to see to it that no public housing was built in the county. If this set of facts could be proved in Du Page County or elsewhere, affirmative relief might be available on constitutional or statutory grounds.

Crow v. *Brown*. In the companion cases of *Crow* v. *Brown* and *Carr* v. *Brown* a district court in Georgia recognized the countywide housing problem, as in *Mahaley*.[9] As part of the remedy, the court required preparation of a countywide plan for public housing in the Atlanta area.

The cases involved two proposed public housing projects in an unincorporated area of Fulton County. The jurisdiction of the Atlanta Housing Authority extended 10 miles into unincorporated Fulton County, although the authority had never built any housing there. In this case, private developers were proposing to build suburban housing for sale to the housing authority under the variant of the program known as turnkey. (The private developer buys land and builds the project, with the understanding that he will sell it, or turn over the key, to the housing authority upon completion.) The county had granted the necessary rezoning before the turnkey arrangement was made. Fulton County officials apparently assumed that luxury housing would be developed on the sites. When the turnkey developers subsequently sought building permits, they were turned down by the county officials who had granted the rezoning. Relying on minutes of meetings and official memoranda, the district court found that the denial of permits was based on the race of the potential occupants. The court held that the refusal to grant the permits constituted a denial of equal protection of the law, under the 14th Amendment of the Constitution. The district court ordered the issuance of building permits for the two public housing projects involved in the case. In addition, the court ordered that a committee be established for the purpose of selecting additional sites for needed low-income housing:

(a)   The Commissioners of Roads and Revenues of Fulton County and other County officials such as the Director of the Department of Planning are to meet with representatives of the Atlanta Housing Authority within 10 days to appoint a joint

committee which will draw up a list of general areas that lie
both within the unincorporated sections of Fulton County
and the jurisdiction of the Atlanta Housing Authority in
which low-rent public housing would be appropriate.

(b)   This joint committee shall, within 30 days after such meeting, draw up such a list with a view toward full compliance
with the national housing policy of balanced and dispersed
public housing.

(c)   Within 60 days after the completion of such a list, the joint
committee shall prepare detailed site evaluation and planning
reports and recommendations for more specific localities
within the general areas that would be appropriate for low-
rent public housing under the national housing policy. Representatives of the City of Atlanta and the federal government
may be called upon for assistance in the preparation of such
report.

(d)   Copies of all lists and reports shall be served upon the Atlanta
Housing Authority, the regional office of HUD, the Commissioners of Roads and Revenues of Fulton County, and this
court.

(e)   Within 30 days after the submission of such reports and
recommendations by the joint committee, the Commissioners
of Roads and Revenues shall meet with representatives of
the Atlanta Housing Authority for the purpose of implementing the recommendations of the joint committee. The results
of that meeting shall be reported to this court.[10]

This opinion and order were affirmed by the Fifth Circuit Court of
Appeals.[11] However, as problems arose in developing and implementing the
county plan, the district court refused to intervene. It indicated that setting up
the planning committee had been a gratuitous effort on the court's part to help
solve the housing problem. For this reason it would not issue additional orders
designed to help the planning process produce low-income housing in suburban
Fulton County.

After the decision in *Crow*, Fulton County established its own housing authority. The county withdrew the jurisdiction of the Atlanta Housing
Authority from portions of the county outside Atlanta, further frustrating
areawide relief.

Gautreaux v. *Chicago Housing Authority.*   The *Gautreaux* case
initially involved discrimination in public housing in the City of Chicago.[12]
The district court decided that the Chicago Housing Authority (CHA) had used
racially discriminatory site selection and tenant selection policies. The court
also issued a strong remedial order requiring that the majority of future public
housing in the city be built in white areas.[13] However, when the plaintiffs

proposed that an additional order be issued to provide for suburban development of public housing, the judge balked.

The Origins of *Gautreaux.*   In 1966 the American Civil Liberties
Union, acting on behalf of a group of public housing tenants and applicants,
filed suit against both HUD and CHA charging racial discrimination in the
site selection procedures followed by the CHA, as well as in their tenant admission procedures. Virtually all public housing for families was built in black
areas of the city, and the few projects built in white neighborhoods were
virtually all white-occupied.

In February 1969 the district court decided that the Chicago
Housing Authority, while not necessarily harboring a "subjective racist attitude,"
had, nevertheless, "intentionally maintained a system of public housing which
discriminated on racial grounds with respect to the selection of sites for
public housing" by confining public housing to black areas of the city.[14]
Several months later the court ordered that for every unit of public housing
built in a black neighborhood, three would have to be built in white neighborhoods. It also ordered the CHA to use its "best efforts" to increase the supply of
public housing in predominantly white neighborhoods "as quickly as possible."[15]

The plaintiffs then activated the case against HUD, which had been
held in abeyance during the CHA part of the case. The district court dismissed
the case against HUD, but the court of appeals reversed that decision.[16]
It found that HUD, like CHA, was liable because the federal agency had subsidized the public housing program and approved the specific sites.

Areawide Relief.   In December 1971 the district court ordered HUD
and the plaintiffs to prepare a plan for relief within 90 days.[17] The court
invited the parties to submit a broad range of alternatives and specified that the
plans need not be limited geographically to the City of Chicago. HUD proposed
that the court order the department to use its "best efforts" to provide desegregated housing opportunities in Chicago. HUD claimed that it had no authority
to plan. The plaintiffs, on the other hand, submitted an areawide plan for
relief as their proposed order.

In seeking desegrated low-income housing on a regional basis, the
plaintiffs proposed that the region be defined as the Chicago "urbanized area."
The urbanized area was urged as appropriate for relief because it excludes rural
areas, which may not be suited to receive subsidized housing for low-income
Chicago residents. At the same time, the urbanized area is large enough to insure
that there would be enough vacant land to build the units necessary for relief
while avoiding excessive concentration of low-income families.

The proposed order specified that in addition to the public housing
units to be provided within the city under the earlier order, units equal in

number to half the units provided within the city would be provided in the urbanized area outside the city. At that time, CHA was under a court order to proceed with 1,500 units inside the city. Therefore, the proposed order identified the initial suburban obligation as one-half that total, or 750 units. Ultimately, the plaintiffs sought the provision of 60,000 units of public housing as the full measure of relief due them. This figure was based on the number of CHA units built on a segregated basis—approximately 30,000. Under the 1969 order and the 1972 proposed order half of the new units would be for the plaintiff class. Residents of the area where the project was built would have first priority for the other half of the units. Thus, it was necessary to provide 60,000 units to provide the plaintiff class with 30,000 new, desegregated units.

Rather than an allocation plan on the Miami Valley model, the proposed order was designed simply to avoid concentration and insure that units would be built throughout the urbanized area. As in the in-city order, three units were to be in white suburban areas for every one in a black area. There were to be no more than 15 percent public housing units in any census tract, nor would any municipality be required to accept public housing units totaling more than four percent of its overall housing stock. Indeed, this ceiling would be reduced to two percent if a municipality provided the necessary approvals voluntarily and proceeded diligently to develop the housing. Further, the units were to be distributed among the three counties in the urbanized area. HUD was not to fund any projects that were not consistent with this framework.

Thus, the plaintiffs' proposal envisioned the development of 60,000 public housing units distributed throughout the Chicago urbanized area. The first stage was to be 750 units. As is customary in public housing, local housing authorities were to be the instruments for developing this housing. There were housing authorities in existence throughout the urbanized area and, although CHA was the only authority which was a defendant in the suit and shown to be guilty of wrongdoing, the plaintiffs suggested that these suburban authorities be given the opportunity to opt into the remedial process. They could do so by signing an agreement with CHA to develop the housing designated for their jurisdiction and obtaining the necessary cooperation agreements locally. If a particular housing authority chose not to participate, the responsibility would shift back to CHA to develop the required housing in that area. Under state law CHA could operate in any community if it was invited to do so by the municipality. The plaintiffs proposed to seek a judicial set-aside of the invitation provision if the local housing authorities did not become a part of the remedial process. CHA and HUD were to use their "best efforts" to provide the suburban units as specified in the order. These "best efforts" might include seeking a judicial set-aside of the cooperation agreement requirement, which might be necessary to permit development of public housing in a particular community.

Status of the Proposed Order. The *Gautreaux* plaintiffs proposed the suburban order because they believed that the city order would fail without a metropolitan approach. The city was more than one-third black by 1970. Projections indicated that by the early 1990s there would be no more white areas in Chicago, under the court's definition of that term. Scattering public housing in white areas of the city might merely accelerate the white flight to the suburbs and subsequent resegregation. Providing public housing in the suburbs at the same time would maximize the chances that this would not happen. In spite of the force of these arguments, however, the district court denied the request for metropolitan relief because:

> . . . the wrongs were committed within the limits of Chicago and solely against residents of the City. It has never been alleged that CHA and HUD discriminated or fostered racial discrimination in the suburbs and, given the limits of CHA's jurisdiction, such claims could never be proved against the principal offender herein. After years of seemingly interminable litigation, plaintiffs now suggest that I consider a metropolitan plan for relief against political entities which have previously had nothing to do with this lawsuit. The factual basis for their request is an opinion of an urbanologist that by the year 2000 the entire geographic area of the City of Chicago will be within the limited public housing area as defined by the judgment order entered on July 1, 1969. This is simply inadequate to support a request to consider imposing obligations upon those who were and are incapable of discriminatory site selection within the City of Chicago.[18]

Instead, the court merely ordered HUD to use its best efforts to cooperate with the Chicago Housing Authority to increase the supply of housing in accordance with earlier orders in the case.

Strategic Questions in *Gautreaux*. The question arises whether, since the original issue was segregation in public housing in Chicago, the plaintiffs in *Gautreaux* were trying to accomplish too much in one lawsuit. Even in 1966, however, it was apparent that full relief might well require a metropolitan approach. In addition, the judge appeared receptive to a suburban approach; the in-city case had been won and there was little to lose in pressing for a suburban order. Future cases starting with central city discrimination might have a better chance for providing access to suburbia if: (1) there is a clear state involvement in the central city discrimination and the state can be named as a party at the outset; (2) discrimination by at least some of the suburbs can be proven, independently; (3) the metropolitan area and the number of suburbs is relatively small; and (4) the central city housing authority has jurisdiction over the surrounding suburbs as well as in Ohio. It is also important to develop a simple plan and implementation mechanism and to establish as a basis for the scheme a clear connection between metropolitan housing patterns and central city discrimination.

Garrett v. *City of Hamtramck.*   Hamtramck, Michigan is a suburb of 27,000 people surrounded by the City of Detroit. It is a low-income and working class community with old housing and industrial and commercial areas. The black population of the city declined substantially in the 1960s, largely as a result of displacement of black families through urban renewal and highway programs. Many of these displacees were unable to relocate in Hamtramck and were forced to move to Detroit or elsewhere. Plaintiffs representing the class of past and future displacees sued the city and HUD. [19] They alleged that the displacement of minorities through public programs, without providing adequate relocation housing, is illegal. As in several other "black removal" cases, the court found that the city and HUD had acted illegally by planning and carrying out projects so as to remove about 500 black households from the area.

Early in 1973 the district court issued a comprehensive remedial order.[20] As in the *Gautreaux* case, the parties were invited to submit plans for relief. The court's order largely adopted the plaintiffs' proposal. It required the city to amend its urban renewal plan in ways that would provide adequate relocation housing. The revised plan was to provide for the construction, not withstanding local ordinances, of at least 430 low- and moderate-income housing units. The court in effect ordered an override of local zoning like that described in the previous chapter. The defendants were also to acquire, by condemnation if necessary, an additional seven acre tract for more housing. At the same time that the city was to provide for substantial new housing construction, it was prohibited from taking actions which might result in "the elimination of housing units in the city, unless a corresponding number of new units . . . are provided within the city."[21]

With these and other implementation provisions, the Hamtramck order provides perhaps the most extensive affirmative relief of any urban renewal housing case. It provides for a specific number of low- and moderate-income housing units to be built, with an override of local zoning if necessary, and it identifies the area within which the initial housing is to be constructed. However, the court did not identify the vehicle for developing the housing; it placed this responsibility on the defendants.

The *Hamtramck* principles might be transferred to other suburban situations. Federal, state and local programs having this effect are all subject to the same constitutional infirmity and remedial pattern. Where suburban jurisdictions use urban renewal or other public programs to remove minorities, the *Hamtramck* order is a useful model for relief. This kind of case will not arise as often as the exclusionary zoning situation, but when it does, the *Hamtramck* pattern should be very helpful. To insure that the remedy is effective, a court might also identify the vehicle for developing the housing and a timetable for implementation.

Corporate Relocation and Employment Discrimination

Communities which refuse to approve subsidized housing may be vulnerable to legal challenge; so may localities which administer these programs on a discriminatory basis. Private companies may also be subject to legal attack if they acquiesce in local exclusionary practices by locating facilities in communities which keep out lower-income housing.

Suburban Action Institute and Title VII. In late 1970 Suburban Action Institute began to raise publicly the linkage between corporate relocations to the suburbs and employment discrimination. Suburban Action sent letters to General Telephone and Electronics and The Western Electric Company urging them to reconsider planned moves from New York City to Connecticut and New Jersey suburbs respectively.[22] Western Electric intended to move to the five acre zoned suburb of Bedminster, New Jersey. Suburban Action told the company that "its move to an exclusionary suburb would deny equal employment opportunity to present and prospective minority employees, as well as to moderate-income employees, and that such a denial might be in violation of Title VII of the 1964 Civil Rights Act."[23] Suburban Action urged Western Electric to "set a model to the nation of responsible corporate behavior" by refusing to move to Bedminster until the town assured them that a large supply of housing would be available for their workers.[24]

In 1971 Suburban Action began pressing the Equal Employment Opportunity Commission to intervene in corporate relocations. It filed a complaint with the EEOC charging RCA with racial discrimination in employment.[25] The institute alleged that the corporation's planned relocation of 1,000 jobs from New York City and Camden, New Jersey to the exclusive suburb of New Canaan, Connecticut would violate the employment discrimination provisions of the 1964 Civil Rights Act. Suburban Action urged the EEOC to exercise its statutory authority and issue a "commissioner's charge" against RCA for engaging in unlawful employment practices. In 1970 two percent of New Canaan's 17,455 people were black. The virtual exclusion of minorities was accomplished largely by zoning laws, including large lot zoning and prohibition of apartments in almost all parts of the community. Minority RCA employees and future applicants would probably be unable to afford to live in New Canaan.

Suburban Action made a strong case on the facts. As discussed in Chapter 15, the EEOC general counsel had made a persuasive legal argument that corporate relocations could violate the civil rights law. However, the EEOC took no action. RCA did not proceed with construction of its facility for reasons which the company claimed had nothing to do with the complaint filed by Suburban Action.[26]

Suburban Action filed additional complaint letters relative to proposed move-outs of AT&T and General Electric.[27] AT&T planned to move office facilities from New York City to Bernards Township, New Jersey. The community prohibited multifamily units and zoned most of its land for one to three acre minimum lot sizes. The township was virtually all-white and upper-income. Because of this pattern, Suburban Action also requested the Federal Communications Commission to initiate disciplinary proceedings against AT&T.[28] The FCC later held hearings on the proposed relocation. A Suburban Action director testified as to the discriminatory impact of the proposed move. This was probably the first hearing held by a regulatory agency to inquire into the relocation policies of a company under the agency's jurisdiction. However, the FCC took no disciplinary action following the hearing.

Suburban Action's complaint against General Electric was also filed with the Office of Federal Contract Compliance (OFCC) of the Department of Labor.[29] Since G.E. was a federal contractor, it was subject to the affirmative action requirements outlined in Chapter 15. G.E. planned to relocate its corporate headquarters from New York City to Fairfield, Connecticut, a predominantly white, affluent community. Hoever, Fairfield is adjacent to Bridgeport, which perhaps weakened the discrimination argument in this case. Although the contrast between Fairfield and Bridgeport demonstrates the exclusionary character of the former, the large number of blacks and lower-income people in Bridgeport makes it feasible for G.E. to secure and retain black employees. Neither the EEOC nor the OFCC took any action in this matter. G.E. moved forward with its relocation plans.

Employment Discrimination Litigation. The next step after administrative complaints is to sue corporations proposing to relocate from central cities to suburbs. The legal basis could be either Title VII of the 1964 Civil Rights Act or the Civil Rights Act of 1866. Title VII was explained in Chapter 15. The 1866 law provides that:

> All persons within the jurisdiction of the United States shall have the same right in every State and Territory to make and enforce contracts . . . as is enjoyed by white citizens. . . . [30]

Several federal courts of appeals have ruled that this provision applies to private acts of employment discrimination. They have interpreted the right to make contracts guaranteed in the law as encompassing the right to obtain contracts of employment. The Civil Rights Act of 1866 thus provides the same protections against employment discrimination as Title VII of the 1964 law. Under Title VII, it is necessary to use the compliance procedure through the administrative process of the EEOC before going to court. The 1866 law may provide a direct route to the federal courts, although some courts have required resort to the administrative machinery of Title VII for any alleged discrimination covered by that law. Other courts have required that complainants justify their not proceeding through EEOC channels before filing a suit under the Civil Rights Act of 1866.

In 1973 black employees filed suit against the Automobile Club of Michigan.[31] The plaintiffs alleged a number of discriminatory actions by the club, including a proposed move of the headquarters from Detroit to the virtually all-white suburb of Dearborn. There was no public transportation from Detroit to the proposed location in Dearborn. Since many of the plaintiffs did not own cars, they would be forced to quit their jobs when the automobile club moved. Whites who lived closer to the proposed site would fill these vacancies. Plaintiffs claimed that this relocation violated their civil rights under the 1866 civil rights law. They requested a permanent injunction against the move but did not seek to impose affirmative housing obligations on the defendant. The case was still pending at the end of 1973.

The Potential of Employment-Discrimination Lawsuits. Because racial minorities are specifically protected by the civil rights acts, suits should be filed on their behalf. Successful suits will benefit other lower-income people as well. Actions should be filed against companies of substantial size, with significant numbers of low- and moderate-income workers, particularly blacks. Although the discussion thus far has focused on relocation from central cities, suits might also be filed challenging all corporate locations and developments at distances from minorities.

If the cases were successful in court, this would alert communities that they would have to provide lower-income housing to attract industrial and commercial development. These developments are perceived by many suburbs as extremely valuable additions to their tax bases. Municipalities compete with each other to bring in the companies. Employment discrimination litigation has a major advantage over direct exclusionary zoning cases in changing the practices of these communities. For once, time is on the side of the plaintiffs. Any delay in the administrative or judicial process merely lengthens the time the community has to wait for the corporation to move in. The municipality has an incentive to move quickly to provide the housing, so it can reap the fiscal harvest of the company's tax payments. If a community does not move fast enough on the housing front, the company may choose to locate its facility elsewhere. Thus, the community may be much more willing to compromise than in an exclusionary zoning case.

Designing a remedy may be simpler in an employment case than in the exclusionary zoning context. The municipality's overall responsibility is not at issue. The amount of housing necessary to provide for the company's low- and moderate-income employees would be an appropriate measure of relief. Before the relocation could take place, this much additional housing would have to be provided.

Making the Public Agencies Do Their Job

It is clear from earlier chapters that public bodies have very significant responsibility and authority to increase suburban access. It is also apparent that this potential is largely untapped. Regional, state and federal agencies have barely begun to use the tools at their command. Because of the difficult political issues involved, prohousing groups have begun to challenge action or inaction by public agencies to compel them to fulfill their obligations. The *Brookhaven* case was an attempt to force the General Services Administration and HUD to obey the executive order governing location of federal facilities as well as their own implementing regulations.

More recently, Suburban Action Institute has filed suit against HUD, the Interior Department and the Tri-State Regional Planning Commission.[32] The suit challenged the validity of a HUD sewer grant and an Interior Department recreational facility grant to New Castle, New York because of the town's exclusionary land use practices. Apartments were prohibited. Most of the town's land was zoned for single family housing on one acre or more. The plaintiffs argued that it was illegal for these federal agencies to provide funds to communities which exclude lower-income people. This kind of suit could have significant impact if the courts will accept the arguments and force withholding of funds.

Chapter Nineteen

School Litigation and Housing

Two kinds of lawsuits related to public schools have been widely discussed in terms of their potential impact on opening the suburbs. First, the school finance cases have challenged the constitutionality of the wide disparity among school districts in per pupil expenditures. In states where these cases are successful, they could lead to major changes in the financing of local schools. The property tax may diminish in importance as a source of school funding. In that event, there would be less fiscal incentive for excluding low- and moderate-income housing.

Secondly, several recent school desegregation cases have considered the need for, and validity of, remedial plans encompassing an area larger than a city. If the courts ultimately require metropolitanwide school desegregation plans, one of the incentives for excluding low- and moderate-income housing from suburbia may be reduced. Where central city blacks are attending suburban schools, the suburbs may be less intent on keeping those families from living in the community.

The School Finance Cases

In *Serrano* v. *Priest* a class action was instituted on behalf of a group of elementary and high school students attending schools in Los Angeles County "to secure equality of educational opportunity."[1] Defendants were the state and county officials responsible for the collection and disbursement of state and county funds for the support of public schools. Plaintiffs alleged that California's method of financing public schools violates the equal protection clause of the 14th Amendment to the federal Constitution, and similar provisions of the California Constitution, in that the great disparity among school districts in per pupil expenditures results in "inferior educational opportunities for children in certain districts."

The California Supreme Court concluded that disparities in taxable

239

valuation among school districts made educational opportunities for a child a function of the relative wealth of their parents and neighbors. State programs for equalization did not reduce these disparities sufficiently to enable California's system of school finance to withstand a challenge of unconstitutionality. *Serrano* has been cited as authority for invalidating state public school finance systems by courts in Minnesota, Texas, Wyoming, Arizona, and new Jersey. These decisions led to speculation about a revolution in financing of public education. They also raised questions about financing of municipal services generally and other noneducational impacts, including the potential for changes in suburban land use patterns.

Then came the U.S. Supreme Court decision in the *Rodriguez* case.[2] The Supreme Court decided that the disparities in per pupil expenditures among Texas districts did not constitute a violation of the U.S. Constitution.

In the *Rodriguez* case, the federal district court found the state's system of financing public schools unconstitutional. The property tax structures and method of distributing state assistance in Texas appear substantially similar to California's. Taxable real property per pupil ranged from under $10,000 to over $100,000 in Texas school districts. A higher tax rate in the poorer districts would produce less revenue than lower rates in the wealthier districts. As in California, state aid in Texas did not mitigate to any appreciable extent the effects of unequal taxable wealth among school districts.

The district court ordered the Texas Legislature to develop a constitutionally acceptable alternative method of school financing. The San Antonio Independent School District appealed the decision to the United States Supreme Court. In March 1973 the Supreme Court reversed the decision of the Texas District Court. In holding that the Texas financing pattern did not violate the plaintiffs' equal protection rights, the Supreme Court found that the system did not disadvantage any group of people or "suspect class" entitled to particular judicial protection. The Court found that the Texas system had not been shown to discriminate against any definable class of poor people or to occasion discrimination depending on the relative wealth of the families in any district.

Nor did the Texas school-financing system impermissibly interfere with the exercise of a fundamental right or liberty, according to the Supreme Court. Though education is one of the most important services provided by the state, it is not within the limited category of rights recognized by the Court as guaranteed by the Constitution. Even if some identifiable quantum of education is arguably entitled to constitutional protection to make meaningful the exercise of other constitutional rights, there was no showing that the Texas system failed to provide the basic minimal skills necessary for that purpose. In addition, the Texas system, though concededly imperfect, bears a rational relationship to a legitimate state purpose. While assuring basic education for every child in the state, it permits and encourages participation in and significant control of each district's schools at the local level. For these and other reasons, the Supreme Court found that the Texas financing system did not violate the U.S. Constitution.

The Supreme Court decision in *Rodriguez* all but foreclosed the possibility of overturning a state's school financing patterns on federal constitutional grounds. Under the principle of this case, the 14th Amendment permits a system where per pupil expenditures vary with the wealth of the local school district. However, some state courts may continue to invalidate gross disparities on state constitutional grounds and require some kind of equalization scheme. If that happens, the dollars per pupil available for education may be similar throughout the state. In addition, *Serrano* and other cases have raised the financing issue to such a high level of public consciousness that many state legislatures have considered various school financing reforms. In spite of *Rodriguez*, some states may make significant alterations. This equalization could affect housing patterns.

Land Use Impact of School Finance Equalization.   To the extent that fiscal motives underlie suburban exclusionary devices, equalizing educational expenditures would lessen the incentives to keep out lower-income families. If per pupil expenditures were equalized among districts, property tax revenues would not determine the resources available for local schools. Since the local schools receive the vast majority of suburban property tax revenues, equalization would make the property tax relatively unimportant. A community would not be harmed financially by the introduction of housing that produced school age children but only small amounts of property taxes.

In sum, if communities really excluded low- and moderate-income housing because it does not pay its way in property taxes, *Seranno*-type decisions might result in these restrictions loosening up. However, as indicated in Chapter 2, it is likely that fiscal motives are only part of the picture. Racial and class prejudices are undoubtedly more powerful motives underlying exclusion. If that is the case, a shift in educational financing would have little or no impact on local zoning and planning decisions related to lower-income families.

Financing changes might help to remove the fiscal argument from the arsenal of justifications available to localities. As a result, rather than causing restrictions to break down, suburbs may merely become more sophisticated in defense of their exclusionary practices. They are already using environmental arguments, which may have a powerful appeal in light of increasing legal protections being afforded the environment. A dramatic example of the potential for perversion here is the suit filed in Chicago under the National Environmental Policy Act to block construction of public housing in white areas of the city because of alleged adverse environmental consequences of poor people living in the neighborhood.[3] With these justifications available to recalcitrant communities it seems unlikely that school financing reform will lead to significant changes in exclusionary suburban patterns.

School Desegregation on a Metropolitan Basis

In several school desegregation cases, plaintiffs have sought judicial recognition that artificial boundaries, such as school districts, cannot be used to justify maintaining a segregated school system. They have argued that if desegregation cannot be accomplished within a single school district, then the court has the duty to adopt a plan covering a larger area. The plan must be capable of achieving desegregation.

The first case to attempt such a multijurisdictional desegregation plan was *Bradley* v. *Richmond*.[4] Early in 1972 the federal district court in Virginia ordered the merger of three school districts. The districts covered the City of Richmond and its two suburban counties. This order followed by several years a remedial order covering only the city of Richmond. The 1972 order was premised on the fact that the city's school system had become identified as black and it was no longer possible to desegregate effectively within the city.

Six months later the court of appeals reversed the district court. It decided that when state-imposed segregation had been completely removed within a school district, further intervention by the district court was not justifiable. The court of appeals found that the last vestiges of state-imposed segregation had been removed in Richmond. The court also held that a district judge did not have the authority to require consolidation of school districts unless there had been a constitutional violation in the establishment or maintenance of each of the school districts. The court of appeals did not believe that any such constitutional violation had been shown.

The case then went to the U.S. Supreme Court. In mid-1973 the Court reached a 4–4 deadlock. This has the effect of affirming the court of appeals decision. The school district merger was not consummated. However, because of the tie vote, there was no Supreme Court opinion in the case. The Court did not indicate what its position would be if the factual or legal history were different. The validity of court-ordered metropolitan school desegreation plans remained an open question after *Bradley* v. *Richmond*.

Ultimately, the Supreme Court may resolve the issue, or at least clarify its position, in *Bradley* v. *Milliken*.[5] While the Richmond case moved up the judicial ladder to the Supreme Court, the Detroit version was moving up and down between the district court and the Sixth Circuit Court of Appeals. It seems destined for resolution by the Supreme Court.

The plaintiffs in the Detroit case charged that the State of Michigan was unconstitutionally interfering with the operation of a voluntary plan for partial high school desegregation in the city. Plaintiffs also alleged that the public schools were segregated on the basis of race as a result of official actions of the local and state defendants. The district court found that the defendants had acted unconstitutionally and ordered that proposed desegregation plans be drawn up. After reviewing alternative plans confined to the City of Detroit, the court concluded: "that the court must look beyond the limits of the Detroit school district for a solution to the problem of segregation in the Detroit public schools is obvious."[6] The court found that it was within the power and duty of the court to order that a plan which was metropolitan in scope be devised where such remedies are shown to be necessary to provide full relief for racial segregation.

On June 14, 1972 the district court issued an order entitled "Ruling on Desegregation Area and Order for Development of Plan for Desegregation"[7] The district court established tentative boundaries for a metropolitan remedy (a three county area) to the pattern of segregation in the Detroit area. The order also provided for a panel of nine members to design plans for integration of the Detroit schools and those of 53 metropolitan school districts.

On December 8, 1972 the court of appeals affirmed the portions of the district court order requiring a remedial plan covering an area larger than the City of Detroit:

> This court, in considering this record, finds it impossible to declare "clearly erroneous" the district judge's conclusion that any Detroit-only desegregation plan will lead directly to a single segregated Detroit school district overwhelmingly black in all of its schools, surrounded by a ring of suburbs and suburban school districts overwhelmingly white in compositon in a state in which the racial composition is 87 percent white and 13 percent black. Big city school systems for blacks surrounded by suburban school systems for whites cannot represent equal protection of the law.
>
> We reject the contention that school district lines are sacrosanct and that the jurisdiction of the district court to grant equitable relief in the present case is limited to the geographical boundaries of Detroit. We reiterate that school districts and school boards are instrumentalities of the state.[8]

Significant questions remained as to the boundaries of the remedial area, the rights of the suburban districts and the nature of the desegregation plan. However, it appeared that the court of appeals' position was firm that the district court was authorized to impose a metropolitan plan if it was necessary to achieve desegregation. This question is likely to be resolved ultimately by the Supreme Court.

Impact of Metropolitan School Desegregation. If *Bradley* v. *Milliken* was affirmed by the Supreme Court and a metropolitan plan implemented, similar cases would probably spring up all over the country. Other cities have black-majority public school systems. Desegregation within these cities is becoming a practical impossibility. Successful "metropolitanization" suits could influence suburban land use patterns. In some cases, communities may decide to open up housing opportunities as long as effective school desegregation has already taken place. This would be particularly likely if the black and white pupils alike fared well in the integrated setting. Other communities might take another route and build higher barriers. Metropolitan desegregation might be so threatening that they would react in a thoroughly defensive way. Perhaps the only real hope is that positive experiences in suburban integrated classrooms would induce lowering of the barriers to permit a wider range of income groups to come into the community.

School Desegregation as a Precedent.   Metropolitan school cases would also be valuable legal precedents for the suburban housing struggle. For example, they would provide support for a metropolitan remedy in a public housing case like *Gautreaux*. If it is impossible to desegregate public housing within the central city, the court should have the authority and the duty to go beyond the artificial barriers of the city limits to provide relief. As indicated in Chapter 18, the plaintiffs made such an argument in *Gautreaux* but the district court was not receptive. A Supreme Court decision affirming a metropolitan school desegregation plan would make the metropolitan argument a much stronger one in the housing context.

Bradley v. *Milliken* also focused on the state role in the operation of public schools. This emphasis may provide a useful precedent for housing cases. As indicated in Chapter 7, about half the states have created housing agencies. If these agencies operate on a discriminatory basis, they might be subject to a metropolitan remedial order. Perhaps the state role in the zoning process could even be used to challenge metropolitan exclusionary zoning patterns and justify an areawide remedy.

Chapter Twenty

Building a Suburban Political Constituency

Litigation is, of course, not the only strategy employed by groups seeking to open the suburbs for lower-income housing. For example, some groups have tried coalition-building instead of confrontation. The Regional Housing Coalition in the Chicago area represents a large scale effort of this kind. The coalition was established in 1972 to develop suburban political support for developing low- and moderate-income housing. Its strategy is to demonstrate to public and private community leaders the need for low- and moderate-income housing in their communities and to enlist their support in the development and implementation of a regional housing plan. The plan would distribute the needed housing on a rational basis throughout the Chicago metropolitan area. The coalition's premise was that the cooperation of individual communities is essential for altering metropolitan housing patterns. A united initiative was thought necessary to change the general suburban political atmosphere from one of antagonism toward low- and moderate-income housing.

The Regional Housing Coalition involves three elements: (1) the Leadership Council for Metropolitan Open Communities, an open housing organization formed by civic leaders in the late 1960s after Martin Luther King's open housing campaign in Chicago; (2) the Northeastern Illinois Planning Commission (NIPC), the regional planning agency for the six county Chicago metropolitan area; and (3) a small group of suburban mayors interested in the housing issue, who served as a steering committee. The coalition received financial support from foundations to carry out its organizational efforts. HUD provided funds for NIPC to undertake the necessary planning. The program was to be a two-year effort to generate support for low- and moderate-income housing and to develop a concrete plan. Implementation was to take place by late 1974.

Originally, the strategy called for first developing alternative general approaches to an allocation plan and then attempting to build support through local input into the refinement of the plan. The coalition later decided that it was necessary to lay the groundwork first by developing support for the general concept of low- and moderate-income housing. To carry the message to local community leaders, a subregional organizational structure was created. There were 11 subregions in the six-county area, six of which were in Cook County (the City of Chicago and five suburban sectors). Each of the five other counties in the metropolitan area constituted a subregion. Members of the steering committee representing various subregions received assistance from the coalition's field staff in building support among public and private community leaders within their subregions.

At the same time, the Northeastern Illinois Planning Commission developed the first stages of a housing allocation plan as part of its work program under its grant from HUD. NIPC determined the need for low- and moderate-income housing in each of the subregions as indicated by current and projected demographic and economic data.

The coalition staff began to design and assist in carrying out an educational program to develop needed support. The educational effort was to overcome stereotypes related to low- and moderate-income housing. This involves replacing the image of massive projects, high crime rates, overcrowding, and poor schools with the more recent reality of subsidized housing, low-rise, low-density on scattered sites. The coalition focused heavily on the opinion leaders, the public and private power actors in individual communities. It directed much of its attention to communities where there was some pre-existing support for low- and moderate-income housing. The goal was to broaden the base of support in communities where there was already receptivity to the program and produce a snowball effect, with other communities agreeing to participate once some communities have made public their support.

The primary arguments the Regional Housing Coalition relied on related to the housing needs of employees and retention of local autonomy. On the latter point, the assertion was that if local communities fail to take action, state and federal intervention may occur, particularly through the courts. One member of the mayors' steering committee explained to his village board that he joined the committee, after declining an initial offer to participate, because:

> I am convinced that our refusal to participate in organized dialogue directed to the housing problem can only isolate us from the problem solving, leaving the solution in the hands of others outside of our community. In this respect, we need only note the many actions completed and underway across the nation which diminish local housing controls. For example, several states have passed laws requiring municipalities to allocate a stated percentage of land to public housing use . . . several states have created state zoning boards with power to override municipal zoning boards . . . and Federal Courts are entering orders which void local housing authority. Certainly the actions of Judge Austin in the Chicago situation is clear warning

that our community is not immune from Federal jurisdiction and an area plan is now being prepared without our participation.

Judge Austin's area plan for housing is being prepared without benefit of what needs actually exist in the metropolitan area. This is not his fault, but ours . . . since the suburban governments have consistently refused to consider the matter, except as to how they can stop it. If this attitude is permitted to continue it should do so only with a full understanding of the consequences. The power of the Federal Judiciary to compel compliance with their mandates is well known to us all . . . rhetoric concerning "home rule," "referendums," impeaching Justices, etc. is a meaningless exercise . . . and beyond rhetoric would be in opposition to our concept of an orderly society under law.

In addition to housing plans by court order, the Federal and State governments are demanding regional plans as the guide to dispensing funds for local projects. Flood control, water supply, traffic, fire and police assistance are but some of the areas that require funding or approval by Federal and State agencies. In this respect, it is clear that all regional problems are related to population . . . both location and density . . . and a regional housing plan is required to interrelate and various studies directed to specific subjects. Such a plan will be developed by the Northeastern Illinois Planning Commission . . . with or without our cooperation. It would seem prudent to make our local needs and circumstances known while the plan is being prepared rather than when it has been completed.

In considering the need for funding or approval by Federal and State agencies for many of our municipal operations, we should not overlook revenue sources such as the State income tax rebate or the Federal revenue sharing program as funds which can be conditioned on compliance with regional plans. Even the flow of private funds, such as mortgage money, can be withheld from a community through Federal or State edict.

The point is, housing plans for the Metropolitan Area are being prepared by the courts and governmental agencies . . . and both groups have the power to implement such plans. I do not believe that the interests of Mount Prospect can be well served by ignoring what is happening or by refusing to discuss the matter with others outside of our community.[1]

Announcing the Plan

On October 1, 1973 the Regional Housing Coalition announced publicly its Interim Balanced Housing Plan. It was not like the Dayton plan, which allocated units to planning areas, or the Twin Cities' Metro Council's plan, which identified priority areas for housing. Instead, it represented a more preliminary effort. The plan measured the need for additional low- and moderate-income housing in the six county area. It identified goals and sought consensus around a general direction rather than a specific formula.

The Regional Housing Coalition plan identifies a need for 230,000 low- and moderate-income housing units in the Chicago metropolitan area for a ten year period. It measures the components of that need in the 11 designated sectors of the region and establishes an initial production target of 10,000 units to be allocated among the sectors. It then asks local officials to recognize the housing need, support the concept of a balanced distribution of the housing and take the initiative in undertaking and implementing plans to meet local needs. Regional goals of the plan include stipulations that:

> . . . Housing opportunities for all income groups should be provided within reasonable access of job opportunities so that every person may, if he so chooses, live in or near the community in which he is employed. . . . Distribution of housing opportunities for low- and moderate-income people should be on a balanced, widespread basis throughout the region, in order to avoid overconcentration. . . .
> . . . Steps should be taken in each community to provide reasonably priced housing in relationship to its own needs and capacities, and to achieve housing balances within its sector.[2]

A central thrust of the coalition's effort is providing housing in reasonable proximity to employment opportunities. This theme is reflected in the regional goals. In addition, the sectors constitute geographic areas within which commuting to work would not be unreasonable in terms of time and distance. Finally, the jobs question was considered in defining the need of a sector. In determining a sector's need, the plan considers people working in the sector whether or not they live there.

A second major theme of the coalition is that "local government should assume the primary role in shaping a response to the shortage of housing in each municipality and sector."[3] In order to move these communities toward consensus, the plan recommended a series of policies. Through these proposed policies the coalition recommended several inclusionary actions for localities to take, including providing an appropriate proportion of low- and moderate-income units (such as 15–20 percent) in new towns, planned unit developments and major new subdivisions for low- and moderate-income people. The policies also encouraged communities to consider the need for lower-income housing in making decisions regarding maximum densities of apartments.

At the time of announcing the plan publicly, the coalition also made a special appeal to the mayors, village presidents and county board presidents in the six county Chicago metropolitan area. The chairman of the Mayors' steering committee wrote to these local officials on behalf of the coalition:

For some time we have involved ourselves in the process of planning in the field of housing, in recognition of the fact that housing problems won't disappear by themselves, and strongly suspecting that if we ignore them, someone else will try to do the job for us.

We'd rather do it ourselves, because we are confident that we are capable of finding solutions which are sensitive to local needs and conditions. But housing is a tough and complicated field, and those solutions will require our combined wisdom and cooperative action. Thus we ask that you, our fellow elected officials at the local and county levels, join us in this effort.[4]

The coalition's plan received the support of civic and professional groups including the League of Women Voters of Illinois, the Chicago Mortgage Bankers Association and the Chicago Chapter of the American Institute of Architects. When the plan was made public, it had also been reviewed and revised by several hundred suburban political leaders as well as civic, business and community groups.

The coalition requested HUD to make available sufficient subsidies to permit development of 10,000 units in the initial fiscal year of implementation. This request emphasized that the plan was flexible enough to make use of either existing or proposed subsidy programs. For example, the coalition urged consideration of implementing a housing allowance experiment in the Chicago area.

Public Education

The Regional Housing Coalition enlisted the assistance of volunteers to work in communities throughout the six-county area. The volunteers attempted to increase public awareness of the housing problem and the need to adopt and implement the plan. The coalition developed a Citizen Action Guide for volunteers to use in this public education effort. The guide indicated the kinds of people and organizations to contact, methods of presenting the plan and possible responses to frequently raised objections and concerns. The guide also encouraged the creation of a speakers' bureau of sympathetic, respected people in the community including representatives of the chamber of commerce, the religious community, the League of Women Voters, local businesses, and organizations of the elderly.

Finally, the Citizen Action Guide outlined a number of specific steps volunteers could take: organizing discussion meetings in people's homes: requesting assistance of the clergy through sermons, endorsements, and the like: mobilizing newspaper support through explanatory articles, editorials and letters to the editor; holding discussions with civic groups; developing strategies to secure the endorsement of the local governing body; collecting endorsement letters and signatures; organizing tours of quality subsidized housing.

In short, the coalition envisioned a three stage process: initiation and formulation of a plan; acceptance of the plan; and, crucially, implementation. The Northeastern Illinois Planning Commission initiated the plan, with the mayors' steering committee and business, labor and citizens' advisory groups participating in this process. The coalition then sought acceptance of the plan through the initial mayors working with other mayors towards presentation to elected councils and boards. Concurrently, the public education campaign proceeded.

The Potential of Voluntary Plans

Instead of challenging exclusionary suburbs, the Regional Housing Coalition's approach seeks to appeal to their self-interest and bring about voluntary acceptance of a measure of lower-income housing. Part of the self-interest motivation for localities is the avoidance of intervention by the courts or other governmental bodies. In fact, a suburban Chicago newspaper carried a cartoon which characterized the coalition's plan as a "do-it-yourself defuser kit." [5] The plan offered the localities an opportunity to respond to housing needs without outside interference and without drastically altering the character of their communities.

The coalition surprised mnay people by reaching the point of developing and announcing its preliminary plan. Its steering committee of mayors remained relatively intact. One mayor who had publicly supported the coalition was reelected, proving that a prohousing position is not necessarily political suicide. There were several housing lawsuits pending which gave credibility to the threat of outside intervention. The NIPC plan was a reasonable one. The coalition staff was responsive to the needs of the mayors' steering committee. There was a moratorium on the subsidy program, so there was no immediate threat of implementation. All these factors helped the coalition to reach the point of going public with the initial plan.

However, implementation may be even harder than in cases where a regional planning body takes the initiative. The public bodies have leverage, such as the A-95 review process, with local communities. The Regional Housing Coalition must depend almost entirely on public education and persuasion. Additional lawsuits might help the cause, but the coalition cannot initiate such challenges. On the other hand, the coalition has a number of mayors and business leaders on board. If they are willing to act aggressively to remove the obstacles to particular projects, the plan may get turned into places for people to live.

Chapter Twenty-One

The Corporate Role

Private industry has long been a major force in shaping suburban development. For just as long, it has been a willing, if sometimes unwitting, partner to the exclusionary practices which have kept lower-income housing out of suburbia. Industry has built the middle- and upper-income housing which characterizes so much of suburbia. It has also spent billions of dollars on plants, shopping centers and other facilities in communities which want them but not their workers. Traditionally, corporations locating in these areas have shown little concern that their low- and moderate-income employees cannot find housing accessible to their jobs. The times are changing. Most companies moving to suburbia want to have housing available there for their lower-income employees. They may still be reluctant to press for lowering barriers to permit the housing, because of the possibility that the community then will not accept the company. These corporations will face a tighter squeeze when unemployment declines and they have an even harder time finding workers for their suburban facilities. In the short run, many companies can afford to ignore the housing problem. In the longer run, the costs may become staggering for employers if suburban housing opportunities are not increased for workers.

Incentives for Corporate Involvement
Increasingly, it is in the interest of private industry to seek development of low- and moderate-income housing in the suburbs. As indicated in Chapter 1, many suburban employers have had trouble getting and keeping employees. The absence of housing for workers nearby makes it difficult to maintain a full work force. A Ford Motor Company executive has pointed out that:

> Zoning that precludes local housing opportunities for large numbers of our workforce imposes hardships on them and raises the cost of doing business. When employees are forced to travel great distances

to their jobs, absenteeism and turnover go up and morale and pro-
ductivity decline.[1]

As the directors of Suburban Action Institute have suggested, hard-
nosed business considerations dictate that business support the drive to open the
suburbs.

> Low- and moderate-income housing in the suburbs, which now hold
> more than 50% of all blue- and white-collar employment in our met-
> ropolitan areas, is no longer just an issue for liberals, or for well-
> intentioned people concerned about the suffering of the poor. It's an
> issue for the leaders of the American economy, the companies traded
> on the New York Stock Exchange.[2]

In short, companies which are located or plan to relocate in suburbia
have a strong economic self-interest in having employees housed nearby. In
addition, more and more companies are recognizing that they have a responsibility to participate in efforts to solve pressing metropolitan problems. Corporate
involvement in this area accelerated after the urban riots of the 1960s dramatized the disastrous implications of the racial and economic polarization of
urban areas. Major companies created or expanded their urban affairs departments or divisions for "corporate responsibility." At least one corporate executive has urged that suburban housing is a critical area in which industry can act to
meet this responsibility, and that "it is incumbent upon corporations to make
a social contribution by seeing to it that new low- and middle-income housing
is built in communities where it is relocating."[3]

If corporations do not respond out of their economic self-interest or
their desire to act in a socially responsible manner, they will probably be subject to increasing pressures to act anyway. As suggested in Chapter 15, federal
agencies may apply employment discrimination laws and executive orders
against corporations seeking to locate in the suburbs. Private groups will initiate
legal action to prevent these moves unless low- and moderate-income housing
is developed for the employees.

Corporate Leverage in Suburbia

For these or other reasons, corporations are likely to become increasingly involved in the development of lower-income housing. If they do so, they
will discover that they have significant leverage at the local level. Suburban politicians aggressively seek to attract new industry; planning commissions offer
variances and other zoning concessions. The companies produce large amounts
of tax revenues for the host community, which pay for schools and other local
public services. In suburban Westchester County, New York private enterprise
pays more than $100 million a year in county and local taxes.[4] Industry also

hires workers and adds its payroll to the community's resources. In short, companies seeking to move to the suburbs are often in a powerful bargaining position relative to potential recipient communities.

Corporate Strategies: Influencing Zoning

Given their leverage with municipal officials, companies can play an important role in altering zoning patterns in order to accommodate lower-income housing. In a related case, Quaker Oats was contemplating establishing a facility in Danville, Illinois in 1967. The company advised local officials that the community would be a more attractive place to locate if it demonstrated its openness to all racial and economic groups. The town immediately passed a fair housing ordinance. Quaker Oats decided in favor of the Danville site.

Although its efforts did not meet with such immediate success, Ford Motor Company used a similar approach in Mahwah, New Jersey. Mahwah is the site of Suburban Action Institute's proposed new community, described in Chapter 17. Ford expressed its support for this planned community at the presentation by Suburban Action before the township planning board. Ford's management strongly supported the requested rezoning and stressed that the "Ford Motor Company management in New Jersey believes that all citizens are entitled to have access to housing at a reasonable price within reasonable reach of their places of employment." [5] The statement went on to say that the "concept of the proposal appears to us to illustrate the type of development that would meet the objectives of the Master Plan and the need for additional moderate-income housing in the Mahwah area." [6]

Ford's leverage in Mahwah did not match Quaker Oats' in Danville because Ford already had its plant in Mahwah and was not likely to pick up and move out if the township refused to rezone. Quaker Oats was negotiating at an earlier stage, when it could still choose among alternative sites. In addition, the Mahwah proposal would have made major changes in the community. It would have more than doubled the population, with a different racial and economic mix than already resided there. As a result, Mahwah did not leap to change its zoning. Even so, the support by Ford could be very useful in further negotiations to avoid or settle a lawsuit, or in designing and implementing remedies.

Corporate Role in the Development Process

Much of the development of low- and moderate-income housing is carried out by private corporations. Most "new town" development is also undertaken by private industry. In addition, suburban-based companies which are not in the development business can help facilitate the construction of low- and moderate-income housing. For example, when they purchase land for their own facility, they can acquire extra land in the community to be used for housing. Companies can also create a seed money fund to give nonprofit sponsors of subsidized housing the initial funds needed to plan a project and get it underway.

New Towns

In addition to building housing in existing suburbs, or helping to facilitate that process, private industry can plan and develop entire new towns with or without federal assistance. Some of the new town developers who have proceeded without government help have set out to create economically and racially integrated communities. Most, however, have not.

The development of new towns is a fairly recent trend. It came about on a significant scale in the 1960s. Defining a new town is difficult as such definitions vary considerably with opinions as to what a new town should be. One definition suggests that a

> New Town must be planned on undeveloped land for a minimum of 20,000 people of varied social, economic and age levels; the land must be held under single ownership or unified control; its design must be part of a regional master plan; and there must be provision for diversified land use and a full range of community services. It should be a self-contained urban entity, preferably with a strong economic base in business and industry.[7]

Although this definition embraces most of the ideals concerning new towns, few of them fit every aspect of this definition. In general, the underlying principles behind new towns are that development should take place in multipurpose units; it should take place under some form of unified ownership or control; it should be preplanned; it should be considered in a regional context; and it should provide a socially balanced community.

Generally, American new towns are not providing such a social balance. For the most part, new town developers have attracted builders of middle- and high-income housing. The developments tend to have superior physical facilities and amenities compared with other suburbs but no greater diversity of population. Many of these builders believe that low-income housing and low-income groups would be detrimental to the sale of higher priced housing. They fear that the economically critical early building stages of the project could be seriously affected. In fact, some developers may even be "basing their investments on the fact that many people want some assurance that communities will remain socio-economically or racially homogeneous."[8]

Some large corporations are, despite these concerns, building some low- and moderate-income housing in their new towns. Towns such as Columbia, Maryland and, to a lesser extent, Reston, Virginia have succeeded in creating racially and economically integrated communities. Part of the reason these places have incorporated diverse groups effectively is that they inform potential residents of the nature of the community. No one is surprised by this mix upon moving in. These communities also attempt to provide such attractive environments that people who would otherwise be reluctant to move there will accept the presence of low- and moderate-income people.

By 1973 Columbia had about 100 moderate-income section 235 townhouses and 200 section 236 rental units. The low-income housing consisted of a small number of rent supplement units in one of the section 236 developments. The Rouse Corporation, the developer of Columbia, had as a goal that 10 percent of the community's housing would serve low- and moderate-income people. This objective was based on the company's assessment of the market in the region.

Because of the relatively high land values in Columbia, subsidized housing was feasible only with a writedown of the cost. The Rouse Corporation provided a writedown of $300 per unit. Columbia developers could not build low-rent public housing because there was no local housing authority in the county in which it was located. Columbia was not a municipality and therefore could not create its own housing authority. Such a public entity is necessary to undertake a public housing program.

Nevertheless, even though a few scattered developers may be including lower-income units, the vast majority do not appear to be following suit, mainly because of the perceived risk of upsetting sales of expensive housing.

Because of the newness of the new town experience in America, it may be too early to evaluate its direction in terms of open access. However, the trend appears ominous. If the developers do not see it in their interest to include low- and moderate-income housing, they will merely become a new kind of exclusionary suburb. In that case, these communities should be subjected to public and private pressures to become inclusionary.

Lobbying and Litigation

Companies which seek to open the suburbs might also seek change through legislation or litigation. For example, joint action by trade associations could help push through state legislation requiring local inclusionary practices. If a company was reluctant to undertake such a task alone, cooperative efforts by trade organizations might result in less exposure and more effectiveness. The chairman of the board of a major New York bank has urged large corporations to move beyond their individual community affairs programs into a "cohesive, visible, efficient and effective unit to meet the housing problems of their employees."[9]

Corporations, individually or jointly, might also make funds available for litigation challenging exclusionary practices. The National Association of Homebuilders considered creating a fund for this purpose. A number of major corporations issue grants to organizations working for social change. They might appropriately use grant funds to support challenges to suburban land use practices.

In short, private industry has all the tools available for increasing suburban access that voluntary organizations have. The business community also has the money and power that civil rights and other prohousing groups do not possess. Only the commitment is lacking.

Conclusion

Where do we go from here? That seems to be the critical question. Public agencies and private groups have tried a variety of strategies for opening the suburbs. The movement is young. It has been slow going, but progress has been made. The barriers have started to fall. Now it's time to ask what approaches and combinations of approaches hold the most promise for the future. In evaluating alternative courses of action it is necessary to weigh several potentially conflicting objectives. First, any approach should attempt to maximize efficiency in providing low- and moderate-income housing. Unnecessary delay permits the costs described in Chapter 1 to continue to mount up.

Second, approaches to opening the suburbs should be manageable. If they involve litigation, for example, they should be within the competence of the court to adminster. Neither the plaintiffs nor the courts should be faced with continuous, complex hearings and numerous court orders before housing can be built. Similarly, if an administrative agency takes an initiative, the approach should be within the administrative capacity of the agency.

Third, local control should be retained as much as possible. This is good policy because most land use decisions have little impact beyond the jurisdiction and should be made at the level closest to those affected. In addition, keeping the maximum amount of local autonomy is good politics. The more limited the intrusion into local decision-making, the less likely that significant opposition will be aroused.

Finally, assessment of suburban strategies requires an estimate of their potential for developing political support. The amount of public support needed for a particular approach is also important. For example, little political support is required to initiate exclusionary zoning litigation, while a broadbased coalition is necessary to pass state zoning appeals legislation. Even in the case of lawsuits, however, support from prohousing forces may be very important in reducing obstruction at the remedial stage.

These, then, are the tradeoffs: efficiency, manageability, local autonomy and political feasibility. Strategies with the most potential are those that maximize this mix of objectives. They could be carried out by public bodies, private groups or by combined efforts with public and private participation.

Job-Related Strategies

One of the most promising directions for the future is the cluster of strategies linking suburban housing to suburban jobs. Already, the crucial need for housing near job sites has prompted the introduction of legislation (the Workers' Residential Rights Act in Illinois), initiation of litigation (the *Michigan Automobile Club* case; the *Brookhaven* case), application of corporate leverage, and adoption of regulations by public agencies designed to protect the rights of workers to live near their jobs.

As a group, the job-linked approaches fare well under the criteria identified at the outset. For example, litigation involving locating federal facilities or private companies in the suburbs may bring relatively quick action if the suit is filed before the move is made. Delay is costly to everyone. The community loses the taxes and other benefits that the facility brings. The company or agency does not have the benefits it seeks from the new location. For a change, the shoe is on the other foot. The wrongdoer pays the price of delay. The community knows that beyond delay, it may lose the facility entirely to another community which will accept low- and moderate-income housing. The pressure is on the locality to settle the case or at least accede to a prompt and reasonable remedy. In spite of efforts by the Suburban Action Institute since 1970 to argue that corporate relocation could constitute employment discrimination, there is no track record on this issue. If the courts will accept these cases without requiring exhaustion of administrative remedies, (Equal Employment Opportunity Commission), jobs-housing cases may become an efficient way to lower suburban barriers.

Job-related approaches are also relatively manageable. In lawsuits, the remedy can relate to the additional low- and moderate-income workers in the community as a result of the new facility. Quantifying the relief is thus fairly simple, as are the provisions for implementation. The pattern is similar with legislation. For example, the proposed Workers' Residential Rights Act in Illinois quantifies the obligations of communities benefiting from employment growth. The bill also sets out how localities are to meet these responsibilities. Although no legislation seeking to open the suburbs can be self-executing, this bill reduces enforcement machinery to a minimum. It does not even provide for a state administrative mechanism, but enables aggrieved parties to go directly to court for relief. The standards are sufficiently concrete that the courts should have little trouble assessing liability or defining a remedy which is relatively easy to administer.

Job-linked strategies constitute an extremely limited intrusion on local prerogatives. Land use control remains almost entirely a local matter. The only change is that if a community wants to recieve the benefits of a corporate or governmental facility locating there, it must make provision for housing the low- and moderate-income workers. The obligation is a modest and reasonable one, clearly defined.

Finally, strategies which press for housing within access of job sites have potential for broadbased political support. Suburban employers who are paying the price of the jobs-housing mismatch want suburban housing opportunities increased. So do unions whose members lose their jobs or pay outrageous commuting costs when the companies move to the suburbs. With the advent of the energy crisis, the costs to employer and employee alike will soar. Evidence of the growing support for job-related housing measures is the response to the Workers' Residential Rights Act in the Illinois legislature. The bill received the overwhelming support of those voting in the house in 1973. The house speaker determined that the bill intruded on home rule powers and therefore needed a three-fifths vote of the entire chamber under the state's constitution. Although the bill therefore did not pass, the strong showing indicated the viability of linking jobs and housing in order to open the suburbs. The variety of vehicles available for making this linkage should encourage both private groups and public bodies to pursue aggressively this cluster of very promising strategies.

Exclusionary Zoning Lawsuits and Related Approaches

Private groups seeking to open the suburbs have devoted much of their energy to zoning and related litigation. It is essential that these confrontations with exclusionary communities continue. Even with all the difficulties inherent in trying to bring about complex social changes through the use of the courts, the judicial process remains one of the best strategies available.

Exclusionary zoning lawsuits can be painfully slow. Much of the pain comes after the case has been decided in favor of the plaintiffs. This is the point at which recalcitrant localities reach into their bag of tricks to delay, and if possible prevent, relief. Through affirmative relief, coupled with implementing mechanisms and continuing supervision of the case, the courts can make zoning litigation a much more efficient approach to overcoming suburban barriers. This is particularly true if the suit is designed to pave the way for development of a large-scale mixed-income community or a regional allocation of lower-income housing with a number of communities sharing the responsibility for removing exclusionary barriers.

As plaintiffs move beyond challenges to a particular local practice or the exclusion of a particular development, manageability becomes an increasingly important issue. Courts must be able to handle the trial necessary to invalidate local actions as well as the remedies necessary to make sure that the housing the plaintiffs are entitled to gets built. Proving the case must not require buying land, designing developments and applying for rezonings in all of the defendant communities. The plaintiffs should only be required to show that the local land use ordinances and practices demonstrate exclusionary patterns and that the effect is the lack of lower-income housing and lower-income people. This kind of proof keeps the judicial process manageable even with multiple defendants.

The case must also be manageable at the remedial stage. Courts should not be able to get off the hook by declaring local practices invalid and enjoining them in the future. The remedial responsibility goes farther, to providing all the relief that is practical. Thus, plaintiffs should present the courts with proposed forms of relief that judges are capable of administering. The set-aside, the override and the mandatory inclusionary approaches are examples of judicially manageable remedies. In addition, these and other forms of judicial relief make it possible for communities to continue making the vast majority of their land use decisions on their own.

Legal action does not require a broad base of political support. Of course, if opposition to the objectives of a lawsuit is overwhelming, this may affect the outcome in court or the extent of obstruction to a judicial decree favorable to the plaintiffs. Generally, however, the degree of public support necessary is far less in the case of a judicial strategy than in one based on legislation or areawide planning. The historical role of the courts has been to protect the rights of the politically powerless, those who cannot generate sufficient public support to guarantee their well-being through the political process. Courts have often been willing to lead in efforts for social change while the more politically sensitive legislatures lag behind. Litigation may even pave the way for legislation. A favorable court decision on exclusionary zoning could create a favorable climate for enacting legislation. This is particularly true if the case involves large-scale developments or regional remedies where suburbanites perceive a real threat from additional judicial action.

Open suburbs activists have already found a number of courts to be sympathetic to the problem of widespread suburban exclusion and ready to provide affirmative relief for the wrongs of the past. Although federal courts have acted aggressively when racial discrimination has been proven, only the state courts have begun to focus in on economic exclusion. For these reasons, litigation challenging exclusionary practices, particularly in receptive state courts, remains an essential tool in the open suburbs movement.

Coordinated Public Strategies

The job-linked cluster of strategies has great potential for participation by public agencies and private groups. Land use litigation is likely to be undertaken as a private initiative, although there is certainly room for public involvement through the judicial route. It is also possible for a county, state or the federal government to develop a coordinated strategy for increasing suburban access. For example, a state could focus its resources, regulatory authority, planning expertise and other activities on the problem of suburban exclusion. In most places, counties do not have the necessary power and resources to mount such an effort. Nor is the federal government likely to undertake the job, in spite of its enormous potential. The suburban constituency is just too strong at the national level.

If a state administration decided to orchestrate a suburban strategy, it would require participation by the housing finance agency, the state planning agency, the department of community affairs, the attorney general, a zoning appeals board and other agencies. Massachusetts and Pennsylvania have perhaps moved the farthest towards such a coordinated approach. Whether the various efforts of each of these states were initiated to complement each other is not clear. At least these states have undertaken multiple approaches to opening up their suburban creatures. Massachusetts has a highly active housing finance agency, the recently upheld zoning appeals act, a limited housing subsidy program, and a planning arm which has involved itself in allocation planning. In Pennsylvania, the Department of Community Affairs has used the carrot and stick aggressively. The attorney general has provided legal support for this effort as well as joining in an exclusionary zoning suit against a number of suburbs in the Philadelphia area. Pennsylvania also created a housing finance agency.

If a state's power could be applied in a coordinated way to provide lower-income housing in suburbia, the job could be done. Through legal confrontation, the carrot and stick, and a state appeals process, a state could remove legal barriers to construction of lower-income housing. With its planning capacity, the state can rationalize the process of locating needed housing. Using its housing finance agency and state subsidy programs, the state could finance, develop, and subsidize the housing in communities where the barriers have fallen and the planners say the housing should go. The state could even engage in "land banking" to assure that the land is available on which to build.

In short, a coordinated state (or federal) thrust could put all the pieces together to develop suburban housing efficiently. It looks that way on paper, anyway. The reality is not quite so promising. First, even if all of the necessary agencies and programs were in place, orchestrating their participation in an open suburbs process would be a monumental task. Anyone who has worked in a bureaucracy knows how difficult it is to coordinate the activities of one agency, much less five or six. The job is even harder when the issue around which the agencies are brought together is not the central purpose of any of them. It would take clear and repeated messages from the top to keep this train on the track.

That brings us to the most important constraint on developing a unified public strategy. Anyone at the top who issued visible orders that the HFA was to build lower-income housing in exclusionary suburbs, following litigation if necessary, or that no state grants were to flow to communities not welcoming lower-income housing, etc., would not occupy that office very long. Such an all-out challenge to the quietude of suburbia would not be tolerated by the populace. It represents far too great an intrusion into local affairs not to spark tremendous opposition. Perhaps the most that is politically feasible is the initiation of piecemeal approaches, coordinated whenever possible.

The Watchdog Function: Forcing Public Bodies to Do Their Jobs

Given the political and institutional constraints inherent in mobilizing a state or federal open suburbs effort, private groups should put pressure on public agencies to meet their responsibilities. The glare of publicity may sometimes be enough. Administrative lobbying may be useful. In many cases, litigation will be necessary. These strategies are likely to be less efficient in getting housing built than an approach initiated by the public bodies directly. Since the political realities are likely to limit the initiative of even the public actors who would like to move aggressively on the housing issue, private groups must fill the vacuum.

The opportunities for influencing public agencies may be even greater at the federal level than with the states. The "feds" have more tools available: e.g., housing subsidies, carrots (grant programs and federal facilities), planning grants and requirements. At the same time, the suburban constituency has as great, or greater, a voice at the federal level as in the states. The result is a vast gap between the federal potential and the government's efforts to open the suburbs. Private groups have started to apply pressure, as in the *Brookhaven* case and Suburban Action Institute's lawsuit against HUD and the Interior Department in New Castle, New York. Much more needs to be done here. Bureaucracies must be made to feel that they are making waves if they do not press for lower-income housing. Agencies should receive political heat if they continue business as usual, administering their programs without regard to the housing needs of lower-income people. At the very least, citizen groups should attempt to prevent the flow of taxpayers' funds to communities where lower-income people cannot live. For example, exclusionary localities should not receive federal or state water and sewer grants to facilitate development of more middle- and upper-income housing. Nor should such a community be the site of federal or state facilities with all the benefits they imply. There are many federal agencies and departments in addition to HUD, GSA and the Interior Department whose expenditures should be enjoined until action is taken by suburban communities to provide lower-income housing. Then it will begin to hurt and some barriers will fall. The Environmental Protection Agency has the power to enjoin a community's actions if they cause air or water pollution. Having ordered a halt to the pollution, EPA should then refuse to make a grant to the community to remedy the situation unless there was an active effort underway to provide lower-income housing. EPA would be in a strong leverage position since the locality would have to eliminate the pollution, and without a housing program the community would have to go it alone on the antipollution program. EPA has not even tried applying such pressure.

Similarly, the Department of Transportation (DOT) and its predecessors have provided enormous benefits to suburbs, and in fact have done as much or more than HUD to encourage the growth of affluent white suburbia. DOT should not continue to assist development of suburban highways unless the communities involved are open or opening. If DOT tries to continue the old patterns, the agency should be exposed, pressured and if necessary, sued.

As "general" and "special" revenue sharing programs replace categorical grants at the federal level, they should also be the subject of vigorous attack. These funds are important to many suburbs because they have few or no strings on them. Because of their lack of conditions, revenue sharing programs represent an additional reward for exclusionary communities.

At the same time, it is essential that pressure be maintained to continue subsidized housing programs, to fund them at high levels and to divert a large portion of these funds towards sponsors (including new community developers) who are willing and able to overcome suburban barriers. In short, private groups should attempt to force public bodies to carry out the kind of coordinated approach these agencies might undertake if it were politically feasible for them to do so. Central cities also should get into the act. They suffer many of the costs of suburban exclusion. For example, the City of Baltimore considered filing suit to stop all new residential construction in Maryland if the suburban counties did not begin to provide lower-income housing. Cities would have to convince the courts that they are appropriate plaintiffs, that they have "standing" to sue in these kinds of cases. If they were successful, cities could become an important force in putting political, administrative and legal pressure on higher levels of government.

The Planning Process:
Setting the Stage

One kind of public body which is beginning to take seriously its responsibility to open up housing opportunities is the metropolitan or regional entity, the council of governments or the planning agency. These organizations are moving quite rapidly from a traditionally passive stance on housing into developing and attempting to implement allocation plans. These plans do not, in themselves, alter zoning patterns or remove other impediments which may price out lower-income housing. They do focus public attention on the issue and identify the responsibility of area municipalities. This puts pressure on local officials to respond favorably to subsidized housing proposals which come before them.

Allocation plans also invite the utilization of other strategies. They may encourage enactment of local or state legislation. If implementation is impeded, lawsuits may be filed by other parties to advance the plan. At the same time, the planners should actively assist in the implementation of the plan, soliciting and assisting developers, seeking subsidy funds, negotiating with recalcitrant communities. With this array of complementary (although not formally coordinated) actions by the various actors in an area, the allocation plan may be an important catalyst in an effort to open the suburbs. These communities may begin to meet their responsibilities, sensing that they will all hang separately if they do not hang together.

Can We Get There From Here?

The patterns of metropolitan economic segregation are deeply entrenched in America. But the negative consequences of separating people by income are becoming greater and ever more visible. More people, institutions and interest groups are being hurt badly by the sins of the past which have continued into the present. As the pain increases, so does the pressure for change. A Ford Motor Company executive argues for zoning changes in Mahwah, New Jersey to permit construction of a mixed-income large-scale development. On the other side of the coin, a local union sues the U.S. Army Electronics Command to keep it from moving from Philadelphia to Fort Monmouth, New Jersey, where there is inadequate low- and moderate-income housing.[1] Meanwhile, state bureaucrats are withholding funds from some exclusionary suburbs and suing others in Pennsylvania and ordering the issuance of comprehensive building permits in Massachusetts. Where public officials are not meeting their responsibilities, Suburban Action and other watchdog groups are challenging them. Civil rights, prohousing and open suburbs groups are also confronting the exclusionary suburbs directly, with lawsuits that often embrace a number of communities and exclusionary practices, seeking remedies that promise to actually provide housing. Builders are sometimes allies in challenging exclusionary and nongrowth provisions. Central cities are also beginning to show signs of willingness to join the struggle as they become more painfully aware that their destiny is tied to the destiny of the suburbs.

At the same time, new directions are coming into view. Land banking may be a useful tool for making land appropriate for lower-income housing available. Churches are looking to use their surplus lands for this purpose. If the barriers are eliminated through litigation or otherwise, this land can then be used for lower-income housing. It may also be possible to use federal surplus lands in this way.

Other approaches being considered include the use of federal revenue sharing funds to write down land costs or otherwise subsidize lower-income housing. And large-scale developers might be required to dedicate land or make a contribution to a public fund to assist in this subsidy process. All of the strategies—those being used as well as those only contemplated so far—build on each other. Part of the leverage in each strategy is the threat that other strategies may be applied.

Can we get there from here? We have to. The odds are long; the time is short; but we are on the road.

Regional Housing Distribution Plans'
A Technical Appendix

The purpose of this appendix is to describe the methodology of allocation plans, examine the technical problems involved in developing such plans, and recommend solutions to those problems. The methodological questions present important issues from both a planning and a political perspective—a technically deficient plan most likely will face more political obstacles in getting adopted than a more exact plan; a poorly conceived plan may prove difficult to implement and may even become counterproductive by directing development towards inappropriate areas. Thus both politicians and planners should be concerned about developing a rational, thoughtful plan even though the most technically competent plan probably only grossly measures the relative ability of areas to absorb low- and moderate-income housing.

      This appendix will discuss the methodological approach taken by six representative allocation models: the initial Miami Valley plan; the revised Miami Valley plan; Washington, D.C. COG; San Bernadino; Denver COG; and Southeastern Wisconsin. The major features of each plan will be examined, including choice of the base number of units being planned for, division of the region involved into planning subareas, choice of criteria, and creation of the mathematical model to finally allocate units to each subarea. In examining these methodological issues the plans will be discussed in turn and in a final section the plans will be compared and recommendations made for resolving the more difficult methodological problems.

Miami Valley Regional Planning
Commission Plan I (1970)
      As the first allocation plan adopted, the 1970 Miami Valley plan takes a relatively simple methodological approach.

      Definition of the Region. At the outset it was assumed that the plan would encompass all five counties in the Miami Valley region. No area was excluded from the plan's reach because of an excessively rural character.

Needs Analysis. As a base for the number of units to be allocated throughout the region, the Miami Valley planners analyzed the number of needed new units of low- and moderate-income housing for each county in the region. Total housing need was determined by adding number of households, extent of overcrowding and a reasonable vacancy rate. Total supply was calculated by first adding the number of dwelling units and the anticipated production of new units; then the number of dilapidated units and the number of other units lost from the supply was calculated and subtracted from the first supply subtotal. To the extent that housing need exceeded total housing supply, a deficit of housing units existed. Such a condition existed in each county in the region.

Each county's deficit was distributed among areas lying within that single county. Except for the interrelationship between the housing markets in the two urban counties in the region, the Miami Valley planners felt there was no justification for placing needed housing units outside the counties where the need existed.

Geographical Subareas. Each county was then split into planning subareas which attempted to follow political boundaries. Planning subareas in densely populated suburban areas followed municipal boundaries; in less densely populated suburban areas, subareas followed township lines. The geographical size of all subareas depended on the intensity of development within that subarea; the more fully developed subareas tended to be smaller geographically. Within the City of Dayton the plan's 21 subareas followed census tract lines, but the units were allocated only to the city as a whole.

Choice of Criteria. Next, six criteria were chosen to allocate units to each subarea within the five counties. These criteria were intended to measure each subarea's ability to absorb new units of low- and moderate-income housing, increase geographic dispersion of such housing, and place the housing where need for units already existed. Factor one distributed an equal number of units to each subarea within that county. Factor two distributed units on the basis of the subarea's proportionate share of the county's households. Factor three distributed units to each subarea based on the inverse rank order of the subarea's income. This factor tended to place units in areas which had a relatively high proportion of the region's wealthy households. A fourth factor tended to place housing where need already existed. This factor calculated the subarea's proportionate share of the county's households earning less than $10,000 ($7,000 in rural counties). Factor four and factor three tended to cancel each other out but the different methods of quantifying these factors—rank ordering versus simple arithmetic proportion—guaranteed that the two factors measured relative ability without the cancelling effect.

The two remaining criteria tended to measure the subarea's ability to absorb new housing in relation to the subarea's capacity to absorb new students in its school system. One of these factors measured the assessed valuation per pupil of each subarea. This factor tended to place units in areas with relatively high assessed valuations. The other school-related factor was pupils in excess of normal capacity, which indicated overcrowding and the need for more classrooms. Again the plan used an inverse rank order for this factor which meant that the most severely crowded districts received fewer dwelling units.

Mathematical Formula. In mathematical terms the above criteria were translated into the actual number of units to be distributed to each planning subarea within each county as follows:

$$HN_1 \, D_1 = A + B + C + D_2 + E + F/ \text{ or } G$$

Where:

$HN_1 \, D_1$ = housing need distribution

A = equal distribution method

B = proportionate share of total households

C = proportionate share of households \$10,000 or \$7,000

D_2 = inverse rank order of number of households \$10,000 or \$7,000

E = direct rank order based on assessed valuation

F = inverse rank order based on pupils in excess of normal capacity

G = composite or average of above methods of distribution

Formulas for the specific methods are:

$$A = \frac{\Sigma \, HN_1}{N_2}$$

$$B = \frac{N_2 HH/PU}{\Sigma HH} = \% \times \delta \, HN_1 = HN_1/PU$$

$$C = \frac{N_2 HH \, < \$10,000 \text{ or } < \$7,000/PU}{\Sigma HH \, < \$10,000 \text{ or } < \$7,000} = \% \times \Sigma \, HN_1 = HN_1/PU$$

$$D_2 = \downarrow\downarrow \frac{R \to S/PU}{\Sigma \, S} = \% \times \Sigma \, HN_1 = HN_1/PU$$

$$E = \downarrow\downarrow\uparrow\uparrow \frac{R \rightarrow S/PU}{\Sigma S} = \% \times \Sigma HN_1 + HN_1/PU$$

$$F = \uparrow\downarrow \frac{R \rightarrow S/PU}{\Sigma S} = \% \times HN_1 = HN_1/PU$$

$$G = \frac{\Sigma A + B + C + D + E + F/PU}{C} = HN_1/PU$$

Where (in addition to above definitions):

ΣHN_1 = total or summation of housing need for county

N_2 = number

HH = households

PU = planning unit

R = ranking position

$\uparrow\downarrow$ = inverse relationship of factors

$\downarrow\downarrow\uparrow\uparrow$ = direct relationship of factors

$\rightarrow$ = yields

S = score

Σ = summation or overall county total

Thus the final allocation for each subarea depended on a simple averaging of each criterion once that criteria has been translated into a numerical score.

Miami Valley Regional Planning Commission II (1973)

After publication of the 1970 census data, MVRPC dramatically revised its allocation model. As previously noted, the 1970 MVRPC model was methodologically quite simple, using an arithmetic average of six single factors to derive the recommended distribution of housing units. In contrast, the 1973 model is perhaps the most complicated plan created to date. It uses 12 factors combined into a single distribution factor by operation of complex statistical tests. Briefly, the formula is: Fair Share = Equal Share + Need Adjustment factor + Ability Adjustment factor + Performance Adjustment factor. The total county need for new units is initially divided equally among planning units in each county; an individual planning unit's share is then adjusted according to its relative need for low- and moderate-income housing, its relative ability to absorb such housing, and its past performance in providing subsidized housing.

Definition of the Region and Geographical Subareas. The MVRPC continued to plan for the region as a whole in its 1973 plan; subareas remained virtually the same.

Needs Analysis. Both the 1970 and 1973 plans calculate the net county housing deficit in the following manner: Housing Deficit $= (HH + O + V) - (HS - (D_1 + $ Unav. Vt$)$. County low and moderate income net need 1970 $= (HH < \$10,000$ or $< \$7,000 +) + V) - (L + M HS_1 - D_1)$.

Where HH = number of households

              O = overcrowded or doubled households

              V = vacancy factor

              D_1 = dilapidated units

              HS_1 = total housing supply

              Unav. Vt   = unavailable vacant houses

              $L + M$ = low and moderate

The factors in these formulas were updated in the 1973 plan to reflect new information available from the 1970 census. Overcrowding was now calculated by the following formulas:

County overcrowding $= SF + (NRH/A \div HH/A). HH < \$5,000$

County low and moderate income overcrowding $= .90.CO.$

Where: (all information below available from 1970 census data)

              SF = subfamilies

              NRH/A = non-relatives to head of household by area

HH/A = number of households in each area

CO = county overcrowding

To update the overcrowding figures to 1973, the 1960–1970 annual rate of change was used to project to 1973. Since a fraction of the total nonrelatives to heads of households was used in 1970, it was assumed that this fraction remained constant until 1973. The same procedures were then followed to derive the 1973 index of overcrowding. As the Miami Valley planners explained: "The basic assumption prevailing within this analysis of overcrowding or undoubling was that this condition is largely a result forced by economic conditions rather than by mere choice. Moreover, it was assumed that the incidence of this phenomenon is even more prevalent in low-income families."

The 1973 plan retained 4.5 percent as the ideal vacancy rate for urban counties and the 4.0 percent vacancy rate for rural counties. The rationale for building this factor into a derivation of need remained the same—vacant units are needed to insure mobility and choice in housing opportunities.

Computing dilapidated units for the 1973 plan proved to be a difficult task; the 1970 census deleted this statistic and therefore a method had to be developed to update 1960 census data. The Miami Valley plan worked in the following manner. The method recommended by the Bureau of the Census in terms of calculating housing condition (substandard housing) was first applied. This entailed summing the number of units which in 1960 lacked some or all plumbing facilities and what the 1960 proportion of deteriorated units with plumbing was of the total, including sound units with plumbing, and applying that percent to the 1970 census figure for total housing units with all plumbing. The next step involved devising a method of deriving dilapidation from substandard housing supply. A basic assumption which was made in the above process was that the number of units lacking some or all plumbing in 1960 included all dilapidated units, plus both sound and deteriorated units lacking plumbing. It was also necessary to construct for 1960 the same component parts of substandard housing supply as defined in 1970. This figure was derived by adding the numbers of sound units lacking only hot water, sound units lacking other plumbing facilities, deteriorating units and dilapidated units. Of this total figure (representing 1960 substandard housing), the percentage representing dilapidation was applied to the 1970 substandard housing figure. The overriding assumption here was that while actual numbers would change, the same proportion would continue to exist.

Choice of Criteria.   The 1973 MVRPC plan adopts new criteria to measure any planning unit's need, ability and performance with respect to low- and moderate-income housing. In the 1970 plan existing need within a subarea was measured by a single factor—the number of low- and moderate-income households in the subarea. In the 1973 plan five factors replace this single indicator: number of low- and moderate-income families; number of renter-occupied housing units with occupants whose incomes are under $10,000 and who pay 25 percent or more of their income in rent; number of housing units lacking some or all plumbing facilities; number of overcrowded housing units (i.e., with 1.51 or more persons per room); and number of occupied units with roomers, boarders and lodgers. Using all these factors was intended to give a more complete picture of actual need within a planning subarea.

To measure a subarea's ability to absorb new housing, the 1973 plan continues to use assessed valuation per pupil and pupils in excess of school capacity. The 1973 plan also measures the amount of vacant land as an allocation criterion. The 1970 plan did not include such a factor. As a consequence, several suburban areas were given large allocations but had little buildable vacant land to fulfill the plan's goals. The 1973 plan attempts to meet this problem by adding the factor acres of suitable vacant land. This factor is defined as vacant land within the 1970 Dayton urbanized area or within municipalities providing or planning to provide water and sewer service. This definition is intended to reflect the amount of an area which might be developable in the foreseeable future.

The 1970 plan did not consider performance in providing assisted low- and moderate-income housing because at the time only four subareas had such housing. In 1973, 19 of the 32 planning units had some subsidized housing. The Miami Valley planners believed that the allocation process should reflect these efforts. Thus the 1973 plan has two indices of performance—public housing units built; and other subsidized units built.

Mathematical Formula. The 1970 plan gave each factor in the allocation process an equal weight and simply averaged all factors to obtain a composite score. In contrast, the 1973 plan weighs criteria in terms of their relative importance and uses a statistical method of combining factors which translates such diverse variables as acres of vacant land, numbers of households, and dollars of assessed valuation into comparable units.

Mathematically, the Miami Valley planners used the statistical methods of computing standard deviations and standard scores to compare the same type of data among subareas and to compare different data in the same subarea. In terms of the allocation process, standard deviation is calculated by the following formula:

$$S_f = \sqrt{\frac{\sum_{=1}^{N_c} (I_{fp} - \bar{I}_f)^2}{N_c}}$$

Where: S_f = standard deviation among planning units for index factor f

I_{fp} = value of index factor f for planning

$\bar{I}_f$ = average value of index factor f

N_c = number of planning units in the county

Standard score is calculated as follows:

$$Z_{fp} = \frac{I_{fp} - \bar{I}_f}{S_f}$$

Where: Z_{fe} = standard score for index factor for planning unit p

$\bar{I}_f$ = average value of index factor f

I_{fp} = value of index factor f for planning unit p

S_f = standard deviation among planning units for index factor f

As the 1973 plan explains, "[i]n order to use the standard scores to derive adjustment factors" they must be converted from units of deviation to units of proportion. The formula used for this conversion is as follows:

$$U_{fp} = \frac{ZZ_{fp}}{\displaystyle\sum_{p=1}^{N_c} |Z_{fp}|}$$

Where: U_{fp} = unweighted adjustment factors for index factor f for planning unit p

Z_{fp} = standard score for index factor f for planning unit p

The purpose of creating adjustment factors is to generate a series of numbers which allocate + 100 percent of the units to be built among those planning subareas having positive standard scores and – 100 percent among those planning subareas which have negative standard scores.

However, since each adjustment index factor only affects a portion of all the units to be allocated to a subarea, the Miami Valley planners employed a system of weighing factors to calculate the ultimate allocation to each subarea. The aim of the weighing process was to "increase the sensitivity of the allocation process both in terms of interrelationships of individual factors and the differences in these interrelationships in individual counties." The weight assigned each index factor was computed by relating the group affected by that factor with the base group of which the affected group was a part. Both the affected group and the base group were quantified and the weight assigned to the index factor is represented by the following mathematical statement:

$$W_f = \frac{A_f}{B_f}$$

Where: W_f = weight to be applied to unweighed adjustment factor (U_{fp})

A_f = size of group affected by index factor f

B_f = size of base group for index factor f

The following chart is a list of base groups and affected groups for each index factor in the second Miami Valley plan.

Factors in the Allocation Process

Index Factor (Planning Unit Data)	Affected Group (County Data)	Base Group (County Data)
Need Factors		
number of low- and moderate-income families*	same as index factor	all families
number of renter-occupied housing units with incomes under $10,000**	same as index factor	all occupied housing units
number of housing units lacking some or all plumbing	same as index factor	all housing units
number of occupied housing units with 1.51 or more persons per room	same as index factor	all occupied housing units
number of occupied housing units with roomers, lodgers & boarders**	same as index factor	all occupied housing units
Ability Factors		
assessed valuation per pupil	number of pupils in public school	total population
number of pupils in excess of capacity	number of pupils in public school	total population
number of households with income below poverty level	all households	all households

Factors in the Allocation Process

Index Factor (Planning Unit Data)	Affected Group (County Data)	Base Group (County Data)
number of acres of suitable vacant land	total population (1975 projection)	total population (1970 actual)
Performance Factors		
number of public housing units actually built	number of families with incomes below poverty level	all families
number of other subsidized units actually built	number of low- & moderate-income families*	all families

  *low- and moderate-income equals: under \$10,000 (Montgomery and Greene Counties)
under \$ 7,000 (Miami, Darke and Preble Counties)

**data not available for Darke County. ·

Once weighed scores are calculated for each criterion, composition adjustment factors for each factor group (need, ability and performance) are computed. The mathematical formula for this operation is:

$$C_{gp} = \frac{\sum\limits_{f=1}^{Ng} U_{fg}\, W_f}{3 \sum\limits_{f=1}^{Ng} W_f}$$

Where: C_{gp} = composition adjustment factor for group *g* for planning unit *p*

            U_{fp} = unweighed adjustment factor *f* for planning subarea *p*

            W_f = weight to be applied to factor *f*

            $N(g)$ = number of index factors in factor *g*

Finally, the fair share proportion of the county's housing allocation can be computed for each subarea:

$$F_p = \frac{1}{N_c} \sum\limits_{g=1}^{3} C_{gp}$$

Where: F_p = fair proportion of the total county housing allocated to sub-area p

N_c = number of planning units in the county: $\dfrac{1}{N_c}$ thus represents an equal share of the county's need

C_{gp} = composite adjustment factor for factor group g for planning unit p

This last formula translates into the original verbal formulation of the 1973 Miami Valley plan:

Fair Share (F_p) = Equal Share $(1/N_c)$ + Need + Ability + Performance

$$\left(\sum_{g=1}^{3} C_{gp} \right)$$

As a final adjustment to this formula, the fair share formula for the county containing Dayton was changed to reflect the fact that Dayton, under the formula, received a negative allocation. Therefore, Dayton's allocation was adjusted up to zero and the allocations of the remaining planning units in the county were adjusted accordingly. Thus the final allocation formulas read:

For Dayton's county

$$D_p = \frac{F_p}{\sum\limits_{p=2}^{14} F_p} (N)$$

For all other counties

$$D_p = F_p (N)$$

Where: N = total county need for low- and moderate-income housing

F_p = fair proportion of total county need allocated to sub-area p

D_p = fair share distribution of low- and moderate-income units to subarea p

Figure D_p was further adjusted to reflect the number of units under construction.

Washington COG Plan (1972)

The Washington COG plan takes a different approach from either of the two Miami Valley plans—the Washington COG plan neither allocates all of the metropolitan area's needed units of low- and moderate-income housing nor does it attempt to average disparate factors such as availability of jobs and vacant land with school capacity. The plan only allocates the number of available HUD subsidized units for the Metropolitan Washington area among the area's local political jurisdictions.

Definition of the Region.   The plan encompasses the whole area for which the COG has jurisdiction.

Needs Analysis.   No overall needs analysis was necessary because the plan only allocates the number of units HUD plans to subsidize in the region.

Planning Subareas.   The subareas within the region are all political jurisdictions, cities and counties. Only 15 such subareas are delineated. Thus, the subareas are generally large geographically. This is partially a consequence of the peculiar lack of many political subdivisions in the Washington area.

Choice of Criteria.   Eight factors were chosen to allocate the subsidized units to the subareas. These factors were in three areas—demand criteria, supply criteria, and locational criteria. The demand criteria, used to describe need in each local jurisdiction, were: (1) the number of overcrowded units indicated by the 1970 census; (2) the number of deficient units as estimated from the 1970 census using methods recommended by the Bureau of the Census; and (3) the number of heads of households making less than $10,000 who commute into each local jurisdiction for jobs as indicated by a survey completed by Washington COG.

Two factors were compouted to indicate the relative capabilities of subareas to accommodate additional units: (1) the number of acres of vacant residential land which now has sewer service or is projected to have sewer service within the next six years; and (2) the number of vacant housing units in the jurisdiction.

Three special locational factors were added to the allocation formula: (1) the potential per capita fiscal resources of each local jurisdiction— as measured by the total real estate value of the jurisdiction, plus all the personal income divided by the local population; (2) the percent of all jobs in the region within 45 minutes commuting time of the local jurisdiction's residents; and (3) the percent of all housing units in each local jurisdiction valued at less than $25,000 or renting for less than $150 per month.

Mathematical Formula.   These factors were translated into a fair share allocation for each jurisdiction by the following equations:

Fair Share = (Demand + Supply) X Modifier

Where: Demand = low- and moderate-income commuters + overcrowding +
                          deficient units

          Supply = vacant residential land + vacant housing units

$$\text{Modifier} = \frac{\text{fiscal resources}}{\substack{\text{low- and moderate-income} \\ \text{housing concentration}}} \times \text{accessibility to employment}$$

$$\substack{\text{Fiscal} \\ \text{Resources}} = \frac{\text{real estate value + personal income}}{\text{population}}$$

In calculating allocations to each subarea actual number of units,
commuters and acres of vacant land were chosen for the demand and supply
factors, rather than local percentages, because the Washington COG planners
felt these numbers adjusted the formula to account for the wide variations
among the sizes of subareas. In contrast, percentage and per capita figures
were used in the special locational factors because these factors were intended
to measure local conditions within the subareas which modified the relative
comparisons of supply and demand.

San Bernardino Government-Subsidized
Housing Distribution Model
The purpose of the San Bernardino allocation plan is to allocate
to each planning district a fair share percentage of the total number of new
government-subsidized dwelling units to be constructed during any given
year in the San Bernardino Valley, and to distribute these units in a manner
consistent with sound planning principles.

Definition of the Region.   Unlike other plans, the area encompassed
by the San Bernardino plan does not include the whole area for which the
agency doing the plan has jurisdiction. Because of the rural nature of the
mountain-desert portion of San Bernardino County, the plan excludes these
regions.

Definition of Subareas.   Unlike other plans, San Bernardino's does
not follow political boundaries in delineating subareas; subareas are amalgama-
tions of census tracts. These groups of tracts, however, attempt to encompass
identifiable communities. Since census tracts often follow political boundaries,
the San Bernardino subareas often are congruent with political subdivisions.

Needs Analysis.   As in Washington COG, no initial analysis of
total housing need was made.

Choice of Criteria. The San Bernardino plan is unique in a third characteristic—the plan creates a two step allocation process. The first step in the model is the interplanning district distribution model. This portion of the plan allocates units among planning subareas. The second step, the "minimodel," distributes units within planning subareas. This portion of the plan is supposed to identify a number of localized areas in which a developer can select a specific site for a project consistent with specific planning goals and political considerations. The minimodel is based upon the geographical base of the elementary school service district.

The San Bernardino interdistrict distribution model closely resembles the 1970 Miami Valley plan. Eight criteria were chosen to represent relative need for and ability to absorb new units of subsidized housing: (1) number of households; (2) number of households with an annual gross income of $10,000 or less; (3) deficient dwellings units affordable by the indicated income group; (4) assessed value per average daily attendance; (5) existing additional school capacity; (6) number of jobs; (7) vacant residential land (in parcels of five acres or more valued at $10,000 per acre or less); and (8) equal share.

Mathematical Formula and the Minimodel. All factors were then expressed for each subarea as a percentage of the region's total. The eight factors were then added together and averaged, giving a percentage figure which represented the final allocation to each planning subarea. Two other ground rules were added to the maximodel. First, no development of single family detached dwelling units shall have more than 40 government subsidized units and no subsidized multiple-unit housing project shall exceed 75 units. Second, all subsidized housing projects or subdivisions shall be separated from each other by a spacing radius of 50 feet per dwelling unit in the project. Thus a project with 20 dwelling units will have no subsidized project closer than 1,000 feet. (The plan provides for waiver of the strict application of this spacing criteria if the proposed project is to be built in a subarea where a deficiency in housing exists.)

The intra-planning-district model divides subareas into neighborhoods to facilitate rational development of housing within planning subareas. The geographical base of these divisions is the elementary school district service area. Five factors are used to place housing within subareas: (1) saturation of schools; (2) availability of mass transportation; (3) location of major job centers; (4) existing subsidized housing; and (5) availability of undeveloped land. Each of the factors was equally weighed on a 1–3–5 point scale as follows:

1. Elementary School Enrollment   Points

   (Capacity to absorb new students, stated as
   percentage of saturation)

100% + saturation	1
80% to 99% saturation	3
60% to 79% saturation	5

2. Local Mass Transportation

No transit within the area	1
Transit along the border of the area	3
Transit within the statistical area	5

3. Major Job Centers

(Job opportunities of varying types)

No job centers within the area	1
Job centers along the border of the area	3
Job centers within the area	5

4. Existing Federally-Subsidized Housing Projects

Housing projects within the area	1
Housing projects bordering the area	3
No housing projects within the area	5

5. Size of Statistical Area as Percentage of Total Study Area

0 to 5.9%	1
6.0% to 7.9%	3
8.0% and over	5

Denver COG Regional Housing Plan

The Denver COG regional housing plan largely adopts the approach taken by the 1970 Miami Valley plan: an initial regionwide needs analysis forms the basis of the plan. The Denver plan differs in that the need factor is expressly divided between low-income need and moderate-income need. Once need is determined, the region is divided into subareas following municipal boundaries. Criteria are then chosen which allocate the needed units to the subareas by averaging all the quantified criteria scores.

Choice of Criteria. Seven allocation criteria were selected by Denver COG: (1) number of deficient housing units measured by number of overcrowded units plus number of housing units lacking some or all plumbing facilities; (2) and (3) low- and moderate-income housing needs measured the number of low- and moderate-income families in the area minus the number of housing units renting or selling for less than stated dollar amounts; (4) ability to absorb the costs of new growth (The total assessed valuation of a sub-area is measured as a percentage of the regional total and this figure is averaged with the percentage share of the region's population for that subarea.); (5) employment opportunities (The numbers for this criteria are generated by adding all the new jobs created between 1960 and 1970 by work place and finding out what percentage each subarea in the region contributed to that employment gain.); (6) a factor for dispersing housing throughout the Denver region and avoiding economic impaction of areas (This criterion was quantified by adding up the total of all the region's households making more than $15,000 and finding out what percentage live in each subarea.); and (7) availability of vacant developable land and housing need (This last criterion has two parts which are averaged together equally: (a) percentage of the region's developable land as measured by all parcels of two acres or more that neither lie in a flood plain nor have a slope greater than 15 percent but are in the Denver urban area; and (b) percentage share of total building permits issued which relates to the land available and actually being used for building.).

Mathematical Model. When every criterion is quantified, the final allocation to subareas is accomplished by a simple averaging of each criterion for each subarea.

Southeastern Wisconsin Regional
Planning Commission: A Short-Range
Action Housing Program

The Southeastern Wisconsin Regional Planning Commission (SEWRPC) allocation plan's purpose was to implement a short-range two year program to disperse 2,000 subsidized housing units throughout the southeastern Wisconsin region. The allocation plan thus only deals with these 2,000 units. The SEWRPC plan uses nine allocation factors: (1) the ratio of severely overcrowded housing for the subarea to the total number of severely overcrowded units in the region; (2) the ratio of minority population in each planning area to the total minority population in the region; (3) the ratio of families with single heads in each planning area to the total number of primary families with single heads in the region; (4) households with six or more persons ratio; (5) average full value of real and personal property per household; (6) total property tax levy in each planning area, divided by the state-equalized value of real and personal property; (7) growth in population; (8) vacant land; and (9) inverse measure of number of low- and moderate-income housing units.

Each of these criteria was then given a weighing factor. For instance, 17 percent of the units were allocated on the basis of overcrowding while 10 percent of the units were allocated on the basis of population growth. Thus, 200 units were allocated throughout the region on the basis of population. If a sub-area had 15 percent of the region's population growth, that subarea was assigned 30 units on the basis of population growth. The final allocation is calculated by adding together all such mathematical calculations.

Selecting an Appropriate Methodology: Choice of Criteria

As the previous discussion of the six plans demonstrates, the criteria chosen attempt to allocate housing units to the planning subareas on the basis of need, ability and previous performance. Explicitly or implicitly, however, each plan recognizes that the criteria chosen can only be proxies for these abstract concepts and, further, that the criteria chosen in many cases can only indirectly measure the intended factor. This subsection will discuss the choice of criteria and the difficulty in collecting uniform regionwide data which attempt to measure need, ability and performance in each subarea.

Need. Measuring need usually involves discovering the status of the present housing stock in each subarea and demand by nonresidents for housing in the subarea. Direct measurement of some aspects of the housing stock is possible from 1970 census data. Data such as number of overcrowded units and number of units lacking some or all plumbing facilities is readily available and can be aggregated for a wide variety of geographical bases. Another indication of need which is relatively easy to obtain is vacancy rate—this data is usually collected by local real estate broker associations. Vacancy rates of under three percent indicate a relatively tight housing market.

The 1970 census, however, does not measure dilapidated units, so several plans have extrapolated this information from 1960 census data using a Census Bureau formula. Even the planners who use this measure admit this method provides only an educated guess at the real number of dilapidated units. Another important indicator of need which is also difficult to obtain is data or numbers of units to be taken out of the housing supply by public action such as urban renewal or highway construction.

Data on commuting patterns also can be a proxy for housing need. The more employees who commute long distance into a subarea, the more likely it is that such employees could not find housing near their employment; thus a plan which does nothing but measure existing housing stock may ignore this important element of need.

Ability. There are a wide range of factors which measure a sub-area's ability to absorb new subsidized housing—fiscal resources, capacity of schools, number of available employment opportunities, and amount of vacant land. Some plans also use population as a measure of ability to absorb new units of housing. Obtaining data on fiscal resources such as property tax and state sales tax rebates is relatively easy; similarly, the census makes population data easy to obtain and school capacity is usually measured yearly by some governmental agency such as a state or county board of education.

Data on vacant land which actually measures land appropriate for residential development and data which measures job opportunities for low- and moderate-income employees, however, are almost impossible to obtain. In fact, the Miami Valley planners rejected jobs as a factor partly because no reliable data were available. Using jobs as a criterion usually creates difficult methodological problems. First, data on jobs for low- and moderate-income people alone are often not disaggregated from statistics giving jobs at all income and skill levels. Second, often the geographical job pool is different than that of the planning area for housing—the housing-planning subarea may have few job opportunities but the adjoining subarea within reasonable commuting distance may have a multitude of job centers. Availability of public transportation will also change the relevant job pool. Third, most plans which use employment criteria assume implicitly that additional job growth will take place where jobs are now located, without taking into account the employment capacity of major job centers, employment trends and industrial growth patterns. Without looking at these factors, housing may be located near job centers where employment is actually declining and the various industries may be obsolete or in need of highly technical skills which low- and moderate-income persons do not generally provide. While major job centers in the outer suburbs may be expected to grow in the future, others in the core city and inner suburbs may be dying out. Thus, if data are available on projected job growth—e.g., location, kinds of jobs—the jobs criterion should incorporate these factors to provide housing with real opportunities for jobs. In light of the difficulties of collecting ideal data which report total number of jobs by income and skill level, number of openings at each level over time, and projected development trends, the best practical solution often is to consider the existing jobs as one of a number of factors in the model.

Total vacant land in acres as an ability criterion, or even total vacant land in parcels over a certain acreage for a certain price, are also unexact measures. This approach ignores problems of vacant land lying in flood plains, current or potential availability of sewer and water service, or plans for vacant land as permanent open space. Thus any plan which uses vacant land as a criterion must attempt to use a more accurate measuring technique than just vacant land in bulk.

Performance. Performance in providing low- and moderate-income housing in each subarea is easy to measure. Census data reveal dollar amount paid for rent per unit and dollar valuation of owner-occupied units. These figures make it easy to determine the existing number of units in each subarea which are affordable by low- and moderate-income families. An assumption is made that generally all such units are so occupied. Census data also provide a test for this assumption by recording income by family size, which allows actual measurement of the numbers of low- and moderate-income families in the subarea.

Another measurement of performance is number of subsidized units actually built in each subarea. Such data should be available from the Department of Housing and Urban Development.

Creation of Subareas

Several factors determine the choice of the geographical base for subareas: subareas must be large enough so that there are enough sites in each subarea to fulfill the plan's goals; political responsibility must be ascertainable during the implementation process; and data must be available so that the criteria chosen can be quantitied. Political jurisdictions such as municipalities or townships usually fulfill these three requirements. In areas where municipalities or townships are too small, groups of these political subdivisions may be appropriate.

Mathematical Formulae

Three major types of mathematical models are used to quantify criteria and then allocate units to each subarea. The first MVRPC approach is the simplest method—each criterion is quantified as a percentage of the region's total for that criterion; then the percentage score for all the criteria are averaged together giving a composite allocation score. A second approach, employed by Denver COG and SEWRPC, used the same type of averaging techniques as does MVRPC. Each criterion, however, is given a weighted score; for instance, 30 percent of the units are allocated on the basis of fiscal ability while 20 percent of the units are allocated on the basis of jobs. The third approach is taken by the revised MVRPC plan. Here all factors are weighted as in the type two plan but are combined in such a manner as to attempt to account for wider fluctuations in certain criteria which may mask other characteristics in certain subareas.

Using standard deviation scores in the mathematical model instead of simple averaging attempts to answer several difficult problems created by the averaging technique. For instance, if vacant land is one criterion and the subarea in question has little suitable vacant land but high relative scores for other criteria, then the subarea may receive a large allocation which it is unable to fulfill. The standard deviation method of scoring recognizes such statistical anomolies and reduces the overall allocation accordingly. This approach, although more difficult to use and explain to the public, may provide real advantages in the implementation stage.

Notes

CHAPTER 1
THE HIGH COST OF SUBURBAN EXCLUSION

1. "Barriers to Minority Suburban Access," statement of Dr. George H. Brown, Director, Bureau of the Census, U.S. Department of Commerce, *Hearings of the United States Commission on Civil Rights,* (Washington, D.C.: Government Printing Office, 1971), pp. 523–65.
2. Ibid.
3. *Report of the National Advisory Commission on Civil Disorders* (Washington, D.C.: 1969).
4. National Commission on Urban Problems, *Building the American City* (Washington, D.C.: Government Printing Office., 1968).
5. John F. Kain, "The Distribution and Movement of Jobs and Industry," *The Metropolitan Enigma* (New York: Anchor Books, 1968), p. 31.
6. National Committee Against Discrimination in Housing, *The Impact of Housing Patterns on Job Opportunities* (New York: National Committee Against Discrimination in Housing, 1968), pp. 24–25.
7. Bureau of Labor Statistics, "Civilian Employment Changes in Selected Large Metropolitan Areas, By Zones, 1968–1971" (Washington, D.C.: G.P.O., 1972).
8. Ibid.
9. Paul Davidoff, Linda Davidoff and Neil Newton Gold, "Suburban Action: Advocate Planning for an Open Society," *AIP Journal,* January 1970, p. 3.
10. Bureau of Labor Statistics, op. cit.
11. Ibid.
12. U.S. Commission on Civil Rights, *Federal Installations and Equal Housing Opportunity* (Washington, D.C.: U.S. Commission on Civil Rights, 1970), p. 4.
13. Regional Plan Association, *Linking Skills, Jobs and Housing in the New York City Region,* (New York: Regional Plan Association, March 1972), p. 6.

14. Ibid., p. 19.
15. Lynne B. Sagalyn and George Sternlieb, *Zoning and Housing Costs* (New Brunswick, N.J.: Rutgers University, Center for Urban Policy Research, 1973), p. 95.
16. John F. Kain, "Housing Segregation, Negro Employment, and Metropolitan Decentralization," *Quarterly Journal of Economics* LXXXII (May 1968): 175–97.
17. Ibid.
18. Bureau of the Census, *Consumer Buying Indicators, Special Report on Household Ownership and Purchase of Automobiles and Selected Household Durables, 1960–67,* Table 2 (Washington, D.C.: Government Printing Office, 1967).
19. Regional Plan Association, op. cit.
20. National Committee Against Discrimination in Housing, op. cit., pp. 28–29.
21. Ibid.
22. Ibid.
23. Ibid.
24. Chicago Urban League, *Research Report: Linking Black Residence to Suburban Employment* (Chicago: Chicago Urban League, 1971), p. 4.
25. National Committee Against Discrimination in Housing, op. cit., p. 29.
26. Bureau of Labor Statistics, op. cit.
27. Ibid.
28. Derived from Illinois Employment Service, *Employment Covered Under the Illinois Unemployment Compensation Act 1957–1970: A Survey By Chicago Postal Zones and Major Suburban Communities,* (Chicago: Illinois Employment Service, 1971).
29. National Committee Against Discrimination in Housing, op. cit., p. 14.
30. Ibid.
31. Neil Newton Gold and Paul Davidoff, "The Supply and Availability of Land for Housing Low and Moderate Income Families," *The Report of the President's Committee on Urban Housing—Technical Studies—Volume II* (Washington, D.C.: Government Printing Office, 1968), p. 304.
32. Judson Gooding, "Roadblocks Ahead for the Great Corporate Move-out," *Fortune,* June 1971, pp. 81–82.
33. William T. Cahill, *Special Message to the Legislature: A Blueprint for Housing in New Jersey* (Trenton, N.J.: Office of the Governor, December 7, 1970), p. 10.
34. Montgomery County Project, *Housing Needs of Montgomery County's Projected Workers* (Bethesda, Maryland: Montgomery County, Maryland Department of Community and Economic Development, 1972), pp. 73–74.
35. The National Jobs-Linked Housing Center, *Jobs and the Missing Link—Housing* (New York, 1973), p. 3.
36. President's Committee on Urban Housing, *A Decent Home* (Washington, D.C.: Government Printing Office, 1968), p. 139.

37. Ibid., p. 376.
38. Ibid.
39. Davidoff, Davidoff and Gold, op. cit., p. 13.
40. Edward Logue, "New York: Are Cities a Bust?", *Look,* April 1, 1969, p. 70.
41. Gold and Davidoff, op. cit.
42. Advisory Commission on Intergovernmental Relations, *Fiscal Balance in the American Federal System: Metropolitan Fiscal Disparities* (Washington, D.C.: Advisory Commission on Intergovernmental Relations, 1967), p. 64.
43. Advisory Commission on Intergovernmental Relations, *Central City— Suburban Fiscal Disparities in the 77 Largest Metropolitan Areas* (Washington, D.C.: Advisory Commission on Intergovernmental Relations, 1972), p. 51.
44. James W. Guthrie, *Schools and Inequality* (Cambridge, Mass.: MIT Press, 1971).
45. Advisory Commission on Intergovernmental Relations, *Fiscal Balance,* p. 60.
46. Guthrie, op. cit.
47. Ibid.
48. James S. Coleman, et al., *Equality of Educational Opportunity* (Washington, D.C.: Government Printing Office, 1966).
49. Muriel Paskin Carrison, "On Bussing: Legitimacy and Public Opinion," *School and Society,* April 1972, p. 224.
50. Rodriguez v. San Antonio Independent School District, 411 U.S. 1 (1973).
51. Advisory Commission on Intergovernmental Relations, *Fiscal Balance,* p. 72.

CHAPTER 2
THE SUBURBAN OBSTACLE COURSE:
BARRIERS TO BUILDING HOUSING
FOR LOWER-INCOME PEOPLE

1. U.S. Department of Commerce, *A Standard State Zoning Enabling Act,* §1 (1926).
2. Ibid.
3. National Commission on Urban Problems, *Building the American City,* pt. III, (Washington, D.C.: National Commison on Urban Problems, 1968) p. 212.
4. Eric J. Branfman, Benjamin I. Cohen and David M. Trubek, "Measuring the Invisible Wall: Land Use Controls and the Residential Patterns of the Poor," *Yale Law Journal* 82, no. 3 (1973): 483.
5. Ibid., p. 501.
6. National Commission on Urban Problems, op. cit., p. 212.
7. Branfman, Cohen, and Trubek, op. cit., pp. 505–6.
8. National Commission on Urban Problems, op. cit., p. 215.

9. Lawrence Sager, "Exclusionary Zoning: Constitutional Limitations on the Power of Municipalities to Restrict the Use of Land." (Presented at the ACLU Biennial Conference, University of Colorado, Boulder, Colorado, June 8–11, 1972, p. 3.

10. Ibid., p. 3.

11. Ibid., p. 3.

12. N. Williams, "Three Systems of Land-Use Controls," *Rutgers Law Review* 25 (1971): 93.

13. Sager, op. cit., p. 3.

14. Sager, op. cit., p. 35.

15. Metropolitan Area Planning Council, *Residential Zoning in the MAPC Region* (Boston: MAPC, 1972), p. 12.

16. National Commission on Urban Problems, op. cit., p. 212.

17. Sager, op. cit., p. 3.

18. Linda Davidoff, Paul Davidoff and Neil N. Gold, "The Suburbs Have to Open Their Gates," *New York Times Magazine,* November 7, 1971, p. 42.

19. National Commission on Urban Problems, op. cit., pp. 214–15.

20. Norman Williams, Jr. and Thomas Norman, "Exclusionary Land Use Controls: The Case of Northeastern New Jersey," *Syracuse Law Review* 22, no. 2 (1971): 476.

21. R.A. Cunningham, "Interrelationship Between Exclusionary Zoning and Exclusionary Subdivision Control," *Michigan Journal of Law Reform* 5 (1972): 351.

22. "Forum," *HUD Challenge,* vol. III, no. 11, November 1972, p. 15.

23. Golden v. Planning Board of Ramapo, 30 N.Y. 2d 359, 285 N.E. 2d 291 (1972).

24. Testimony of Dale F. Bertsch, Executive Director, Miami Valley Regional Planning Commission, *Hearings Before the United States Commission on Civil Rights,* June 14–17, 1971, (Washington, D.C.: Government Printing Office, 1971), p. 35.

25. David M. Trubek, Hearing Exhibit No. 32, *Hearings Before United States Commission on Civil Rights,* p. 853.

26. Mary E. Brooks, *Lower-Income Housing: The Planner's Response,* (Chicago: American Society of Planning Officials, 1972), p. 40.

27. National Commission on Urban Problems, op. cit., p. 217.

CHAPTER 3
INTRODUCTION TO PUBLIC STRATEGIES

1. Village of Euclid v. Ambler Realty Co., 272 U.S. 365 (1926).

CHAPTER 4
INCLUSIONARY ZONING AT THE
COUNTY LEVEL

1. Fairfax County, Va., Code § 30–1 88 et. seq. (1961); and DeGroff Enterprises, Inc. v. Board of County Supervisors, Law No. 25609 (Fair-

fax County Civ. Ct., November 11, 1971), *aff'd* Va. (August 30, 1973).

2. Don Loomis, "Profile of an Affluent Suburb," *House and Home* (Washington, D.C.: McGraw-Hill News, September 1971), p. 8.

3. Ibid., p. 8.

4. Carol J. Cunningham and James M. Scott, *Land Development and Racism in Fairfax County* (Fairfax, Va.: The Washington Suburban Institute, 1970), p. 6.

5. Reverend Gerald Hopkins, Transcript of the Eighth Conference on Exclusionary Land Use Problems, Washington, D.C., October 5, 1971, p. 3.

6. Ibid.

7. Fairfax County, Va., Code § 30-2.2.2. (2) a.

8. Ibid., § 30-15.3 par. 6.

9. Ibid., § 30-2.2.2 (2) a.

10. Ibid., § 30-2.2.2 (2) b (1) (a).

11. Ibid., § 30-2.2.2 (2) b (2).

12. Ibid., § 30-2.2.2 (2) b (4) and § 30-15.3 par. 6.

13. Fairfax County, Va., Code § 30-15.3 par. 6.

14. Ibid.

15. Ibid.

16. Ibid.

17. DeGroff Enterprises, Inc. v. Board of County Supervisors, No. 25609 (Fairfax County Civ. Ct., November 11, 1971).

18. Board of Supervisors v. DeGroff Enterprises, No. 8118, (Va. Sup. Ct., August 30, 1973).

19. James Birchheld, "The Moratorium," *Washington Evening Star,* November 17, 1972, p. C-1.

20. Fairfax County, Va., Code § 30-2.2.2 (2) d.

21. William Morrill, Transcript of Eighth Conference on Exclusionary Land Use Problems, Washington, D.C., October 5, 1971, p. 4.

22. Robert C. Alexander, "State Housing Finance Agencies Face Difficult Problems During Housing 'Freeze' and Pending Federal Housing Re-evaluation," *Journal of Housing* 30, no. 3 (March 1973): 123.

23. Montgomery County, Md., Code, Chap. 25A, "Housing, Moderately Priced."

24. Richard S. McKernon, County Attorney, Montgomery County to James P. Gleason, County Executive, memorandum concerning "Legality of Moderate Priced Dwelling Unit Bill No. 3-72 and Zoning Text Amendment Application No. F-803," October 25, 1972, p. 6, Center for Urban Affairs, Northwestern University, Evanston, Illinois.

25. Montgomery County, Md., Code, Chap. 25A, "Housing, Moderately Priced."

26. Ibid.

27. Los Angeles, Cal., Proposed Ordinance for the Addition of § 12.39 A, entitled "Requirements," to the Municipal Code, December 5, 1972.

28. Los Angeles, Cal., Proposed Ordinance for the Addition of § 12.39, en-
    titled "Requirements," to the Municipal Code, December 5, 1972.
29. Los Angeles, Cal., Proposed Ordinance for the Addition of § 12.39 (D)
    1, entitled "Modifications," to the Municipal Code, December 5,
    1972.
30. City Attorney, Los Angeles, Cal., City Plan Case No. 23798, p. 4.
31. Eloise Blake, Staff Report on Ordinance, City Plan Case No. 23798.

CHAPTER 5
ALLOCATING HOUSING ON A REGIONAL BASIS

1. Miami Valley Regional Planning Commission, *A Housing Plan for the
    Miami Valley* (Dayton, O.: Miami Valley Regional Planning Commis-
    sion 1970).
2. Metropolitan Council of the Twin Cities Area, *Interim Housing Allocation
    Proposal* St. Paul, Minn., December 1971); San Bernardino County
    Planning Department, *Government Subsidized Housing Distribution
    Model* (San Bernardino, Calif., January 1972); Southeastern Wis-
    consin Regional Planning Commission, *A Short-Range Action
    Housing Program for Southeastern Wisconsin—1972 and 1973*
    (Waukesha, Wis., July 1972); Metropolitan Washington Council of
    Governments, *A Fair Share Housing Formula for Metropolitan
    Washington,* (Washington, D.C., January 1972); Denver Regional
    Council of Governments, *A Regional Housing Plan: Policies and
    their Implementation* (Denver, Col., December 1972).
3. U.S. Congress, testimony of Paul Davidoff, Board of Governors, American
    Institute of Planners, *Hearings on H.R. 9688* 92d Cong., 1st sess.,
    pt. 2, House, Committee on Banking, 1971, p. 674.
4. Howard A. Glickstein, Staff Director, United States Commission on Civil
    Rights to HUD Secretary George Romney, July 26, 1971, Center
    for Urban Affairs, Northwestern University, Evanston, Ill.; see
    also statement of George Romney, quoted in Metropolitan Wash-
    ington Council of Governments, op. cit., p. 2.
5. Petition of Association for Equal Opportunity, Bucks County Interfaith
    Housing Corporation, Housing Association of South Jersey, et al.
    to Delaware Valley Regional Planning Commission (1972), Center
    for Urban Affairs, Northwestern Universty, Evanston, Illinois.
6. 40 U.S.C. § 461, quoted in Petition of Association for Equal Opportunity,
    et al., op. cit., p. 10.
7. Dale F. Bertsch and Ann M. Shafor, "A Regional Housing Plan: The Miami
    Valley Regional Planning Commission Experience," *Planners Note-
    book* 1, no. 1, (April 1971): 4–5.
8. Editorial quoted in Denver Regional Council of Government, "COG Adopts
    Regional Housing Plan," *COG Notes: Monthly Progress Report,* 6,
    no. 1 (January 1973): 1.
9. R. Ann Siracusa, San Bernardino County Planning Department to Lois

Craig, *City Magazine,* April 7, 1972, Center for Urban Affairs,
   Northwestern University, Evanston, Ill.

10. Denver Regional Council of Governments, "Aurora, Lakewood Adopt
   Housing Plan," *COG Notes: Monthly Progress Report,* 6, no. 5
   (May 1973): 2.
11. San Bernardino County Planning Department, op. cit., p. 3.
12. Miami Valley Regional Planning Commission, op. cit., pp. 3–4.
13. Metropolitan Washington Council of Governments, op. cit., p. 4.
14. Miami Valley Regional Planning Commission, op. cit., p. 27.
15. San Bernardino County Planning Department, op. cit., pp. 4, 7.
16. Metropolitan Council of the Twin Cities Area, op. cit., p. 2.
17. Ibid.
18. Miami Valley Regional Planning Commission, *The Miami Valley Region's
   Housing Plan* (Dayton, O.: Miami Valley Regional Planning Commission, 1973).
19. Metropolitan Council of the Twin Cities Area, *Metropolitan Development
   Guide: Housing: Policy Planning Program* (St. Paul, Minn.:
   Metropolitan Council of the Twin Cities Area, 1973), p. 44.
20. San Bernardino County Planning Department, op. cit., p. 1.
21. Nancy Reeves, Housing Planner, Metropolitan Council of the Twin Cities
   Area to Leonard Rubinowitz, April 17, 1973, Center for Urban
   Affairs, Northwestern University, Evanston, Illinois.

CHAPTER 6
STATE REGULATION OF LAND USE

1. Massachusetts Ann. Laws, Chap. 40B § 20–23 (Supp. 1971).
2. SB. 1355, State of Connecticut, January Session (1971); HB 509,
   State of Wisconsin (1973).
3. American Law Institute, "A Model Land Development Code," Tentative
   Draft No. 3, April 22, 1971.
4. Commonwealth of Massachusetts, Senate, Order 933, 1967.
5. Commonwealth of Massachusetts, Senate, Legislative Research Council,
   Restricting the Zoning Power to City and County Governments,
   Rept. 1133, 1968.
6. Ibid., p. 118.
7. Commonwealth of Massachusetts, Department of Community Affairs,
   Proposed Housing Policy and Action Program: Under Section 3
   of Chapter 23B of the Massachusetts General Laws, Rept. 5010,
   January 10, 1972, p. 11.
8. Ibid., p. 28.
9. Commonwealth of Massachusetts, House, Committee on Urban Affairs,
   Rept. 5429, June 1969, p. 2.
10. Massachusetts Ann. Laws, Chap. 40B § 20–23 (Supp. 1971).
11. Ibid., § 20.
12. Ibid.
13. Ibid.

14. Ibid., § 21.
15. Ibid., § 22.
16. Ibid.
17. Ibid., § 23.
18. Ibid., § 21.
19. Board of Appeals of Hanover v. Housing Appeals Committee, Department of Community Affairs, No. 7754, (Sup. Jud. Ct. of Massachusetts, March 22, 1973).
20. Ibid., p. 21.
21. Ibid., p. 28.
22. Ibid., p. 39.
23. Massachusetts Ann. Laws, Chap. 40B § 20–23 (Supp. 1971).
24. Board of Appeals of Hanover v. Housing Appeals Committee, Department of Community Affairs, op. cit., p. 20.
25. Ibid., p. 35.
26. MacDonald Barr, "The Massachusetts Zoning Appeals Law: Lessons of the First Three Years," submitted for presentation at the American Society of Planning Officials Conference, August, 1972, Appendix B. Updated in letter from MacDonald Barr, Coordinator of Planning and Program Development, Massachusetts Department of Community Affairs to Sarah R. Wolff, March 1, 1973, Center for Urban Affairs, Northwestern University, Evanston, Illinois.
27. Ibid.
28. *Housing and Renewal Index*, September 25, 1972, p. 3.
29. Massachusetts Ann. Laws, Chap. 40B, § 20.
30. Commonwealth of Massachusetts, Department of Community Affairs, *Regional Housing Planning Circular*, Boston: Department of Community Affairs, January 17, 1973.
31. Massachusetts Ann. Laws, Chap. 40B § 21.
32. Liz Gallere, "Suburban Stall: Housing for the Poor Blocked Despite Curb on 'Snob Zoning' Laws," *Wall Street Journal*, October 17, 1972.
33. Gallere, op. cit.
34. Ibid.
35. Robert Engler, *Subsidized Housing in the Suburbs: Legislation or Litigation?*, Boston: Massachusetts Department of Community Affairs, June 1971, p. 10.
36. Ibid., pp. 18–22.
37. HB 1449, Commonwealth of Massachusetts (1973); HB 3779, Commonwealth of Massachusetts (1973); HB 4845, Commonwealth of Massachusetts (1973).
38. Metropolitan Area Planning Council, *774 Plus Two: An Interpretive Analysis of Chapter 774 and a Review of Activities*, Planning Information Series: Housing (Boston: Metropolitan Area Planning Council, 1972), p. 6.
39. SB 1335, State of Connecticut, January Session (1971).
40. Ibid., § 4.
41. Ibid., § 5a.

42. David M. Trubek, "Will State Courts and Legislatures Eliminate Exclusion-
    ary Land Use Controls?", Hearings before the U.S. Commission on
    Civil Rights, June 14–17, 1971, (Washington, D.C.: Government
    Printing Office, 1971), p. 843.
43. State of Wisconsin, Assembly, Municipalities Committee, Subcommittee on
    Housing, *Housing in Wisconsin: A State Response,* December 1972.
44. Ibid., p. 18.
45. HB 509, State of Wisconsin (1973).
46. Ibid., § 2e (1.).
47. HB 709, State of Illinois (1973).
48. American Law Institute, op. cit.
49. Ibid., Art. 7, Land Development Regulation.
50. Ibid., Art. 8, Land Development Planning.
51. Ibid., Art. 7, Pt. 7, § § 7–701, 702.
52. Ibid., Art. 7, Pt. 3, § 7–302.
53. Ibid., Art. 7, Pt. 3, § 7–301 (4).
54. Ibid., Art. 7, Pt. 5, § 7–502 (5).
55. Ibid., Art. 7, Pt. 4, § 7–404 (3).
56. Ibid., Art. 7, Pt. 4, § 7–405.
57. Chap. 72–317, Laws of Florida (1972).
58. Ibid., § 380.06 (8) (e).
59. State of New Jersey, Hackensack Meadowlands Development Commission,
    *Master Plan, Hackensack Meadowlands District Zoning Regula-
    tions,* Art. VII, December 28, 1971, p. 3.
60. State of New Jersey, Senate, Proposed *State Land Use Planning and
    Development Act,* Bill 803, introduced by Senators William
    B. Knowlton and Richard J. Coffee, May 12, 1969.
61. Ibid.
62. Vermont Revised Statutes Chap. 91 § 4382.
63. Cal Govt. Code § 65302 (c).

CHAPTER 7
STATE FINANCING AND DEVELOPMENT
OF HOUSING

1. R.C. Alexander, "Fifteen State Housing Finance Agencies in Review,"
   Journal of Housing, January 1972, p. 9.
2. R.C. Alexander, "State Housing Finance Agencies Face Difficult Problems
   During Housing 'Freeze' and Pending Federal Housing Re-Evaluation," *Journal of Housing,* March 1973, p. 120.
3. *Summary of State Housing Finance/Development Agency Program,* Washington, D.C.: HUD, Subsidized Mortgage Insurance Division, February 1973.
4. R.C. Alexander, "Fifteen State Housing Finance Agencies," p. 9.
5. Ibid., pp. 11–12.
6. R.C. Alexander, "State Housing Finance Agencies Face Difficult Problems,"
   p. 122.

7. R.C. Alexander, "Fifteen State Housing Finance Agencies," p. 13.

8. Ibid.

9. S.H. Schonberg, "How to Twist Arms: The Rockefeller Way," *New York Times,* April 11, 1968, p. 1.

10. N.Y. Unconsol. Laws § 6252 and § 6255 (7) and § 6255 (9) (McKinney, 1968).

11. N.Y. Unconsol. Laws § 6266 (3) (McKinney, 1968).

12. Herbert M. Franklin to the Metropolitan Clearinghouse, June 5, 1973, Center for Urban Affairs, Northwestern University, Evanston, Illinois.

13. R. Beckham, "Detour Ahead," *Journal of Housing,* May 1973, p. 227.

14. Ibid., p. 232.

15. L. Greenhouse, "Low-Income State Housing Due in Rural Westchester," *New York Times,* June 21, 1973, p. 24.

16. L. Greenhouse, "Suburbs Fighting State Agency's Plan to Override Local Zoning," *New York Times,* June 17, 1972, p. 9.

17. Ibid., p. 24.

18. R. Beckham, op. cit., p. 233.

19. L. Greenhouse, "Low-Income State Housing Due," p. 26.

20. L. Greenhouse, "Suburbs Fighting," p. 9.

21. Ibid.

22. C. Benjamin, "Community Reaction to the Urban Development Corporation" (Unpublished paper on file at Center for Urban Affairs, Northwestern University, Evanston, Illinois).

23. R. Beckham, op. cit., p. 232.

24. L. Greenhouse, "Housing Projects Backed in Towns," *New York Times,* January 23, 1973, p. 34.

25. "Fair Share in New York State," *Trends in Housing,* Fall 1972, p. 4.

26. Interview with UDC official in New York City, December 29, 1972, Center for Urban Affairs, Northwestern University, Evanston, Illinois.

27. *New York Times,* July 31, 1972, p. 32.

28. L. Greenhouse, "Westchester Towns Pressed on Housing," *New York Times,* January 17, 1973, p. 17.

29. Ibid.

30. "New Community in Westchester Will Be Environmental Landmark," *Suburban Action News,* November 14, 1972, p. 1.

31. L. Greenhouse, "Rural Westchester Town Torn by Housing Plan," *New York Times,* December 27, 1972, p. 11.

32. "Ed Logue Drops the H-Bomb on Westchester County," *City,* Winter 1972, p. 7.

33. Herbert M. Franklin to the Metropolitan Clearinghouse, op. cit., p. 1.

34. Ibid., p. 2.

35. William T. Cahill, *Special Message to the Legislature: A Blueprint for Housing in New Jersey* (Trenton, N.J.: Office of the Governor, December 7, 1970), p. 17.

36. Ibid.

37. *Housing and Renewal Index,* January 8, 1973, p. 1.
38. SB 608, State of Illinois (1973).
39. *Summary of State Housing Finance/Development Agency Program,* op. cit.
40. R.C. Alexander, "State Housing Finance Agencies Face Difficult Problems,"
    p. 120.
41. Ibid., pp. 120–21.

CHAPTER 8
THE STATE'S CARROTS AND STICKS

1. P.L. (1967) § 996 et. seq., 32 P.S. § 5101 et. seq., "Land and Water
   Conservation and Reclamation Act," Act of January 19, 1968,
   ("Project 500" Act).
2. J. Shane Creamer, Attorney General to Hon. William Wilcox, Secretary,
   Department of Community Affairs, Commonwealth of Pennsylvania, Reviewing an opinion of John P. Fernsler, former Deputy
   Attorney General (transmitted in a memorandum dated December
   17, 1698), January 13, 1972.
3. P.L. (1967) § 996 et seq., 32 P.S. § 5116 (4) (9v), "Land and Water Conservation and Reclamation Act," Act of January 19, 1968.
4. J. Shane Creamer to Hon. William H. Wilcox, op. cit., p. 3.
5. Ibid., p. 6 and 9.
6. J. Shane Creamer, Attorney General to Hon. William H. Wilcox, Secretary,
   Department of Community Affairs, Commonwealth of Pennsylvania, May 5, 1972, p. 1.
7. Ibid., pp. 4–5.
8. D. Giovannetti, "Zoning Power Tested in Upper St. Clair," *Pittsburgh
   Press,* December 20, 1972.
9. State of Pennsylvania, Department of Community Affairs, *Advisory Panel
   Report,* (State of Pennsylvania: Harrisburg, May 1973).
10. *Housing and Renewal Index,* September 25, 1973.
11. State of Pennsylvania, Department of Community Affairs, Regional Program
    Evaluation Committee, *Regional Staff Report,* February 14,
    1972.
12. Richard J. Fox, President of the Fox Companies to Henry Rentschler,
    Chairman, Board of Supervisors, Tredyffrin Township, Berwyn,
    Pennsylvania, March 6, 1972.
13. A.L. Hydeman, Executive Deputy Secretary, Department of Community
    Affairs, Commonwealth of Pennsylvania, to Karl C. Smith, Janu-
    ary 17, 1972.
14. William H. Wilcox, "We're Out to End Exclusionary Zoning," *Philadelphia
    Inquirer,* February 15, 1972.
15. Ibid.
16. James Crutchfield, "State Official Hits Exclusive Suburb Zoning," *Pitts-
    burgh Post-Gazette,* November 16, 1972.

CHAPTER 9
ALLOCATION PLANNING AT THE
STATE LEVEL

1. *Housing and Renewal Index,* May 22, 1973, p. 4.
2. Commonwealth of Massachusetts, Department of Community Affairs, *Regional Housing Planning Circular,* (Boston: Department of Community Affairs, January 17, 1973).
3. William T. Cahill, *Special Message to the Legislature: A Blueprint for Housing in New Jersey* (Trenton, N.J.: Office of the Governor, December 7, 1970), pp. 12–13.
4. Ibid., p. 18.
5. William T. Cahil, *Special Message to the Legislature, New Horizons in Housing,* (Trenton, N.J.: Office of the Governor, March 27, 1972), pp. 28, 33.
6. Ibid., p. 7.
7. Ibid., p. 32.
8. Ibid.

CHAPTER 10
THE STATE AS PLAINTIFF

1. Commonwealth v. County of Bucks, 22 Bucks County L. Rep. 179 (Ct. C.P. 1972).
2. Commonwealth v. County of Bucks, 22 Bucks County L. Rep. 179, Brief for Plaintiffs (Ct. C.P. 1972), p. 99.

CHAPTER 11
ADMINISTRATION OF FEDERAL
HOUSING PROGRAMS

1. G. Lefcoe, *Affirmative Marketing, Environmental Requirements, and Project Selection Criteria, Crisis '72.* A Symposium presented by Sanford R. Goodkin and Title Insurance and Trust Co., (September, 1972).
2. Shannon v. United States Department of Housing and Urban Development, 436 F. 2d 809 (3rd Cir. 1970).
3. 436 F. 2d at 825.
4. 436 F. 2d at 827.
5. Richard M. Nixon, *Statement by the President on Federal Policies Relative to Equal Housing Opportunity,* (Washington, D.C.: Office of the White House Press Secretary, June 11, 1971), p. 11.
6. Gautreaux v. Romney, 448 F. 2d 731 (7th Cir. 1971).
7. D. Maxwell, "HUD's Project Selection Criteria—A Cure for 'Impermissible Color Blindness'?", *Notre Dame Lawyer* 48, part 1 (1972), p. 92.
8. U.S. Congress, House Committee on Banking and Currency, Subcommittee on Housing *Settlement Cost, Mortgage Foreclosure, Housing Abandonment, and Site Selection Policies,* statement of George

Romney, Secretary of Housing and Urban Development, 42d
Cong. 2d Sess. February 1972, p. 39.
9. Ibid.
10. 37 Fed. Reg. No. 2 (January 5, 1972).

CHAPTER 12
FEDERAL CARROT AND STICK: HUD

1. Richard M. Nixon, *Statement by the President on Federal Policies Relative to Equal Housing Opportunity,* (Washington, D.C.: Office of
the White House Press Secretary, June 11, 1971), p. 7.
2. Francis D. Fisher, Regional Administrator, Department of Housing and
Urban Development to Ted Bates, Mayor of Warren, Michigan,
March 9, 1970.
3. "U.S. Picks Warren as Prime Target in Move to Integrate all Suburbs," *Detroit News,* July 21, 1970, p. 1.
4. Housing and Urban Development Act of 1965, § 702, Publ. L. No. 89–117;
42 U.S.C. § 3101 (1964), *as amended*, (Supp. V, 1965–69).
5. *Housing Affairs Letter,* Sept. 28, 1973, p. 6.
6. Housing Act of 1961, § 702; Pub. L. No. 87–70; 42 U.S.C. § 1500 a
(1964), *as amended* (Supp. V, 1965–1969).
7. Edward M. Levin, Jr., Acting Assistant Regional Administrator for Metropolitan Planning and Development to Ervin L. Welch, City Manager,
Kettering, Ohio, December 7, 1970.
8. *Housing Affairs Letter,* June 1, 1973, p. 3.

CHAPTER 13
FEDERAL PLANNING PROGRAMS
AND REQUIREMENTS

1. 40 U.S.C. § 461 (1970). This is usually referred to as the section 701
program, after the section of the statute creating it.
2. Ibid.
3. 40 U.S.C. § 461 (a) (1970).
4. U.S. Department of Housing and Urban Development, *Comprehensive
Planning Assistance Requirements and Guidelines for a Grant,
HUD Handbook 1,* (Washington, D.C.: Government Printing
Office, March 1972) CPM 6041. 1A, Ch. 4 § 5.
5. Ibid.
6. Edward M. Levin, Jr., Acting Assistant Regional Administrator for Metropolitan Planning and Development, Chicago Regional Office of
HUD, to George C. Berteau, Chairman, Southeastern Wisconsin
Regional Planning Commission, March 31, 1971.
7. Ibid.
8. Ibid.
9. "HUD—Regional Planning Agency Clash Over the Issue of Low-Cost Housing," *Planning,* vol. 37, no. 6, July 1971.
10. Ibid.

11. Ibid.
12. Richard M. Nixon, *Statement by the President on Federal Policies Relative to Equal Housing Opportunity*, (Washington, D.C.: Office of the White House Press Secretary, June 11, 1971), p. 7.
13. G. Gordon, "Perspectives on Office of Management and Budget Circular A-95." Presented at the 1972 Annual Meeting of the American Society for Public Administration, Statler Hilton Hotel, New York, New York, March 21–25, 1972, p. 1.
14. *Title IV of the Intergovernmental Cooperation Act of 1968*, P.L. 90–577, 82 Stat. 1098.
15. Office of Management and Budget, Circular No. A 95, Revised Transmittal Memorandum No. 2 § 1 (a) (March 8, 1972).
16. Ibid., at § 2 (a) (1) (d).
17. Ibid., at § 5 (d).
18. Belkin, "Intergovernmental Co-operation," *City,* vol. 6, no. 1, Winter 1972, p. 8.
19. Paul A. Meaney, Executive Director, Division of Fair Employment Practices, State of California to all federal funding agencies, undated.
20. I. Sikorsky, "A-95: Deterrent to Discriminatory Zoning," *Civil Rights Digest,* August 1972, p. 19.
21. Ibid.
22. John A. Buggs, U.S. Commission on Civil Rights, to Mr. Dwight Ink, Office of Management and Budget, September 20, 1971.
23. Land Use Policy and Planning Act, § 203 (a) (3) (c) (1973).
24. U.S. House, Committee on Interior and Insular Affairs, Subcommittee on the Environment, *Subcommittee Print No. 1, Land Use Planning Act,* § 104 (b) (4), 1973.
25. Ibid., § 412 (e).

CHAPTER 14
FEDERAL CARROT AND STICK: LOCATION
OF GOVERNMENT FACILITIES

1. R. Cassidy, "GSA Plays the Suburban Game on a Grand Scale," *City,* Fall 1971, p. 12.
2. Ibid., pp. 13–14.
3. Ibid., p. 12.
4. Ibid., p. 14.
5. Housing Opportunities Council of Metropolitan Washington, "HEW Agencies Recent Rockville Move Described as 'Great Whitener,'" *Housing Opportunities in the National Capital Area* (Washington, D.C.: Housing Opportunities Council of Metropolitan Washington, June, 1970), p. 3.
6. "US Move Cuts Jobs for Capital Blacks," *Trends in Housing,* Special Report 1– (New York: National Committee Against Discrimination in Housing, 1970), p. 2.

7. William A. Schmidt to all Regional Administrators of GSA, March 14, 1969, published in 34 *Fed. Reg.* 8273 (May, 1969).

8. U.S. Commission on Civil Rights, *Federal Installations and Equal Housing Opportunity,* (Washington, D.C.: Government Printing Office, 1972), pp. 7–9.

9. Executive Order No. 11. 512 § 2 (a) (6) (1970).

10. U.S. Commission on Civil Rights, op. cit., p. 15.

11. 36 *Fed. Reg.* 22873 § 6 (1971).

12. 36 *Fed. Reg.* 22873 § 9 (g) (1971).

13. U.S. Congress, House, Judiciary Committee, Civil Rights Oversight Sub-Committee, *Federal Government's Role in the Achievement of Equal Opportunity in Housing:* Statement of GSA Administrator Robert L. Kunzig, 92nd Cong., 2d sess. 1972.

14. *Housing and Renewal Index,* July 10, 1973, p. 4.

15. Cassidy, op. cit., p. 14.

16. Ibid.

17. Brookhaven Housing Coalition, et. al., v. Robert L. Kunzig, Administrator, General Services Administration, Civil No. 71–C–1001, (E.D.N.Y., filed on April 19, 1972).

18. Ibid.

19. Brookhaven Housing Coalition, et. al., v. Robert L. Kunzig, Administrator, General Services Administration, Civil No. 71–C–1001 (E.D.N.Y., filed on July 20, 1972).

CHAPTER 15
FEDERAL ENFORCEMENT OF CIVIL
RIGHTS PROVISIONS

1. Executive Order No. 11063 (1970).

2. Civil Rights Act of 1964, § 601, 42 U.S.C. § 2000 d.

3. Richard M. Nixon, *Statement by the President on Federal Policies Relative to Equal Housing Opportunity* (Washington, D.C.: Office of the White House Press Secretary, June 11, 1971), p. 5.

4. *Housing Affairs Letter,* September 28, 1973, p. 6.

5. Kennedy Park Homes v. Lackawanna, 318 F. Supp. 669 (W.D.N.Y.), *aff'd* 436 F. 2d 108 (2d Cir. 1970); *cert. den.* 401 U.S. 1010 (1971).

6. United States v. City of Black Jack, Missouri, Civil No. 71C–372 (E.D. Mo. 1971); see also 467 F. 2d 1208 (8th Cir. 1972).

7. Nixon, op. cit., p. 6.

8. 436 F. 2d at 115.

9. United States v. City of Parma, No. C73–439 (N.D. Ohio 1973).

10. *Housing Affairs Letter,* May 4, 1973, p. 7.

11. United States v. City of Parma, op. cit.

12. 42 U.S.C. § 3608 (d) (5) (Supp. V, 1965–1969).

13. Griggs v. Duke Power Company, 401 U.S. 424 (1971).

14. Ibid., p. 432.
15. Ibid.
16. 42 U.S.C. § 703.
17. Stanley P. Herbert, General Counsel, to William H. Brown III, Chairman,
    Equal Employment Opportunity Commission, "Employment Dis-
    crimination by Relocation of Plant and Corporate Headquarters,"
    July 7, 1971, p. 3.
18. Diaz v. Pan American Airways, 442F. 2d 385 (5th Cir. 1971).
19. William H. Brown, III, Chairman EEOC, "Corporate Location and the
    Urban Crisis." (Speech to the Suburban Action Institute, October 5,
    1970), p. 15.
20. Stanley P. Herbert to William H. Brown, III, op. cit., p. 2.
21. Samuel M. Convissor, "The Role of Business and Industry in Housing."
    (Presented at Danforth Foundation Regional Housing Conference,
    St. Louis, Missouri, November 5, 1971), p. 10.
22. Contractors Ass'n v. Shultz, 442 F. 2d 159 (3rd Cir. 1971).
23. 41 C.F.R., § 60–2 (1971).
24. C.F.R. § 60–2.11 (1971).
25. A. Blumrosen, "The Duty to Plan for Fair Employment: Plant Location in
    White Suburbia," *Rutgers Law Review* 25, pt. 2 (1972): 404.

CHAPTER 16
INTRODUCTION TO PRIVATE
SECTOR STRATEGIES

1. "The Battle of the Suburbs," *Newsweek,* Nov. 15, 1971, p. 61.

CHAPTER 17
EXCLUSIONARY ZONING LITIGATION

1. Appeal of Girsh, 437 Pa. 237, 263 A. 2d 395 (1970).
2. Southern Burlington County NAACP v. Township of Mount Laurel, 119
    N.J. Super. 164, 290 A 2d 465 (1972).
3. Lionshead Lake, Inc. v. Township of Wayne, 13 N.J. Super. 490 (1951),
    rev'd, 10 N.J. 165 (1952).
4. Vickers v. Township Committee of Gloucester Township, 37 N.J. 232,
    181 A. 2d 129 (1962), *cert. denied* 371 U.S. 233 (1963).
5. Bristow v. City of Woodhaven, 35 Mich. App. 205, 192 N.W. 2d 322
    (1971).
6. Derry Borough v. Shomo, 289 A. 2d 513 (Pa. Comm. 1972).
7. Simon v. Town of Needham, 311 Mass. 560, 42 N.E. 2d 516 (1942).
8. National Land and Investment Co. v. Easttown Township Board of
    Adjustment, 419 Pa. 504, 215 A. 2d 597 (1965).
9. Appeal of Concord Township (Kit-Mar Builders, Inc.), 439 Pa. 466, 268 A.
    2d 765 (1970).
10. Board of County Supervisors of Fairfax County v. Carper, 200 Va. 653,
    107 S.E. 2d 390 (1959).

11. Schere v. Township of Freehold, 292 A 2d 35 (N.J. Super. Ct. 1972).
12. Oakwood at Madison, Inc. v. Township of Madison, 117 N.J. Super. 11, 283 A. 2d 353 (1971).
13. Southern Burlington County NAACP v. Township of Mount Laurel, 119 N.J. Super. 164, 290 A. 2d 465 (1972).
14. Dailey v. City of Lawton, 425 F. 2d 1037 (10th Cir. 1970), *aff'g* 296 F. Supp. 266 (W.D. Okla. 1969).
15. 296 F. Supp. at 269.
16. Sisters of Providence v. City of Evanston, 335 F. Supp. 396 (N.D. Ill. 1971).
17. 335 F. Supp. at 404.
18. Park View Heights Corp. v. City of Black Jack, 335 F. Supp. 899 (E.D. Mo. 1971) *rev'd,* 467 F. 2d 1208 (8th Cir. 1972); G&D Holland Construction Company v. City of Marysville, 12 Cal. App. 3d 989, 91 Cal. Rep. 227 (1970).
19. Southern Alameda Spanish-Speaking Organization (SASSO) v. City of Union City, California, 424 F. 2d 291 (9th Cir. 1970), *aff'g* 314 F. Supp. 967 (N.D. Cal. 1970).
20. 424 F. 2d at 295.
21. No. 51590 (N.D. Cal., July 31, 1970).
22. James v. Valtierra, 402 U.S. 137 (1971).
23. Richard F. Bellman and Alice Baker, *Summary of Recent Court Challenges to Exclusionary Land Use Practices,* pp. 5–6 (Washington, D.C.: National Committee Against Discrimination in Housing, 1972).
24. National Land and Investment Co. v. Easttown Township Board of Adjustment, 419 Pa. 504, 215 A. 2d 597 (1965).
25. Appeal of Concord Township (Kit-Mar Builders, Inc.), 439 P. 466, 268 A. 2d 765 (1970).
26. Commonwealth v. County of Bucks, 22 Bucks County L. Rep. 179 (Ct. C.P. 1972), *appeal docketed* Commonwealth Ct. Pa. 27 T.D. 1972, brief for Appellants, at 45–47.
27. Green v. County School Board, 391 U.S. 430 (1968) at 439.
28. Kennedy Park Homes v. Lackawanna, 318 F. Supp. 669 (W.D.N.Y. 1969) at 697, *aff'd,* 436 F 2d 108 (2d Cir. 1970), *cert. denied,* 401 U.S. 1010 (1971).
29. 318 F. Supp. at 697–98.
30. Ibid. at 697, citing U.S. v. Louisiana, 380 U.S. 145 (1965).
31. Southern Alameda Spanish-Speaking Organization (SASSO) v. City of Union City, 424 F. 2d 291 (9th Cir. 1970).
32. No. 51590 (N.D. Cal., July 31, 1970).
33. Southern Burlington County NAACP v. Township of Mount Laurel, 119 N.J. Super. 164, 290 A. 2d 465 (1972).
34. 119 N.J. Super. at 179, 290 A. 2d at 474.
35. 119 N.J. Super. at 178, 290 A. 2d at 473.
36. 342 F. Supp. 827 (N.D. Ill. 1972), *aff'd*   F. 2d   (7th Cir. 1973).
37. Metropolitan Housing Development Corporation v. Village of Arlington Heights, Civil No. 72C–1453 (N.D. Ill., filed June 12, 1972), plaintiff's complaint at p. 23.

38. Garden Cities Development Corporation, Application for Zoning Amendment to the Township Committee of the Township of Mahwah, New Jersey, September 6, 1972.
39. Ibid.
40. *Housing and Renewal Index,* August 5, 1973, p. 3.
41. "New Community in Westchester Will be Environmental Landmark," *Suburban Action News,* November 14, 1972, p. 1.
42. *Housing and Renewal Index,* March 19, 1973, p. 4; *Housing and Renewal Index,* May 8, 1973, p. 2.
43. Village of Euclid v. Ambler Realty Co., 272 U.S. 365 (1926).
44. Duffcon Concrete Products v. Borough of Cresskill, 1 N.J. 509 at 513, 64 A. 2d 347 at 349–50 (1949).
45. Molino v. Mayor and Council of the Borough of Glassboro, 116 N.J. Super, 195 at 204, 281 A. 2d 401 at 406 (1971).
46. Oakwood at Madison, Inc. v. Township of Madison, 117 N.J. Super. 11, 283 A. 2d 353 (1971).
47. National Land and Investment Co. v. Easttown Township Board of Adjustment, 419 Pa. 504 at 527–28, 215 A. 2d 597 at 610 (1965).
48. Appeal of Girsh, 437 Pa. 237, 263 A. 2d 395 (1970).
49. 437 Pa. at 244–45, 263 A. 2d at 398–99 (1970).
50. Appeal of Concord Township (Kit-Mar Builders, Inc.), 439 Pa. 466 at 474–75, 476, 268 A. 2d 765 at 768–69 (1970).
51. Commonwealth of Pennsylvania and Bucks County Interfaith Housing Corporation, et al. v. County of Bucks, et al., 22 Bucks Co. L. Rep. 179 (Ct. C.P. 1972), *appeal docketed* Commonwealth Ct. Pa., 27 T.D. 1972.
52. Ibid., Brief for Appellants at 48–49.
53. Bradley v. Milliken, 338 F. Supp. 582 (E.D. Mich. 1972), *aff'd* F 2d (6th Cir. 1972), rehearing en banc granted, F. 2d (1973).
54. Planning for People Coalition v. County of DuPage, Civil No. 71–C587 at 32 (N.D. Ill., filed September 14, 1971).
55. Accion Hispana Inc. v. Town of New Canaan, Civil No. B312, (D. Conn., filed June 14, 1971).
56. Ibid., Plaintiff's Complaint, at 28–29.
57. Cornwall Estates Co. v. Town of Cornwall, Civil N. 72–3291 (S.D.N.Y., filed August 2, 1972).
58. Ibid., Plaintiff's Complaint at 36–39.
59. Fair Housing Development Fund Corporation v. Burke, Civil No. 71–328 (E.D.N.Y. filed July 18, 1972).
60. Ibid., Plaintiff's Complaint at 19.

CHAPTER 18
RELATED INCLUSIONARY LITIGATION

1. Moody v. Bangor Township, Civil Action No. 3100, (E.D. Mich. 1972).
2. Mahaley et al. v. Cuyahoga Metropolitan Housing Authority, 355 F. Supp. 1245 (1973); opinion supplemental, D.C. 355 F. Supp. 1257 (1973).

3. Ibid., 355 F. Supp. at 1249.

4. 355 F. Supp. at 1264.

5. 355 F. Supp. at 1266.

6. 355 F. Supp. at 1269.

7. Cuyahoga Metropolitan Housing Authority, *Study Reflecting Need in Cuyahoga County Communities for Public Housing and Proposed Production Plan,* (Cleveland: Cuyahoga Metropolitan Housing Authority, June 1973), p. 4.

8. Gautreaux v. Chicago Housing Authority, 342 F. Supp. 827 (N.D. Ill. 1972).

9. Crow v. Brown, 332 F. Supp. 392 (N.D. Ga. 1971) *aff'd.* 457 F. 2d 788 (5th Cir. 1972).

10. 332 F. Supp. at 395.

11. Crow v. Brown, 457 F. 2d 788 (5th Cir. 1972).

12. Gautreaux v. Chicago Housing Authority, 296 F. Supp. 907 (N.D. Ill. 1969).

13. Ibid., 304 F. Supp. 736 (N.D. Ill. 1969).

14. Ibid., 296 F. Supp. at 914.

15. Ibid., 304 F. Supp. 736 (N.D. Ill. 1969).

16. Ibid., 448 F. 2d 731 (7th Cir. 1971).

17. Gautreaux v. Romney, No. 66 C1460 (N.D. Ill.) 1971. Unpublished Order Entered 12/23/71.

18. Gautreaux v. Chicago Housing Authority, Romney, No. 66 C1459, No. 66 C1460 (Consolidated), slip opinion dated September 11, 1973 (N.D. Ill.).

19. Garrett v. Hamtramck, 335 F. Supp. 16 (E.D. Mich. 1971).

20. Ibid., 357 F. Supp. 925 (E.D. Mich. 1971).

21. Ibid. at 932.

22. *Suburban Action News,* Nov. 4, 1970; *Suburban Action News,* January 30, 1971.

23. *Suburban Action News,* Nov. 4, 1970.

24. Ibid.

25. Paul Davidoff and Neil Gold to William H. Brown III, Chairman of the U.S. Equal Employment Opportunity Commission, March 3, 1971.

26. Eugene E. Beyer, Jr., Staff Vice President and General Attorney, RCA, to Patrick J. Schauer, Northwestern University, February 27, 1973.

27. *Suburban Action News,* June 2, 1971; *Suburban Action News,* July 14, 1971.

28. Paul Davidoff and Neil Gold to Dean Burch, Chairman, Federal Communications Commission, and William H. Brown III, Chairman of the U.S. Equal Employment Opportunity Commission, June 2, 1971.

29. Paul Davidoff and Neil Gold to William H. Brown III, Chairman of the U.S. Equal Employment Opportunity Commission, July 12, 1971.

30. 42 U.S.C. § 1981.

31. Bell v. Automobile Club of Michigan, cited in *Potomac Institute Memorandum* 73–1 (January 2, 1973): 4.

32. Evans v. Lynn, 73 Civ. 3475 (MP) (S.D.N.Y., filed August 8, 1973).

CHAPTER 19
SCHOOL LITIGATION AND HOUSING

1. Serrano v. Priest, 5 Cal. 3d 584, 487 P. 2d 1241 (1971).
2. Rodriguez v. San Antonio Independent School District, 411 U.S. 1 (1973).
3. Nucleus of Chicago Homeowners' Association (NO–CHA) v. Romney, 72 C 1197 (N.D. Ill., filed May 12, 1972).
4. Bradley v. Richmond, 324 F. Supp. 396. 400 (E.D. va. 1971), *rev'd* 462 F 2d 1058 (4th Cir. 1972) cert. den. U.S.   (1973).
5. Bradley v. Milliken, 338 F. Supp. 582 (E.D. Mich. 1972), *aff'd,* F 2d (6th Cir. 1972), rehearing en banc granted, F2d (1973).
6. Ibid., "Ruling on Propriety of Considering a Metropolitan Remedy to Accomplish Desegregation of the Public Schools of the City of Detroit." Interlocutory Order of District Court, E.D. Michigan, March 28, 1972, p. 5.
7. Ibid., "Ruling on Desegregation Area and Order for Development of Plan of Desegregation," Interlocutory Order of District Court, E.D. Michigan, June 14, 1972.
8. Ibid., Nos. 72–1809, 72–1814 (6th Cir. 1972), advance sheet at 66.

CHAPTER 20
BUILDING A SUBURBAN POLITICAL CONSTITUENCY

1. Mayor Robert D. Teichert to the Mount Prospect Village, Illinois Board, October 3, 1972.
2. Regional Housing Coalition, *An Interim Plan for Balanced Distribution of Housing Opportunities for Northeastern Illinois,* (Chicago: Regional Housing Coalition, 1973), p. 8.
3. Ibid., p. 22.
4. Jack Pahl, Chairman, Mayors' Steering Committee, Regional Housing Coalition, to Mayors, Village Presidents, County Board Chairmen, September 26, 1973.
5. *The Herald,* October 3, 1973, p. 10.

CHAPTER 21
THE CORPORATE ROLE

1. Charles H. Pillon, Regional Civic and Governmental Affairs Manager, Ford Motor Company. (Statement made at Mahwah Township, N.J. Planning Board Meeting, Monday, December 11, 1972).
2. Suburban Action Institute, "Ford Motor Statement Supports New Mixed Income Community in Mahwah, N.J.," *Suburban Action News,* December 14, 1972, p. 3.
3. Samuel M. Convissor, "The Role of Business and Industry in Housing." (Presented at Danforth Foundation Conference on Developing and

Implementing a Regional Housing Policy, St. Louis, Missouri, November 5, 1971), p. 10.

4. J. Feron, "Businessmen Told To Aid on Housing," *New York Times,* November 18, 1973, p. 16.

5. Pillon, op. cit.

6. Ibid.

7. James A. Clapp, *New Towns and Urban Policy* (New York: Donellan Publishing Co., 1971), pp. 248–49.

8. Ibid.

9. Feron, op. cit.

CONCLUSION

1. Local 1498, American Federation of Government Employees, AFL-CIO v. U.S. Army Electronics Command, No. 73–1739 (E.D. Pa., filed August 1, 1973).

Bibliography

BOOKS, CHAPTERS IN BOOKS, MONOGRAPHS

Anderson, Robert. *American Law of Zoning*. San Francisco: Lawyers Cooperative, 1968.

Armstrong, Regina Belz. *Linking Skills, Jobs and Housing in the New York Urban Region*. New York: Regional Plan Association, 1972.

Babcock, Richard F. *The Zoning Game: Municipal Practice and Policies*. Madison: University of Wisconsin Press, 1969.

Baron, Harold M. *Building Babylon: A Case of Racial Controls in Public Housing*. Evanston: Northwestern University, Center for Urban Affairs, 1971.

Bellman, Richard F., and Baker, Alice. *Summary of Recent Court Challenges to Exclusionary Land-Use Practices*. Washington, D.C.: National Committee Against Discrimination in Housing, 1972.

Bennett, William S., Jr., and Falk, Frank. *New Careers and Urban Schools*. New York: Holt, Rinehart, and Winston, 1970.

Bosselman, Fred, and Callies, David. *The Quiet Revolution in Land Use Control*. Washington, D.C.: Council on Environmental Quality, 1971.

Brooks, Mary E. *Exclusionary Zoning*. Chicago: American Society of Planning Officials, 1970.

——. *Lower-Income Housing: The Planners' Response*. Chicago: American Society of Planning Officials, 1972.

Center for Urban Social Science Research. *The Roles of the States in Solving Urban Problems*. New Brunswick, N.J.: Rutgers University, Center for Urban Social Science Research, 1969.

Clapp, James A. *New Towns and Urban Policy*. New York: Donellan Publishing Co., 1971.

Conin, Joseph M., and Hailer, Richard M. *Organizing an Urban School System: A Study of the Boston School Department*. Cambridge, Mass.: McBer and Co., 1970.

309

Coons, John E. *et al. Private Wealth and Public Education.* Cambridge, Mass.: Harvard University Press, 1970.

Cunningham, Card J., and Scott, James M. *Land Development and Racism in Fairfax County.* Fairfax, Va.: Washington Suburban Institute, 1970.

Daly, Charles V. *The Quality of Inequality: Urban and Public Schools.* Chicago: University of Chicago, Center for Policy Study, 1968.

de Leeuw, Frank. *The Demand for Housing: A Review of Cross-Section Evidence.* Washington, D.C.: Urban Institute, undated.

———. *Time Lags in the Rental Housing Market.* Washington, D.C.: Urban Institute, 1970.

de Leeuw, Frank, and Ekanem, Nkanta. *The Supply of Rental Housing.* Washington, D.C.: Urban Institute, undated.

de Leeuw, Frank *et al. The Design of a Housing Allowance.* Washington, D.C.: Urban Institute, 1970.

De Vise, Pierre. *Chicago's Widening Color Gap.* De Paul University, December, 1967.

Dorsen, Norman, ed. *The Rights of Americans: What They Are—What They Should Be.* New York: Pantheon Books, 1970.

Downs, Anthony. *Opening Up the Suburbs.* New Haven: Yale University Press, 1973.

———. *Urban Problems and Prospects.* Chicago: Markham Publishing Company, 1970.

Eicher, Edward P., and Kaplan, Marshall. *The Community Builders.* Berkeley: University of California Press, 1967.

Finkler, Earl. *Nongrowth as a Planning Alternative: A Preliminary Examination of an Emerging Issue.* Chicago: American Society of Planning Officials, 1972.

Franklin, Herbert M. *Controlling Urban Growth—But for Whom.* Washington, D.C.: Potomac Institute, 1973.

Gruen, Nina. *Low and Moderate Income Housing in the Suburbs.* New York: Praeger, 1972.

Guthrie, James W. *Schools and Inequality.* Cambridge, Mass.: MIT Press, 1971.

Havighurst, Robert. *Education in Metropolitan Areas.* Boston: Allyn and Bacon, 1971.

———. *Metropolitanism: Its Challenge to Education.* Chicago: University of Chicago Press, 1968.

Hecht, James L. *Because It Is Right: Integration in Housing.* Boston: Little, Brown and Company, 1970.

Heinberg, John. *The Transfer Cost of a Housing Allowance: Conceptual Issues and Benefit Patterns.* Washington, D.C.: Urban Institute, 1971.

Holleb, Doris. *Social and Economic Information for Urban Planning.* Vols. I and II. Chicago: University of Chicago, Center for Urban Studies, 1969.

Hurwitz, Emanuel Jr., and Tesconi, Charles A., Jr. *Challenges to Education.* New York: Dodd, Mead and Company, 1972.

Kaster, Lewis R., and Berman, Stanley, Co-Chairmen. "Packaging Subsidized Housing Deals," *Real Estate Law and Practice Course Handbook Number 51.* New York: Practicing Law Institute, 1972.

Lauber, Daniel. *Recent Cases in Exclusionary Zoning.* Chicago: American Society of Planning Officials, 1973.

Levin, Melvin R., and Shank, Alan. *Educational Investment in an Urban Society: Costs, Benefits, and Public Policy.* Chicago: University of Chicago Press, 1968.

Lowry, Ira S. *Housing Assistance for Low-Income Urban Families: A Fresh Approach.* New York: New York City Rand Institute, 1971.

McKeever, J. Ross, ed. *Community Builders Handbook.* Washington, D.C.: Urban Land Institute, 1968.

Meyerson, Martin, and Banfield, Edward. *Politics, Planning and the Public Interest.* New York: Free Press, 1955.

Mogulof, Melvin B. *Governing Metropolitan Areas.* Washington, D.C.: Urban Institute, 1971.

National Academy of Sciences. *Freedom of Choice in Housing: Opportunities and Constraints.* Washington, D.C.: National Academy of Sciences, 1972.

——. *Urban Growth and Land Development: The Land Conversion Process.* Washington, D.C.: National Academy of Sciences, 1972.

National Committee Against Discrimination in Housing. *Jobs and Housing: A Study of Employment and Housing Opportunities for Racial Minorities in Suburban Areas of the New York Metropolitan Region* (Interim Report). New York: National Committee Against Discrimination in Housing, 1970.

National Housing and Development Law Project. *Handbook on Housing Law.* Berkeley, Calif.: National Housing and Development Law Project, 1970.

National Urban Coalition. *Guide to Federal Low and Moderate-Income Housing and Community Development Programs.* Washington, D.C.: National Urban Coalition, 1971.

Nenno, Mary K. *Housing in Metropolitan Areas: Roles and Responsibilities of Five Key Actors.* Washington, D.C.: National Association of Housing and Redevelopment Officials, 1973.

Neutze, Max. *The Suburban Apartment Boom.* Baltimore: Johns Hopkins Press, 1968.

Rose, Harold M. *Social Processes in the City: Race and Urban Residential Choice.* Washington, D.C.: Association of American Geographers, 1969.

Rubinowitz, Leonard S. "A Question of Choice: Access of the Poor and the Black to Suburban Housing," in *The Urbanization of the Suburbs,* edited by Louis H. Masotti and Jeffrey K. Hadden, pp. 329–66. Beverly Hills: Sage Publications, 1973.

Specer, Richard. *Increasing State and Regional Power in the Development Process.* Chicago: American Society of Planning Officials, 1970.

Stein, Clarence. *Toward New Towns for America.* Cambridge: MIT Press, 1966.

Sumichrast, Michael, and Frankel, Sara A. *Profile of the Builder and His Industry.* Washington, D.C.: National Association of HomeBuilders, 1970.

Taggart, Robert, III. *Low-Income Housing: A Critique of Federal Aid.* Baltimore: Johns Hopkins Press, 1970.

Technical Assistance Corporation for Housing. *Development of Low, Moderate and Middle Income Housing in Glencoe: A Feasibility Study.* Chicago: Technical Assistance Corporation for Housing, 1972.

Toll, Seymour. *Zoned American.* New York: Grossman Publishers, 1969.

Turner, Michael. *Exclusionary Zoning: The State's Role–Case Study of Massachusetts Low and Moderate Income Housing Law.* Champaign: University of Illinois Bureau of Community Planning, 1970.

Wilson, James Q., ed. *The Metropolitan Enigma.* Garden City, N.Y.: Anchor Books, 1970.

ARTICLES IN PROFESSIONAL JOURNALS

Alexander, R.C. "Fifteen State Housing Finance Agencies in Review." *Journal of Housing,* January 1972, pp. 9–17.

Aloi, Frank, and Goldberg, Arthur A. "Racial and Economic Exclusionary Zoning: The Beginning of the End?" *Urban Law* (1971), pp. 9–62.

Aloi, Frank, Goldberg, Arthur A., and White, James M. "Racial and Economic Segregation by Zoning: Death Knell for Home Rule?" *University of Toledo Law Review* 1 (Winter 1969): 65–108.

American Institute of Planners. "A–95 Used to Address Housing Imbalance." *AIP Newsletter,* June 1972, pp. 11–12.

——— . "Model Land Development Code," *AIP Newsletter* 6 (1971): 8–9.

Aumenta, Jerome. "Domestic Land Reform." *City,* January-February 1971, pp. 56–57.

Babcock, Richard F. "Comments on the Model Land Development Code." *Urban Law Annual* (1972), pp. 59–68.

——— . "Let's Stop Romancing Regionalism," *Planning* 38 (1972): 120–124.

Babcock, Richard F. and Bosselman, Fred. "Suburban Zoning and the Apartment Boom." *University of Pennsylvania Law Review* III (1963): 1040–1091.

Bass, G.A., and Freilich, R.H. "Exclusionary Zoning: Suggested Litigation Approaches." *Urban Law* 3 (1971): 244–263.

Beckham, Robert. "The Experimental Housing Allowance Program." *Journal of Housing,* January 1973, pp. 12–17.

Beckman, Norman, and Langdon, Bruce. "National Growth Policy: Legislative and Executive Actions 1970-71." *Urban Land Institute Research Monograph.* 18 (1972).

Bertch, Dale F., and Shafor, Ann M. "A Regional Housing Plan: The Miami Valley Regional Planning Commission Experience." *Planner's Notebook* 1, no. 1 (April 1971).

Blumrosen, Alfred W. "The Duty to Plan for Fair Employment: Plant Location in White Suburbia." *Rutgers Law Review* 25 (1971): 383–404.

Borschenstein, Warren. "Design for Socially Mixed Housing." *Journal of the American Institute of Planners* 37 (1971): 311–318.

Bowe, William J. "Regional Planning Versus Decentralized Land-Use Controls—Zoning for the Megalopolis," *De Paul Law Review* 18 (1968): 144–166.

Branfman, Eric J., Cohen, Benjamin I., and Trubek, David M. "Measuring the Invisible Wall: Land Use Controls and the Residential Patterns of the Poor." *Yale Law Journal* 82 (January 1973): 483–508.

Comment. "Discriminatory Zoning: Legal Battleground of the Seventies." *American University Law Review* 21 (1971): 157–183.

——. "Exclusionary Zoning: A Legislative Approach." *Syracuse Law Review* 22 (1971): 583–597.

——. "Standing to Appeal Zoning Determinations: 'The Aggrieved Person' Requirement." *Michigan Law Review* 64 (April 1966): 1070–1085.

——. "Standing to Challenge Exclusionary Local Zoning Decisions: Restricted Access to State Courts and the Alternative Federal Forum." *Syracuse Law Review* 22 (1971): 598–626.

——. "The Constitutionality of Local Zoning." *Yale Law Journal* 79 (April 1970): 896–925.

——. "The Equal Protection Clause and Exclusionary Zoning After *Valtierra* and *Dandridge.*" *Yale Law Journal* 81 (November 1971): 61–86.

Davidoff, Linda and Paul. "Opening the Suburbs: Toward Inclusionary Land Use Controls," *Syracuse Law Review* 22 (1971): 509–536.

Davidoff, Paul, "Entire Township Zoning Ordinance Struck Down as Exclusionary." *AIP Newsletter* November 1971, pp. 9–10.

Davidoff, Paul; Davidoff, Linda; and Gold, Neil Newton. "Suburban Action: Advocate Planning for an Open Society." *AIP Journal* January 1970, pp. 12–21.

Davidoff, Paul, and Gold, Neil N. "Exclusionary Zoning." *Yale Review of Law and Social Action* 1 (Winter 1970): 56–63.

Downs, Anthony. "Suburban Housing: A Program for Expanded Opportunities." *Real Estate Review,* Spring 1971, pp. 4–11.

Drachman, Roy P. "Federal Land Use Controls?" *Urban Land,* November 1972, pp. 22–23.

Dreyfus, Daniel. "Needed: A National Land Use Policy." *Civil Engineering* 42 (1972): 52–54.

Finnell, Gilbert L. "Saving Paradise: The Florida Environmental Land and Water Management Act of 1972." *Urban Law Annual* (1973): 103–136.

Fisher, Francis D. "The Carrot and the Stick: Conditions for Federal Assistance." *Harvard Journal on Legislation* 6 (May 1969): 401–412.

Haar, Charles. "Regionalism and Realism in Land-Use Planning." *University of Pennsylvania Law Review* 105 (1957): 515–537.

Hendel, Robert A. "The 'Aggrieved Person' Requirement in Zoning." *William and Mary Law Review* 8 (1967): 294–307.

Holland, D.K. "National Growth Policy: Notes on the Federal Role." *Urban Law Annual* (1973): 59.

Kain, John F. "Housing Segregation, Negro Employment, and Metropolitan Decentralization." *Quarterly Journal of Economics* 82 (May 1968): 175–197.

Krasnowiecki, Jan Z. "Model Land Use and Development Code." *Urban Law Annual* (1971): 101–116.

——. "Zoning Litigation and the New Pennsylvania Procedures." *University of Pennsylvania Law Review* 120 (June 1972): 1029–1157.

Krochalis, Richard. "State-wide Land Use Planning." *Urban Land,* September 1972, pp. 8–13.

Land Use Planning Reports, vol. 1, no. 1 (March 1973).

Langendorf, Richard. "Residential Desegregation Potential." *Journal of the American Institute of Planners* 35 (1969): 90–96.

Law Project Bulletin. "HUD Complaint Procedures," *Law Project Bulletin* 2 (December 1972): 1–4.

Lefcoe, George. "From Capitol Hill: The Impact of Civil Rights Litigation on HUD Policy." *Urban Law* 4 (Winter 1972): 112–131.

Lilley, William. "Cities and Suburbs." *National Journal,* January 22, 1972, pp. 162–163.

Marcus, Norman. "Exclusionary Zoning: The Need for a Regional Planning Context." *New York Law Forum* 16 (1970): 732–740.

Michelman, Frank I. "The Supreme Court 1968 Term Foreword: On Protecting the Poor Through the Fourteenth Amendment." *Harvard Law Review* 83 (1969): 7–59.

Milwaukee Tenants Union. *Newsletter* (July 1972).

Mogulof, M.B. "Federal-Regional Councils: A Potential Instrument for Planning and Joint Action." *Social Service Review* 44 (June 1970): 132–146.

Mullarkey, Mary J. "The Evolution of a New Community, Problems of Government." *Harvard Journal on Legislation* 6 (May 1969): 462–483.

National Housing and Human Development Alliance. *NHHDA Newsletter* 1 (December 1972).

Note. "Extending Standing to Non-Residents—A Response to the Exclusionary Effects of Zoning Fragmentation." *Vanderbilt Law Review* 24 (March 1971): 341–366.

——. "Low-Income Housing in the Suburbs: The Problem of Exclusionary Zoning." *University of Florida Law Review* 34 (1971): 58–86.

——. "Regional Impact of Zoning: A Suggested Approach." *University of Pennsylvania Law Review* 114 (1966): 1251–1259.

——. "The Responsibility of Local Zoning Authorities to Non-Resident Indigents." *Stanford Law Review* 23 (April 1971): 774–798.

——. "Segregation and the Suburbs: Low-Income Housing, Zoning, and the Fourteenth Amendment." *Iowa Law Review* 56 (1971): 1298–1322.

Plager, Sheldon. "Judicial Review 1970: Policy, Planning and the Courts." *Journal of American Institute of Planners* 37 (1971): 174–191.

Poverty Law Reports. "New Developments." *Poverty Law Reports* 77 (October 1971): 68–69.

Reilly, William K. "New Directions in Federal Land Use Legislation." *Urban Law Annual* (1973): 29–58.

Reilly, William K., and Schulman, S.J. "The State Urban Development Corporation: New York's Innovation." *The Urban Lawyer* 1 (Summer 1969): 129–145.

Rivkin, Malcolm. "Breaking Through the Suburban Barrier." *Urban Land* (May 1971): 9–14.

Rosenberg, Wolfgang H. "New York State's Urban Development Corporation is an Action Agency." *Journal of Housing* 27 (December 1970).

Rubinowitz, Leonard S. "Exclusionary Zoning: A Wrong in Search of a Remedy." *University of Michigan Journal of Law Reform* 6 (Spring 1973): 625–669.

Sager, Lawrence G. "Tight Little Islands: Exclusionary Zoning, Equal Protection, and the Indigent." *Stanford Law Review* 21 (April 1969): 767–800.

Savings and Loan News. "The Attack on Snob Zoning." *Savings and Loan News* (November 1970): 30–36.

Shadur, Milton. "Judicial Supervision of Housing Policies and Plans." *Poverty, Planning, Participation and Law* (November 1969): 18–40.

Sherer, Samuel A. "Snob Zoning: Developments in Massachusetts and New Jersey." *Harvard Journal on Legislation* 7 (1970): 246–270.

Shields, Geoffrey, and Spector, L. Sanford. "Opening Up the Suburbs: Notes on a Movement for Social Change." *Yale Review of Law and Social Action* 2 (1972): 300–333.

Sikorsky, I. "A–95: Deterrent to Discriminatory Zoning." *Civil Rights Digest* (August 1972), pp. 17–19.

Silverman, Jane A. "Chicago's Gautreaux Cases." *Journal of Housing* 29 (May 1972): 236–240.

Stegman, Michael A. "National Housing and Land-Use Policy Conflicts." *Journal of Urban Law* (May 1972): 629–667.

Walsh, Robert E. "Are Local Zoning Bodies Required by the Constitution to Consider Regional Needs?" *Connecticut Law Review* 3 (1971): 244–267.

Zucotti, John. "Social Implications of Land Use Legislation." *Urban Land* (July/August 1973): 9–12.

U.S. GOVERNMENT PUBLICATIONS

Advisory Commission on Intergovernmental Relations. *Fiscal Balance in the American Federal System: Metropolitan Fiscal Disparities.* Washington, D.C.: Advisory Commission on Intergovernmental Relations, 1967.
Coleman, James S., et al., *Equality of Educational Opportunity.* Washington, D.C.: Government Printing Office, 1966.
Congressional Quarterly. "Growing Issue: Communities vs. Low-Income Housing." *Congressional Quarterly,* January 8, 1972, pp. 95–107.
Department of Housing and Urban Development. *Comprehensive Planning Assistance Requirements and Guidelines for a Grant HUD Handbook 1,* Washington, D.C.: Government Printing Office, March 1972.
——. *Direct Housing Allowance for Low Income Families.* Washington, D.C.: Office of Research and Technology, 1971.
——. *Direct Housing Assistance: The Administrative Agency.* Washington, D.C.: Office of Research and Technology, 1972.
——. *Direct Housing Assistance: The Demand Experiment.* Washington, D.C.: Office of Research and Technology, 1972.
——. *Direct Housing Assistance: An Experimental Program.* Washington, D.C.: Office of Research and Technology, 1972.
——. *Direct Housing Assistance: The Supply Experiment.* Washington, D.C.: Office of Research and Technology, 1972.
——. *Equal Opportunities Procedure: A HUD Handbook.* Washington, D.C.: Government Printing Office, 1970.
——. *Fair Housing Law and Other Federal Civil Rights Law.* Washington, D.C.: Department of Housing and Urban Development, 1969.
——. *Fair Housing U.S.A.* Washington, D.C.: Government Printing Office, 1971.
——. *First Annual Report of the Experimental Housing Allowance Programs.* Washington, D.C.: Office of Policy Development and Research, 1973.
——. *Summary of Citizen Complaint Procedures in Effect as of November 14, 1972.* Washington, D.C.: Department of Housing and Urban Development, 1972.
——. *Your Housing Rights–Live Where You Want to Live.* Washington, D.C.: Government Printing Office, 1969.
Downs, A. "Statement: Residential Segregation by Income and Race–Its Nature, Its Relation to School, and Ways to Ameliorate It." In *"Equal Educational Opportunity": Hearings before the Select Committee on Equal Educational Opportunity of the United States Senate, part 5–DeFacto Segregation and Housing Discrimination, Washington, D.C., August 25–27, September 1, 1970,* pp. 2966–2988. Washington, D.C.: Government Printing Office, 1971.
Environmental Protection Agency. *Guidelines: Water Quality Management Planning.* Washington, D.C.: Government Printing Office, 1971.
Federal Housing Administration. *FHA Techniques of Housing Market Analysis.* Washington, D.C.: Federal Housing Administration, 1970.

Fed. Reg. 37, Fed. Reg. 6700. Advertising Guidelines for Fair Housing. Department of Housing and Urban Development, 1972.

Jackson, Samuel. "New Communities." *HUD Challenge,* August 1972, pp. 1–4.

——. "Fair Housing and Fair Planning." *HUD News,* April 18, 1972.

National Commission on Urban Problems. *Building the American City.* Washington, D.C.: National Commission on Urban Problems, 1968.

Nixon, Richard M. *Statement by the President on Federal Policies Relative to Equal Housing Opportunity.* Washington, D.C.: Office of the White House Press Secretary, June 11, 1971.

Office of Equal Opportunity. *Fair Housing Law and Other Federal Civil Rights Laws and Executive Orders Relating to the Programs of the U.S. Department of HUD.* Washington, D.C.: Government Printing Office, 1969.

President's Committee on Urban Housing. *A Decent Home.* Washington, D.C.: Government Printing Office, 1968.

Report of the National Advisory Commission on Civil Disorders. New York: Random House, 1967.

Romney, George. "The Real City." *HUD News,* June 14, 1971.

——. Statement at Press Conference on Equal Housing Opportunity. *HUD News,* June 14, 1971.

Trubek, David M. "Will State Courts and Legislatures Eliminate Exclusionary Land Use Controls?" Testimony before U.S. Commission on Civil Rights, Washington, D.C., June 16, 1971.

U.S., Commission on Civil Rights. *District of Columbia Advisory Committee to the Movement of Federal Facilities to the Suburbs.* Washington, D.C.: U.S. Commission on Civil Rights, 1971.

——. *Federal Installations and Equal Housing Opportunity.* Washington, D.C.: U.S. Commission on Civil Rights, 1970.

——. *Hearing Before the United States Commission on Civil Rights, June 14–17, 1971.* Washington, D.C.: Government Printing Office, 1971.

STATE AND LOCAL GOVERNMENT PUBLICATIONS

Board of Appeals of Hanover v. Housing Appeals Committee in the Department of Community Affairs and others. Supreme Judicial Court of Massachusetts, no. 7754, March 22, 1973.

Cahill, William T. *A Special Message to the Legislature: New Horizons in Housing.* Trenton, N.J.: Office of the Governor, March 27, 1972.

Committee on Urban Affairs, Commonwealth of Massachusetts. *Report of the Committee on Urban Affairs on the Attached Legislation.* Commonwealth of Massachusetts, House, no. 5429, June 1969.

Corman, Maurice. *The Massachusetts Solution: The Legislative Approach to the Problem of Exclusionary Zoning.* Boston: Massachusetts Department of Community Affairs, 1972.

Department of Community Affairs. Commonwealth of Massachusetts. "Community Housing News" 2 (October 1972).

——. Commonwealth of Massachusetts. Memorandum on the Law for Subsidized Housing Permits, September 30, 1971.

——. Commonwealth of Massachusetts. Regional Housing Planning Circular, January 17, 1973.

——. *"Report of the Department of Community Affairs Relative to a Proposed Housing Policy and Action Program": Under Section 3 of Chapter 23B of the Massachusetts General Laws.* Commonwealth of Massachusetts, House, no. 5010, January 10, 1972.

Department of Local Government Affairs. *The Office of Housing and Buildings: The State's Agency for the Provision of Low Income Housing in Illinois.* Springfield, Ill.: Department of Local Government Affairs, 1971.

Engler, Robert. *Subsidized Housing in the Suburbs: Legislation or Litigation?* Boston: Department of Community Affairs, 1972.

Governor's Advisory Commission on Housing and Community Development. *Ohio's Housing Agenda for Action.* Columbus, Ohio: State Department of Development, 1972.

Governor's Housing Task Force, Commonwealth of Pennsylvania. *Better Housing: A Social Priority for Pennsylvania,* Pt. I. Harrisburg, Pa.: Governor's Housing Task Force, 1969.

Illinois Legislative Commission on Low Income Housing. *For Better Housing in Illinois—Report of the Legislative Commission on Low Income Housing.* Chicago: Illinois Legislative Commission on Low Income Housing, 1967.

Joint Legislative Committee on Metropolitan and Regional Area. *Coordinating Governments through Regionalism and Reform.* Vol. 1. Land Use Control: Modern Techniques for Modern Problems. Albany, N.Y.: Joint Legislative Committee on Metropolitan and Regional Area, 1971.

Legislative Research Council. *Report of the Legislative Research Council Relative to Restricting the Zoning Power to City and County Governments.* Boston: Commonwealth of Massachusetts, Senate, no. 1133, 1968.

Mallach, Alan. *Housing in New Jersey: Needs and Programs.* Trenton, N.J.: New Jersey Department of Community Affairs, 1968.

Massachusetts House of Representatives. *Report of the Department of Community Affairs Relative to a Proposed Housing Policy and Action Program.* Boston: Commonwealth of Massachusetts, House, no. 5010, 1972.

Model Cities Department of City of Kansas City, Missouri. *The Direct Housing Allowance Experiment of Model Cities in Kansas City, Missouri.* Kansas City: Model Cities Department, 1972.

New Jersey Department of Community Affairs, Community Development Planning Program. *The Housing Crisis in New Jersey.* Trenton, N.J.: New Jersey Department of Community Affairs, 1970.

——. *New Jersey Laws Affecting Housing Sponsors.* Trenton, N.J.: New Jersey Department of Community Affairs, 1971.

New York State Office of Planning Coordination. *New York State Planning Law Revision Study: Study Document No. 4.* Albany, N.Y.: Office of Planning Coordination, 1970.

State of New Jersey, Hackensack Meadowlands Development Commission. *Master Plan–Hackensack Meadowlands District Zoning Regulations.* Hackensack, N.J.: State of New Jersey, 1971.

PLANNING AGENCY PUBLICATIONS

Delaware Valley Regional Planning Commission. *Delaware Valley Planning News,* vol. 7, no. 1. (Philadelphia, Pa.: Delaware Valley Regional Planning Commission), January 1973.

——. *DVRPC Response to Petition from Bucks County Legal Aid Society.* Philadelphia, Pa.: Delaware Valley Regional Planning Commission, December 22, 1971.

Development Research Associates. *Housing Needs in the San Diego Region.* San Diego, California: Comprehensive Planning Organization of San Diego County, 1972.

——. *Organization for Housing Action in the San Diego Region: Analysis of Organizational Forms.* San Diego, California: Comprehensive Planning Organization of San Diego County, 1972.

Illinois Housing Development Authority. *Illinois Housing Needs, 1970–1980.* Springfield, Ill.: Illinois Housing Development Authority, 1972.

Los Angeles County Regional Planning Commission. *Los Angeles County Preliminary Housing Element.* Los Angeles: Los Angeles County Regional Planning Commission, 1971.

Marin County Planning Department. *Don't Leave It to Elsewhere: The Marin County-Wide Initial Housing Element 1970.* San Rafael, Calif.: Marin County Planning Department, 1970.

——. *The Marin County Initial Housing Element 1971.* San Rafael, Calif.: Marin County Planning Department, 1971.

Metropolitan Area Planning Council. *Guides for Progress: Development Opportunities for Metropolitan Boston.* Boston: Metropolitan Area Planning Council, 1968.

——. *Housing Metropolitan Boston.* vol. I. Housing Needs and Housing Supply, 1950–1980. Boston: Metropolitan Area Planning Council, 1969.

——. *The Role of the Suburban Nonprofit Corporation: Working Paper No. 7.* Boston: Metropolitan Area Planning Council, 1972.

——. *774 Plus Two: An Interpretive Analysis of Chapter 774 and a Review of Activities.* Boston: Metropolitan Area Planning Council, 1972.

——. *Subsidized Housing in the Boston Region as of December 31, 1971.* Boston: Metropolitan Area Planning Council, 1972.

Metropolitan Council of the Twin Cities Area. *Distribution and Types of Subsidized Housing in the Twin Cities Metropolitan Area: Housing Report Number 1.* St. Paul, Minn.: Metropolitan Council of the Twin Cities Area, 1971.

——. *Housing Review Manual.* St. Paul, Minn.: Metropolitan Council of the Twin Cities Area, 1972.

——. *Indications of Housing Quality in the Twin Cities Metropolitan Area: Housing Report Number 2.* St. Paul, Minn.: Metropolitan Council of the Twin Cities Area, 1971.

——. *Metropolitan Development Guide: Housing: Policies, System Planning Program.* St. Paul, Minn.: Metropolitan Council of the Twin Cities Area, 1971.

——. *Metropolitan Development Guide: Housing: Policy Planning Program.* St. Paul, Minn.: Metropolitan Council of the Twin Cities Area, 1973.

——. *Regional Relocation Clearinghouse: News from the Council's Housing Program.* St. Paul, Minn.: Metropolitan Council of the Twin Cities Area, undated.

——. *Report of the Housing Advisory Committee.* St. Paul, Minn.: Metropolitan Council of the Twin Cities Area, 1973.

——. *Summaries of Acts of the 1971 Minnesota State Legislature Affecting the Powers and Duties of the Metropolitan Council.* St. Paul, Minn.: Metropolitan Council of the Twin Cities Area, undated.

——. *Summary of 1971 Minnesota Housing Legislation: Housing Report Number 4.* St. Paul, Minn.: Metropolitan Council of the Twin Cities Area, 1972.

——. *Twin Cities Metropolitan Area Municipal Housing Profile: Housing Report Number 3.* St. Paul, Minn.: Metropolitan Council of the Twin Cities Area, December 1971.

Metropolitan Planning Commission, Kansas City Region. *A Decent Home For All: Housing Action in the Kansas City Metropolitan Region.* Kansas City, Mo.: Metropolitan Planning Commission, Kansas City Region, 1971.

——. *Operation Breakthrough: A Preliminary Program for the Kansas City Metropolitan Region.* Kansas City, Mo.: Metropolitan Planning Commission, Kansas City Region, 1971.

Metropolitan Washington Council of Governments. *COG's EMPIRIC Activity Allocation Model . . . How It Works.* Washington, D.C.: Metropolitan Washington Council of Governments, 1969.

——. "Fair Share Formula Adopted to Meet Area Housing Needs." In *Council of Governments Regional Report.* Washington, D.C.: Metropolitan Washington Council of Governments, 1972.

——. *A Fair Share Housing Formula for Metropolitan Washington.* Washington, D.C.: Metropolitan Washington Council of Governments, 1972.

——. *Housing Policies and Programs for Metropolitan Washington–1971.* Washington, D.C.: Metropolitan Washington Council of Governments, 1971.

——. *Housing Policies and Programs for Metropolitan Washington, 1972.* Washington, D.C.: Metropolitan Washington Council of Governments, 1972.

———. *Implementation of Balanced Housing Policies. The A-95 Housing Review Manual.* Washington, D.C.: Metropolitan Washington Council of Governments, 1973.

———. *Summary of Fair Targets and Units Recommended for Funding in Metropolitan Washington.* Washington, D.C.: Metropolitan Washington Council of Governments, 1973.

Miami Valley Regional Planning Commission. *Advisory Bulletin*, no. 6 (1969).

———. *Advisory Bulletin*, no. 7 (1969).

———. *Advisory Bulletin*, no. 8 (1970).

———. *Advisory Bulletin*, no. 9 (1971).

———. *County Summary Sheets, Housing Plan Progress, for Montgomery, Drake, Preble, Miami, and Green Counties.* Dayton, O.: Miami Valley Regional Planning Commission, 1971.

———. *Housing Needs in the Miami Valley Region 1970 and 1975.* Dayton, O.: Miami Valley Regional Planning Commission, undated.

———. *A Housing Plan for the Miami Valley Region.* Dayton, O.: Miami Valley Regional Planning Commission, 1970.

———. *A Housing Plan for the Miami Valley Region: A Summary.* Dayton, O.: Miami Valley Regional Planning Commission, 1970.

———. *A Housing Profile of the Miami Valley Region.* Dayton, O.: Miami Valley Regional Planning Commission, 1969.

———. *A Housing Profile of the Miami Valley Region.* Dayton, O.: Miami Valley Regional Planning Commission, 1972.

———. *Initial Housing Element.* Dayton, O.: Miami Valley Regional Planning Commission, 1969.

———. *The Miami Valley Region's Housing Plan.* Dayton, O.: Miami Valley Regional Planning Commission, 1973.

———. *Population and Household Projections 1970-2000.* Dayton, O.: Miami Valley Regional Planning Commission, 1969.

———. *Population, Housing, Income in the Miami Valley Region.* Dayton, O.: Miami Valley Regional Planning Commission, 1972.

———. *Special Project Proposal: Facilitating the Compatability of Low and Moderate-Income Housing.* Dayton, O.: Miami Valley Regional Planning Commission, 1971.

———. *A Time for Decision.* Dayton, O.: Miami Valley Regional Planning Commission, undated.

Northeastern Illinois Planning Commission. *Housing for Families of Low and Moderate Income.* Chicago: Northeastern Illinois Planning Commission, 1972.

———. *A Regional Armature for the Future.* Chicago: Northeastern Illinois Planning Commission, 1968.

———. *Suggested Procedures for Communities Wishing to Develop Subsidized Housing.* Chicago: Northeastern Illinois Planning Commission, 1972.

———. *Zoning Provisions and Practices and the Effect on Moderately Priced Housing.* Chicago: Northeastern Illinois Planning Commission, 1971.

Planning Department, County of Santa Clara. *The Joint Housing Element: 1971, Santa Clara County.* San Jose, Calif.: Planning Department, City of Santa Clara, 1971.

San Bernardino County Planning Department. *Government Subsidized Housing Distribution Model for Valley Portion San Bernardino County California.* San Bernardino, Calif.: San Bernardino County Planning Department, 1972.

San Diego County Comprehensive Planning Organization. *Initial Housing Element.* San Diego, Calif.: San Diego County Comprehensive Planning Organization, 1970.

San Diego Planning Department. *A Decent Home for Every San Diegan.* San Diego, Calif.: San Diego Planning Department, 1971.

Southeastern Wisconsin Regional Planning Commission. *A Short-Range Action Housing Program for Southeastern Wisconsin*—1972 and 1973. Waukesha, Wisc.: Southeastern Wisconsin Regional Planning Commission, 1972.

MISCELLANEOUS: PAPERS, SPEECHES, CONFERENCE REPORTS, UNPUBLISHED MATERIAL

Papers

Barr, MacDonald. "The Massachusetts Zoning Appeals Law: Lessons of the First Three Years." Submitted for an American Institute of Planners Conference, August 1972.

Bertsch, Dale F. "Regional Housing: New Pressures for Good and Bad." Paper presented at the 1972 Conference on Public Administration, March 21–25, 1972, New York, New York.

Franklin, Herbert M. "Urban Growth Policy in the Courts: The Quest for New Ground Rules." Paper delivered to the 1971 Planning Conference, American Society of Planning Officials, March 1971, New Orleans, Louisiana.

Jentsch, Robert W. "Political Involvement: An Approach to Usable Plans." Paper presented at the 54th Conference of the American Institute of Planners, October 1971, San Francisco, California.

Sager, Lawrence G. "Exclusionary Zoning: Constitutional Limitations on the Power of Municipalities to Restrict the Use of Land." Paper prepared for ACLU Biennial Conference, June 8–11, 1972, University of Colorado, Boulder, Colorado.

Speeches

Babcock, Richard F. "Let's Stop Romancing Regional Planning." Address given at University of Notre Dame, February 16, 1972.

Babcock, Richard F., and Bosselman, Fred P. "The Contest for Public Control Over Land Development: A Rough Intergovernmental Game for

the Seventies." Regents' Lecture presented at the University of
California, Los Angeles, April 16, 1970.

Babcock, Richard and Weaver, Clifford. "Exclusionary Suburban Zoning:
One More Black Rebuff to the Latest Liberal Crusade." Address
at Fisk University, April 7, 1972.

Bosselman, Fred P. "Capitalizing on Civil Rights: A Strategy for Apartment
Builders." Address delivered at the National Association of
Home Builders International Apartment Conference, Chicago,
Illinois, September 24, 1971.

Downs, Anthony. "The Role of Governors and States in Coping with Urban
Problems in the 1970s." Speech presented at the Conference of
Republican Governors, Hot Springs, Arkansas, December 12, 1969.

Jackson, Samuel C. "Fair Housing and Fair Planning." Remarks before the
American Society of Planning Officials 1972 National Planning
Conference, Detroit, Michigan, April 18, 1972.

Levin, Edward M. "HUD Programs and Citizen Participation: A Widespread
Search for Involvement." Address given at Second Annual Institute on Law and Planning, Urbana-Champaign, Illinois, November
23, 1969.

Polikoff, Alexander. "Urban Change Through the System." Address given
February, 1970. Reprinted in *Occasional Papers 3*. Chicago: Roger
Baldwin Foundation, 1971.

Romney, George. Remarks prepared for delivery at the 29th Annual Con-
vention Exposition of the National Association of Home Builders,
Houston, Texas, January 8, 1973.

Van Dusen, Richard C. "HUD News." Remarks prepared for delivery before
the Denver Regional Council of Governments Urban Growth Conference, Denver, Colorado, March 14, 1972.

Conference Reports

Summary of Proceedings—National Conference on Housing. Regional Issues
and Strategies. St. Louis: August 1971.

Testimony of the Planning for People Coalition before the Illinois State Zoning
Law Study Commission. Springfield, Illinois: February 9, 1971.

Summaries of the Clearinghouse on Exclusionary Land Use Problems. Washington, D.C. and New York: 1970–1973.

About the Author

Leonard S. Rubinowitz is a member of the faculty of Northwestern University's Center for Urban Affairs. He is a graduate of Yale Law School where he was a member of the Board of Editors of the Yale Law Journal. He taught for a year in an inner city school in Bridgeport, Connecticut. His past experience also includes that of Special Assistant to the Midwest Regional Administrator of HUD. There he was engaged in seeking increased housing choice for low and moderate-income people and racial minorities within metropolitan areas. He has contributed numerous articles on housing and zoning to law journals. His continuing research interest is the definition and implementation of housing strategies.